HOW T[O] [GET A]

J**O**B IN

SEATTLE/ PORTLAND

THE INSIDER'S GUIDE

THOMAS M. CAMDEN
SARA STEINBERG

SURREY BOOKS
230 East Ohio Street
Suite 120
Chicago, Illinois 60611

HOW TO GET A JOB IN SEATTLE/PORTLAND—The Insider's Guide.
Published by Surrey Books, Inc., 230 E. Ohio St., Chicago, IL 60611.
Telephone: (312) 751-7330.

This book is manufactured in the United States of America.

1st Edition. 1 2 3 4 5

Library of Congress Cataloging-in-Publication data:

Camden, Thomas M., 1938-
        How to get a job in Seattle/Portland: the insider's guide /
Thomas M. Camden, Sara Steinberg.
        532p.   cm.
        Includes bibliographical references.
        ISBN 0-940625-10-5: $15.95
        1. Job hunting—Washington—Seattle. 2. Professions—
Washington—Seattle. 3. Business enterprises—Washington—Seattle—
Directories. 4. Job hunting—Oregon—Portland. 5. Professions—
Oregon—Portland. 6. Business enterprises—Oregon—Portland—
Directories. I. Steinberg, Sara   II. Title.
HF5382.75.U62S453   1990   90-32167
650.14'09795'49—dc20   CIP

AVAILABLE TITLES IN THIS SERIES — all $15.95

How To Get a Job in Atlanta by Thomas M. Camden, Diane C. Thomas,
    and Bill Osher, Ph.D.
How To Get a Job in Chicago by Thomas M. Camden and Susan Schwartz.
How To Get a Job in Dallas/Fort Worth by Thomas M. Camden and
    Nancy Bishop.
How To Get a Job in Europe by Robert Sanborn, Ph.D.
How To Get a Job in Houston by Thomas M. Camden and Bob Sanborn.
How To Get a Job in Los Angeles/San Diego by Thomas M. Camden and
    Karen Tracy Polk.
How To Get a Job in New York by Thomas M. Camden and
    Susan Fleming-Holland.
How To Get a Job in San Francisco by Thomas M. Camden and
    Evelyn Jean Pine.
How To Get a Job in Seattle/Portland by Thomas M. Camden and
    Sara Steinberg.
How To Get a Job in Washington, DC, by Thomas M. Camden and
    Karen Tracy Polk.

Single copies may be ordered directly from the publisher. Send check or money
order plus $2.00 per book for postage and handling to Surrey Books at the
above address. For quantity discounts, please contact the publisher.

Editorial production by Bookcrafters, Inc., Chicago
Cover design by Hughes Design, Chicago.
Typesetting by On Track, Chicago.

ACKNOWLEDGMENTS

The authors would like to thank the following people for their help: Researcher/Fact Checkers Suzanne Nichols, Joycelee McAteer, Iris A. Moore, Ann Pollack-Gomes, Paulette Buchanan, Joe Morales, and Sue Giacometti; and typists Brenda Donovan, Grace Engler, and Maura Brady.

Thanks also goes to Publisher Susan Schwartz, Production Editor Gene DeRoin, Art Director Sally Hughes, and Drs. Bill Osher and Robert Sanborn, editorial contributors.

Note to Our Readers

We, the authors and editors, have made every effort to supply you with the most useful, up-to-date information available to help you find the job you want. Each name, address, and phone number has been verified by our staff of fact checkers. But offices move and people change jobs, so we urge you to call before you write, and write before you visit. And if you think we should include information on companies, organizations, or people that we've missed, please let us know.

LOOKING FOR A JOB?

THESE BOOKS, COVERING 9 MAJOR MARKETS (PLUS EUROPE), CAN HELP.

HOW...

to get the job you want: Each book gives you up to 1,500 major employers, numbers to call, and people to contact

WHERE...

to get the job you want: How to research the local job market and meet the people who hire

PLUS...

how to use: Local networks and professional organizations; advice on employment services; how to sell yourself in the interview; writing power resumes and cover letters; hundreds of names and numbers, many available nowhere else!

FOR EASIER ORDERING CALL 1-800-326-4430

CONTENTS

1 How To Get the Most from This Book *Page 1*

What this book can and can not do for you. What you absolutely shouldn't skip. Outlook for the Seattle/Portland area in the 1990s. Tips for newcomers, and how to find your way around. Chambers of Commerce.

2 Establishing an Objective: How To Discover What You Want To Do *Page 17*

The importance of knowing what you want to do. Questions to help you clarify your job objective. Helpful books on life/career planning. Books for recent graduates, mid-life career changers, older job hunters, and women. Professional vocational analysis: where to find it, what it costs, pros and cons. What to expect from career counselors. Lists of career counselors, colleges, and social service agencies offering testing and guidance. Resources for starting your small own business. Resources for women.

3 Writing a Resume That Works
Page 50

The resume—what it is, what it can and can not do for you. The basics of a good resume. Pros and cons of hiring someone else to write your resume. Firms that prepare resumes: what they cost, what they offer. What NOT to do with a resume. Cover letters. Choosing a resume format. Sample resumes and cover letters.

4 Researching the Seattle/Portland Job Market
Page 71

The importance of doing your homework. The public library, the best friend a job hunter ever had. Locations and phone numbers of local libraries. The Big Four directories and how they can help you. Over 100 other directories that might come in handy. Area newspapers and how to use them. Pros and cons of answering want ads. General business magazines. Local feature publications. Trade magazines—how to use them. Job-hunt publications. Job telephone hotlines.

5 Developing a Strategy: The ABCs of Networking
Page 110

The importance of having a strategy. How long will it take to find a job? Tried and true advice about nurturing your ego. Establishing a job-hunting schedule. Networking—the key to a successful job search. The exploratory interview. Developing professional contacts. How to keep yourself organized. How to identify and contact hiring authorities. Books on job-hunting strategy. A unique list of selected networking groups in the Seattle/Portland area: professional organizations, trade groups, clubs, and societies, with addresses, phone numbers, and contact persons (where possible).

6 Using Professional Employment Services
Page 149

Employment agencies—what they can and can not do for you, how they charge, how to get the most from them. Listing of selected employment agencies and their specialties. Career consultants; some words to the wise and questions to ask before retaining one. Executive search firms—how they operate, pros and cons; selected list. Social service and government employment agencies.

7 How To Succeed In an Interview
Page 174

The interview objective and how to prepare. Mastering the five-minute resume. The interview as a sales presentation. Steps to a successful interview. What interviewers look for. Handling the interview, anticipating tough questions, and making sure you get your own questions answered. What to do following the interview. Books on interviewing. How to use your references.

8 What To Do If Money Gets Tight
Page 187

Reviewing your assets and liabilites. Pros and cons of part-time and temporary work. Books on part-time and flexible employment. List of selected sources for part-time work. How to sign up for unemployment benefits.

9 Where To Turn If Your Confidence Wilts
Page 197

Tips for dealing with rejection. What to do if you get fired. Dealing with emotional stress. Guidelines for seeking professional counseling or therapy. Selected crisis and mental health centers. Career transition issues. Beating the job-hunt blues.

10 Selecting the Right Job for You
Page 210

You don't have to jump at the first offer. What you should find out before accepting any job offer. Finding the right employment "culture." Tips on negotiating salary. How to compare job offers— sample checklist. What to do after you finally accept a job.

11 Where Seattle/Portland Works
Page 217

Names, addresses, and phone numbers of the Seattle/Portland area's top 1,900 employers, arranged by industry, with descriptions and contacts, where possible. Useful professional organizations, professional publications, and directories. Candid interviews and helpful hints.

Employers Index   *Page 495*

General Index   *Page 514*

How To Get the Most from This Book

So you want to get a job in the Seattle or Portland area? Well, you've picked up the right book. Whether you're a recent graduate, new in town, or an old hand at the great Pacific Northwest Job Search; whether or not you're currently employed; even if you're not fully convinced that you *are* employable—this book is crammed with helpful information.

It contains the combined wisdom of two top professionals: Tom Camden, a personnel professional who currently is an officer of Enterchange, a nationally known career consulting firm; and Sara Steinberg, a Puget Sound-based freelancer who specializes in writing about the employment market.

Tom contributes expert advice on both basic and advanced job search techniques, from how to write a resume to suggestions for racking up extra points in an employment interview. Sara combines her knowledge of the Pacific Northwest working world with an impressive network of contacts developed while living in the Seattle metropolitan area. Whether you're looking for a job in the city or the suburbs, her extensive listings will save you hours of research time.

Other Seattle/Portland area insiders have contributed tips, warnings, jokes, and observations in candid, behind-the-scenes interviews. All of which is to say that we have done our level best to pack more useful information between these covers than you'll find anywhere else. We would love to guarantee that this book is the only resource you will need to find the job of your dreams, but we are not miracle workers. This is a handbook, not a Bible. There's just no getting around the fact that finding work takes work. You are the only person who can land the job you want.

What we *can* do—and, we certainly hope, have done—is to make the work of job hunting in Seattle or Portland easier and more enjoyable for you. We have racked our brains, and those of many others, to provide you with the most extensive collection of local resources in print.

To get the most from this book, first browse through the Table of Contents. Acquaint yourself with each chapter's major features, see what appeals to you, and turn to the sections that interest you the most.

It may not be necessary or useful for you to read this book from cover to cover. If you're currently employed, for example, you can probably skip Chapter 8—What To Do If Money Gets Tight. If you have no interest in using a professional employment service, you'll only need to browse through Chapter 6.

There are certain parts of this book, however, that no one should overlook. One of them is Chapter 4—Researching the Seattle/Portland Area Job Market. Unless you're a professional librarian, we'd bet money that you won't be able to read this chapter without discovering at least a few resources that you never knew existed. We've tried to make it as easy as possible for you to get the inside information that can put you over the top in an employment interview.

Chapter 5 is another Don't Miss—especially our unique listing of organizations that you should know about to develop your network of professional contacts. We also strongly suggest that you read Chapter 7, even if you think you already know all about how to handle an interview. And then, of course, there's Chapter 11—listings of the Seattle/Portland area's top 1,900 employers of white-collar workers.

There's another thing you should know about to get the most from this book. Every chapter, even the ones you don't think you need to read, contains at least one helpful hint or insider interview that is set off from the main text. Take some time to browse through them. They contain valuable nuggets of information and many tips that have never before appeared in print.

Keep in mind that no one book can do it all for you. While we've touched on the basic tasks of any job search—self-analysis, developing a resume, researching the job market, figuring out a strategy, generating leads, interviewing, and selecting the right job—we don't have space to go into great detail on each and every one of them. What we *have* done is to supply suggestions for further reading. Smart users of this book will follow those suggestions when they need to know more about a particular subject.

Electronic bulletin board profiles Washington communities

Want to narrow your job search to a particular county, town, or city in Washington State? If you have an IBM-compatible personal computer and a modem, a free call will give you access to 191 community profiles on the Electronic Bulletin Board, a service of Washington State's Business Assistance Center.

A call to (206) 753-3333 can bring up information on 39 counties and 174 cities and towns on your PC screen. Profiles average six pages and include data on the community's economy, demographics, educational resources, transportation, and government, plus a local economic development contact.

For more information, call Imbert Matthee at (206) 586-5297.■

Job Outlook for the Seattle/Portland Area

What's the economic outlook as the Seattle and Portland areas enter the 1990s? We would love to be able to look into our crystal ball and tell you exactly what jobs have the most promising future, but it's not that easy. We can, however, point to some key trends.

But first, we'd better point you in the right direction, geographically speaking. The scope of this insider's employment guide includes metropolitan Seattle and Portland, but it doesn't stop there. Our focus will take in the Greater Seattle area, commonly known as Puget Sound. For our purposes, Puget Sound will refer to the major cities of Seattle, Tacoma, Olympia, and Everett, plus suburban areas and nearby smaller cities.

SEATTLE/PUGET SOUND AREA

While it may rain a bit here at times (all right—a *lot* of the time), the Seattle metropolitan area is consistently top-rated as a great place to live, work, play, and raise a family. The region boasts gorgeous scenery, clean air, and reasonably priced housing in relationship to income.

Puget Sound is an area of recent economic growth and falling unemployment. In 1988, the strongest year economically since 1984, employment grew 4.5 percent, twice the national average, while population gained 3.7 percent. Seattle continued above-average economic growth in 1989, according to The Grant Thornton Index. The projected outlook for growth includes the arrival of 100,000 new residents in the greater Puget Sound area in the next decade.

Many human resource specialists believe there is a job here for anyone who wants it. Most frequently mentioned as perennial openings to fill: technical, general management, secretarial, general office, and sales. Puget Sound led the nation in new manufacturing jobs created from June 1988 to June 1989. Federal job opportunities are also plentiful, as Seattle is a regional federal headquarters.

In an up and down economy, one cannot project a certain future. The one certainty is that the fortunes of the Puget Sound area will be based on the global economy. In 1989, the state of Washington averaged 38,400 jobs tied to foreign investment.

Puget Sound is a growth area due to its tremendous Pacific Rim trade, a significant manufacturing base, and its role as entree to the Western Canadian market.

Because of its expansive waterways, this area does a lot of exporting and importing. Port of Seattle is the nation's second most active port, and other ports along Puget Sound are thriving. Largely due to the port business, Alaska is one of the state's top trading partners. In a recent study, doing business with Alaska accounted for 52,250 jobs in Puget Sound, led by services, fish harvesting and processing, and manufacturing.

It is generally presumed that the Puget Sound area is overly dependent on the fortunes of its extraordinarily successful aereospace industry, the Boeing Company. Besides Boeing aircraft, Washington's three major exports include lumber and wood products (pulp and paper production employed 17,000 workers in 1988, up 1 percent over 1987) and agricultural products. Despite dwindling supplies of old growth timber, the industry's two leading exporters, Weyerhaeuser and TT Rayonier, exported about $1 billion in forest products in 1989.

The U.S.-Canada Free Trade Agreement leaves Puget Sound with a new regional trade and transportation challenge to meet in the air, sea, and on land. Canadians are fast becoming consumers seeking American goods. This, of course, will create employment opportunities in the transportation industry.

Seattle has also proven itself as a place where small businesses can do big business. In a recent nationwide poll, the city was named the second most popular place to locate a business. All 150 mid-sized Puget Sound companies surveyed by a Seattle personnel placement service in January 1989 said they planned to create new jobs in 1989 and beyond. Venture capital investments (granted to already established small businesses) in Puget Sound appear to be increasing at a rate of 25 percent.

Downtown Seattle office buildings absorbed a record-tying 1.4 million square feet of new office space in 1988. The suburbs and cities close to Seattle are also in the throes of expansion.

The best King County growth area is Federal Way, which has experienced a surge of activity over recent years. The boom is also spilling over into Pierce County (Tacoma). Sudden growth at Boeing and Weyerhaeuser, plus increased activity at the Port of Tacoma, have fueled this trend.

On the Eastside, across Lake Washington, expansion is largely attributed to high-tech industry. The Eastside's Technology Corridor stretches from Bothell to Everett. It consists of a new cluster of separate business parks, each housing mostly high-tech companies. They have attracted more than 160 companies and employ approximately 4,500 workers.

Excluding aerospace, software and biomedical technology are Washington's fastest growing industries, according to the Department of Trade and Economic Development. The Puget Sound region as a whole has the third largest concentration of software companies in the U.S. Washington Software Association reports a booming industry, employing an estimated 7,000 people. Once considered almost a cottage industry, there are now dozens of companies. The world's three premier operating systems for nonframe computers—OS/2, MS-DOS, and UNIX—are products of Microsoft in Redmond.

Puget Sound is one of the nation's few bodies of saltwater that still produces uncontaminated seafood. Tacoma has two seafood plants and two frozen food distribution plants. Port of Tacoma is strategically located between Alaska and the growing seafood market of the United States.

Seattle is the home of the state's largest educational institution. The University District is a special "city" unto itself, revolving around the student population. Community colleges are large, both north, south, and central, including Everett, Bellevue, and Tacoma.

Evergreen State College, part of the popular West Olympia area, is a unique progressive educational alternative, keeping pace with the changing times and needs of the students.

Nestled as it is on sky-blue waters between the two snow-capped mountain ranges of the Cascades and Olympics, a lot of Puget Sound's work revolves around play. Seattle Center, built for a World's Fair, is the biggest recreational employer. The Woodland Park Zoo, Pioneer Square, the Museum of Flight, and the aquarium afford job opportunities year-round.

In sports, Seattle has it all, with major-league football, basketball, and baseball teams. Sports and athletic clubs thrive throughout the area; the Sporting House Athletic Club in Federal Way has 1,500 adult members. Two large sports domes (Seattle and Tacoma) help boost the already healthy tourist industry.

Seattle offers a large choice of careers in the arts. It is home to the Seattle Opera, Seattle Symphony, and the Northwest Ballet. Many local theaters employ actors, such as The Repertory and The Cirque. Seattle's nightclubs are also lively and often unique, booking individual musicians and groups nightly.

Olympia, in Thurston County, was once just the quiet, largely wooded home of Olympia Beer and the state capitol. It is now booming with a 2.4 percent population growth. NPA Data Services of Washington, DC, has projected that Thurston County will be the nation's fifth fastest growing county between now and the end of the century, jumping from a population of 149,300 to 220,116.

One reason for the projected growth is that Thurston County still offers a rural way of life close enough to big cities to provide modern-day necessities. Moreover, cities that are state capitals are popular growth areas since they provide a stable economy.

PORTLAND AREA

In the past, the Northwest was associated primarily with the lumber industry. When that industry experienced a recession in the early 1980s, there were few employment alternatives. Oregon has finally pulled out of that recession and is experiencing what some feel is a metamorphosis. But Oregonians still remember the exodus of people when the timber and high-tech industries laid off thousands.

In 1979, there were 1,051,000 workers in the state. During the next four years their numbers declined until, by the beginning of 1984, only 963,600 workers remained, a drop of about 86,000. This represents a city the size of Salem, Oregon's capital.

Even though there is a growing recovery, the timber industry is still not out of trouble. It has attracted national attention with the controversial spotted owl issue. Environmentalists would like to see all old-growth timber cutting terminated. The other side feels that would mean a major economic setback and a loss of thousands of jobs again. A number of small communities around the Portland area are fighting for their very existence, while the issue is being held up in the courts.

Despite the old-growth timber issue, some economists see Oregon as one of the West's most economically stable states. The decline in lumber employment is being offset, they feel, by the growth of high-tech, construction, and service industries. There is a demand for millwrights, mechanics, nurses, secretaries, accountants, and electrical engineers However, a random sampling of job hunters that we spoke to said they encountered a preference by employers to hire native Oregonians over newcomers.

The city of Portland is one of the area's biggest employers. Portlanders have watched their city build a transit mall, a downtown public square, a light-rail system, a 37-acre river front park, and the Justice Center (jail) from tax money used for development purposes.

Portland has been innovative in broadening its industrial base. It has developed manufacturing of aluminum and metal fabrication plants, as well as a shipyard (Hyster and Freightliner). There is also a substantial imported and home-based electronics industry.

When it comes to quality of life and governmental attitude toward business, chief executive officers rank Portland among the best in the country, according to a nationwide poll to determine the best cities in which to locate a business. This was offset only by the limited availability of existing commercial sites.

Many wonder what new direction Portland will take next. Some speculate that with the "information" industry in expansion, the Rose City may become a center for the supercomputing industry, data networking, or even biotechnologies.

Beaverton, a bedroom community southwest of Portland, is the proud home of the Mentor Graphics Corporation, a pioneer in electronics design automation (EDA). Their hold on one-third of the international EDA market makes this corporation the world's leading supplier of work stations that electronically design circuit boards.

The Japanese are becoming major Oregon employers, with 15 different plants already built by Japanese companies in Oregon and southwest Washington. In 1988, approximately 3,000 people were employed in these plants.

With unemployment at 5 percent and a 13 percent increase in new home construction, developers see Oregon as a growing economy. Businesses are encouraged and can be assisted financially in Oregon through lottery funds designated to lure new businesses and assist in economic development. Funds are funneled through the Oregon Economic Development Department, the state's small business advocate.

Oregon's new minimum wage laws went into effect September 1989, with a boost from $3.35 to $3.85 an hour. In January 1990 the minimum rose again to $4.25 an hour and will reach $4.75 an hour on Jan. 1, 1991.

On that optimistic note, we hope to provide you with the resources you need to find the job you want. Good luck from both of us, and happy hunting.

New in Town?

Have you just moved to the Seattle or Portland area? In addition to this book, you could probably use some personalized assistance.

In the greater Seattle area:

The **Travelers Aid Society** (909 Fourth, Seattle, WA 98104, (206) 461-3888) offers referral services for newcomers.

The **Greater Seattle Chamber of Commerce** (600 University, Suite 1200, Seattle, WA 98101, (206) 461-7200) publishes various guides describing Seattle's business climate.

The **Seattle-King County Convention and Visitors Bureau** (666 Stewart St., Seattle, WA 98101, (206) 461-5840) offers free maps of downtown Seattle, King County, and Washington State.

Check with the **East King County Convention and Visitor's Bureau** (515 116th N.E., Bellevue, WA 98004, (206) 455-1926) for information on the Bellevue/Eastside area.

The **Tacoma-Pierce County Chamber of Commerce** (950 Pacific Ave., Suite 300, Tacoma, WA 98402, (206) 627-2175) publishes a number of useful directories.

The **Tacoma-Pierce County Visitor and Convention Bureau** (950 Pacific Ave., Suite 450, Tacoma, WA 98402, (206) 627-2836) provides free maps and brochures.

The **Olympia-Thurston County Chamber of Commerce** (1000 Plum St. S.E., Olympia, WA 98501, (206) 357-3362) will provide important information about the business climate of the state's capital.

The **Olympia Visitor and Convention Bureau** (316 Schmidt Place, Tumwater, WA 98501, (206) 357-3370) has free maps and brochures available.

In addition, the **State Capitol Visitor Services Bureau** (14th and Capitol Way, Olympia, WA 98504, (206) 586-3460) publishes a "Newcomer's Guide" and provides free information on Olympia and Washington State.

By calling the **Washington State Tourist Information Hotline** (800-544-1800), you can have mailed to you the "Destination Washington Guide Book," which lists Chambers of Commerce, hotels, motels, and various events.

For the greater Portland area, check out the **Portland/Oregon Visitors Association** (26 S.W. Salmon St., Portland, OR 97204, (503) 222-2223).

Free information from the **Oregon State Tourist Information Center** (Jantzen Beach Center, 12345 N. Union, Portland, OR 97217, (503) 285-1631) includes maps, brochures, and the "Oregon Guidebook."

For statewide assistance, contact the **Oregon Tourism Office** in Salem at (800) 547-7842).

Finding Your Way Around the Area

SEATTLE AREA

If you need help in the Seattle area, you're not alone. Seattle outgrew its bus system long ago. Although a monorail operates between Seattle Center and downtown Seattle, the only other transportation choices are Metro city buses or private car.

Seattle is working hard to keep up with the influx of people to the central business district by adding more off-street parking spaces. Monthly parking costs can run from $46 to $120. Cost of parking by day averages $3.76 for two hours, and $7.45 for all-day parking. As one moves out from the city center into other districts, such as Queen Ann, First Hill, Magnolia, University, and Northgate, the parking costs are lower and sometimes free.

A lot of people have reported paying as much as $100 in total costs to repossess their vehicle after parking in a restricted area. Look for signs indicating the hours parking is allowed, for a parking area during the daytime may become a rush-hour lane for a.m. and p.m. commuters.

Perhaps the most efficient transportation system is the ferry network. With a ferry terminal on the Seattle waterfront downtown, those who commute to and from the islands, such as Bremerton, find the going easiest of all.

METRO, the municipal authority responsible for King County transportation, reports that driving into Seattle from the Eastside over the Mercer Island or the floating bridge can take 45 minutes in rush-hour traffic.

Depending on where in the suburbs one lives, the commute up and down I-5 every weekday can average one to two hours.

These phone numbers should come in handy:

Airport Express Grayline
720 S. Forest St.
Seattle, WA 98134
(206) 626-6088 or (206) 624-5813
Runs between downtown area hotels and SeaTac Airport; also residential service. $10 round trip; $5.50 one way. In operation between 5:45 a.m. and 12 a.m.

Amtrak Station
303 S. Jackson St.
Seattle, WA 98104
(206) 382-4125

METRO (Municipality of Metropolitan Seattle)
821 Second St.
Seattle, WA 98104
Bus & route info: (206) 447-4800
(includes Park & Ride locations)
Speech/hearing impaired (206) 684-2029
Carpool & vanpool (206) 625-4500
Bus service for the greater Seattle area. Free zone downtown. Handicapped and bicycle equipped.

Shuttle Express
805 Lenora St.
Seattle, WA 98121
(206) 622-1424 or 1-800-942-0711
Home pick-up in King County to SeaTac Airport.

Taxis
Checker Cab (206) 622-8333
North End Taxi (206) 363-3333 or (206) 624-6666
Yellow Cab (206) 622-6500

How To Get a Job

Washington State Ferries
Information, schedules, tolls (206) 464-6400
Toll-free numbers: 1-800-542-0810; 1-800-542-7052
Bremerton-Winslow schedules (206) 464-6990
Edmonds-Kingston schedules (206) 464-6960

TACOMA AREA

Pierce Transit
3701 96th S.W.
Tacoma, WA 98499
Bus route/ride share info (206) 581-8000
Hearing impaired (206) 582-7951
Shuttle for elderly & handicapped (206) 581-8100
Bus service throughout greater Tacoma area.

Taxis
Pierce Taxi (206) 582-3455
Yellow Cab (206) 472-3303

OLYMPIA/LACEY AREA

Capital Aeroporter Tours & Charter
PO Box 2163
Olympia, WA 98507
(206) 754-7113
Regular service to SeaTac International Airport from five
downtown hotels. Home and hotel pick-up in Olympia; h
only in Tacoma.

Intercity Transit
PO Box 659
Olympia, WA 98507
Bus route info (206) 786-1881
Car & vanpool info (206) 786-8800
Dial-A-Ride van (206) 943-7777
Routes throughout greater Olympia area. Downtown free
Vanpool and Dial-A-Ride van for elderly and handicappe
Free ride matching for carpooling.

Olympia Bus Depot
107 E. Seventh
Olympia, WA 98501
(206) 357-5541

Taxis
Lacey City Taxi (206) 357-5757
Red Top Taxi (206) 357-3700

12

PORTLAND AREA

You can choose among a varied and interesting array of transportation options for getting around the greater Portland area. City leaders take pride in a balanced transport system that keeps motor traffic in check. The results: first-rate air quality and a "rush hour" of less than 20 minutes on most traffic arteries.

Portland's new light-rail system, MAX, runs between downtown Portland and the eastern suburb of Gresham. This Tri-Met system is so successful that it has drawn at least one investigating foreign delegation each week since it went into operation.

Due to MAX, the many bridges that span the Columbia river, and an overall well-planned transportation system, rush hour is usually a calm affair, especially on the Sunset Highway going west and the stretch of I-5 between Vancouver and Portland. Commuters also get an assist from the Eastside Freeway (205), where traffic south of Portland can be diverted to bypass downtown and exit onto I-5 in the Vancouver area. Half of all those who consider Portland their home live within the city proper, so there is no imposing commute.

Getting from the airport to downtown Portland is a breeze. Taxis, shuttles, limousines, and buses are all readily available to make the 20-minute drive. Choose from five car rental agencies inside the airport terminal or nine more within a mile or so. A number of hotels offer courtesy vehicles, while shuttles run regularly from the airport to Portland and its surrounding suburbs. Tri-Met buses are also an option.

These listings should be useful:

Amtrak Station
800 N.W. Sixth
Portland, OR 97204
General info (503) 241-4270
Toll-free 1-800-872-7245

Tri-Met
4012 S.E. 17th St.
Portland, OR 97202
General info (503) 233-3511
24-hour recorded info (503) 228-7246
Tri-Met buses serve Clackamus, Multnomah, and Washington counties. MAX, the light rail, runs between Gresham and downtown Portland.

Chambers of Commerce

Most major chambers of commerce publish material that is especially helpful to newcomers or anyone who wants to be better informed about a community. These brochures and maps are available free or for a nominal charge and provide much of what you want to know about area businesses, city services, transportation, public schools, utilities, and entertainment. If you have a question that's not answered in one of the publications, ask one of the chamber's representatives.

SEATTLE/PUGET SOUND AREA

Greater Seattle Chamber of Commerce
600 University, Suite 1200
Seattle, WA 98101
(206) 461-7200
Publishes various directories that are updated regularly, a quarterly newsletter to members, and makes available extensive demographic information. The Chamber sponsors Roundtable Meetings, where business people can meet to network on an informal basis, and monthly Brown Bag and Afternoon Seminars. Brown Bag Seminars cost $10.00 for members and $20.00 for non-members. Afternoon Seminars, held from 4-6:30 p.m., are $15.00 for members and $30.00 for non-members.

Tacoma-Pierce County Chamber of Commerce
950 Pacific Ave., Suite 300
Tacoma, WA 98402
(206) 627-2175
Publishes "Membership Directory," "Manufacturers Directory," and "Major Employees Directory" for entire Puget Sound area. Sponsors monthly small business breakfasts for members and non-members. Members-only meet for a small business social the third Thursday of every month.

Olympia-Thurston County Chamber of Commerce
1000 Plum St. S.E.
Olympia, WA 98501
(206) 357-3362
Publishes monthly "Impact Newsletter" for members, describing the Chamber's goals and objectives.

Auburn Chamber of Commerce
24 B St. N.E.
Auburn, WA 98002
(206) 833-0700

Bellevue Chamber of Commerce
10500 N.E. Eighth St., Suite 750
Bellevue, WA 98004
(206) 454-2464

Chinatown Chamber of Commerce
508-1/2 Seventh Ave. S.
Seattle, WA 98104
(206) 623-8171

Greater Federal Way Chamber of Commerce
34400 Pacific Highway S.
Federal Way, WA 98003
(206) 838-2605

Issaquah Chamber of Commerce
145 N.W. Gilman Blvd.
Issaquah, WA 98027
(206) 392-7024

Kirkland Chamber of Commerce
301 Kirkland Ave.
Kirkland, WA 98033
(206) 822-7066

Northshore Area Chamber of Commerce
18120 Bothell Way N.E., Suite A5
Bothell, WA 98011
(206) 486-1245

Southwest King County Chamber of Commerce
225 Tukwila Parkway
Tukwila, WA 98188
(206) 244-3160

PORTLAND AREA

Portland Chamber of Commerce
221 N.W. Second
Portland, OR 97209
(503) 228-9411
Publishes a directory of members and businesses for $17.50; a
relocation packet, including maps, events, and resources for
$5.00; a business directory for $15.00; and a manufacturers'
directory for $15.00.

Beaverton Chamber of Commerce
4800 S.W. Griffith Dr. #100
Beaverton, OR 97005
(503) 644-0123

Canby Chamber of Commerce
231 N.W. Second
Holly Mall, PO Box 35
Canby, OR 97031
(503) 266-4600

Forest Grove Chamber of Commerce
2417 Pacific Ave.
Forest Grove, OR 97116
(503) 357-3006

Gresham Chamber of Commerce
150 W. Powell, PO Box 696
Gresham, OR 97030
(503) 665-1131

Hillsboro Chamber of Commerce
334 S.E. Fifth Ave.
Hillsboro, OR 97123
(503) 648-1102

Lake Oswego Chamber of Commerce
47 N. State St.
Lake Oswego, OR 97034
(503) 636-3634

Milwaukie Chamber of Commerce
15010 S.E. McLoughlin Blvd.
Milwaukie, OR 97267
(503) 654-7777

Oregon City Chamber of Commerce
500 Abernathy Road
Oregon City, OR 97045
(503) 656-1619

Tigard Chamber of Commerce
12420 S.W. Main St.
Tigard, OR 97223
(503) 639-1656

Tualatin Chamber of Commerce
18622 S.W. Boones Ferry
Tualatin, OR 97062
(503) 692-0780

Wilsonville Chamber of Commerce
8880 S.W. Wilsonville Rd.
Wilsonville, OR 97070
(503) 682-0411

Establishing an Objective: How To Discover What You Want to Do

One of the most common mistakes job seekers make is not establishing an *objective* before beginning the job search. Practically everyone wants a job that provides personal satisfaction, growth, good salary and benefits, prestige, and a desirable location. But unless you have a more specific idea of the kind of work you want to do and are qualified to do, the chances are high that your job search will be less than satisfactory.

Many of our readers already have a clear objective in mind. You may want a job as a systems analyst, paralegal, production assistant, sales manager, or any one of the thousands of other occupations at which Oregonians and Puget Sounders work. That's all well and good—in fact, *establishing an objective is a necessary first step in any successful job search.*

But anyone who's looking for work, or thinking about changing jobs or careers, can benefit from a thorough self-appraisal. What follows is a list of highly personal questions designed to provide you with insights you may never have considered, and to help you answer the Big Question, "What do I want to do?"

To get the most from this exercise, write out your answers. This will take some time, but it will help to ensure that you give each question careful thought. The more effort you put into this exercise, the better prepared you'll be to answer the tough questions that are bound to come up in any job interview. The exercise also will serve as the foundation for constructing a decent resume—a subject we'll discuss in more detail in the next chapter.

When you've completed the exercise, consider sharing your answers with a trusted friend or relative. Self-analysis is a difficult task. Although we think we know ourselves, we seldom have the objectivity to see ourselves clearly, to outline our personal and professional strengths and weaknesses, to evaluate our needs, and to set realistic objectives. Someone who knows you well can help.

Questions About Me

1. Taking as much time as necessary—and understanding the purpose of this appraisal—honestly describe the kind of person you are. Here are some questions to get you started. Are you outgoing or are you more of a loner? How well disciplined are you? Are you quick-tempered? Easygoing? Are you a leader or a follower? Do you tend to take a conventional, practical approach to problems? Or are you more imaginative and experimental? How sensitive are you to others?
2. Describe the kind of person others think you are.
3. What do you want to accomplish with your life?
4. What role does your job play in that goal?
5. What impact do you have on other people?
6. What are your accomplishments to date? Are you satisfied with them?

18

7. What role does money play in your standard of values?
8. Is your career the center of your life or just a part of it? Which should it be?
9. What are your main interests?
10. What do you enjoy most?
11. What displeases you most?

Questions About My Job
1. Beginning with your most recent employment and then working back toward school graduation, describe *in detail* each job you had. Include your title, company, responsibilities, salary, achievements and successes, failures, and reason for leaving.
2. How would you change anything in your job history if you could?
3. In your career thus far, what responsibilities have you enjoyed most? Why?
4. What kind of job do you think would be a perfect match for your talents and interests?
5. What responsibilities do you want to avoid?
6. How hard are you really prepared to work?
7. If you want the top job in your field, are you prepared to pay the price?
8. What have your subordinates thought about you as a boss? As a person?
9. What have your superiors thought about you as an employee? As a person?
10. Can your work make you happier? Should it?
11. If you have been fired from any job, what was the reason?
12. How long do you want to work before retirement?

Your answers to these highly personal questions should help you to see more clearly who you are, what you want, what your gifts are, and what you realistically have to offer. They should also reveal what you don't want and what you can't do. It's important to evaluate any objective you're considering in light of your answers to these questions.

People who are entering the job market for the first time, those who have been working for one company for many years, and those who are considering a career change need more help in determining their objectives. Vocational analysis, also known as career planning or life planning, is much too broad a subject to try to cover here. But we can refer you to some excellent books.

CAREER STRATEGY BOOKS

Applegath, John. *Working Free: Practical Alternatives to the 9 to 5 Job.* New York: AMACOM, 1984.

Beatty, Richard H. *The Complete Job Search Book.* New York: John Wiley & Sons, 1988.

Blackledge, Walter L., et al. *The Job You Want—How to Get It.* New York: SW Publishers, 1984.

Bloch, Deborah P. *How to Get and Get Ahead on Your First Job.* New York: National Textbook, 1988.

Bolles, Richard N. *The Three Boxes Of Life and How to Get Out Of Them.* Berkeley, CA: Ten Speed Press, 1983.

Bolles, Richard N. *The 1990 What Color Is Your Parachute?* Berkeley, CA: Ten Speed Press, 1990. The bible for job hunters and career changers,this book is revised every year and is widely regarded as the most useful and creative manual available.

Borchard, David C. *Your Career: Choices, Chances, Changes.* New York: Kendall-Hunt, 1988.

Camden, Thomas M. *Get That Job! How to Succeed in a Job Search.* Hinsdale, IL: Camden & Associates, 1981.

Camden, Thomas M. *The Job Hunter's Final Exam.* Chicago: Surrey Books, 1990.

Clawson, James G., et al. *Self-Assessment and Career Development.* Englewood Cliffs, NJ: Prentice-Hall, 1985.

Davidson, Jeffrey P. *Blow Your Own Horn: How to Market Yourself and Your Career.* New York: Simon & Schuster, 1988.

Figler, Howard. *The Complete Job-Search Handbook.* New York: Holt, Rinehart, and Winston, 1988.

Fink, Edward J. *Building a Career in the Business World.* New York: Vantage Press, 1984.

Green, Gordon W., Jr. *Getting Ahead At Work.* DC: Carol Publishing Group, 1988.

Haldane, Bernard. *Career Satisfaction and Success: A Guide to Job Freedom.* New York: AMACOM, 1982.

Jackson, Tom. *Guerrilla Tactics in the Job Market.* New York: Bantam Books, 1981. Filled with unconventional but effective suggestions.

Krannich, Ronald L. *Network Your Way to Career & Job Success.* Vienna, VA: Impact, 1989.

Levinson, Harry. *Designing and Managing Your Career.* Boston: Harvard University Press, 1988.

Lewis, Adele. *Fast Track Careers for the 90's.* New York: Scott Foresman, 1989.

Mazzei, George. *Moving Up: Digging In, Taking Charge, Playing the Power Game and Learning to Like It.* New York: Poseidon Press, 1984.

Miller, Arthur F., and Ralph T. Mattson. *The TRUTH About You: Discover What You Should Be Doing With Your Life.* Old Tappan, NJ: Fleming H. Revell Co., 1977.

Noble, John. *The Job Search Handbook.* Boston: Bob Adams, 1988.

Wood, Orrin G. *Your Hidden Assets—The Key to Getting Executive Jobs.* Homewood, IL.: Dow Jones-Irwin, 1984. Written by the co-founder of a job-changing workshop developed for Harvard Business School alumni; an upscale book.

If you're **still in college or have recently graduated,** the following books will be of particular interest:

Briggs, James I. *The Berkeley Guide to Employment for New College Graduates.* Berkeley, CA: Ten Speed Press, 1984.

Fox, Marcia R. *Put Your Degree to Work: The New Professional's Guide to Career Planning.* New York: Norton, 1988.

Holton, Ed. *The M.B.A.'s Guide to Career Planning.* Princeton, NJ: Peterson's Guides, 1989.

Kalt, Neil C. *Flight Path: How to Get the Job that Launches Your Career After College.* New York: Simon & Schuster, 1989.

King, James B. *Negotiating the Briar Patch: Resume & Job Search Strategies for the College Graduate.* New York: Kendall-Hunt, 1986.

Osher, Bill, and Sioux Henley Campbell. *The Blue Chip Graduate: A Four Year College Plan For Career Succcess.* Atlanta: Peachtree Publishers, 1987.

For those of you involved in a **mid-life career change,** here are some books that might prove helpful:

Birsner, E. Patricia. *The Forty Plus Job Hunting Guide.* New York: Arco, 1987.

Harper, Maxwell J. *How to Get the Job You Want After Forty.* Pilot Books, 1988.

Hecklinger, Fred J., and Bernadette M. Curtin. *Training for Life: A Practical Guide to Career and Life Planning.* New York: Kendall-Hunt, 1984.

Montana, Patrick J. *Stepping Out, Starting Over.* New York: National Center for Career Life Planning, 1988.

For workers who are **nearing retirement age** or have already reached it, here are two books that might be useful:

Morgan, John S. *Getting a Job After Fifty.* Princeton, NJ: Petrocelli, 1988.

Myers, Albert, and Christopher P. Anderson. *Success Over Sixty.* New York: Summit Books, 1984.

And for **handicapped** job seekers, this title could prove helpful:

Lewis, Adele, and Edith Marks. *Job Hunting for the Disabled.* Woodbury, NY: Barrons, 1983.

For **women** in the work force, these titles will be of interest:

Berryman, Sue E. *Routes Into the Mainstream: Career Choices of Women and Minorities.* New York: National Center for Research in Vocational Education, 1988.

Morrow, Jodie B., and Myrna Lebov. *Not Just a Secretary: Using the Job to Get Ahead.* New York: Wiley Press, 1984.

Nivens, Beatrice. *The Black Woman's Career Guide.* New York: Anchor Books, 1987.

Senter, Dr. Sylvia, Marguerite Howe, and Dr. Donald Saco. *Women at Work: A Psychologist's Secret to Getting Ahead in Business.* New York: Coward, McCann & Geoghegan, 1982.

Wyse, Lois. *The Six-Figure Woman (and How to Be One)*. New York: Linden Press, 1984. How to break into top corporate management.

What Color Is Your Parachute?

What Color Is Your Parachute? author Richard Bolles presents "Two Weeks of Life/Work Planning" the first Friday through the third Friday of August every year in Bend, Oregon. Workshop topics include: New Ways To Figure Out What You Want To Do With Your Life; New Ways To Define Future Objectives for Your Life; and New Ways To Make Your Objectives Achievable.

For more information, contact:
What Color Is Your Parachute?
PO Box 379
Walnut Creek, CA 94596
(415) 935-1865 (Mon.-Fri., 10-4)■

Professional Vocational Analysis

It would be great if there were some psychological test that would confirm without a doubt who you are and precisely what job, career, or field best suits you. Unfortunately, there isn't. Yet professionals in vocational planning have literally dozens of tests at their disposal designed to assess personality and aptitude for particular careers.

The test most commonly used is probably the Strong-Campbell Interest Inventory (SCII). This multiple-choice test takes about an hour to administer and is scored by machine. The SCII has been around since 1933. The most recent revision, in 1981, made a serious and generally successful attempt to eliminate sex bias.

The SCII offers information about an individual's interests on three different levels. First, the test provides a general statement about the test-taker's interest patterns. These patterns suggest not only promising occupations but also characteristics of the most compatible work environments and personality traits affecting work. Second, the test reports how interested a person is in a specific work activity compared with other men and women. Finally, the occupational scales compare the test-taker with satisfied workers in some 90 different occupations. If you think you'd enjoy being a librarian, for example, you can compare yourself with other librarians and see how similar your likes and dislikes are. The occupational scales indicate the degree of probability, confirmed by extensive research, that you'll be satisfied with the choice of a particular occupation.

Personality/vocational tests come in a variety of formats. Many are multiple choice; some require you to finish incomplete sentences; others are autobiographical questionnaires. No single test should ever be used as an absolute. Personality tests are more important for generating discussion and for providing data that can be used in making judgments.

In the Seattle/Portland area, vocational guidance and testing are available from a variety of sources. The most comprehensive service is generally provided by private career counselors and career consultants. Their approaches and specialties vary greatly. Some primarily provide testing while others also offer long-term programs that include counseling, resume writing, preparing for the job interview, and developing a job marketing campaign. Fees usually range from $50 to several thousand dollars.

It's best to find a professional who specializes in the type of vocational help you need. You don't want to spend hundreds of dollars on a lengthy job search when you only need several counseling sessions and tests. The list that follows gives you some idea of what counselors and consultants offer. Telephone these professionals to find out whether their services fit your needs.

Although the terms are often used synonymously, there is a difference between a career counselor and consultant. Most professionals use the title "counselor" if they have a counseling degree in psychology, social work, or marriage, family, and child counseling and are licensed by the state. Career counselors may also have an advanced degree in career development. Professionals who aren't licensed often call themselves "career consultants." This field attracts people from a wide variety of backgrounds, education, and levels of competency. That's why it's important to talk to people who have used the service you are considering, and check with the Better Business Bureau to make sure the service is not beset with complaints.

Because career counseling and consulting firms are private, for-profit businesses with high overhead costs, they usually charge more for testing than local community colleges or social service agencies (lists follow in this chapter). A fuller discussion of services offered by career consultants is provided in Chapter 6. Also in Chapter 6 is a list of more social service agencies, some of which offer vocational testing.

What To Expect from a Career Counselor

What kind of help can you expect from a career counselor that you can't find on your own?

For one thing, counselors offer an objective viewpoint, says one licensed professional career counselor we know. "You may not be able to discuss everything with family, friends, and especially coworkers if you happen still to be working. A trained professional can serve as a sounding board and offer strategies and information that you can't get elsewhere. We can essentially help a person become more resourceful."

This particular career counselor usually spends four sessions with individuals who want to establish a sense of direction for their careers. Here's what sessions cover:

❚ Exploring problems that have blocked progress and considering solutions.

❚ Establishing career objectives and determining strengths and areas to work on.

❚ Writing a career plan that outlines a strategy to achieve goals.

❚ Preparing an ongoing, self-directed plan to explore career goals.

"A counselor should help people develop methods and a framework from which to base continual exploration about what they want from a career, even after they are employed," our counselor friend says.

All too often people look for "quick fixes" in order to get back to work, she says. "In haste, they may not take time to reflect on where their career is going, to make sure they look for a job that will be challenging and satisfying."

CAREER COUNSELORS AND CONSULTANTS

SEATTLE/PUGET SOUND AREA

Barnhart, Rosemary
1415 Harrison N.W., Suite 201
Olympia, WA 98502
(206) 754-3473
Contact: Rosemary Barnhart
Counseling for employed and unemployed, job search skills,
interest testing. $35 per hour. Thirty- to 40-hour
comprehensive evening program for career changers offered
every six weeks for $295. One-day workshop, "Re-entering
the Job Market," and two-evening workshop, "Finding a State
Job," offered periodically for $45.

Bertino, Susan, Ph.D.
13216 Military Road S.
Seattle, WA 98168
(206) 242-5410
Contact: Susan Bertino
Battery of vocational and interest-assessment tests costs $200.
Career planning counseling available at $60 per hour.

Career and Business Concepts
10900 N.E. Eighth
Bellevue, WA 98004
(206) 451-7996
Contact: Merlin McIntire
A Christian approach to professional and vocational
development. Phase I includes five sessions covering
personality typology, transferable skills testing, and outlining
of basic needs and goals; $395 fee. Phase II consists of four
sessions devoted to interviewing and self-marketing skills;
$325 fee. Free follow-up session after 45 days on the job is
included in the cost of either Phase I or Phase II.

Career Discovery
515 116th N.E., Suite 101
Bellevue, WA 98004
(206) 451-2878
Contact: Jan Reha
Services include individual counseling at $60 per session,
career assessment, some outplacement.

Career Improvement Group
150 Nickerson
Seattle, WA 98109
(206) 281-8044
Contact: Dennis Buckmaster
Conducts free workshop on the career planning process and
offers general overview of the area job market. Series of seven

workshops offered, covering all aspects of the job search, of which any combination may be taken. Workshops average $16 to $25 per hour. Private one-on-one counseling available for $70 per hour.

Career Improvement Group
10900 N.E. Eighth St., Suite 900
Bellevue, WA 98004
(206) 451-7996
Contact: Jack Wilson
Free workshop on job market review. Vocational workshops on the hidden job market, job search skills, self-marketing, resume writing, interviews. Career counseling at $70/hour.

Career Management Consultants
4556 University Way N.E.
Seattle, WA 98105
(206) 547-2448
Career exploration, interest assessment, job search and marketing skills. $45 hourly.

Career Management Institute
8404 27th W.
Tacoma, WA 98466
(206) 565-8818
Contact: Ruthann Reim
Career counseling for $50 per hour. Career life planning packages include battery of eight vocational and psychological tests and three hours of counseling for $250 or six hours of counseling for $450.

Career Transition Services
555 116th N.E., Suite 140
Bellevue, WA 98004
(206) 455-3313
Contact: Larry Kraft
No testing. Emphasis on career transitions. Three-session program covers self-evaluation and interest evaluation, new career goals and the job search, and development of a self-marketing plan. Cost is $990. Continuing counseling available for $150 per hour.

Center for Life Decisions
1216 Pine, Suite 200
Seattle, WA 98101
(206) 623-7223
Contact: Larry Gaffin
All aspects of career counseling, with some testing. Emphasis on matching inner values with work setting and helping people find socially and environmentally responsible employment.

DeWitt, Diane W., Ph.D.
2025 112th N.E., Suite 200
Bellevue, WA 98004
(206) 454-0800
Contact: Diane DeWitt
Vocational testing. Career counseling for $90 per hour. Free
telephone consultation.

Individual Development Center
1020 E. John
Seattle, WA 98102
(206) 329-0600
Contact: Mary Lou Hunt
All aspects of career exploration and planning, job search
skills. Set of seven to eight vocational/personality tests plus
three hours of counseling for $290. Counseling alone runs $65
hourly.

Lerbakken and Associates
10116 36th Ave. Court S.W., #12
Tacoma, WA 98499
Contact: Rik Lerbakken
Vocational rehabilitation. Career counseling for career
changers only, $55 per hour. Package of take-home tests plus
two hours of counseling available for $110.

Louderback and Associates
801 Second Ave., Suite 211
Seattle, WA 98104
(206) 343-5828
Contact: Judith Louderback
Comprehensive career planning and counseling. Testing for
needs, capabilities, functional flexibility, and personality is
required before counseling begins. Testing costs $100.
Counseling covers the development of new perspectives and
options, setting long- and short-term goals and priorities, and
unique approaches to researching the job market and self-
marketing. Total program ranges from $1,000 to $2,700.

Potentials Development
1223 N.E. Ballinger Place
Seattle, WA 98155
(206) 364-0737
Contact: Patrick Neils
Testing package, including several hours of tests that can be
taken at home, nine-page computerized analysis of tests, and
one hour of consultation available for $125.

Professional Dynamics
10116 36th Ave. Court S.W.
Tacoma, WA 98499
(206) 584-7888

Contact: Sue Hoff
also:
150 Nickerson, Suite 108
Seattle, WA 98103
(206) 286-9387
Contact: Kathy Papac
also:
317 Fourth Ave. E., Suite 311
Olympia, WA 98501
(206) 352-1992
Contact: Ed Hopkins
Vocational rehabilitation, some individual career counseling
and testing, vocational aptitude testing, career changes.
$50/hour.

Total Career Services
309 South G St.
Tacoma, WA 98405
(206) 383-3714
Contact: Steve Duchesne
Vocational testing and interest assessment included in the $50
hourly rate for career counseling and planning.

TRAC Associates
2722 Eastlake Ave. E., Suite 250
Seattle, WA 98102
(206) 324-9422
also:
2502 Tacoma Ave. S.
Tacoma, WA 98402
(206) 272-9299
Contact: Jack Fioto
Full range of aptitude testing, interest assessment, and
personality profiles. Packages of testing and analysis of results
range from $250 to $350. Individual career counseling costs
$50 per hour. Workshops on resume writing and interviewing,
including a video playback exercise, are also available.

Vocational Resources
19655 First Ave. S., Suite 204
Seattle, WA 98148
(206) 824-1850
Contact: Debra Stearns
also:
1700 Cooper Point Road
Olympia, WA 98502
(206) 754-1485
Contact: Chris Simmons
Vocational rehabilitation. Vocational testing, interest
assessment package available for $200. Career counseling runs
$50 to $60 hourly.

PORTLAND AREA

Career Guidance Specialists
15800 S.W. Boones Ferry Road
Lake Oswego, OR 97035
(503) 625-7513
Contact: Renette Meltebeke
Counseling for career skills discovery, resume assistance. $40 per 90-minute session.

Kevane, R.A., and Associates
Career Advisory Services
111 S.W. Columbia
Portland, OR 97201
(503) 222-9055 or (206) 693-4341
Contact: Jim Ellis
Free initial consultation. Services include assessment of skills and talents, career guidance, professional marketing interview techniques, mid-career evaluation.

New Perspectives Counseling
1962 N.W. Kearney
Portland, OR 97209
(503) 222-5442
Contact: Elaine Cornick
Offers career counseling, resumes, help with job search in hidden job market. $50/hour.

Self-Marketing
8555 S.W. Beaverton Hillsdale Highway
Portland, OR 97225
(503) 293-8103
No counseling. One-day comprehensive workshop on job hunting includes videotaped mock interview practice, problem-solving sessions on common job-search pitfalls, resume assistance. Fee is $79.95.

**Who's good?
Who's not?**

A listing in this book does not constitute an endorsement of any consulting firm or vocational testing service. Before embarking on a lengthy or expensive series of tests, try to get the opinion of one or more people who have already used the service you're considering. You can also contact the following:

Better Business Bureau of Greater Seattle (206) 448-8888

Tacoma Better Business Bureau Inquiries (206) 383-5561

Olympia Better Business Bureau (206) 754-4254

Portland Better Business Bureau (503) 226-3981

See also our Chapter 4 sidebar on a new BBB "instant info" service in Seattle.

Human Rights Department, Discrimination Complaints and Contract Compliance:

Seattle (206) 684-4500

Tacoma: Contract compliance (206) 591-5825 Discrimination complaints (206) 591-5151

Washington State Attorney General's Office, Consumer and Business Fair Practices Division (206) 464-6684 or 1-800-551-4636

Attorney General's Office, Consumer Complaints, Salem, Oregon (503) 378-4320■

COLLEGES OFFERING VOCATIONAL TESTING AND GUIDANCE

SEATTLE/PUGET SOUND AREA

Evergreen State College
Career Development Office
317 E. Fourth, Suite 305
Olympia, WA 98501
(206) 438-0744
Contact: Wendy Freeman, Director
Career counseling, peer support groups, job research programs,

and vocational testing are available free to students and alumni only. Job listings and library are open to the general public.

LH Bates Vocational-Technical Institute
1101 S. Yakima
Tacoma, WA 98405
(206) 596-1519
Contact: Arnand Yapachino, Counselor
Classes ranging from advertising and marketing to diesel mechanics. Vocational testing, career counseling, seminars available free to students and non-students.

Metropolitan Business College
615 Second Ave.
Seattle, WA 98104
(206) 624-3773
Contact: Shaun Dale, Assistant Director
Offers classes in accounting, secretarial, and computer skills. All courses touch on job-search skills. Career counseling and placement services available to students and alumni only.

North Seattle Community College
Career and Employment Services
9600 College Way North
Seattle, WA 98103
(206) 527-3685
Contact: Susan Walters Shanahan, Director
Blind job-board listings, referrals, resume critiquing, job search and skills workshops, career exploration and counseling, SIGI and Work Occupational Information Services (WOIS) computer programs are available to students and recent alumni. Vocational testing is administered for a small fee.

Pacific Lutheran University
Career Services
111 Ramstad
Tacoma, WA 98447
(206) 535-7459
Contact: Beth Ahlstrom, Director
Career counseling, planning, self-directed search surveys, vocational testing, resume writing, workshops, job listings are available to students and alumni only.

Pierce College
Career Center
9401 Far West Drive S.W.
Tacoma, WA 98498
(206) 964-6590
Contact: Nancy Raeback, Career Center Coordinator
In addition to career planning classes offered for credit, free vocational testing, job-search skills workshops, and career counseling are available for students. Non-students may take

31

the Strong Campbell test for $25 and may also make free
search of career opportunities listings for private and public
sectors; this information is updated monthly.

Seattle Central Community College
Career Placement Office
1701 Broadway
Seattle, WA 98122
(206) 587-5422
Contact: Bob Tarpchinosf, Director
Career Planning Class is offered quarterly for credit. General
assistance, handouts, and job listings are available to students
and non-students at the Career Placement Office. Vocational
testing, including the Strong Campbell test for an $8 fee and
the Meyers test, is available to students and non-students
through the Testing Office (587-6913). No interpretation is
included. The Computerized Career Library includes the SIGI
Plus program; call 587-3852 for details.

Seattle Pacific University
Career Development Center
3307 Third Ave. W.
Seattle, WA 98119
(206) 281-2018
Contact: Lisl Helms, Program Administrator
Career counseling, recruiting, co-op internship programs
(students attend school part time and work part time in their
chosen field), resume formating, and SIGI Plus computer
programs available for students only, free of charge. Students
may also attend periodic workshops, some of which may
include testing for a small fee. Career Resource Library and job
listings are open to the general public.

Seattle University
Career Development Center
McGoldrick Building
Seattle, WA 98122
(206) 296-6080
Job listings, career counseling, resume writing, recruitment
programs, and SIGI computer program available to students,
alumni, and students of other Jesuit schools only.

Shoreline Community College
Employment Services
16101 Greenwood Ave. N., Room 2120
Seattle, WA 98133
(206) 546-4610
Contact: Corky Olson, Director
Free workshops on resume writing, cover letters, job search,
interviews. Job-line numbers and job-listings board are open to
students and alumni (defined as anyone who has taken at least
one class for credit) only. Clipboard job announcements are

available to the public. Career counseling and vocational testing are available at the Counseling Center on an ongoing basis for students and alumni and on a short-term basis for members of the community. Counseling is free; $15 fee is charged for testing.

South Puget Sound Community College
Counseling and Career Center
2011 Mottman Road S.W.
Olympia, WA 98502
(206) 754-7711
One-on-one career counseling for students only. Interest inventory testing and six-hour career planning workshops are available to students and non-students. Workshop fee is $10.

South Seattle Community College
Career Planning Office
6000 16th Ave. S.W.
Seattle, WA 98106
(206) 764-5369
Contact: Anne Galarosa, Instructor
Career counseling, WOIS computer program, vocational testing, and interest assessment available. Charge for vocational testing is $7, which includes one session with a counselor. Job listings available at the Student Union Building. All services are open to students and non-students.

St. Martin's College
Career Planning/Placement
700 College St.
Lacey, WA 98503
(206) 438-4382
Testing and counseling for students only. No fees. Placement office, open to public, offers job listings in 21 different categories and copies of "Occupational Outlook Handbook" outlining types of jobs and respective salaries available in the Puget Sound area.

Tacoma Community College
Career Center
5900 S. 12th
Tacoma, WA 98465
(206) 566-5027
Contact: Susan Mitchell, Advisor
Offers wide range of services including vocational testing, WOIS and SIGI computer programs, and career counseling. Two-hour workshops on "The Hidden Job Market," "Resume Writing," "The Employment Interview," and "Applying for a Government Job" are held quarterly. All services are available free to students and non-students.

How To Get a Job

Trend College
819 E. Olympia Ave.
Olympia, WA 98506
(206) 357-9313
Contact: Frank Boronat, Career Development Coordinator
This business college offers courses and programs in all aspects
of business. Employment Assistance Program, which includes
testing, counseling, job search, and help with resume/cover-
letter writing and interviewing, is available only to students
and alumni.

University of Puget Sound
Career Development
Collins Memorial Library
1500 N. Warner
Tacoma, WA 98416
(206) 756-3250
Contact: Jack Roundy, Director
Career counseling, skills workshops, vocational testing, and
interest assessment surveys available to students and alumni
only. Job Room with job listings is open to the public.

University of Washington
Placement Center
301 Loew Hall, FH-30
Seattle, WA 98195
(206) 543-0535
Contact: Jean Hernandez, Associate Director
Available to students only. Full range of services, including
library with company binders, career counseling, skills
workshops, and recruitment programs. Alumni may have full
access to the Placement Center's programs and resources for
$20 per quarter. Non-students may subscribe to a weekly job
listing update for $35 per quarter.

University of Washington Extension
Career Counseling
University Extension Building
5001 25th N.E.
Seattle, WA 98195
(206) 543-2300
Contact: Cheryl Roberts, Program Coordinator
Career exploration, planning, job search. Counseling for $65
per hour. Three-counseling-session program, including testing,
for $195. Six-session program with testing for $390. No testing
without counseling. Available to non-students only.

PORTLAND AREA

City University
12600 S.W. 72nd Ave.
Tigard, OR 97223

(503) 620-2900
Offers business administration, accounting, and management
degrees. No formal career services department. Job
announcements are listed, however, and are open to the
public.

Clackamas Community College
Career and Job Development Office
19600 S. Molalla Ave.
Oregon City, OR 97045
(503) 657-6958
Contact: Gail Laferriere, Career Development Specialist or
Sheri Schoenborn, Placement Specialist
One of the best career resources in Oregon. Extensive library.
Vocational testing, including Edwards, Strong Campbell, and
Myers Briggs, available for nominal fees. Free interest
assessment. Discover, Career Finder, Microskills, and Career
Information computer programs available; job placement
service is also computerized. Individual career counseling.
Workshops for youth, seniors, displaced homemakers,
students, and non-students on every aspect of the job search,
from resumes to self-marketing. Videos on these subjects also
available. All services are free and available to students and
non-students.

Clark College
Career Planning Center
1800 E. McLoughlin Blvd.
Vancouver, WA 98663
(206) 699-0155
Contact: Donna Wolther, Career Resources Specialist
Vocational testing available for nominal fee. Two full-time
career counselors provide free counseling. Periodic job-search
skills workshops.

Columbia Christian College
Education Office
9101 E. Burnside St.
Portland, OR 97216
(503) 257-1206
Contact: Dr. Marshall Gunselman, Director of Teacher
Education
Workshops on resume writing, job search, mock interviews, job
placement assistance available to students pursuing a Teacher's
Certificate only. Job listings notebook includes teaching
positions throughout the state.

Concordia College/Portland
2811 N.E. Holman St.
Portland, OR 97221
(503) 280-8512
Contact: Paul Linneman

No formal career center. Placement Board in Student Services open to the public.

Lewis and Clark College
Career Planning Center
0615 S.W. Palatine Hill Road
Portland, OR 97219
(503) 293-2770
Contact: Sara Hamilton, Director
Some vocational testing. Career counseling, job-search skills workshops, job listings, Alumni Network. Free lifetime services available to students and alumni only.

Marylhurst College
Student Services
Highway 43
Marylhurst, OR 97036
(503) 620-2442 or 1-800-634-9982
Life Planning Studies Program taught by certified career counselors. Individual career counseling available for students and non-students. No testing. Job clipboard open to the public.

Oregon Institute of Technology
Career Placement
3201 Campus Drive
Klamath Falls, OR 97601
(503) 882-6321 or 1-800-343-6653
Contact: Ted Dobson, Director
Job-search and self-marketing workshops. Career counseling. Free services for students only and for up to six months after graduation.

Pacific University
2043 College Way
Forest Grove, OR 97116
(503) 357-6151 or 1-800-635-0561 Ext. 2201
Contact: David Stout, Assistant Dean of Faculty
Some vocational testing. Resume writing, interviewing, job-search workshops. Career counseling. Internships and externships (worksites outside the community and/or country). All services for students only.

Portland Community College
Career Resource Center
12000 S.W. 49th Ave.
Portland, OR 97219
(503) 244-6111
Contact: Linda Rock, Counselor
Cam Kozlowski, Job Placement Service Director
Vocational testing free for students upon referral by a counselor; $5 per test for non-students. Free career counseling

and access to computerized interest-assessment programs for students and non-students. Job Placement Service for students only.

Portland State University
Career Center
1633 S.W. Park Ave.
Portland, OR 97207
(503) 725-4613
Contact: Mary Cumpston, Director
For students only. Four areas of emphasis are: 1) student employment—new temporary and part-time listings daily; 2) career planning—includes computerized career guidance programs, career counseling, and a three-credit course called "Discovering Career Paths"; 3) enhancing job search skills; and 4) information—videos, library, company notebooks.

Reed College
Career Advising Office
3203 S.E. Woodstock Blvd.
Portland, OR 97202
(503) 777-7291
Contact: Patricia Cassidy, Director
For students only. Career exploration and development, individual counseling, job search skills workshops, alumni programs, job listings.

University of Portland
Career Services
5000 N. Willamette Blvd.
Portland, OR 97203
(503) 283-7911
Contact: Clarice Wilsey, Placement Specialist
Vocational testing, Microskills, and SIGI Plus. Resume writing and interview workshops. Career counseling and placement services. Free services for students and alumni only. However, non-students may subscribe to a weekly newsletter that lists teaching vacancies in the state. Subscription is $7.50 for three months, $15 for six months.

Warner Pacific College
2219 S.E. 68th Ave.
Portland, OR 97125
(503) 775-4366
Contact: Mary Vandiver, Director

SOCIAL SERVICE AGENCIES OFFERING VOCATIONAL TESTING AND GUIDANCE

Be sure to check out the listings of Social Service Agencies and Government Agencies in Chapter 6.

How To Get a Job

SEATTLE/PUGET SOUND AREA

Community Youth Services
824 Fifth Ave. S.E.
Olympia, WA 98501
(206) 943-0780
Contact: Paula Raven, Program Manager
Vocational testing, classroom and on-the-job training.

Education Opportunities and Resource Center (EORC)
622 Tacoma Ave. S.
Tacoma, WA 98402
(206) 572-5960
Contact: Marcia Petersen, Inter-Agency Coordinator
Provides free vocational testing, interest assessment, and
career counseling, by appointment, to Pierce County
residents. Job listings and government grant applications
available.

Employment Opportunities Center
4726 Rainier South
Seattle, WA 98118
(206) 725-8200
Contact: Harry Wong
This private, non-profit agency serves the Asian population in
the Seattle metropolitan area. Job listings, some testing,
bilingual counseling, pilot programs in job-search skills are
available free of charge.

Morningside
PO Box 1937
Olympia, WA 98507
(206) 943-0512
Contact: Richard Craighead, Job Developer
Serves income-eligible disabled clients. Vocational testing, on-
the-job training programs, referrals, placement, monthly
evaluation. Counseling available through Thurston County
Mental Health Department.

YWCA
220 Union Ave. S.E.
Olympia, WA 98501
(206) 352-0593
Job search workshops, vocational testing, career counseling,
support groups. Career exploration programs for displaced
homemakers.

YWCA of Seattle/King County
Program Center—Employment Services
1118 Fifth Ave.
Seattle, WA 98101
(206) 461-4862

also:
Eastside Branch
1420 156th Ave. N.E.
Bellevue, WA 98007
(206) 644-7361
North Area Branch
12531 28th Ave. N.E.
Seattle, WA 98125
(206) 364-6810
Job board organized by category. Free workshops every
Tuesday afternoon, covering resume writing, job-search skills,
interviews. Vocational testing for $25 fee. Career counseling is
free to homeless and is available on a sliding scale to others.

PORTLAND AREA

Employment Training and Business Services
PO Box 215
Marylhurst, OR 97036
(503) 635-4591
Some vocational testing. Career assessment, job search, and
interview workshops. Career counseling. Available free of
charge to low-income residents of Clackamas County.

Goodwill Industries of the Columbia-Willamette
1831 S.E. Sixth
Portland, OR 97214
(503) 238-6100
Contact: Karen DuVall, Public Relations
Training and employment programs for disabled, including
counseling, vocational testing, mock interviews, assistance with
resumes, outplacement. Services by referral only.

Human Solutions
2900 S.E. 122nd Ave.
Portland, OR 97236
(503) 248-5200
Training and employment programs, vocational testing, job
matching program.

Job Opportunity Bank
2710 N.E. 14th Ave.
Portland, OR 97212
(503) 288-1602
Non-profit community service organization of Ecumenical
Ministries of Oregon, which provides "job-search skills,
services, and group support to persons in the process of career
change."

Network
1950 Fort Vancouver Way
Vancouver, WA 98663

(206) 696-8409
Funded by the Job Training Partnership Act. Provides
vocational testing, career exploration and counseling, and on-
the-job training to income-eligible residents of Clark, Cowlitz,
Wahkiakum, and Skamania counties in Washington State.

Thinking of Starting Your Own Small Business?

Many basic questions about starting your own small
company can be answered by the **U.S. Small Business
Administration.** This federal program will mail free
information on a variety of topics, including loan programs, tax preparation, government contracts, and
management problems.

Although simple questions can be answered by telephone, you'll learn more by dropping by one of the
main offices to meet with staff members or volunteers
from SCORE (Service Corps of Retired Executives). You
may be matched up with a retired professional in your
field who can share information that will help you get
started. In addition, members of ACE (Active Corps of
Executives), a volunteer group of working professionals,
are on hand to offer assistance.

These volunteers conduct free seminars covering
major topics of interest to new business owners. Programs are scheduled regularly at the main offices; others
are held at community colleges and elsewhere in the
community.

The **Small Business Administration** also operates **Small Business Development Centers** throughout Washington State and Oregon. For more information about the Centers, call the District Offices listed
below.

SEATTLE/PUGET SOUND AREA

Small Business Administration/SCORE District Office
915 Second Ave., Room 1792, Mail Code 1013
Seattle, WA 98174
(206) 442-8403

**Small Business Administration/SCORE Regional
Office**
2615 Fourth Ave., Suite 440
Seattle, WA 98121
(206) 442-2872

Small Business Administration/SCORE Tacoma Office
950 Pacific Ave., Suite 300
Tacoma, WA 98402
(206) 627-2175

Check out Chapter 5 to learn about the range of
networking organizations for Seattle/Portland area
entrepreneurs.
The following small business centers may also be of
assistance:

**City of Tacoma Department of Community
Development**
Department of Business Assistance and Economic
Development
747 Market St.
Tacoma, WA 98402
(206) 591-5200
Contact: Bob Remen, Economic Development Specialist
Programs for businesses requiring loan assistance; low-interest
programs.

Downtown Seattle Association
1402 Third Ave.
1010 Joseph Vance Building
Seattle, WA 98101
(206) 623-0340
Represents business in downtown Seattle. Information on
promotion and marketing available. Publishes bi-monthly
newsletter for members.

Downtown Tacoma Association
950 Pacific Ave., Suite 400
Tacoma, WA 98402
(206) 572-4200
Information on demographics, promotion, and development.
Publishes quarterly newsletter for membership of downtown
Tacoma businesses.

Economic Development Council
721 Columbia S.W.
Olympia, WA 98501
(206) 754-6320
Contact: Kathy Combf
This private, non-profit agency provides small businesses with
information on site selection, recruiting, financing, attracting
investments, among others. One-on-one, case-by-case
consultations are free of charge.

How To Get a Job

Home Based Business Association
PO Box 111132
Tacoma, WA 98411
Contact: John Schultz
Support and networking organization for people operating home-based businesses. Bi-monthly newsletter. Meetings with speakers nine times per year.

Independent Business Association
920 108th N.E., Suite #3
Bellevue, WA 98004
(206) 453-8621 or 1-800-562-9989 if calling from outside the greater Seattle area
Contact: Gary Smith, Executive Director
Lobbying association and legislative hotline for small businesses in Washington State. Monthly newsletter.

King County Minority and Women's Business Enterprises
King County Courthouse, Room E224
516 Third Ave.
Seattle, WA 98104
(206) 296-7617
Helps enhance contracting opportunities with King County. For certified companies owned by minorities or women only.

Seattle-King County Economic Development Council
2510 Columbia Center
701 Fifth Ave.
Seattle, WA 98104
(206) 386-5040
Contact: Laurie Owen, Business Development Coordinator
This private, non-profit agency acts as a resource and information clearinghouse for businesspeople. The Business Development Group will help new businesses find land or office space. The Marketing Development Group helps suppliers hook up with manufacturers. "The Business Help Center" is a directory listing of resources available to small businesses in the Seattle-King County area.

Tacoma Small Business Development Center
950 Pacific Ave.
Tacoma, WA 98402
(206) 272-7232
Contact: Neil Delisante

Tacoma-Pierce County Small Business Incubator
3202 Portland Ave.
Tacoma, WA 98404
(206) 272-0068
Contact: Gary Waller, Manager
Privately owned and operated service for fledgling businesses.

Offers secretarial support, answering service, and graphics. Copier and copying materials are available. Businesses may rent space in the Incubator's building or use the services only for low monthly fee.

Washington State Business Assistance Center
919 Lakeridge Way S.W.
Olympia, WA 98502
(206) 753-5632
Hotline: 1-800-237-1233
Contact: Brian Teller
General resources center for small businesses. Information on licensing, child care. Mediation and consultation available for businesses having trouble with state agencies.

Washington State Office of Minority and Women's Business Enterprises
406 S. Water, Mail Stop FK-11
Olympia, WA 98504
(206) 753-9693
Certification of businesses owned by minorities and/or women. Loan assistance. Publishes the "OMBE Directory," listing certified companies owned by minorities and/or women, available for $10 quarterly.

Washington State Small Business Development Center
721 Columbia Ave.
Olympia, WA 98501
(206) 753-5616
Contact: Neil Miller
Funded by Washington State University, the center provides general start-up assistance to small businesses. Information on budgeting, regulations, and financing.

Women Business Owners
12601 S.E. 255th Place
Kent, WA 98031
(206) 447-2371
Contact: Darlene Garner, Coordinator
Networking organization for women who own a business or part of a small business. Monthly luncheon meetings with keynote speakers. Monthly newsletter for members.

Women Entrepreneurs Network (East Sound Chapter)
PO Box 5536
Bellevue, WA 98006
(206) 340-1679
Contact: Gilla Bachellerie
also:
Women Entrepreneurs Network (West Sound Chapter)
3010 17th St.
Bremerton, WA 98312

How To Get a Job

(206) 479-7946
Contact: Debi Andrews
Support, information, and networking group for women who own businesses or are considering starting one. Each chapter publishes a monthly newsletter.

PORTLAND AREA

Small Business Administration
1220 S.W. Third
Portland, OR 97204
(503) 221-2682

Small Business Administration/SCORE
222 S.W. Columbia, Suite 500
Portland, OR 97201
(503) 221-3441

Portland Development Commission (PDC)
1120 S.W. Fifth Ave., Suite 1100
Portland, OR 97204
(503) 796-5301
The Business Resource Directory lists all agencies in the Portland metropolitan area that provide assistance to businesses. JOBNET is a service designed to link up employers with employment assistance and services. The PDC also gives direct assistance to manufacturing and industrial firms.

Small Business Development Center
221 N.W. Second Ave.
Portland, OR 97209
(503) 228-9411
Three major areas of emphasis are: 1) counseling, consulting, and training. Free, confidential one-on-one counseling. Consulting topics include compiling a business plan, how to turn your idea into a viable business, how to market your business, and how to gain financial assistance; 2) classes, plus more than 50 different workshops taught by local businesspeople at locations throughout the greater Portland area; and 3) a small business management curriculum, with 54 hours of instruction covering marketing, financial management, organization, and business systems and controls. Nominal fee for some workshops and individual counseling beyond that which is included in the initial introduction to the program.

Small Business Development Center Network
99 W. 10th, Suite 216
Eugene, OR 97401
(503) 726-2250
Write or call for more information about the Small Business Development Centers located throughout the state of Oregon.

Need a hand getting your business off the ground?

Small businesses are perhaps the backbone of Oregon's economy, with 95 percent of all firms employing less than 50 employees. In a unique partnership with these businesses, the **Oregon Small Business Development Center Network** offers new business owners an inexpensive—often free—opportunity to develop ownership skills, solve start-up problems, locate customers, and grow profitable businesses.

The three metropolitan Portland centers listed below offer free ongoing business consulting. Visitors may browse each center's extensive business library of small business management books, magazines, journals, directories, legal and regulatory manuals, audio and video tapes, and hands-on computer labs.

Clackamas Community College
Harmony Center, 7616 S.E. Harmony Road
Milwaukie, OR 97222
(503) 656-4447
Contact: Bob Ellis, Director:
The **Greenhouse Program** nurtures new businesses by teaching essential technical, marketing, and financial skills. It includes weekly seminars and individual counseling.

Mt. Hood Community College, Center for Business Development
26000 S.E. Stark
Gresham, OR 97030
(503) 667-7658
Contact: Don King, Director
Because women outnumber men

in starting businesses, this center offers two women-only workshops. The **Women's Business Management Program** combines monthly workshops with on-site consultations for women-owned businesses. The **Starting a Business Confidently** series is for start-ups.

Portland Community College
Portland Chamber of Commerce Building
221 N.W. Second Ave.
Portland, OR 97209
(503) 273-2828
Contact: Hal Bergmann, Director
The **Preparing for Outrageous Ownership** program offers more than 60 hours of instruction in business design skills.■

Resources for Women

A career counselor we know who focuses on women job hunters states, "Women are too often resistant to asking for help. They feel they must tough it out. A woman facing a major transition—newly widowed, newly divorced, reentering the work force, or starting to work for the first time—needs help and support. Fortunately, in the Puget Sound area and in Portland there are wonderful resources available for women. My advice: Get help."

The following resources specialize in meeting the needs of women. Don't forget to check out the Social Service Agencies listed earlier in this chapter and in Chapter 6, and the networking organizations listed in Chapter 5 for additional support and information.

SEATTLE/PUGET SOUND AREA

Apprenticeship and Nontraditional Employment for Women
3000 N.E. Fourth, Building L
Renton, WA 98056
(206) 235-2212

This agency provides training in nontraditional jobs for women ages 16 through 60. It is a five-month program, five days a week. The training includes job skills, and courses in carpentry, welding, cement masonry, tying steel, trade math, blueprint reading and drawing, mechanical and electrical theory and practice, basic carpentry, and construction techniques. This program is only open to low-income women and must meet federal Job Training Partnership Act guidelines. All expenses are paid, including schooling, child care, books, tools, and job-related transportation.

City of Seattle Office for Women's Rights
700 Third Ave., Suite 940
Seattle, WA 98104
(206) 684-0390
This office provides economic, political, and social support for Seattle's women. More than 250 jobs are listed, many of which are nontraditional jobs for women. The agency also publishes the "Referrals and Resources Guide," which lists over 250 agencies for women in the Seattle and King County areas. The guide may be purchased for $4.

City of Tacoma Human Rights Department
Office of Women's Rights
747 Market St.
Tacoma, WA 98402
(206) 591-5161 or (206) 591-5158
Provides information on jobs in the City of Tacoma. Female firefighter recruitment program.

Displaced Homemakers
Pierce College Training Institute
10206 126th St. East
Puyallup, WA 98374
(206) 964-6732
Contact: Evelyn Jackson
A program for women who are separated, widowed, divorced, or the spouse of a disabled man and were or have been married for at least 10 years or are at least 35 years old. Two-week sessions cover self-esteem, motivation, interest assessment, and job-search techniques. On-the-job training and/or educational assistance are available as part of the Individual Training Program.

**King County Department of Human Resources—
Women's Program**
414 Smith Tower
Seattle, WA 98104
(206) 296-5220
Contact: Elaine Ko
Comprehensive legal, medical, housing information and referral services available. Job Bank and job listings.

Washington Women United
1063 Capitol Way South, Room 213B
Olympia, WA 98501
(206) 754-9880
Organization composed of associations and individuals who
work to address women's issues in the State of Washington.
Lobbying, networking, information clearinghouse, job listings.

Washington Women's Employment & Education
1525 Fourth Ave., Suite 510
Seattle, WA 98101
(206) 447-9786
also:
1517 Fawcett St.
Tacoma, WA 98402
(206) 627-0527
Serves low-income women, women on welfare, and heads of
household with no income. Financial assistance available for
transportation and child care. GED classes. Three-week course
in resume writing, interviewing, and job skills.

Women's Yellow Pages
Geha Sorger, Editor/Publisher
7318 15th Ave. N.E.
Seattle, WA 98115
(206) 522-5894 or (206) 726-9687
Available from New Media Productions (same address/phone)
for $5.95, or from Puget Sound area bookstores. Lists women-
owned businesses, as well as women professionals; includes
helpful articles on such topics as financial investment, creating
your own business, etc. Also available from this publisher is a
calendar of events for women's organizations throughout Puget
Sound, published quarterly for $7. Washington residents add
sales tax when ordering items by mail.

YWCA
220 Union Ave. S.W.
Olympia, WA 98501
(206) 352-0593
Provides job-opening lists for city, county, state, and
educational institutions. Twice-monthly workshops: "Accessing
the Hidden Job Market in Thurston County" and "Successful
Interviewing Skills"; cost for each is $20. Free Discovery
Program for displaced homemakers. Also provides referral and
information services for job seekers. See also listing for the
YWCA of Seattle-King County under Social Service Agencies
earlier in this chapter; many suburbs and smaller municipalities
have their own branches.

PORTLAND AREA

Displaced Homemakers
Clackamas Community College
19600 S. Molalla Ave.
Oregon City, OR 97045
(503) 657-6958
Contact: Gail Laferriere, Career Development Specialist
Extensive Displaced Homemakers program at one of Oregon's
most successful and well used career resource centers.
Vocational testing, full range of computer programs, individual
career counseling, workshops, placement.

**Institute For Managerial & Professional Women
(IMPW)**
PO Box 40324
Portland, OR 97240
(503) 230-2129
Throughout the year, this not-for-profit organization schedules
workshops and other programs to help women build
managerial and professional skills. Provides applied
management experience for members.

**Oregon Business & Professional Women/Oregon
BPW/USA**
PO Box 69106, University Station
Portland, OR 97201
(503) 227-1165
Groups meet monthly in various communities throughout
Oregon, providing valuable contacts and helping members to
develop leadership skills. Scholarship program for women
wishing to return to school to be more productive in the job
market. Works with legislature to obtain financial equality for
women.

Women's Yellow Pages
1208 S.W. 13th St., Suite 212
Portland, OR 97205
(503) 223-9344
This free publication lists more than 1,500 women-owned
businesses, women's groups, and women in the Portland area
with skills to share. Entries include name, address, phone
number, skills, interests, and line of business.

YWCA
1111 S.W. 10th Ave.
Portland, OR 97205
(503) 223-6281
Women's Resource Center provides information and referral
service, Job Finders classes, counseling. Job board includes
government, social services, and private sector.

3

Writing a Resume
That Works

Volumes have been written about how to write a resume. That's because, in our opinion, generations of job seekers have attached great importance to the creation and perfection of their resumes. Keep in mind that *no one ever secured a job offer on the basis of a resume alone.* The way to land a good position is to succeed in the employment interview. *You have to convince a potential employer that you're the best person for the job. No piece of paper will do that for you.*

The resume also goes by the name of *curriculum vita* ("the course of one's life"), or *vita* ("life") for short. These terms are a little misleading, however. A resume cannot possibly tell the story of your life, especially since, as a rule, it shouldn't be more than two pages long. The French word *résumé* means "a summing up." In the American job market, a resume is a concise, written summary of your work experience, education, accomplishments, and personal background—the essentials an employer needs to evaluate your qualifications.

A resume is nothing more or less than a simple marketing tool, a print ad for yourself. It is sometimes useful in generating interviews. But it is most effective when kept in reserve until *after* you've met an employer in person. Sending a follow-up letter *after* the interview, along with your resume, reminds the interviewer of that wonderful person he or she met last Thursday.

The Basics of a Good Resume

The resume is nothing for you to agonize over. But since almost every employer will ask you for one at some point in the hiring process, make sure that yours is a good one.

What do we mean by a good resume? First, *be sure it's up to date and comprehensive.* At a minimum it should include your name, address, and phone number; a complete summary of your work experience; and an education profile. (College grads need not include their high school backgrounds.)

In general, your work experience should include the name, location, and dates of employment of every job you've held since leaving school, plus a summary of your responsibilities and, most important, your accomplishments on each job.

If you're a recent graduate, or have held several jobs, you can present your experience chronologically. Begin with your present position and work backward to your first job. If you haven't had that many jobs, organize your resume to emphasize the skills you've acquired through experience.

A second rule of resume writing is to *keep the resume concise.* Most employers don't want to read more than two pages, and one page is preferable. In most cases your resume will be scanned, not read in detail. Describe your experience in short, pithy phrases. Avoid large blocks of copy. Your resume should read more like a chart than a short story.

There are no hard and fast rules on what to include in your resume besides work experience and education. A statement of your objective and a personal section containing date of birth, marital status, and so on, are

51

optional. An employer wants to know these things about you, but it's up to you whether to include them in your resume or bring them up during the interview. If you have served in the military, you ought to mention that in your resume.

Your salary history and references, however, should *not* be included in your resume; these should be discussed in person during the interview.

Keep in mind that a resume is a sales tool. Make sure that it illustrates your unique strengths in a style and format you can be comfortable with. Indicate any unusual responsibilities you've been given, or examples of how you've saved the company money or helped it grow. Include any special recognition of your ability. For example, if your salary increased substantially within a year or two, you might state the increase in terms of a percentage.

Third, *keep your resume honest.* Never lie, exaggerate, embellish, or deceive. Tell the truth about your education, accomplishments, and work history. You needn't account for every single work day that elapsed between jobs, however. If you left one position on November 15 and began the next on February 1, you can minimize the gap by simply listing years worked instead of months.

Fourth, *your resume should have a professional look.* If you type it yourself or have it typed professionally, use a high-quality office typewriter with a plastic ribbon (sometimes called a "carbon" ribbon). Do not use a household or office typewriter with a cloth ribbon.

If your budget permits, consider having your resume typeset professionally or typed on a good-quality word processor. In either case you have a choice of type faces, such as boldface, italics, and small caps. You can also request that the margins be justified (lined up evenly on the right and left sides, like the margins of a book).

No matter what method you use to prepare your resume, be sure to *proofread it* before sending it to the printer. A misspelled word or typing error reflects badly on you, even if it's not your fault. Read every word out loud, letter for letter and comma for comma. Get a friend to help you.

Do *not* make copies of your resume on a photocopy machine. Have it printed professionally. The resume you leave behind after an interview or send ahead to obtain an interview may be photocopied several times, and copies of copies can be very hard to read. You should also avoid such gimmicks as using colored paper (unless it's very light cream or light gray) or using a paper size other than 8 1/2 x 11".

Our purpose here is not to tell you how to write the ideal resume (there is no such thing) but rather to provide some general guidelines. The following books are full of all the how-to information you'll need to prepare an effective resume and are available from bookstores or your local library.

BOOKS ON RESUME WRITING

Bostwick, Burdette. *Resume Writing.* New York: John Wiley and Sons, 1985.

Corwen, Leonard. *Your Resume: Key to a Better Job.* New York: Arco, 1984.

Coxford, Lola M. *Resume Writing Made Easy.* New York: Gorsuch, 1989.

Foxman, Loretta D., and Walter L. Polsky. *Resumes That Work: How to Sell Yourself On Paper.* New York: John Wiley and Sons, 1988.

Krannich, Ronald L. *High Impact Resumes and Letters.* Vienna, VA: Impact, 1988.

Lewis, Adele. *How to Write a Better Resume.* Woodbury, NY: Barron's Educational Series, 1989.

Nadler, Burton Jay. *Liberal Arts Power: How to Sell It on Your Resume.* Princeton, NJ: Peterson's Guides, 1985.

Parker, Yana. *The Resume Catalog.* Berkeley, CA: Ten Speed Press,

Should You Hire Someone Else To Write Your Resume?

In general, if you have reasonable writing skills, it's better to prepare your own resume than to ask someone else to do it. If you write your own job history, you'll be better prepared to talk about it in the interview. "Boiler plate" resumes also tend to look and sound alike. On the other hand, a professional resume writer can be objective about your background and serve as a sounding board on what you should and shouldn't include. You might also consider a professional if you have trouble writing in the condensed style that a good resume calls for.

Here is a list of Seattle/Portland area firms that will assist you in preparing your resume. Many career counselors and consultants also provide resume preparation; you may wish to contact those listed in Chapter 2. Remember that a listing in this book does *not* constitute an endorsement. Before engaging a professional writer, ask for a recommendation from someone whose judgment

53

you trust—a personnel director, college placement officer, or a knowledgeable friend. Check with the Better Business Bureau and other consumer advocates listed in Chapter 2 to see if there have been any complaints made about the resume service you are considering.

How to choose a professional

Before engaging a professional to help you write your resume, run through the following checklist of questions.

▌ **What will it cost?** Some firms charge a set fee. Others charge by the hour. Though many firms will not quote an exact price until they know the details of your situation, you should obtain minimum and maximum costs before you go ahead.

▌ **What does the price include?** Does the fee cover only writing? Or does it include typesetting? Most firms will charge extra for printing.

▌ **What happens if you're not satisfied?** Will the writer make changes you request? Will changes or corrections cost extra?

▌ **How do this writer's fees and experience stack up against others?** It's wise to shop around before you buy writing services, just as you would when purchasing any other service.■

PROFESSIONAL RESUME PREPARERS

SEATTLE/PUGET SOUND AREA

A AAPRO Resume Company
13353 Bellevue Redmond Road
Bellevue, WA 98005
(206) 643-2349
Fee: $10 to $600, depending on nature of project. Includes 25 copies of final resume. Help with cover letters, salary histories, reference listings, and follow-up letters also available. Straight typing available for $20 per hour.

A Professional Resume and Writing Service
825 Legion Way S.E., Suite D

Olympia, WA 98501
(206) 754-6330
Contact: Stephanie Brooks
Fee: $9 for standard high-school student's information sheet to
$300 for bound presentations.

A Professional Resume and Writing Service
506 Second Ave.
Smith Tower, Suite 2001
Seattle, WA 98104
(206) 587-6272
Contact: Claudia Quate
Fee: $10 to $300 for initial interview, drafting, and final
printing of resume.

A Professional Resume and Writing Service
19105 36th Ave. W.
Alderwood Business Center
Building #2, Suite 210
Lynwood, WA 98036
(206) 527-4800
Contact: Jim Esson
Fee: $20 to $200, depending on nature and extent of
background. Includes interview, composition, editing, laser
printing.

A Professional Resume and Writing Service
7406 27th St. W., #212
Tacoma, WA 98466
(206) 564-7662
Contact: Dave Hanson
Fee: $5 to $300, depending on extent of background and
number of pages. Discounts on revisions. $15 to $20 per page
for straight typing.

Action Resume Service
809 E. 56th
Tacoma, WA 98404
(206) 473-2452
Contact: Linda Edwards
Fee: $45 for one-page standard resume and cover letter. $75
for standard profile for company managers. $250 for executive
profile.

Career Management Resources
1750 112th Ave. N.E.
Seattle, WA 98004
(206) 454-6982
Contact: Tom Washington
Fee: Free initial interview. $150 to $250 for composition of
resume with client, editing, production of final resume.
Revisions are done on a $45-per-hour basis.

Career Services Group
2111 N. Northgate Way, Suite 206
Seattle, WA 98133
(206) 361-0934
Contact: Michael B. Wright
Fee: $10 to $300, depending on extent of project. Fees for revisions vary. Free lifetime storage on disk.

Dorothy's Unique Resume Service
1420 Auburn Way S.
Auburn, WA 98002
(206) 228-8489
Contact: Tom Cadero
Fee: $100 includes initial interview, composition with client, cover letter, two final copies. $25 for revisions.

Executive Resumes
(206) 622-0117
By appointment only.
Contact: Milly Culp
Fee: $95 for their budget resume. Fee for the Executive Resume Service, which includes one interview, writing and revisions with client, and marketing strategy, depends on extent of project.

Executive West Lazer Printed Resumes
4700 42nd S.W., Suite 670
Seattle, WA 98116
(206) 932-2825
Contact: Sheree Lucchesi
Fee: $25 for compilation of data, proof copy, editing, and final version. Add $.50 per page for laser typeset copies. Add $2.50 for permanent disk storage. $5 fee for reinsertion of disk includes revisions and copies.

Island Wordsmith, The
10140 N.E. High School Road
Bainbridge, WA 98110
(206) 842-9343
Contact: Brian Dunn
Fee: Free 5- to 10-minute interview. $300 for finished package. Additional writing, editing, and consultation available at $40 per hour. Digital typesetting for $30 hourly.

Mattley Resumes
8815 S. Tacoma Way, #118
Tacoma, WA 98408
(206) 581-7207
Contact: Mrs. Mattley
Fee: $20 to $150. Standard package, including interview, rough draft, editing, final resume, runs approximately $70. File is kept on disk for one year.

Office Overload
8419 34th Ave. W.
Tacoma, WA 98466
(206) 564-7930
Contact: Janell Wight
Fee: $20 per hour. Standard resume, including interview,
composition, and printing, averages $40. For formatting and
printing only, fee averages $30.

Resumes by Ed Bagley
4109 Bridgeport Way W., Suite D
Tacoma, WA 98466
(206) 565-6484
Contact: Ed Bagley
Fee: Executive services range from $75 to $400, depending on
scope of project.

Sixth Avenue Center
4313 Sixth Ave. S.E.
Lacey, WA 98503
(206) 459-5157
Contact: Anne Waldron
Fee: $20 for single page, $30 for two pages. Includes three
copies on bond paper; free revisions.

PORTLAND AREA

A Business/Creative Writing and Resume Service
510 S.W. Third, Suite 434
Portland, OR 97204
(503) 274-0587
Various resumes: bound, cover letters, follow-ups. Minimum of
$35.

A Professional Resume and Writing Service
320 S.W. Stark
Portland, OR 97204
(503) 295-6295

Advanced Resume Concepts
4755 S.W. Watson
Beaverton, OR 97005
(503) 646-0499
Free initial consultation. Complete writing services,
typesetting with bound format if desired. A rewrite with 25
copies on parchment linen paper with matching envelopes
and computer storage for future updates, fee $65.

American Resume Service
10175 S.W. Barbar Blvd.
Portland, OR 97219
(503) 244-5252

also:
2124 N.E. Sandy Blvd.
Portland, OR 97232
(503) 235-5100
Free consultation. Complete resume services, including target market, cover letters, and follow-ups. Works within client's budget.

Letter Perfect
12150 S.W. First St.
Beaverton, OR 97005
(503) 626-6137
Laser-set first page $29.95, second page $17.55. Typed or word-processed resumes. Also business letters, brochures, flyers. Ten-minute free consultation; otherwise $39.

National Resume Service
2104 S.E. Tamarack
Portland, OR 97214
(503) 235-5582

Resume Plus
1800 S.W. Beaverton-Hillsdale Highway
Beaverton, OR 97201
(503) 644-5699
Career counseling, rewrites, updates, cover letters, and follow-ups.

Resumes
8305 S.E. Monterey Ave., No. 220
Portland, OR 97266
(503) 635-4606
also:
320 S.W. Stark, No. 506
Portland, OR 97204
(503) 295-6295

Resume writing tips—for free

At the **Seattle Public Library's Career Information and Job Search Center** (1000 Fourth Ave., Second Floor, (206) 386-4636) you can pick up a free copy of their "Guide to Resume Writing." This booklet, as well as information on area firms and many other job-hunting resources, is also available at the Library's many other branches, which are listed in Chapter 4.■

What NOT To Do with Your Resume Once You Have It Printed

Do not change your resume except to correct an obvious error. Everyone to whom you show the resume will have some suggestion for improving it: "Why didn't you tell 'em that you had a scholarship?" or "Wouldn't this look better in italics?" The time to consider those kinds of questions is *before* you go to the typesetter. Afterward, the only thing to keep in mind is that there is no such thing as a perfect resume, except typographically.

A second point to remember: DO NOT send out a mass mailing. If you send letters to 700 company presidents, you can expect a response of from 7 to 9 percent—and 80 percent of the responses will be negative. The shotgun approach is expensive; it takes time and costs money for postage and printing. You'll get much better results if you are selective about where you send your resume. We'll discuss this at greater length in Chapter 5. The important thing is to concentrate on known hiring authorities in whom you are interested.

The power of verbs

Gary J. has been an engineer in Portland for 20 years. During those years he has changed jobs seven times, enhancing his career with each move. Gary realized early that using powerful, active verbs to describe his accomplishments made his resume stand out. Here are some sample verbs that job seekers in various career areas might use to help build a more effective resume.

Advertising/ Promotion
Generated
Recruited
Tailored
Sparked

Communications
Facilitated
Edited
Consulted
Disseminated

Creative
Devised
Effected
Originated
Conceived

Management
Controlled
Headed
Implemented

Methods and Controls	Public Relations/ Human Relations
Restructured	Monitored
Cataloged	Handled
Verified	Sponsored
Systematized	Integrated
Negotiations	
Engineered	**Resource-fulness**
Mediated	Rectified
Proposed	Pioneered
Negotiated	Achieved■

Always Include a Cover Letter

Never, never send your resume without a cover letter. Whether you are answering a want ad or following up an inquiry call or interview, you should always include a letter with your resume. If at all possible, the letter should be addressed to a specific person—the one who's doing the hiring—and not "To Whom It May Concern."

A good cover letter, like a good resume, is *brief*—usually not more than three or four paragraphs. No paragraph should be longer than three or four sentences. If you've already spoken to the contact person by phone, remind him or her of your conversation in the first paragraph. If you and the person to whom you are writing know someone in common, the first paragraph is the place to mention it. You should also include a hard-hitting sentence about why you're well qualified for the job in question.

In the next paragraph or two, specify what you could contribute to the company in terms that indicate you've done your homework on the firm and the industry. Finally, either request an interview or tell the reader that you will follow up with a phone call within a week to arrange a mutually convenient meeting.

Remember that the focus of your job search is to sell yourself as a match to fit an employer's needs. You should emphasize that you match the company's needs throughout all of your communication—your resume, phone calls, cover letters, and follow-up letters.

Choosing a Resume Format

There are a number of different methods for composing a quality resume. Every career counselor and resume compiler has his or her own favorite method and style. As the person being represented by the resume, *you* must choose the style and format that best suits and sells you. Many resume books will use different terms for the various styles. We will highlight the three most popular types.

1. *The chronological resume* is the traditional style, most often used in the workplace and job search; that does not mean it is the most effective. Positive aspects of the chronological resume include the traditionalist approach that employers may expect. It also can highlight past positions that you may wish your potential employer to notice. This resume is also very adaptable, with only the reverse chronological order of items as the essential ingredient.

2. *The functional resume* is most common among career changers, people reentering the job market after a lengthy absence, and those wishing to highlight aspects of their experience not related directly to employment. This resume ideally focuses on the many skills one has used at his or her employment and the accomplishments one has achieved. It shows a potential employer that you can do and have done a good job. What it doesn't highlight is where you have done it.

3. *The combination resume* combines the best features of a functional resume and a chronological resume. This allows job seekers to highlight skills and accomplishments while still maintaining the somewhat traditional format of reverse chronological order of positions held and organizations worked for.

Here are some sample resumes and cover letters to help you with your own. The books listed earlier in this chapter will supply many more examples than we have room for here.

SAMPLE CHRONOLOGICAL RESUME

GEORGE P. BURDELL
555 Maple Avenue
Seattle, WA 98105
(206) 555-2436

OBJECTIVE

Position in technical management.

WORK EXPERIENCE

SAMPO CORPORATION   1978-1990

Manager, Marketing & Planning-(Taiwan)   1988-1990
- **Supervised** operations & staff of **new products development.**
- Instrumental in **making decisions** regarding **OEM new products** with clients such as: IBM, NCR, TI, Xerox, Quadram, etc.
- **Developed 4 new products:** Low-cost display monitor, oscilloscope, and two DEC-compatible terminals.
- Accomplishment: IPD **sales volume** in 1989: **$45,000,000; 50% increase** from 1987.

Manager, Pacific Northwest   1986-1988
- Generated **$3,000,000 in sales** of OEM display monitors to IBM(NC), NCR(SC), Quadram, Digital Control, & other local accounts.

Sales Engineer—(Seattle, WA)   1985-1986
- Successfully collaborated with OEM engineers to **develop** monitors for computer & laser games such as Jungle King & Dragon's Lair.

Production Engineer—(Tacoma, WA)   1983-1985
- Member of team credited with building **Washington's first TV manufacturing plant.**
- **Involvement in this $7,000,000** project ranged from conceptualization to production of 600, 19" color sets daily.

Circuit Design Engineer-(Taiwan)   1978-1983
  I Designed PIF, deflection & remote control circuit
  for color TV.

EDUCATION

University of Washington, Seattle, WA: **MBA in marketing,** 1986

Evergreen State College, Olympia, WA: **B.A.,** 1977

REFERENCES

Furnished upon request

SAMPLE FUNCTIONAL RESUME

KATHY JONES
256 Sarasota Drive
Portland, OR 97229
(503) 555-5902

OBJECTIVE: Seek position as an
administrative assistant,
utilizing my adminstrative,
organizational, and computer skills.

SKILLS

Administrative
- I Independently straightened out a major client's account for an advertising agency.
- I Kept books and managed funds in excess of $80,000 for a non-profit corporation.
- I Managed two rental properties.

Organizational
- I Set up procedure for assigned experiments and procured equipment for a research laboratory.
- I Planned course syllabi, assessed weaknesses of individual students to facilitate learning.

63

Computer
- Managed data input and generated monthly reports.
- Completed courses in FORTRAN and BASIC.

EMPLOYMENT

Computer Operator, Woolco, Portland, OR
(1988-Present)

Trouble-shooter in accounting, Cargill, Wilson,
and Acree, Portland, OR (1986)

Instructor, Math Dept., Lewis & Clark College (1982-85)

EDUCATION

M.S., Mathematics   Oregon Graduate Institute   (1981)

B.A., Mathematics   Pacific University   (1979)

REFERENCES

Furnished upon request.

SAMPLE COMBINATION RESUME

SUSAN SKINNER
122 Pine St.
Olympia, WA 98501
(206) 555-0011

OBJECTIVE: Software development position utilizing software and computer skills.

EDUCATION: **UNIVERSITY OF WASHINGTON**
GPA 3.7/4.0
M.S., Information and Computer Science 12/86

CORNELL UNIVERSITY (NEW YORK) GPA 3.5/4.0
A.B., Mathematics 5/81

QUALIFICATIONS:

Career-related projects:
- Designed and implemented multitasking operating system for the IBM-PC.
- Implemented compiler for Pascal-like language.
- Implemented simulation project using tasking in Ada.
- Designed electronic mail system using PSL/PSA specification language.
- Designed menu-based interface for beginning UNIX users.

Languages and operating systems:
- Proficient in **Ada, Modula-2, Pascal, COBOL.**
- Familiar with C, Fortran, Lisp, Prolog, dBaseIII, SQL, QBE.
- Working knowledge of IBM-PC hardware and 8088 assembly language.

I Experienced in **UNIX, MS-DOS, XENIX,** CP/M operating systems.

Hardware:

I IBM-PC (MS-DOS, Xenix), Pyramid 90x (UNIX), Cyber 990 (NOS), Data General MV/10000 (UNIX, AOS/VS).

WORK EXPERIENCE:

Neil Araki Programming Services— Olympia, WA   10/86-Present

I **UNIX Programmer—** Responsible for porting MS-DOS database applications to IBM-PC/AT running Xenix System V. System administration.

Strathmore Systems— Seattle, WA   11/83-9/86

I **Computer Programmer—** Performed daily disk backup on Burroughs B-1955 machine. Executed database update programs and checks. User assistance.

I From 8/81 to 11/83, held full-time positions as **Computer operator** for organizations in Ithaca, NY, and Seattle, WA.

REFERENCES

Furnished upon request.

SAMPLE COVER LETTER

3420 Salmon Court S.E.
Gresham, OR 97030
June 26, 1990
(503) 555-6886

Ms. Jacqueline Doe
Wide World Publishing Company
1400 N.E. Holman St.
Portland, OR 97221

Dear Ms. Doe:

As an honors graduate of Lewis and Clark College
with two years of copy editing and feature writing
experience with the *Gresham Outlook,* I am confident
that I would make a successful editorial assistant with
Wide World.

Besides my strong editorial background, I offer
considerable business experience. I have held summer
jobs in an insurance company, a law firm, and a data
processing company. My familiarity with word
processing should prove particularly useful to Wide
World now that you're about to become fully
automated.

I would like to interview with you as soon as possible
and would be happy to check in with your office about
an appointment. If you prefer, your office can contact
me between the hours of 11 a.m. and 3 p.m. at (503)
555-6886.

Sincerely,

Valerie Jones

SAMPLE/COVER LETTER

2239 Forest Park Blvd.
Lacey, WA 98503
May 31, 1990

Advertiser
Box 1826
The Olympian
1268 E. Fourth Ave.
Olympia, WA 98501

Dear Employer:

Your advertisement in the May 29 issue of *The
Olympian* for an entry-level bookkeeper seems perfect
for someone with my background. I am about to
graduate from Lacey High School in a business
preparatory course that includes two semesters of
accounting.

As you can see from my resume, my work experience
consists mainly of miscellaneous summer employment
and part-time jobs while in school. But I hope to offset
my lack of experience with hard work, enthusiasm, and
a desire to succeed.

My activities with Junior Achievement should give
you an idea of my aptitude for business. I would
appreciate the opportunity of an interview at your
convenience.

Sincerely,

Jim Clark
(206) 555-4414

SAMPLE COVER LETTER

228 Meadow Rd. S.W.
Tacoma, WA 98499
December 1, 1989

Dear Mike:

Just when everything seemed to be going so well at my job, the company gave us a Christmas present that nobody wanted—management announced that half the department will be laid off before the end of the year. Nobody knows yet just which heads are going to roll. But whether or not my name is on the list, I am definitely back in the job market.

I have already lined up a couple of interviews. But knowing how uncertain job hunting can be, I can use all the contacts I can get.

You know my record—both from when we worked together at 3-Q and since then. But in case you've forgotten the details, I've enclosed my resume.

I know that you often hear of job openings as you wend your way about Tacoma and Seattle. I'd certainly appreciate your passing along any leads you think might be worthwhile.

My best to you and Fran for the Holidays.

Cordially,

Emily Noir
(206) 555-9876

Seven ways to ruin a cover letter

1. Spell the name of the firm incorrectly.
2. Don't bother to find out the name of the hiring authority. Just send the letter to the president or chairman of the board.
3. If the firm is headed by a woman, be sure to begin your letter, "Dear Sir." Otherwise, just address it, "To Whom It May Concern."
4. Make sure the letter includes a couple of typos and sloppy erasures. Better yet, spill coffee on it first, then mail it.
5. Be sure to provide a phone number that has been disconnected, or one at which nobody is ever home.
6. Tell the firm you'll call to set up an appointment in a few days; then don't bother.
7. Call the firm at least three times the day after you mail the letter. Get very angry when they say they haven't heard of you. ∎

Researching the Seattle/Portland Job Market

To a large extent, the success of your job search will depend on how well you do your homework. Once you've figured out what kind of job you want, you need to find out as much as you can about which specific companies might employ you. Your network of personal contacts can be an invaluable source of information about what jobs are available where. But networking can't do it all; at some point, you'll have to do some reading. This chapter fills you in on the directories, newspapers, and magazines you'll need in your search, and notes the libraries where you can find them.

Libraries

Public libraries are an invaluable source of career information. Everything from books on resume writing to *Standard and Poor's Register of Corporations, Directors, and Executives* can usually be found in the business and economics sections.

Save time by checking with the reference librarians on what is available and where to find it. These staff members will be especially cooperative if you first ask them when their "slow" periods are. These are the times when they can give you their undivided attention.

SEATTLE/PUGET SOUND AREA LIBRARIES

The **Seattle Public Library** (1000 Fourth Ave., Seattle, WA 98104, (206) 386-4636) is a mine of career information. In the Career Information and Job Search Center on the second floor can be found current career reference materials, including books, government documents, pamphlets, and directories. The library's free "Guide to Resume Writing" is available here as well as a list of Civil Service job announcements. The Business Department, also on the second floor, offers a broad collection of information on local businesses and financial markets. Reference librarians are helpful and well informed, if somewhat overworked.

You can also find job-hunting information at the following branches of the Seattle Public Library:

Ballard
5711 24th Ave. N.W.
Seattle, WA 98107
(206) 684-4089

Beacon Hill
2519 15th S.
Seattle, WA 98144
(206) 684-4711

Broadview
12755 Greenwood Ave. N.
Seattle, WA 98133
(206) 684-7519

Columbia
4721 Rainier Ave. S.
Seattle, WA 98118
(206) 386-1908

Douglass-Truth
23rd & Yesler Way
Seattle, WA 98122
(206) 684-4704

Fremont
731 N. 35th
Seattle, WA 98103
(206) 684-4084

Green Lake
7364 E. Green Lake Drive N.
Seattle, WA 98115
(206) 684-7547

Greenwood
8016 Greenwood N.
Seattle, WA 98103
(206) 684-4086

Henry
425 Harvard Ave. E.
Seattle, WA 98102
(206) 684-4715

High Point
6338 32nd Ave S.W.
Seattle, WA 98126
(206) 684-7454

Holly Park
6805 32nd Ave. S.
Seattle, WA 98118
(206) 386-1905

Lake City
12501 28th Ave. N.E.
Seattle, WA 98125
(206) 684-7518

**Madrona Sally
Goldmark**
1134 33rd Ave.
Seattle, WA 98122
(206) 684-4705

Magnolia
2801 34th Ave. W.
Seattle, WA 98199
(206) 386-4225

Montlake
2300 24th Ave. E.
Seattle, WA 98102
(206) 684-4720

Northeast
6801 35th Ave N.E.
Seattle, WA 98115
(206) 684-7539

Queen Anne
400 W. Garfield
Seattle, WA 98119
(206) 386-4227

Rainier Beach
9125 Rainier S.
Seattle, WA 98118
(206) 386-1906

Southwest
9010 35th Ave. S.W.
Seattle, WA 98126
(206) 684-7455

University
5009 Roosevelt Way N.E.
Seattle, WA 98105
(206) 684-4063

Wallingford Wilmot
4423 Densmore N.
Seattle, WA 98103
(206) 684-4088

West Seattle
2306 42nd Ave S.W.
Seattle, WA 98116
(206) 684-7444

The **King County Library System** (300 Eighth Ave. N., Seattle, WA 98109, (206) 684-6644) includes 36 branches throughout the county. Many of these have their own job rooms and local resource collections. Call for more information about the branch closest to you.

Although the **Tacoma Public Library** (1142 Broadway, Tacoma, WA 98402, (206) 591-5666) does not have a job services center per se, it does boast a fairly extensive local business and information reference collection. The branches listed below may offer local resource information as well.

Fern Hill
765 S. 84th
Tacoma, WA 98408
(206) 591-5620

Kobetich Branch
212 Browns Point Blvd. N.E.
Tacoma, WA 98422
(206) 591-5630

McCormick
3722 N. 26th
Tacoma, WA 98407
(206) 591-5640

South Tacoma
3411 S. 56th
Tacoma, WA 98409
(206) 591-5670

Moore
215 S. 56th
Tacoma, WA 98408
(206) 591-5650

Swan Creek
3928 Portland Ave.
Tacoma, WA 98421
(206) 594-7805

Mottet
3523 East G
Tacoma, WA 98404
(206) 591-5660

Swasey
7001 Sixth Ave.
Tacoma, WA 98406
(206) 591-5620

The **Timberland Regional Library** system's 27 branches serve the southwest portion of Washington State.

A free gold mine for job hunters is the collection of written, videotaped, and computer software resources at Educational and Job Information Centers (EJIC). Here you can view or check out videotapes on job-hunting topics. Utilizing the Centers' personal computers and software, you can assess your career skills, set up your resume, learn popular word processing systems, and even learn to type.

EJICs are located at six Timberland branches, including the Lacey Timberland Library in Thurston County (listed below), and in Snohomish County, the Evergreen branch of Everett Public Library (9512 Evergreen Way, Everett, WA 98203, (206) 259-8797).

Olympia-area branches of the Timberland Regional Library system are listed below. For more information on other branches call 1-800-562-6022.

Lacey Timberland Library
4516 Lacey Blvd.
Lacey, WA 98503
(206) 491-3860

Tumwater Timberland Library
5131 Capitol Blvd.
Tumwater, WA 98501
(206) 943-7790

Olympia Timberland Library
Eighth and Franklin
Olympia, WA 98501
(206) 352-0595

Although the **Washington State Library** (State Capitol Campus, Olympia, WA 98504 (206) 753-5590) does not have an official career information center, it houses a vast collection of resources that could be very helpful in getting to know the ins and outs of Washington State.

PORTLAND AREA LIBRARIES

The **Multnomah County Library's** Central Library branch
maintains files on local firms, including their annual reports
and pertinent news clippings. You can also find job-hunting
information at the following branches:

Central Library
801 S.W. Tenth Ave.
Portland, OR 97205
(503) 223-7201

Albina Branch
3605 N.E. 15th
Portland, OR 97212
(503) 221-7701

Belmont Branch
1038 S.E. 39th
Portland, OR 97214
(503) 221-7712

Capitol Hill Branch
10723 S.W. Capitol
Highway
Portland, OR 97219
(503) 221-7721

**Gregory Heights
Branch**
7921 N.E. Sandy Blvd.
Beaverton, OR 97213
(503) 221-7730

Gresham Branch
410 N. Main St.
Gresham, OR 97030
(503) 665-2222

Hillsdale Branch
1525 S.W. Sunset Blvd.
Beaverton, OR 97201
(503) 221-7735

Holgate Branch
7905 S.E. Holgate
Beaverton, OR 97206
(503) 221-7740

Hollywood Branch
3930 N.E. Hancock
Portland, OR 97212
(503) 221-7725

Midland Branch
805 S.E. 122nd
Portland, OR 97233
(503) 221-7727

North Portland Branch
512 N. Killingsworth
Portland, OR 97217
(503) 221-7702

Rockwood Branch
17917 S.E. Stark
Gresham, OR 97030
(503) 665-9440

Sellwood-Moreland Branch
7904 S.E. Milwaukie
Portland, OR 97202
(503) 221-7732

St. Johns Branch
7510 N. Charleston
Portland, OR 97203
(503) 221-7716

Woodstock Branch
6008 S.E. 49th
Portland, OR 97206
(503) 221-7742

Want to investigate a prospective employer?

The Better Business Bureau (BBB) of Greater Seattle has an **"instant information" number** that can be called 24 hours a day: **(206) 448-6222.**

Using a touch-tone telephone, code in a company's phone number to hear a pre-recorded reliability report. This free service, the first of its kind in the country, provides reports on the performance and practices of about 3,000 businesses in Washington State and nationwide.

Directories

When you're beginning your homework, whether you're researching an entire industry or a specific company, there are four major sources of information with which you should be familiar. All four of these "gospels" are available at the **Seattle Public Library** (1000 Fourth Ave.) and the **Multnomah County Central Library** (801 S.W. Tenth Ave. in Portland). Check your local branch library as well.

Standard and Poor's Register of Corporations, Directors, and Executives (Standard and Poor's Publishing Co., 25 Broadway, New York, NY 10004) is billed as the "foremost guide to the business community and the executives who run it." This three-volume directory lists more than 38,000 corporations and 70,000 officers, directors, trustees, and other bigwigs.

Each business is assigned a four-digit number called a Standard Industrial Classification (S.I.C.) number, which tells you what product or service the company provides. Listings are indexed by geographic area and also by S.I.C. number, so that it's easy to find out all the companies in the Puget Sound area that produce, say, industrial inorganic chemicals.

You can also look up a *particular* company to verify its correct address and phone number, its chief officers (that is, the people you might want to contact for an interview), its products, and, in many cases, its annual sales and number of employees. If you have an appointment with the president of XYZ Corporation, you can consult *Standard and Poor's* to find out where he or she was born and went to college—information that's sure to come in handy in an employment interview. Supplements are published in April, July, and October.

The **Thomas Register of American Manufacturers and Thomas Register Catalog File** (Thomas Publishing Co., One Penn Plaza, New York, NY 10119) is published annually. This 16-volume publication is another gold mine of information. You can look up a certain product or service and find out every company that provides it. (Since this is a national publication, you'll have to weed out companies that are not in the Pacific Northwest, but that's easy.) You can also look up a particular company to find out about branch offices, capital ratings, company officials, names, addresses, phone numbers, and more. The *Thomas Register* even contains five volumes of company catalogs. Before your appointment with XYZ Corporation, you can bone up on its product line with the *Thomas Register*.

Moody's Complete Corporate Index (Moody's Investor Service, 99 Church St., New York, NY 10007) gives you the equivalent of an encyclopedia entry on more than 20,000 corporations. This is the resource to use when you want really detailed information on a certain company. *Moody's* can tell you about a company's history—when it was founded, what name changes it has undergone, and so on. It provides a fairly lengthy description of a company's business and properties, what subsidiaries it owns, and lots of detailed financial information. Like the directories above, *Moody's* lists officers and directors of companies. It can also tell you the date of the annual meeting and the number of stockholders and employees.

The **Million Dollar Directory** (Dun & Bradstreet, Inc., 3 Sylvan Way, Parsippany, NJ 07054) is a three-volume listing of approximately 120,000 U.S. businesses with a net worth of more than half a million dollars. Listings appear alphabetically, geographically, and by product classification and include key personnel. Professional and consulting organizations such as hospitals and engineering services, credit agencies, and financial institutions other than banks and trust companies are not generally included.

So much for the Big Four directories. The following listings contain more than 100 additional directories and guides, most with a local focus, that may come in handy:

NATIONAL/REGIONAL DIRECTORIES

Advanced Technology in the Pacific Northwest
(Quantix Data Services, Inc., PO Box 247, West Linn, OR 97068)
Lists nearly 1,080 manufacturers of high-technology products and equipment, including computers, aerospace and aviation equipment, electronics, and audio/video equipment. Includes address, phone number, key personnel, number of employees, and description of product or service provided. Indexed alphabetically and by product.

Adweek Directory of Advertising, Western Edition
(*Adweek Magazine,* 820 Second Ave., New York, NY 10017)
Includes directories of ad agencies and public relations firms as well as guides to media, advertising, and marketing services.

Alaska/Puget Sound Trade Directory
(Greater Seattle Chamber of Commerce, 1200 One Union Square, Seattle, WA 98101)
Annual directory.

Almanac of American Employers: A Guide to America's 500 Most Successful Large Corporations
(Contemporary Books, Inc., 180 N. Michigan Ave., Chicago, IL 60601)
Alphabetical profiles of major corporations, including information about benefits, job turnover, and financial stability.

Aviation Telephone Directory: Pacific and Western States
(Directional Media Systems, Inc., 535 W. Lambert Road, Suite D, Brea, CA 92621)
Includes alphabetical list of related firms, state-by-state listings of airports and airport services, plus listing of aviation products and services.

Career Guide: Employment Opportunities Directory
(Dun and Bradstreet, Inc., 3 Sylvan Way, Parsippany, NJ 07054)
Employment information on companies with at least 1,000 employees, including hiring practices and disciplines hired geographically.

College Placement Annual
(College Placement Council, 62 Highland Ave., Bethlehem, PA 18017)
Occupational needs of more than 1,200 corporations and government employers.

Consultants and Consulting Organizations Directory
(Gale Research Co., Book Tower, Detroit, MI 48226)
Descriptions of 6,000 firms and individuals involved in
consulting, indexed geographically.

Corporate Technology Directory
(Corporate Technology Information Services, Inc., 1 Market
St., PO Box 281, Wellesley Hills, MA 02181)
Profiles of high-technology corporations, including address,
phone, ownership, history, brief description, sales, number of
employees, executives, and products. Indexed by company
names, geography, technology, and product.

Dictionary of Occupational Titles
(U.S. Dept. of Labor, 200 Constitution Ave., N.W., Washington,
DC 20210)
Occupational information on job duties and requirements;
describes almost every conceivable job.

**Directory of Western Book Publishers and
Production Services**
(Bookbuilders West, 170 Ninth St., San Francisco, CA 94103)
Listing of book publishers in the western states.

Directory of Women-Owned Businesses
(National Association of Women Business Owners, 2000 P St.,
N.W., Suite 511, Washington, DC 20036)
Free directory lists women-owned businesses by state;
describes products and services.

Dun and Bradstreet State Sales Guide
(Dun and Bradstreet, Inc., One Diamond Hill Road, Murray
Hill, NJ 07974)
Covers all businesses in each state that are included in Dun
and Bradstreet's national "Reference Book."

Employment Opportunities Directory
(Dun's Marketing Services, 1 Penn Plaza, New York, NY
10119)
Designed for those beginning a career; describes job prospects
at hundreds of companies.

Encyclopedia of Associations
(Gale Research Press, Book Tower, Detroit, MI 40226)
Directory of state and national associations, indexed by topic,
key word, organization name, and geography.

Engineering, Science, and Computer Jobs
(Peterson's Guides, 166 Bunn Drive, Princeton, NJ 08540)
Lists specific companies within these industries.

Environmental Organizations Directory
(Environmental Protection Agency, Region 10, 1200 Sixth
Ave., MS: MD-108, Seattle, WA 98101)
Profiles regional voluntary organizations; EPA regional offices;
state, local, and provincial environmental and pollution
control agencies. Entries include organization name, address,
phone, regional representative, and a brief narrative on the
organization's purpose, goals, committees, local chapters.

Fortune Double 500 Directory
(Time, Inc., 1271 Avenue of the Americas, New York, NY
10002)
Lists the 500 largest and the 500 second-largest industrial
corporations, along with the 500 largest commercial banks,
utilities, life insurance companies, diversified financial
companies, retailers, transportation companies, and diversified
service companies. Arranged by annual sales.

Grocery Commercial Food Industry Directory
(GroCom Group, Inc., PO Box 10378, Clearwater, FL 34617)
Profiles 2,500 manufacturers, wholesalers, brokers, distributers,
and other suppliers of food and beverage products and food
industry-related products.

Guide: Building Construction Material Prices
(Worley-McGowan Co., 16710 N.E. 79th, Suite 103, Redmond,
WA 98052)
Lists approximately 1,000 suppliers of construction
equipment, products, and services in Alaska, Oregon, and
Washington.

Hi-Tech Buyers Guide Covering Local Sources in the Western States
(Directories of Industry, Inc., 9371 Kramer Ave., Westminster,
CA 92683)
Alphabetical listings of electronics, computer, aerospace, and
industrial high-technology manufacturers. Cross-referenced by
products.

Hispanic Media Guide, USA: Directory of Hispanic Print, Radio & TV Media in the U.S.
(Directories International, Inc., 150 Fifth Ave., Suite 610, New
York, NY 10011)
Profiles media outlets serving Hispanics, including information
about parent companies, address, and contact. Organized by
state.

Job Openings
(Publication #510K, Consumer Information Center, Dept. G,
Pueblo, CO 81009)
Free 80-page booklet, revised monthly, highlights occupations

with large numbers of openings and indicates where they are located.

Mix Annual Directory, The
(*Mix* Publications, 6400 Hollis St., Suite 12, Emeryville, CA 94608)
Includes directory of Northwest recording studios.

National Directory of Addresses and Telephone Numbers
(General Information, Inc., 401 Parkplace Center, Kirkland, WA 98033)
Includes names, addresses, phone numbers and fax numbers of national corporations, financial institutions, colleges and universities, government agencies, and other businesses and organizations. Cost is approximately $50 plus handling fee.

National Trade & Professional Associations of the United States
(Columbia Books, Inc., 1350 New York Ave., NW, Suite 207, Washington, DC 20005)
Alphabetical profiles of associations, including address, phone, affiliations, history, publications, meetings, and annual budget. Indexed by subject, geography, budget, and acronym.

Occupational Outlook Handbook
(U.S. Dept. of Labor, 200 Constitutional Ave. N.W., Washington, DC 20210)
Describes in clear language what people do in their jobs, the training and education they need, earnings, working conditions, and employment outlook.

Pacific Builder and Engineer—Buyers Guide and Directory
(Vernon Publications, Inc., 109 W. Mercer St., Seattle, WA 98119)
Listing of heavy construction equipment manufacturers, distributors, and equipment-financing companies in Washington, Oregon, and Montana.

Pacific Coast Aviation Directory
(E.A. Brennan & Co., 15111 East Whittier Blvd., Whittier, CA 90603)
State-by-state listing of airports and port firms as well as listings of other services.

Pacific Coast Oil Directory
(Petroleum Publishers, Inc., PO Box 129, Brea, CA 92621)
Listing of energy producers and operators, engineers, contractors, media, agencies, associations, and educational opportunities in the West.

Pacific Northwest Grain and Feed Association—
Official Directory
(Pacific Northwest Grain and Feed Association, 200 S.W.
Market St., Suite 1005, Portland, OR 97201)
Profiles grain, feed, milling, and seed firms for Washington,
Oregon, Montana, and Idaho. Includes company name,
address, phone, names and titles of key personnel, activity.

Pacific Northwest Publishers Directory
(Pacific Northwest Book Publishers Association, PO Box 31236,
Seattle, WA 98103)
Over 900 publishers in the Pacific Northwest.

Pacific Stock Exchange Guide
(Commerce Clearing House, Inc., 4025 W. Peterson Ave.,
Chicago, IL 60646)
Lists members, associate members, and member organizations.
Also stocks and bonds admitted to trading on the Exchange,
with descriptions and class of stock or bond.

Peterson's Annual Guide to Careers and Employment
for Engineers, Computer Scientists, and Physical
Scientists
(Peterson's Guides, Inc., 166 Bunn Drive, Princeton, NJ
08540)
Describes 800 government agencies, technical firms, and
manufacturers that hire engineers, computer scientists, and
physical scientists.

Purchasing Line Card
(Cobro NW, 11 143rd S.E., Lynwood, WA 98037)
Profiles nearly 6,500 manufacturers, distributors, and
manufacturer's representatives in the electronics industry in
Idaho, Oregon, and Washington.

Shelton's Retail Directory
(Phelon, Shelton & Marsar, 15 Industrial Ave., Fairview, NJ
07022)
Directory of the largest department stores, women's specialty
stores, chain stores, and resident buying offices. Geographical
listings plus alphabetical index.

Sibbald Guides
(Sibbald Corp., O'Hare Plaza, 5725 E. River Road, Suite 575,
Chicago, IL 60631)
Leading public corporations and financial institutions and large
privately held companies.

Western Association News—Hotel/Facilities
Directory
(Western Association News, 1516 S. Pontius Ave., Los Angeles,

CA 90025)
Lists 200 hotels and meeting facilities in 14 western states.

Western Bank Directory
(Western Banker Publications, Inc., 1299 Fourth St., Suite 308,
San Rafael, CA 94901)
Banks and branch offices in 11 western states.

Western Media Contacts
(*Bulldog Reporter,* 2115 Fourth St., Suite B, Berkeley, CA 94710
(415) 644-0873)
Profiles newspapers, magazines, television and radio stations,
and West Coast bureaus in California, Nevada, Arizona,
Washington, and Oregon. Published in March and September;
price of $245 includes one revised update.

Western Mining Directory
(*Mining Record Newspaper,* Howell Publishing Co., 311 Steele
St., Suite 208, Denver, CO 80206)
Mining companies listed alphabetically and by state. Includes
key personnel, address, phone, ownership, and mines.

Western Packaging Directory
(*Good Packaging Magazine,* Erich Printing & Lithography, 1315 E.
Julian St., San Jose, CA 95116)
Alphabetical listing of packaging companies, including all
western offices. Cross-indexed by products and services.

Western Travel Sales Guide
(Cabell Travel Publications, 11411 Cumpston St., North
Hollywood, CA 91601)
Travel agencies listed by state, plus listing of tour operators,
consultants, airlines, and others in the travel industry. Listings
include names of key staff people. Alphabetical index.

Who's Who in Electronics
(Harris Publishing Co., 2057 Aurora Road, Twinsburg, OH
44087)
Alphabetical listing of manufacturers plus geographical index
and industrial purchasing section.

PUGET SOUND AREA DIRECTORIES

Advanced Technology in Washington State
(Commerce Publishing Corp., 157 Yesler Way, Suite 317,
Seattle, WA 98104)
Profiles companies that provide advanced technology products
and services. Includes company name, address, phone, name
and title of contact, key personnel, number of employees,
product or service.

Directory of Attorneys of King County
(*Daily Journal of Commerce,* 83 Columbia St., Seattle, WA 98104)
Covers attorneys and law firms in King County, as well as
federal, county, and city judges, court reporters, county
officers, and county legal officers for all counties in
Washington.

Directory of Certified Minority and Women's Business Enterprises
(Washington Office of Minority and Women's Business
Enterprises, 406 S. Water, MS: FF-11, Olympia, WA 98504)
Lists over 2,000 certified professional, commercial, industrial,
and consumer firms owned by minorities and/or women.
Entries include company name, address, phone, name of
contact, status of certification as a minority- or woman-owned
firm, and product or service provided.

Directory of Licensed Hospitals
(Washington State Department of Social and Health Services,
Eastside Plaza, Building A, ET-31, Olympia, WA 98504)
Profiles nearly 110 licensed hospitals located throughout
Washington. Includes hospital name, address, phone, county,
license number, number of beds, type of ownership, name of
administrator.

Directory of Major Employers: Central Puget Sound Region
(Greater Seattle Chamber of Commerce, 600 University St.,
Suite 1200, Seattle, WA 98101)
Alphabetical directory covering approximately 750 businesses,
medical and educational institutions, government and social
agencies with over 100 employees. Entries include company
name, address, phone, name of principal officer, annual sales,
number of employees, names of parent and subsidiary
companies, line of business, market area served.

Directory of Major Manufacturers: Central Puget Sound Region
(Greater Seattle Chamber of Commerce, 600 University St.,
Suite 1200, Seattle, WA 98101)
Alphabetical listing of nearly 300 manufacturers having more
than 100 employees. Includes company name, address,
phone, name of principal officer, number of employees, and
description of product.

Directory of Planning and Community Development Agencies
(Washington State Department of Community Development,
Ninth and Columbia Building, MS: GH-51, Olympia, WA 98504)
Listing of 400 planning agencies at federal, county, and local
levels.

Directory of Seattle-King County Manufacturers
(Greater Seattle Chamber of Commerce, 600 University St.,
Suite 1200, Seattle, WA 98101)
Approximately 2,000 listings that include company name,
address, phone, name of principal executive, number of
employees, list of products, and annual gross sales. Indexed by
product and SIC number.

Greater Seattle Area Computer Directory
(The Data Center, Box 2401, Seattle, WA 98111)
Profiles 7,500 data processing installations. Includes company
name, address, phone, contact, type of hardware used, type of
software, number of employees, line of business. Indexed by
hardware and industry.

International Trade Directory: Washington, the State
(Hirshman Publishing, 13615 E. Lake Kathleen Drive S.E.,
Renton, WA 98056, (206) 271-6073.)
Covers over 3,100 manufacturers, agricultural producers and
brokers, timber products firms, fish brokers, and others
involved in international trade, as well as 850 international
trade support services firms. Cost is $88.

List of Approved Contractors
(Seattle Regional Office, Small Business Administration, 2615
Fourth Ave., Room 440, Seattle, WA 98121)
Geographical listing of over 150 minority contractors offering
industrial and commercial services and products.

**Marine Directory—Greater Puget Sound and
Washington Coast**
(Jeremy Mattox and Associates, Inc., 2591 Perkins Lane West,
Seattle, WA 98199)
Profiles companies, organizations, associations, and
government agencies involved in the maritime industry
around Puget Sound and Washington coastal areas. Includes
attorneys, engineers, tug and barge companies, and port
facilities. Entries include name, address, phone, names and
titles of key personnel and service. Organized by organization
name, personal name, and service.

Metro Washington Media
(Public Relations Plus, PO Drawer 1197, New Milford, CT
06776)
Washington media outlets listed by type. Includes name,
address, phone, and key personnel. Alphabetical index.

Meyer Dyne Business Profiles for Washington State
(Meyer Dyne, Inc., 679 Lincoln Ave., St. Paul, MN 55105)
Listing of over 330 private and publicly held companies in
Washington. Entries include company name, address, phone,

key personnel, description of products and services, SIC
numbers, number of employees.

**National Electrical Contractors Association—
Washington Construction Industry Directory**
(National Electrical Contractors Association, 711 Sixth Ave. N.,
#10, Seattle, WA 98109)
Free directory lists address, phone, and key personnel for
electrical and general contractors, architects, engineers,
inspectors, and utility suppliers in Washington State. For mail
orders call (206) 284-2150.

**Official Seattle Area Computer Buyers and Vendors
Guide**
(The Data Center, PO Box 2401, Seattle, WA 98111)
Profiles nearly 500 sellers of computer and data processing
equipment, suppliers of software, and other materials for data
processing activities in the Seattle area.

Puget Sound Finderbinder Media Directory
(Finderbinder, The McConnell Co., 200 W. Mercer St., Suite
201, Seattle, WA 98119)
Outlets listed by type of media. Includes general information,
brief description, circulation, subscription price, key staff
members, and ad information. Indexed by orientation and
format.

Seattle Chinese Business Directory
(Seattle Chinese Post, Inc., PO Box 3468, Seattle, WA 98114)
Alphabetical listing of nearly 1,000 businesses located or
interested in the Chinese community in Seattle. Entries
include company name, address, phone, products or services
provided. In Chinese and English.

**State of Washington Supervisor of Banking—Annual
Report**
(Division of Banking, Washington State Department of
General Administration, General Administration Building,
Room 219, Olympia, WA 98504)
Profiles the nearly 500 chartered and commercial banks and
trust companies and over 200 industrial loan and consumer
finance companies in Washington State.

**Tacoma/Pierce County Chamber of Commerce—
Membership Directory and Buyer's Guide**
(Tacoma/Pierce County Chamber of Commerce, Box 1933,
Tacoma, WA 98401)
Alphabetical listing of more than 2,200 manufacturing, service,
and professional member firms. Includes company name,
address, phone, name and title of key representatives, product
or service.

Washington Education Directory
(Barbara Krohn and Associates, Securities Building, #835, Seattle, WA 98101)
Lists all State Department of Education offices, public school systems, public and private schools, colleges and universities. Includes name, address, phone, name of chief executive officer, and estimated enrollment for schools and school systems. For associations, gives name, phone, and names of key personnel. Indexed by school system name and by subject.

Washington Food Dealer—Grocery Industry Directory
(Washington State Food Dealers' Association, 8288 Lake City Way, N.E., Box 15300, Seattle, WA 98115-0030)
Lists over 100 buying offices and 4,000 grocery stores, supermarkets, and convenience stores. Buyers' guide section includes advertising by suppliers to the industry.

Washington Health Care Association Directory
(Washington Health Care Association, 2120 State Ave., N.E., Olympia, WA 98506)
Lists over 230 long-term health care facilities. Available to members only.

Washington Libraries: Directory of Libraries
(Washington State Libraries, MS AJ-11, Olympia, WA 98504)
Entries include library name, key personnel, population served, hours of operation, circulation.

Washington Manufacturers Register
(Database Publishing Co., 523 Superior, Newport Beach, CA 92660)
Over 4,400 listings, including company name, address, phone, key personnel, numbers of employees, products and services.

Washington State Agricultural Suppliers Directory
(Agricultural Development Division, Washington State Department of Agriculture, General Administration Building, #406, Olympia, WA 98504)
Profiles nearly 700 firms supplying raw and processed agricultural products from Washington. Also lists state wineries and commodity commissions.

Washington State Broadcasters Directory
(Washington State Association of Broadcasters, 1001 Fourth Ave., Suite 3200, Seattle, WA 98154)
Lists all radio and television stations in Washington. Entries include call letters, address, phone, general manager, and affiliation. Categorized by city of license and alphabetically by call letters.

Washington State Software Industry Directory
(Washington State Software Association, PO Box 8364, Kirkland, WA 98034)
Profiles of companies in the software industry. Includes name of company, address, phone, FAX, number of employees, key personnel, primary activities, and description of three principal products or services.

Women's Yellow Pages
(New Media Publications, 7318 15th Ave. N.E., Seattle, WA 98115, (206) 726-9687)
Lists women-owned businesses and women professionals; includes articles of interest to women. Cost is $5.95. Also available is quarterly calendar of events for women's organizations.

PORTLAND AREA DIRECTORIES

Annual Report of the Finance Section
(Administrator, Division of Finance and Corporate Securities, Oregon Department of Insurance and Finance, 21 Labor and Industries Building, Salem, OR 97310, (503) 378-4140)
List of banks, trust companies, state-chartered credit unions, consumer finance, and savings and loan institutions. Order from Cashier; cost is $10.

Directory and Statistics of Oregon Libraries
(Library Development Division, Oregon State Library, State Library Building, Salem, OR 97310)
Includes almost 400 public, academic, and special libraries: name, address, phone, contact, number of employees, financial and statistical data.

Directory of Economic Development Organizations in Oregon
(Council for Economic Development in Oregon, 529 S.W. Third Ave., Suite 500, Portland, OR 97267)
Profiles public and private organizations, and federal, state, and local government agencies concerned with economic development in Oregon.

Directory of Human Services
(United Way of the Columbia-Willamette, 718 W. Burnside St., Portland, OR 97209)
Community service agencies and organizations. Three regional editions cover Multnomah County, Clackamas County, and Washington County. Includes agency or organization name, address, phone, hours, services offered, eligibility requirements, application procedures, fees, accessibility, and area served.

Directory of Mineral Producers in Oregon
(Oregon Department of Geology and Mineral Industries, 1400 S.W. Fifth Ave., Room 910, Portland, OR 97201)
Nearly 550 mineral producers in the state, classified by type of product.

Directory of Oregon Manufacturers
(Oregon Economic Development Department, 595 Cottage St. N.E., Salem, OR 97310, (503) 373-1241)
Profiles some 7,000 manufacturers, including products, number of employees, executives, home offices. Various formats, including mailing labels and computer diskettes. Cost is $60.

Guide to Oregon Foundations
(United Way of the Columbia-Willamette, 718 W. Burnside St., Portland, OR 97209)
Covers about 285 foundations based in Oregon and national foundations particularly active in Oregon. Entries include foundation name, address, name of contact, restrictions on grants, total grants, and range of size of individual grants. Includes sample grants; tells whether letter or interview is preferred as first contact.

Largest Employers of the Portland Metro Area
(Portland Chamber of Commerce, 221 N.W. Second Ave., Portland, OR 97209)
Lists about 190 public and private firms with at least 250 employees in the Portland area. Includes address, phone, name and title of chief executive officer, products or services.

MacRae's Industrial Directory Oregon
(MacRae's Blue Book, Inc., Business Research Publications, Inc., 817 Broadway, New York, NY 10003)
Some 4,800 listings, including company name, address, phone, names of key personnel, number of employees, products, services, gross sales.

Manufacturers Directory for the Portland Metro Area
(Portland Chamber of Commerce, 221 N.W. Second Ave., Portland, OR 97209)
Profiles more than 700 manufacturers with 25 or more employees.

Oregon Arts Index
(Portland Metropolitan Chamber of Commerce, 221 N.W. Second Ave., Third Floor, Portland, OR 97209)
Includes information about impact of the arts on the local economy; lists art galleries and arts groups. Available for $5.

Oregon Association of Nurserymen—Directory and Buyer's Guide
(Oregon Association of Nurserymen, 2780 S.E. Harrison, Suite 102, Portland, OR 97222)
Covers growers and wholesalers of flowering plants, nursery crops, fruit trees, etc., and landscaping and landscape maintenance firms.

Oregon Computer Consultants Association—Professional Skills and Services Directory
(Oregon Computer Consultants Association, PO Box 5365, Portland, OR 97228; (503) 227-0791)
Free alphabetical listing of member computer consulting firms in the state of Oregon. Includes company name, address, phone, name and title of contact, services, products supported. Also available at some bookstores and computer retail outlets.

Oregon Media Guide
(Center for Urban Education, 1135 S.E. Bancroft, Portland, OR 97201)
Guide to Oregon's newspapers, radio and television stations. Entries include name, address, phone, channel or frequency, coverage, hours, key personnel.

Oregon School Directory
(Oregon Department of Education, 700 Pringle Parkway S.E., Salem, OR 97310)
Lists public and private schools, community colleges, colleges and universities, special and federal schools, associations, commissions, and councils.

Portland Area Computer Directory
(The Data Center, Box 2401, Seattle, WA 98111)
Lists about 4,000 data processing installations in western Oregon. Entries include company name, address, phone, contact, type of hardware and software used, line of business, number of employees.

Portland Chamber of Commerce—Membership Directory and Buyer's Guide
(Portland Chamber of Commerce, 221 N.W. Second Ave., Portland, OR 97209)
Lists company name, address, phone, key personnel, product or service, and number of employees for over 3,000 firms.

Resource Guide of Oregon High Technology
(Hillsboro Chamber of Commerce, 334 S.E. Fifth St., Hillsboro, OR 97123)
Electronic, computer, and other high-tech companies in Oregon and southwestern Washington. Lists firm name, address, phone, names of key personnel, product or service.

Roster of Licensed Landscaping Business and Licensed Landscape Contractors
(Landscape Contractors Board, Oregon Department of Commerce, Labor and Industries Building, Room 403, Salem, OR 97310)
Alphabetical listing of almost 1,000 firms.

Women's Yellow Pages
(*Progressive Woman,* 1208 S.W. 13th St., Suite 212, Portland, OR 97205, (503) 223-9344)
Free publication profiles over 1,500 women-owned businesses, women's groups, and women in the Portland area. Includes name, address, phone, skills, interests, line of business.

Cooperatives are big business in Puget Sound

The activities of cooperatives touch virtually every resident of Washington State. If you are interested in exploring the job opportunities they offer, start by contacting the **Puget Sound Cooperative Federation,** trade association for the region's cooperatives, which has 35 member organizations (521 Wall St., Seattle, WA 98121, (206) 448-6557).

To give you an idea of the scope of Seattle-area cooperatives, here are a few you may wish to research:

The nation's largest consumer co-op, with more than two million members, is **Recreational Equipment, Inc. (REI),** with corporate offices at 6750 S. 228th St., Kent, WA 98032, (206) 395-3780.

Group Health Cooperative of Puget Sound serves one of every 11 Washington State residents; membership is 425,000 and growing. The Personnel Department operates 24-hour job lines for non-nursing (206-448-2745), nursing (206-448-2743), and medical receptionist (206-448-2744) positions.

About 30 percent of all farm products in the nation are marketed through cooperatives such as

Associated Grocers, Inc. (3301 S. Norfolk St., Seattle, WA 98118 (206) 762-2100) and **Darigold, Inc.** (635 Elliott Ave. W., Seattle, WA 98119, (206) 284-7220).

The **Puget Consumers Co-op,** with several branches throughout Seattle, and **The Meat Shop** offer additive-free food. There are also about 250 financial co-ops in the Puget Sound area.■

Newspapers

Answering want ads is one of several tasks to be done in any job search, and generally among the least productive. According to Forbes magazine, only about 10 percent of professional and technical people find their jobs through want ads. Like any other long shot, however, answering want ads sometimes pays off. Be sure to check not only the classified listings but also the larger display ads that appear in the Sunday business sections of the major papers. These ads are usually for upper-level jobs.

Help-wanted listings generally come in two varieties: open advertisements and blind ads. An **open ad** is one in which the company identifies itself and lists an address. Your best bet is *not* to send a resume to a company that prints an open ad. Instead, you should try to identify the hiring authority (see Chapter 5) and pull every string you can think of to arrange an interview directly.

The personnel department is in business to screen out applicants. Of the several hundred resumes that an open ad in a major newspaper is likely to attract, the personnel department will probably forward only a handful to the people who are actually doing the hiring. It's better for you to go to those people directly than to try to reach them by sending a piece of paper (your resume) to the personnel department.

Blind ads are run by companies that do not identify themselves because they do not want to acknowledge receipt of resumes. Since you don't know who the companies are, your only option in response to a blind ad is to send a resume. This is among the longest of long shots and usually pays off only if your qualifications are exactly suited to the position that's being advertised.

Just remember that if you depend solely on ad responses, you're essentially conducting a passive search, waiting for the mail to arrive or the phone to ring. Passive searchers usually are unemployed a long time.

Newspaper business sections are useful not only for their want ads but also as sources of local business news and news about personnel changes. Learn to read between the lines. If an article announces that Big Bucks, Inc., has just acquired a new vice-president, chances are that he or she will be looking for staffers. If the new veep came to Big Bucks from another local company, obviously that company may have at least one vacancy, and possibly several.

MAJOR NEWSPAPERS IN SEATTLE/PUGET SOUND AREA

Herald, The
Grand and California
Everett, WA 98206
(206) 339-3000
Daily newspaper serving Snohomish County.

Morning News Tribune
1950 S. State St.
Tacoma, WA 98405
(206) 597-8511
Tacoma's daily paper. Sunday's edition has extensive job classified ads.

Olympian, The
1268 E. Fourth Ave.
Olympia, WA 98501
(206) 754-5400
Daily paper serving Olympia.

Seattle Post-Intelligencer
101 Elliott Ave. W.
Seattle, WA 98119
(206) 448-8000
Seattle Times
Fairview Ave. N. and John St.
Seattle, WA 98109
(206) 464-2111
The *Post-Intelligencer* is Seattle's daily morning paper; the *Times* comes out in the afternoon. Both have business sections that track local developments. The two papers publish together on Sundays. Sunday editions include an extensive business section and help-wanted ads.

MAJOR NEWSPAPER IN PORTLAND AREA

Oregonian, The
1320 S.W. Hampton, Suite 232
Portland, OR 97223
(503) 684-2074
Daily morning newspaper.

OTHER NEWSPAPER RESOURCES

There are many other outstanding daily and weekly
newspapers in the major metropolitan areas, plus suburban
and community papers. Most carry want ads and all feature
stories and items about local businesses and business people
that will give you more input for your job search.

SEATTLE/PUGET SOUND AREA

Aberdeen Daily World
315 S. Michigan St.
Aberdeen, WA 98520
(206) 532-4000

Ballard News Tribune
(weekly)
2208 N.W. Market St.,
#202
Seattle, WA 98107
(206) 783-1244

Beacon Hill News
(weekly)
2720 S. Hanford St.
Seattle, WA 98144
(206) 723-1300
also:
Capitol Hill Times
(weekly)
(206) 323-5777 *461-1331*
News
(206) 723-1300
Outlook
(206) 545-7173
South District Journal
(weekly)
(206) 723-1300
Times
(206) 723-1300
University Herald
(weekly)
(206) 545-7173

Bellevue Journal-American
1705 132nd Ave. N.E.
Bellevue, WA 98005
(206) 455-2222
Daily newspaper serving the
Eastside.

Bellingham Herald (daily)
1155 N. State St.
Bellingham, WA 98225
(206) 767-2600

Bremerton Sun
645 Fifth St.
Bremerton, WA 98310
(206) 377-3711
Daily newspaper serving Kitsap
and Mason counties.

Daily Chronicle, The
321 N. Pearl
Centralia, WA 98531
(206) 736-3311
Daily paper serving Centralia,
Chehalis, and Lewis counties.

Edmonds Enterprise
(weekly)
PO Box 997
Lynnwood, WA 98046
(206) 775-7521

Facts
PO Box 22015
Seattle, WA 98122
(206) 324-0552

Federal Way News
1634 S. 312th St.
Federal Way, WA 98003
(206) 839-0700

Herald
PO Box 16069
Seattle, WA 98116
(206) 932-0300

**Highline Times/Des
Moines News** (weekly)
207 S.W. 150th St.
Burien, WA 98166
(206) 242-0100

**Kirkland Courier
Review** (weekly)
**Sammamish Valley
News** (weekly)
PO Box 716
Redmond, WA 98073
(206) 885-4178

Lynnwood Journal
7627 196th S.W.
Lynnwood, WA 98036
(206) 775-2400
Monthly, consumer and
community news.

News Tribune (weekly)
PO Box 596
Everett, WA 98206
(206) 568-4121

Northwest Dispatch
1108 S. 11th St.
Tacoma, WA 98405
(206) 272-7587
Black community weekly.

Olympia News (weekly)
PO Box 366
Olympia, WA 98507
(206) 943-2950

Passage
PO Box 47111
Seattle, WA 98146
(206) 323-0354

Peninsula Gateway (weekly)
7521 Pioneer Way
Gig Harbor, WA 98335
(206) 851-9921

Pierce County Herald
(weekly)
822 E. Main St.
Puyallup, WA 98372
(206) 841-2481

**Queen Anne/Magnolia
News**
225 W. Galer
Seattle, WA 98119
(206) 282-0900
Weekly, Republican
orientation.

Seattle Medium
2600 S. Jackson
Seattle, WA 98104
(206) 323-3070
Weekly newspaper serving
Seattle's black community.

Skagit Valley Herald (daily)
1000 E. College Way
Mt. Vernon, WA 98273
(206) 424-3251

**South Pierce County
Dispatch** (weekly)
PO Box 248
Eatonville, WA 98328
(206) 832-4411

Suburban Times
PO Box 99669
Tacoma, WA 98499
(206) 473-2920

Valley Daily News
600 S. Washington
Kent, WA 98032
(206) 872-6000
Daily paper serving Kent,
Auburn, and Renton.

Weekly, The
1931 Second Ave.
Seattle, WA 98101
(206) 441-5555
Seattle's most popular
current affairs and cultural
events newspaper.
Extensive classified
section. Published on
Wednesdays.

**West Seattle/White Center
News** (weekly)
3600 W. Alaska St.
Seattle, WA 98126
(206) 932-0300

Whidbey News Times
3098 300th W.
Oak Harbor, WA 98227
(206) 675-6611
Weekly general interest, local
news for Whidbey Island and
other San Juan islands.

PORTLAND AREA

Argus
150 S.E. Third
Hillsboro, OR 97123
(503) 648-1131
Twice-weekly community
newspaper.

Bee, The (weekly)
8113 S.E. Thirteenth Ave.
Portland, OR 97202
(503) 235-8335

Canby Herald (weekly)
PO Box 250
Canby, OR 97013
(503) 266-6831

Catholic Sentinel
PO Box 18030
Portland, OR 97218
(503) 281-1191
Weekly religious
newspaper.

**Clackamas County
Review** (weekly)
PO Box 1520
Clackamas, OR 97015
(503) 656-4101

Columbian, The (daily)
701 W. Eighth St.
Vancouver, WA 98666
(206) 694-3391

Forest Grove News Times
(weekly)
PO Box 408
Forest Grove, OR 97116
(503) 357-3181

Gresham Outlook, The
PO Box 880
Gresham, OR 97030
(503) 665-2181
Twice-weekly community
newspaper.

Hillsboro Aloha Breeze
(weekly)
West Valley Courier (weekly)
PO Box 588
Hillsboro, OR 97123
(503) 648-1131

Lake Oswego Review
(weekly)
111 Southwest A Ave.
Lake Oswego, OR 97034
(503) 635-8811

Skanner, The (weekly)
PO Box 5455
Portland, OR 97228
(503) 287-3562
Portland's largest
circulated minority-
oriented newspaper.

St. Johns Review
(weekly)
8410 N. Lombard St.
Portland, OR 97203
(503) 286-0321

Tigard Times (weekly)
Valley Times (weekly)
PO Box 370
Beaverton, OR 97075
(503) 684-0360

West Linn Tidings (weekly)
PO Box 189
West Linn, OR 97068
(503) 635-8811

Willamette Week
2 N.W. Second Ave.
Portland, OR 97209
(503) 243-2122

**Number One is
always hiring**

In the greater Seattle area, **The
Boeing Company,** a major aircraft
manufacturer, is the largest employer.
Boeing has approximately 156,000
employees and is always hiring,
reports Bob Jorgensen,
Communications Manager, due to its
need to replace the 8,000 to 10,000
employees who retire each year.
Boeing has aerospace manufacturing
facilities in Everett, Seattle, Renton,
Bellevue, Kent, and Tukwila.

The Commercial Division
accounts for 90 percent of Boeing's
business, delivering approximately
29 airplanes a month. This division,
says Lee Lathrop in Corporate Public
Relations, has a large backlog of
commercial orders, totaling $60
billion as of November 1989.

On new contracts received, each
stage in the manufacturing process
calls for employees with different
skills. Designers, for example, are
eventually replaced by machinists,
etc., as the job progresses. Whereas
Boeing makes every effort to transfer
employees such as these designers to
other contracts for which their skills

will again be needed, it is not always possible; thus ensues a fluctuating employment scene.

Jorgensen emphasizes that big Boeing order announcements in the media do *not* mean Boeing is hiring for that contract. Best advice is to call Boeing's job hotline:

Job Hotline: (206) 394-3111
Within Washington State:
1-800-525-2236■

General Business Magazines and Newspapers

The smart job seeker will want to keep abreast of changing trends in the economy. These periodicals and newspapers will help you keep up with the national and the Seattle/Portland business scenes.

NATIONAL/REGIONAL

Business Week
1221 Ave. of the Americas
New York, NY 10020
(212) 997-1221

Business West
450 Sacramento St.,
Suite 210
San Francisco, CA 94111
(415) 956-6262
Bi-monthly magazine
about business on the
Pacific Rim.

Forbes
60 Fifth Ave.
New York, NY 10011
(212) 620-2200
Bi-weekly.

Fortune
1271 Ave. of the Americas
New York, NY 10020
(212) 586-1212
Published 26 times per
year.

Money
Time Life Building
1271 Ave. of the Americas
New York, NY 10020
(212) 522-1212
Monthly.

Newsweek
444 Madison Ave.
New York, NY 10022
(212) 350-4000

Time Magazine
1271 Ave. of the Americas
New York, NY 10022
(212) 586-1212
Weekly.

Venture
35 W. 45th St.
New York, NY 10036
(212) 682-7373
Monthly.

Wall St. Journal
600 S. 334th
Federal Way, WA
(206) 838-4400
Daily newspaper.

Working Woman
342 Madison Ave.
New York, NY 10173
(212) 599-2080
Monthly.

SEATTLE/PUGET SOUND AREA

Daily Journal of Commerce
PO Box 11050
Seattle, WA 98104
(206) 622-8272
Daily newspaper covering construction, business, and industry throughout the Pacific Northwest. Specializes in legal notices and all King County court and auditor records.

Pacific Northwest Executive
Graduate School of Business Administration
University of Washington
336 Lewis Hall, MS: DJ-10
Seattle, WA 98195
(206) 543-1819
Free quarterly magazine.

Puget Sound Business Journal
101 Yesler Way, Suite 200
Seattle, WA 98104
(206) 583-0701
Weekly newspaper, covering business news for the Puget Sound area. "Top 25" lists from each issue are compiled into annual "Book of Lists."

Seattle Business Magazine
3000 Northup Way, #200
Bellevue, WA 98004
(206) 827-9900
Monthly magazine, focusing on regional business issues.

Washington Business
1414 S. Cherry St.
Olympia, WA 98507
(206) 943-1600
Bi-weekly magazine published by the Association of Washington Businesses.

Washington CEO
2505 Second Ave., Suite 602
Seattle, WA 98121
1-800-783-WCEO

PORTLAND AREA

Business Journal, The
10 N.W. 10th Ave.
Portland, OR 97209
(503) 233-0074
Weekly newspaper, covering Portland area business news; also publishes "Top 25" lists and annual "Top 25 Book."

Daily Journal of Commerce
2014 N.W. 24th Ave.
Portland, OR 97210
(503) 226-1311
Newspaper, providing business and legal news; published five times a week.

Northwest Investment Review
400 S.W. Sixth Ave., Suite 1115
Portland, OR 97204
(503) 224-6004
Weekly magazine, reporting on economic markets and corporate development in the Northwest.

Oregon Business Magazine
208 S.W. Stark, Suite 500
Portland, OR 97204
(503) 223-0304

Pacific Marketer
PO Box 19031
Portland, OR 97219
(503) 235-7040
Monthly newsletter, containing contact names and marketing opportunities in the Pacific Rim for agriculture, food, computer, forest products, and other industries.

Portland Life and Business Magazine
816 S.W. First Ave.
Portland, OR 97204
(503) 274-7640

Western Investor
Willamette Publishing, Inc.
400 S.W. Sixth, #1115
Portland, OR 97204
(503) 222-0577
Quarterly investment magazine.

Local Feature Magazines and Newspapers

The following periodicals do not necessarily cover business news, but can be valuable sources of information about the Seattle/Portland area itself, information you need to be a well-informed resident of the Pacific Northwest.

SEATTLE/PUGET SOUND AREA

Northwest Living
130 Second Ave. S.
Edmonds, WA 98020
(206) 774-4111
Bi-monthly lifestyle and outdoors magazine.
also:
Destination Washington
The annual official Washington State travelers' guide.

Pacific Northwest Magazine
222 Dexter Ave. N.
Seattle, WA 98109
(206) 682-2704
Monthly magazine about lifestyles in the Northwest.

Pacific Northwest Quarterly
4045 Brooklyn Ave. N.E.
University of Washington
Seattle, WA 98105
Quarterly magazine about the history of the Pacific Northwest.

Puget Soundings
4119 E. Madison
Seattle, WA 98112
(206) 324-2059
Bi-monthly publication of the Seattle Junior League, covering local issues.

Seattle Arts Newsletter
305 Harrison St.
Seattle, WA 98109
(206) 684-7171
Free monthly guide published by the Seattle Arts Commission.

Seattle Folklife Society Journal
6556 Palatine Ave. N.
Seattle, WA 98103
(206) 782-0505
Semi-annual guide to folklife in the Northwest.

Seattle Home and Garden
222 Dexter Ave. N.
Seattle, WA 98109
(206) 682-2704

Seattle Magazine
320 Aurora Ave. N.
Seattle, WA 98109
(206) 682-3555
Monthly magazine, covering Northwest public affairs, travel, business, and lifestyles.

Washington
901 Lenora St.
Seattle, WA 98121
(206) 328-5000
Bi-monthly magazine, covering the beauty and bounty of Washington.

also:
Tastes of the Pacific
Northwest
Tastes of Washington
Washington's Almanac

PORTLAND AREA

Northwest Magazine
1320 S.W. Broadway
Portland, OR 97201
(503) 221-8228
Weekly newspaper insert,
focusing on Northwest
interests.

Northwest Palate, The
PO Box 10860
Portland, OR 97210
(503) 228-4897
Bi-monthly newsletter,
covering wine, food, and
lifestyles in Oregon,
Washington, and Idaho.

Oregon Historical
Quarterly
Oregon Historical Society
1230 S.W. Park Ave.
Portland, OR 97205
Quarterly journal, focusing
on history and culture of
the Pacific Northwest,
particularly the state of
Oregon.

Oregon Magazine
421 S.W. Fifth, Suite 520
Portland, OR 97204
(503) 274-4393
Bi-monthly regional magazine.

Pacific Northwest
Magazine
1020 S.W. Taylor
Portland, OR 97205
(503) 248-9308
Sales office. Editorial offices
located in Seattle.

Portland Guide Magazine
4475 S.W. Scholls Ferry Rd.
Portland, OR 97225
(503) 297-3050

This Week Magazine
6960 S.W. Sandburg St.
Tigard, OR 97223
(503) 620-4140
Weekly general editorial
magazine.

Trade Magazines

Every industry or service business has its trade press—
that is, editors, reporters, and photographers whose job
it is to cover an industry or trade. You should become
familiar with the magazines of the industries or professions that interest you, especially if you're in the interviewing stage of your job search. Your prospective employers are reading the industry trade magazines; you
should be, too.

Trade magazines are published for a specific business
or professional audience; they are usually expensive
and available by subscription only. Many of the maga-

zines we've included here are available at the libraries we listed earlier in this chapter. For those that are not to be found at the library, call up the magazine's editorial or sales office and ask if you can come over to look at the latest issue.

Most of the following magazines have editorial offices in the Seattle/Portland region, reporting area news about the people and businesses in their industry. The majority carry local want ads and personnel changes. Additional trade magazines are listed in Chapter 11 under specific career categories. For a complete listing of the trade press, consult the *Ayer Directory of Publications* in the reference section of most libraries.

SEATTLE/PUGET SOUND AREA TRADE MAGAZINES

Northwest Computer News
PO Box 242
Renton, WA 98055
Monthly computer magazine.

Northwest Computing
PO Box 75061
Seattle, WA 98125
(206) 547-3620
Monthly computer magazine.

Northwest Construction News Daily
3000 Northup Way, #200
Bellevue, WA 98004
(206) 827-9900
Daily bulletin of contemplated construction, bid calls, and contract awards in the Northwest.

Pacific Builder and Engineer
3000 Northup Way, #200
Bellevue, WA 98004
(206) 827-9900
Semi-monthly magazine, covering all phases of heavy, engineered construction in Washington, Oregon, Idaho, and Montana.

Puget Sound Computer User
3530 Bagley Ave. N.
Seattle, WA 98103
(206) 547-4950
Monthly magazine for the non-technical business person.

Seattle Actors' Handbook
600 E. Pine, #692
Seattle, WA 98122

Seattle Ad Federation Guide
PO Box 12065
Broadway Station
Seattle, WA 98102
(206) 382-9220

Washington Builder
1800 Arthur St., Box 266
Louisville, KY 40217
Tri-quarterly publication of
the Home Builders
Association of Washington
State.

Washington Engineer
University of Washington
Engineering Students'
Council
230 Mechanical
Engineering Building
Seattle, WA 98195
Published eight times per
year.

**Washington Food
Dealer**
8288 Lake City Way N.E.,
Box 15300
Seattle, WA 98115
(206) 522-4474
Monthly magazine,
covering stores,
operations, equipment,
consumer trends,
merchandising ideas, and
more.

Washington Pharmacist
1420 Maple Ave. S.W., #101
Renton, WA 98055
(206) 228-7171
Bi-monthly magazine, covering
statewide and national news
and trends in the industry.

**Washington Plumbing and
Heating Contractor**
11732 First Ave. N.E.
Seattle, WA 98125
(206) 363-9647

**Washington State Journal
of Nursing**
83 S. King St., #500
Seattle, WA 98104
(206) 622-3613
Bi-monthly magazine, covering
nursing in Washington. The
Washington State Nurses'
Association also publishes
Washington Nurse eight times
per year.

PORTLAND AREA TRADE MAGAZINES

Animator, The
Northwest Film & Video
Center, Oregon Art
Institute
1219 S.W. Park Ave.
Portland, OR 97205
(503) 221-1156
Quarterly newsletter on
film, video, media, and
computer arts education.

Chain Saw Age
3435 N.E. Broadway
Portland, OR 97232
(503) 287-6113
Monthly magazine,
covering outdoor power
equipment trade.

Commercial Review
1725 N.W. 24th
Portland, OR 97210
(503) 226-2750
Weekly agricultural magazine.

Competitive Advantage, The
PO Box 10091
Portland, OR 97210
(503) 274-2953
Monthly newsletter, targeting
sales and marketing
professionals.

Daily Shipping News
2014 N.W. 24th
Portland, OR 97210
(503) 227-4545
Covers world trade and
transportation.

Digger, The
2780 S.E. Harrison, #102
Milwaukie, OR 97222
(503) 653-8733
Monthly magazine for the
Northwest nursery
industry.

Export Report
Western Wood Products
Association.
Yeon Building, 522 S.W.
Fifth Ave.
Portland, OR 97204
(503) 224-3930
Monthly, featuring
statistical reports on the
volume of softwood
lumber exports by species
and major destinations.

Forest World
World Forestry Center
410 S.W. Canyon Road
Portland, OR 97221
(503) 228-1367
Quarterly forestry
magazine.

Northwest Electrician
Route 2, Box 137
Pendleton, OR 97801
(503) 443-7991
Monthly.

Oregon Congress-PTA
Oregon Congress of
Parents & Teachers
Association
531 S.E. 14th
Portland, OR 97214
(503) 234-3928
Education magazine
published seven times
yearly.

Oregon Education
Oregon Education Association
One Plaza Southwest, 6900 S.W.
Haines Road
Tigard, OR 97223
(503) 684-3300
Newsletter published monthly
during the academic year.

Oregon Food Journal
Northwestern Food Merchants,
Inc.
3000 Market St. Plaza N.E., No.
541
Salem, OR 97309
(503) 363-3768
Magazine serving the Oregon
and southwest Washington
grocery industry, published six
times yearly.

Oregon Grange Bulletin
Oregon State Grange
1313 S.E. 12th Ave.
Portland, OR 97214
(503) 236-1118
Monthly agricultural magazine.

Oregon Optometry
Oregon Optometric Association
2410 Sunset Drive
Forest Grove, OR 97116
(503) 357-5984
Quarterly journal.

Oregon Pharmacist
1460 State St.
Salem, OR 97301
(503) 585-4887
Monthly magazine.

Oregon Publisher
7150 S.W. Hampton, Suite 232
Portland, OR 97223
(503) 684-2074
Quarterly journalism magazine.

Pacific Northwest Grain and Feed Association Newsletter
200 S.W. Market St., #1005
Portland, OR 97201
(503) 227-0234
Bi-weekly.

Portland Physician Scribe
4540 S.W. Kelly
Portland, OR 97201
(503) 222-9977
Twice-monthly tabloid on social, political, and economic aspects of medicine.

Resource Recycling
PO Box 10540
Portland, OR 97210
(503) 227-1319
"North America's recycling journal," published seven times yearly.

Topicator
Topicator/Lake Moor Publishers, Inc.
PO Box 1009
Clackamas, OR 97015
(503) 653-1002
Classified guide to advertising, communication, and marketing periodicals, published six times a year.

Visions
Oregon Graduate Center, Office of External Affairs & Development
19600 N.W. Von Neumann Drive
Beaverton, OR 97006
(503) 690-1096
Science and technology quarterly magazine.

Western Lumber Facts
Western Wood Products Association
Yeon Building, 522 S.W. Fifth Ave.
Portland, OR 97204
(503) 224-3930
Monthly magazine, featuring lumber industry statistics on production, orders, shipments, etc.

Job-Hunt Related Publications

The following newspapers and magazines contain only job listings and job-related information and advice.

AAR/EEO Affirmative Action Register
8356 Olive Blvd.
St. Louis, MO 63132
(314) 991-1335
"The only national EEO recruitment publication directed to females, minorities, veterans, and the handicapped."
Monthly magazine consists totally of job listings.

Community Jobs
1516 P St. N.W.
Washington, DC 20036
(202) 667-0661
Monthly nationwide listings of jobs with community organizations and advocacy groups.

Contract Engineer Weekly
CE Publications, Inc.
PO Box 97000
Kirkland, WA 98083
(206) 823-2222
Weekly magazine of job opportunities for contract engineers.

Federal Jobs Digest
PO Box 594
Millwood, NY 10546
Elaborate listing of job opportunities with the federal government.

International Employment Hotline
PO Box 6170
McLean, VA 22106
(703) 573-1628
Monthly listing of overseas jobs. Provides a resume service for subscribers.

JOBNET
Association of Washington Cities
1076 S. Franklin
Olympia, WA 98502
(206) 753-4137
Monthly listings of job opportunities with the cities and towns of Washington.

Legal Employment Newsletter
Pacific Edition
PO Box 36601
Grosse Point, MI 48236
Newsletter lists open Washington legal positions as well as career opportunities in the public-private sector throughout the West.

National and Federal Legal Employment Report
Federal Reports
1010 Vermont Ave., N.W.
Washington, DC 20005
(202) 393-3311
Monthly in-depth listings of attorney and law-related jobs in federal government and with other public and private employers throughout the United States.

National Arts Job Bank
Western States Arts Foundation
141 East Palace Ave.
Santa Fe, NM 87501
(505) 988-1166
Twice-monthly publication of arts-related job, internship, and apprenticeship openings for the western United States.

Opportunities in Non-profit Organizations
ACCESS: Networking in the Public Interest
67 Winthrop St.
Cambridge, MA 02138
(617) 495-2178
Monthly listings of non-profit jobs around the country, organized by type of non-profit.

Pacific Northwest Employment Directory
Jobs Unlimited
2315 El Capitan Way
Everett, WA 98208
(206) 353-7782

Washington Labor Market
Washington State Employment Security Department
MS: KG-11
Olympia, WA 98504
(206) 438-4818
Monthly publication with extensive labor market information for the state.

Job Telephone Hotlines

Here's a way to find out about job openings by "letting your fingers do the walking." Just dial any of the numerous telephone job banks and listen to taped recordings that describe available positions and how to apply (asterisks denote hotlines without recorded messages). Although some of these job hotlines are sponsored by particular professional associations (see Chapter 5), many are available at no charge other than what you might spend at a pay telephone or for a long-distance telephone call. Area job information lines include:

SEATTLE/PUGET SOUND AREA

Bangor Naval Base (206) 396-4779
Boeing Co. (206) 394-3111, or within Washington State 1-800-525-2236
Federal Government (206) 442-4365
Fort Lewis (206) 967-5377
Hewlett-Packard (206) 334-2244
Highline Community College* (206) 878-3710
IBM Central Employment* (206) 587-3192
Internal Revenue Service (206) 442-2639
Kaiser Aluminum* (206) 455-5466
King County (206) 296-5209
McChord A.F.B.(206) 984-2277
Metro (Municipality of Metropolitan Seattle) (206) 684-1313
Olympia, City of (206) 753-8442
Pierce College* (206) 964-6585
Pierce County (206) 591-7466
Port of Seattle (206) 728-3290
Puget Sound Naval Shipyard 1-800-562-5972
Seattle Community College (206) 587-5454
Seattle, City of (206) 684-7999
Seattle, Port of (206) 728-3290
Sheraton Hotel(206) 621-8677
Snohomish County (206) 259-0686
Tacoma Community College* (206) 566-5014
Tacoma, City of (206) 591-7466
Tektronix* (206) 885-0900
Thurston County (206) 754-5499
United Parcel Service (206) 621-6329
University of Washington (206) 543-6969
US West PNB (206) 345-6126
Veterans:
   ***King County Veteran's Aid Bureau** (206) 296-7656
   ***Seattle Veteran's Action Center** (206) 684-4708
   ***Seattle Veterans Administration** (206) 624-7200
   ***Tacoma Veterans Administration** (206) 383-3851
   ***All other VA benefits and programs** 1-800-552-7480

Washington State Personnel:
  Olympia (206) 586-0545,
  Seattle (206) 464-7378
Weyerhaeuser (206) 924-5630 (after tone, dial 8449)

PORTLAND AREA

Allstate Insurance* (503) 641-6600
Blue Cross/Blue Shield (503) 225-5402
Boeing of Portland (503) 661-8318
Freightliner (503) 283-8657
Great Northern Products* (503) 227-1947
GTE* (503) 526-2737
Hewlett Packard (206) 896-2493
Intel Corp.* (503) 681-8080
Meier & Frank* (503) 241-5776
Metro Service District (503) 220-1177
Multnomah County (503) 248-5035
Multnomah Education Services District* (503) 255-1841,
  Ext. 207
Nike   (503) 644-4224
Pacific Power & Light (503) 464-6800
Pacific Telecom (206) 699-5990
Port of Portland (503) 231-5478
Portland General Electric (503) 226-7441
Portland Public Schools (503) 280-5156
Portland State University* (503) 777-0746
Portland, City of (503) 248-4573
Reed College (503) 777-7706
Safeway (503) 657-6400
Standard Insurance (503) 248-2884
Tri-Met (transit) (503) 238-4840
U.S. Post Office (503) 294-2270
U.S. West Direct (503) 242-8593
United Grocers (503) 652-7522
University of Portland* (503) 283-7332
Willamette Industries* (503) 227-5581

Developing a Strategy: The ABCs of Networking

The successful job search doesn't happen by accident. It's the result of careful planning. Before you rush out to set up your first interview, it's important to establish a strategy—that is, to develop a plan for researching the job market and contacting potential employers.

This chapter and Chapter 7 will cover specific techniques and tools that you'll find useful in your search. But before we get to them, a few words are in order about your overall approach.

It's Going to Take Some Time

Looking for a new job is no easy task. It's as difficult and time-consuming for a bright young woman with a brand-new MBA as it is for a 50-year-old executive with years of front-line experience. Certainly, every once in a while someone lucks out. One of Tom's clients established a record at Camden and Associates by finding a new position in four days. But most people should plan on two to six months of full-time job hunting before they find a position they'll really be happy with.

According to *Forbes* magazine, the older you are and the more you earn, the longer it will take to find what you're looking for—in fact, up to six months for people over 40 earning more than $40,000. People under 40 in the $20,000-$40,000 bracket average two to four months.

Your line of work will also affect the length of your search. Usually, the easier it is to demonstrate tangible bottom-line results, the faster you can line up a job. Lawyers, public relations people, and advertising executives are harder to place than accountants and sales people, according to one top personnel specialist.

Be Good to Yourself

Whether or not you're currently employed, it's important to nurture your ego when you're looking for a new job. Rejection rears its ugly head more often in a job search than at most other times, and self-doubt can be deadly.

Make sure you get regular exercise during your job search to relieve stress. You'll sleep better, feel better, and perhaps even lose a few pounds.

Take care of your diet and watch what you drink. Many people who start to feel sorry for themselves tend to overindulge in food or alcohol. Valium and other such drugs are not as helpful as sharing your progress with your family or a couple of close friends.

Beef up your wardrobe so that you look and feel good during your employment interviews. There's no need to buy an expensive new suit, especially if you're on an austerity budget, but a new shirt, blouse, tie, pair of shoes, or hairstyle may be in order.

Maintain a positive outlook. Unemployment is not the end of the world; few people complete a career without losing a job at least once. Keep a sense of hu-

111

mor, too. Every job search has its funny moments. It's OK to joke about your situation and share your sense of humor with your friends and family.

Life goes on despite your job search. Your spouse and kids still need your attention. Try not to take out your anxieties, frustrations, and fears on those close to you. At the very time you need support and affirmation, your friends may prefer to stay at arm's length. You can relieve their embarrassment by being straightforward about your situation and by telling them how they can help you.

Put Yourself on a Schedule

Looking for work is a job in itself. Establish a schedule for your job search and stick to it. If you're unemployed, work at getting a new job full time—from 8:30 a.m. to 5:30 p.m. five days a week, and from 9 a.m. to 12 noon on Saturdays. During a job search, there is a temptation to use "extra" time for recreation or to catch up on household tasks. Arranging two or three exploratory interviews will prove a lot more useful to you than washing the car or cleaning out the garage. You can do such tasks at night or on Sundays, just as you would if you were working.

Don't take a vacation during your search. Do it after you accept an offer and before you begin a new job. You might be tempted to "sort things out on the beach." But taking a vacation when you're unemployed isn't as restful as it sounds. You'll spend most of your time worrying about what will happen when the trip is over.

Even if you're currently employed, it's important to establish regular hours for your job search. If you're scheduling interviews, try to arrange several for one day so that you don't have to take too much time away from your job. You might also arrange interviews for your lunch hour. You can make phone calls during lunch or on your break time. You'd also be surprised at how many people you can reach before and after regular working hours.

Tax deductible job-hunting expenses

A certified public accountant offers the following tips on deducting job-hunting expenses on the income tax form. To qualify for certain deductions, you must hunt for a job in the same field you just left, or in the field that currently employs you. For example, someone who has worked as a public school teacher could not be compensated for the cost of getting a real estate license and seeking a broker's job.

If you are unemployed or want to switch jobs, expenses can be deducted on the Income Tax Statement of Employee Business Expenses or itemized on Schedule A of Form 1040. Expenses you can deduct include preparing, printing, and mailing resumes; vocational guidance counseling and testing; and the standard government reimbursement for miles driven to and from job interviews. Telephone, postage, and newspaper expenses are also deductible. While seeking work out of town, additional deductions are allowed for transportation, food, and lodging.■

Watch Your Expenses

Spend what you have to spend for basic needs such as food, transportation, and housing. But watch major expenditures that could be delayed or not made at all. The kids will still need new shoes, but a $200 dinner party at a fancy place could just as well be changed to sandwiches and beer at home.

Keep track of all expenses that you incur in your job search, such as telephone and printing bills, postage, newspapers, parking, transportation, tolls, and meals purchased during the course of interviewing. These may all be tax deductible.

Networking Is the Key To a Successful Job Search

The basic tasks of a job search are fairly simple. Once you've figured out what kind of work you want to do, you need to know which companies might have such jobs and then make contact with the hiring authority. These tasks are also known as researching the job market and generating leads and interviews.

Networking, or developing your personal contacts, is a great technique for finding out about market and industrial trends and is unsurpassed as a way to generate leads and interviews. *Networking is nothing more than asking the people you already know to help you find out about the job market and meet the people who are actually doing the hiring.*

Each adult you know has access to at least 300 people you do not know. Of course, a lot of them will not be able to do much in the way of helping you find a job. But if you start with, say, 20 or 30 people, and each of them tells you about 3 other people who may be able to help you, you've built a network of 60 to 90 contacts.

Mark S. Granovetter, a Harvard sociologist, reported to Forbes magazine that "informal contacts" account for almost 75 percent of all successful job searches. Agencies find about 9 percent of new jobs for professional and technical people, and ads yield another 10 percent or so.

Box 7457
University of Washington
Seattle, WA 98195
April 11, 1990

Dr. Norman Hartman
President
Combined Opinion Research
1204 Pacific Ave.
Tacoma, WA 98402

Here's an example of a networking letter

Dear Dr. Hartman:

    Dr. Obrigon Partito, with whom I have studied these past two years, suggested that you might be able to advise me of opportunities in the field of social and political research in the Seattle/Tacoma area.

I am about to graduate from the University of Washington at Seattle with a B.A. in American History and am a member of Phi Beta Kappa. For two of the last three summers, I have worked in the public sector as an intern with the Association of Washington Cities in Seattle and with Senator Claghorn in Washington. Last summer I worked as a desk assistant at UPI's Seattle office.

I am eager to begin full-time work and would appreciate a few minutes of your time to discuss employment possibilities in the field of social and political research. I will be finished with exams on May 24 and would like to arrange a meeting with you shortly thereafter.

I look forward to hearing from you, and in any case I will be in touch with your office next week.

Sincerely,

Steven Sharp
(206) 555-9876■

How To Start

To begin the networking process, draw up a list of all the possible contacts who can help you gain access to someone who can hire you for the job you want. Naturally, the first sources, the ones at the top of your list, will be people you know personally: friends, colleagues, former clients, relatives, acquaintances, customers, and club and church members. Just about everyone you know, whether or not he or she is employed, can generate contacts for you.

Don't forget to talk with your banker, lawyer, insurance agent, dentist, and other people who provide you with services. It is the nature of their business to know a lot of people who might help you in your search. Leave no stone unturned in your search for contacts. Go through your Christmas card list, alumni club list, and any other list you can think of.

On the average, it may take 10 to 15 contacts to generate 1 formal interview. It may take 5 or 10 of these formal interviews to generate 1 solid offer. And it may take 5 offers before you uncover the exact job situation you've been seeking. You may have to talk to 250 people before you get the job you want. The maximum may be several hundred more.

Don't balk at talking to friends, acquaintances, and neighbors about your job search. In reality, you're asking for advice, not charity. Most of the people you'll contact will be willing to help you, if only you tell them *how*.

The Exploratory Interview

If I introduce you to my friend George at a major Portland bank, he will get together with you as a favor to me. When you have your meeting with him, you will make a presentation about what you've done in your work, what you want to do, and you will ask for his advice, ideas, and opinions. That is an exploratory, or "informational," interview. As is true of any employment interview, you must make a successful sales presentation to get what you want. You must convince George that you are a winner and that you deserve his help in your search.

The help the interviewer provides is usually in the form of suggestions to meet new people or contact certain companies. I introduced you to George. Following your successful meeting, he introduces you to Tom, Dick, and Mary. Each of them provides additional leads. In this way, you spend most of your time *interviewing*, not staying at home waiting for the phone to ring or the mail to arrive.

A job doesn't have to be vacant in order for you to have a successful meeting with a hiring authority. If you convince an employer that you would make a good addition to his or her staff, the employer might create a job for you where none existed before. In this way, networking taps the "hidden job market."

To make the most of the networking technique, continually brush up on your interviewing skills (we've provided a refresher course in Chapter 7). Remember, even when you're talking with an old friend, you are still conducting an exploratory interview. Don't treat it as casual conversation.

Developing Professional Contacts

Friends and acquaintances are the obvious first choice when you're drawing up a list of contacts. But don't forget professional and trade organizations, clubs, and societies—they are valuable sources of contacts, leads, and information. In certain cases, it isn't necessary for you to belong in order to attend a meeting or an annual or monthly lunch, dinner, or cocktail party.

Many such groups also publish newsletters, another valuable source of information on the job market and industry trends. Some professional associations offer placement services to members, in which case it may be worth your while to join officially. At the end of this chapter, we've provided a list of selected organizations that might prove useful for networking purposes.

If you're utterly new to the area and don't as yet know a soul, your job will naturally be tougher. But it's not impossible. It just means you have to hustle that much more. Here are some first steps you should take. Start attending the meetings of any professional society or civic organization of which you've been a member in the past. Find a church, temple, or religious organization that you're comfortable with and start attending. Join a special interest group. It could be anything from The Sierra Club to Parents Without Partners.

If you're just out of college (even if you flunked out), work through your alumni association to find out who else in the Seattle/Portland area attended your alma mater. If you were in a fraternity or sorority, use those connections. If you're not a member of any of the groups mentioned above, now's the time to join—or to investigate some of the networking groups that follow.

Once you've taken the trouble to show up at a meeting, be friendly. Introduce yourself. Tell people you talk to what your situation is, but don't be pushy. You've come because you're interested in this organization and what it stands for. Volunteer to serve on a committee. You'll get to know a smaller number of people much better, and they'll see you as a responsible, generous person, a person they'll want to help. Do a bang-up job on your committee and they'll want to help all the more.

You've already got lots of contacts

Networking paid off for Liz, a young woman eager to make her way in banking or a related industry. She told us why she's glad she took the time to talk with her friends and neighbors about her job search.

"I was having dinner with close friends and telling them about my job search," says Liz. "During the conversation, they mentioned a banker friend they thought might be hiring. As it turned out, the friend didn't have a job for me. But he suggested I come in, meet with him, and discuss some other possibilities. He put me in touch with an independent marketing firm, servicing the publishing industry. The owner of the firm was looking for someone with my exact qualifications. One thing led to another, and pretty soon I had landed exactly the position I wanted." ■

Keeping Yourself Organized

The most difficult part of any job search is getting started. A pocket calendar or engagement diary that divides each work day into hourly segments will come in handy.

You will also want to keep a personal log of calls and contacts. You may want to develop a format that's different from the one shown here. Fine. The point is to keep a written record of every person you contact in your job search and the results of each contact.

Your log (it can be a notebook from the dime store) will help keep you from getting confused and losing track of the details of your search. If you call someone who's out of town until Tuesday, say, your log can flag this call so it won't fall between the cracks. It may also come in handy for future job searches.

Your log's "disposition" column can act as a reminder of additional sources of help you'll want to investigate.

You'll also have a means of timing the correspondence that should follow any interview.

CALLS AND CONTACTS

Date	Name & Title	Company	Phone	Disposition
2/10	Chas. Junior, V.P. Sales	Top Parts	(703) 277-5500	Interview 2/15
2/10	E. Franklin Sales Manager	Frameco	466-0303	Out of town until 2/17
2/10	L. Duffy Dir. Marketing	Vassar Inc.	826-6112	Out of office. Call in aft.
2/10	P. Lamm Sls. Dir.	Golfco Ent.	(301) 386-9100	Busy to 2/28 Call then.
2/10	E. Waixel VP Mktg. & Sales	Half'n'Half Foods	(818) 338-1055	Call after 2

If you're unemployed and job hunting full time, schedule yourself for three exploratory interviews a day for the first week. Each of these meetings should result in at least three subsequent leads. Leave the second week open for the appointments you generated during the first. Maintain this pattern as you go along in your search.

We can't emphasize too strongly how important it is that you put yourself on a job-searching schedule, whether or not you're currently employed. A schedule shouldn't function as a straitjacket, but it ought to serve as a way of organizing your efforts for greatest efficiency. Much of your job-hunting time will be devoted to developing your network of contacts. But you should also set aside a certain portion of each week for doing your homework on companies that interest you (see Chapter 4), and for pursuing other means of contacting employers (we'll get to these in a minute).

As you go through your contacts and begin to research the job market, you'll begin to identify certain employers in which you're interested. Keep a list of them. For each one that looks particularly promising, begin a file that contains articles about the company, its annual report, product brochures, personnel policy, and the like. Every so often, check your "potential employer" list against your log to make sure that you're contacting the companies that interest you most.

119

Go for the Hiring Authority

The object of your job search is to convince the person who has the power to hire you that you ought to be working for him or her. The person you want to talk to is not necessarily the president of the company. It's the person who heads the department that could use your expertise. If you're a salesperson, you probably want to talk with the vice-president of sales or marketing. If you're in data processing, the vice-president of operations is the person you need to see.

How do you find the hiring authority? If you're lucky, someone you know personally will tell you whom to see and introduce you. Otherwise, you'll have to do some homework. Some of the directories listed in Chapter 4 will name department heads for major companies in the Portland or Seattle areas. If you cannot otherwise find out who heads the exact department that interests you, call the company and ask the operator. (It's a good idea to do this anyway, since directories go out of date as soon as a department head leaves a job.)

Use an introduction wherever possible when first approaching a company—that's what networking is all about. For those companies that you must approach "cold," use the phone to arrange a meeting with the hiring authority beforehand. Don't assume you can drop in and see a busy executive without an appointment.

And *don't* assume you can get to the hiring authority through the personnel department. If at all possible, you don't want to fill out any personnel forms until you have had a serious interview. The same goes for sending resumes (see Chapter 3). In general, resumes are better left behind, *after* an interview, than sent ahead to generate a meeting.

Telephone Tactics

Cold calls are difficult for most job seekers. Frequently, a receptionist or secretary, sometimes both, stands between you and the hiring authority you want to reach. One way around this is to call about a half-hour after closing. There's a good chance that the secretary will be off to happy hour, and the boss will still be finishing up the XYZ project report. Only now there will be no one to run interference for him or her.

Generally, you're going to have to go through a support staffer, so the first rule is to act courteously and accord him or her the same professional respect you'd like to be accorded yourself. This person is not just a secretary. Often, part of his or her job is to keep unsolicited job hunters out of the boss's hair. You want this intermediary to be your ally, not your adversary. If possible, sell what a wonderfully qualified person you are and how it is to the company's advantage to have you aboard.

If you're not put through to the hiring authority, don't leave your name and expect a return call. Instead, ask when there's a convenient time you might call back, or allow yourself to be put on hold. You can read job-search literature or compose cover letters while you wait. Be sure and keep your target's name and title and the purpose of your call on a card before you, however. You don't want to be at a loss for words when you're finally put through.

Other Tactics for Contacting Employers

Direct contact with the hiring authority—either through a third-party introduction (networking) or by calling for an appointment directly—is far and away the most effective job-hunting method. Your strategy and schedule should reflect that fact, and most of your energy should be devoted to direct contact. It's human nature, however, not to put all your eggs in one basket. You may want to explore other methods of contacting potential employers, but they should take up no more than a quarter of your job-hunting time.

Calling or writing to personnel offices may occasionally be productive, especially when you know that a company is looking for someone with your particular skills. But personnel people, by the nature of their responsibility, tend to screen out rather than welcome newcomers to the company fold. You're always better off going directly to the hiring authority.

Consider the case of a company that runs an ad in *The Wall Street Journal*. The ad may bring as many as 600 responses. The head of personnel asks one of the secretaries to separate the resumes into three piles according to age: "under 30," "over 30," and "I don't know." The personnel chief automatically eliminates two of the three stacks. He or she then flips through the third and eliminates all but, say, eight resumes. The personnel specialist will call the eight applicants, screen them over the phone, and invite three for a preliminary interview. Of those three, two will be sent to the hiring authority for interviews. That means that 598 applicants never even got a chance to make their case.

Statistically, fewer than one out of four job hunters succeed by going to personnel departments, responding to ads (either open or blind, as described in Chapter 4), or using various employment services. Some do find meaningful work this way, however. We repeat, if you decide to use a method other than networking or direct contact, don't spend more than 25 percent of your job-hunting time on it.

As you might expect, many books have been written on job-hunting strategy and techniques. Here is a sampling of them.

SELECTED BOOKS ON JOB-HUNTING STRATEGY

Baker, Nancy C. *The Mid-Career Job Change and How to Make It*. New York: Vanguard Press, 1980.
Bolles, Richard N. *The Three Boxes of Life and How to Get Out of Them*. Berkeley, CA: Ten Speed Press, 1983.
Bolles, Richard N. *What Color Is Your Parachute?* Berkeley, CA: Ten Speed Press, 1990.
Camden, Thomas M. *Get That Job! How to Succeed in a Job Search*. Hinsdale, IL: Camden and Associates, 1981.
Camden, Thomas M. *The Job Hunter's Final Exam*. Chicago: Surrey Books, 1990.
Figler, Howard. *The Complete Job Search Handbook*. New York: H. Holt & Co., 1988.
Gerberg, Robert Jameson. *The Professional Job Changing System*. New York: Performance Dynamics, Inc., 1981.
Haldane, Bernard. *Career Satisfaction and Success: A Guide to Job Freedom*. New York: AMACOM, 1982.
Hart, Lois Borland. *Moving Up—Women and Leadership*. New York: AMACOM, 1980.
Higginson, Margaret V., and Thomas L. Quick. *The Ambitious Woman's Guide to a Successful Career*. New York: AMACOM, 1980.
Kisiel, Dr. Marie. *Design for a Change—A Guide to New Careers*. New York: Franklin Watts, 1980.
Kleiman, Carol. *Women's Networks*. New York: Ballantine, 1981.
Peskin, Dean B. *Sacked*. New York: AMACOM, 1979.
Pettus, Theodore. *One On One—Win the Interview, Win the Job*. New York: Random House, 1981.

There follows a selected list of more than 150 organized groups, ready-made for networking, forming relationships, and learning inside information about business and commerce in the Seattle/Portland area. Pick the groups (arranged by the two geographical areas) that fit best into your career game plan, and work through them to help you land the job you want.

A complete list of groups suitable for networking is beyond the scope of this book, but to broaden your networking efforts in the Seattle area, check out **Greater Seattle Area Clubs and Organizations.** This publication, which lists approximately 1,300 professional, social, and service clubs and organizations in the greater Seattle area, is available through the Education Department of the Seattle Public Library.

SELECTED SEATTLE/PORTLAND AREA PROFESSIONAL ORGANIZATIONS, TRADE GROUPS, NETWORKS, CLUBS, AND SOCIETIES

SEATTLE/PUGET SOUND AREA

Administrative Management Society
c/o Dean's TOPS
633 Securities Building
Seattle, WA 98101
(206) 623-8677
Contact: Nancy Schroeder
Professional association for office managers. Newsletter and monthly dinner meetings.

Altrusa Club of Seattle
PO Box 70231
Seattle, WA 98107
(206) 789-1889
Contact: Judith Taylor
International service club of women professionals and executives that organizes community service projects. Several Puget Sound chapters. Membership by invitation only.

American Association of Retired Persons
9750 Third Ave. N.E., Suite 400
Seattle, WA 98115
(206) 526-7918
Contact: Jean Nalibow
Promotes independence and enhanced quality of life for persons 55 and older. Conducts older worker programs.

American Association of University Women
2433 E. Interlaken Blvd.
Seattle, WA 98112
(206) 626-3737
For women college graduates.

American Businesswomen's Association
PO Box 58528
Seattle, WA 98138(206) 641-8362
Contact: Eileen Heyn
Promotes professional, educational, cultural, and social
advancements of businesswomen. Monthly meetings.

American Electronics Association
11812 Northcreek Parkway N., Suite 205
Bothell, WA 98011
(206) 486-5720
Contact: Terry Byington or Brad Melton
National trade organization, serving electronics software
industry. Monthly programs for member companies. Publishes
bi-monthly local newsletter, plus monthly national newsletter,
salary surveys, and operating ratio surveys.

American Institute of Aeronautics and Astronautics, Pacific Northwest Section
c/o Boeing Commercial Airplane Co.
Boeing Box 3707 MS:4R-36
Seattle, WA 98124
(206) 393-0400
Contact: Norm Baullinger, Membership Chairman
International professional organization. Publishes newsletter
and meets 10 times per year.

American Institute of Architects, Seattle Chapter
1911 First Ave.
Seattle, WA 98101
(206) 448-4938
Southwest Washington Chapter
502 S. 11th St.
Tacoma, WA 98402
(206) 627-4006
Contact: Rebecca Keene
Olympia Chapter
McCleary Mansion
111 W. 21st Ave., Suite 11
Olympia, WA 98501
(206) 943-6012
Contact: Mary D. Mauerman
Professional association of licensed architects. Networking
meetings, monthly newsletters, job file, and resume file.

American Society for Information Science, Pacific Northwest Chapter
Children's Hospital and Medical Center, Hospital Library
PO Box C-5371
Seattle, WA 98105
(206) 526-2118
Contact: Tamara Turner

Organization for diverse group of professionals involved in information science, theory, research, product development. Quarterly *Points Northwest* newsletter.

American Society for Public Administration
1120 G St., Suite 500
Washington, DC 20036
(202) 393-7878
Professional association for government managers. Training programs, luncheon meetings, and monthly newsletter. Phone national office for local contacts.

American Society for Training and Development, Puget Sound Chapter
217 Ninth Ave. N.
Seattle, WA 98109
(206) 623-8632
Contact: Pam Miller, President
Not-for-profit education service society operating as a resource for Puget Sound organizations. Monthly newsletter.

American Society of Women Accountants
314 Lloyd Building
Seattle, WA 98101
(206) 467-8645
Contact: Susan Paulsen, President
Everett and Tacoma chapters. Continuing education seminars, monthly dinner meetings, newsletter.

American Women's Society of Certified Public Accounting, Seattle Chapter
PO Box 2442
Seattle, WA 98111
(206) 644-4800
Contact: Lauren Thomas, President
Ongoing resume file. Monthly newsletter includes job listings. Monthly meetings.

Associated Builders and Contractors of Western Washington
11911 N.E. First St., Suite 3
Bellevue, WA 98005
(206) 646-8000
Contact: Kathleen Garrity
Association representing contractors, subcontractors, suppliers, and service professionals primarily in open shop, light industrial, and multi-family businesses. Monthly meetings, monthly magazine.

Associated General Contractors of Washington
1200 Westlake N.
Seattle, WA 98109

(206) 284-0061
Contact: Richard C. Bristow, Executive Director
Southern District
3820 S. Pine
Tacoma, WA 98409
(206) 472-4476
Contact: Roland Dewhurst, Executive Director
Non-profit association for general contractors, subcontractors,
suppliers, and service providers. Monthly dinner board
meetings open to all members. Personnel Mart resume service.

**Associated Women Contractors, Suppliers and Design
Professionals**
217 Ninth Ave. N.
Seattle, WA 98109
(206) 364-4095
Contact: Elizabeth Eurick
Statewide organization for women and men in all aspects of
the building industry; voting members must be business
owners.

Association for Women in Computing
PO Box 179
Seattle, WA 98111
(206) 292-1000, Ext. 3133
Contact: Pamela Perrott
Organization of consultants, sales representatives,
programmers, analysts, others. Education, job bank, monthly
meetings.

Association of Professional Mortgage Women
c/o First American Title
Fourth and Blanchard Building
Seattle, WA 98121
(206) 728-0400
Contact: Pat Hamilton-Bell
Non-profit educational association for women and men
sponsors seminars and holds monthly dinner meetings.

Association of Washington Business
PO Box 658
Olympia, WA 98507
(206) 943-1600
Contact: Don C. Brunell

Building Industry Association of Washington
Associated Services
PO Box 1909
Olympia, WA 98507
Contact: Diane Johnson, Administrative Assistant

Business and Professional Women's Organization
12032 Pinehurst Way N.E.
Seattle, WA 98125
(206) 361-5048
Contact: Milly Alspach
Some 58 local chapters promote economic equity for working women. Monthly meetings.

Coalition of Labor Union Women
111 Second Ave. N.
Seattle, WA 98109
(206) 281-8901
Contact: Patricia Agostino
National organization, supporting women's involvement with unions. Monthly meetings.

Commercial Real Estate Women
c/o Colleen Price
1425 Fourth Ave., Suite 914
Seattle, WA 98101
(206) 455-2900
Contact: Margaux Mason
Networking resources in all areas of commercial real estate, including law, accounting, and property management. Monthly luncheons with speakers.

Consulting Engineers Council of Washington
508 Tower Building
Seattle, WA 98101
(206) 623-5936
Contact: Jack Morell, Executive Director
Organization of consulting engineering firms, representing approximately 2,500 employees engaged in the private practice of engineering. The office maintains a resume interchange. Monthly newsletter. Meetings three times per year.

Executive Women International
4401 E. Marginal Way S.
Seattle, WA 98134
(206) 464-6391
Contact: Janet L. Dillow
Membership by invitation only. Promotes advancement of women in business leadership. Projects assist women in need. Monthly meetings.

Fashion Group of Seattle
314 Lloyd Building
Seattle, WA 98101
(206) 441-8282
Contact: Linda Albo
Regional affiliate of New York-based international organization

127

for women in retail and wholesale, apparel design and manufacturing, and interior design. Membership by invitation, but guests are welcome at monthly meetings.

Insurance Women of Puget Sound
PO Box 374
Lynnwood, WA 98046
(206) 485-9552
Contact: Lilla Howard, President
Open to anyone in the insurance industry. Monthly meetings, employment referral service. Monthly newsletter includes job announcements.

International Association for Financial Planning
3229 Eastlake Ave. E.
Seattle, WA 98102
(206) 324-3208
Contact: Mary Lynne McDonald, President (206) 858-8102
Broad-based forum of personal and corporate financial planners. Monthly meetings include at least one hour of continuing education. Several annual educational symposia. Quarterly newsletter.

Jewish Federation of Greater Seattle, Business and Professional Division
2031 Third Ave.
Seattle, WA 98121
(206) 443-5400
Contact: M. Cordova Laytner
Helps women take on leadership roles.

National Academy of Television Arts and Sciences, Washington Chapter
217 Ninth Ave. N.
Seattle, WA 98109
(206) 682-3576
Contact: Marion Simpson, Chapter Administrator
Association of television professionals. Periodic program meetings. Monthly newsletter.

National Association of Accountants, Seattle Chapter
800 Fifth Ave., Floor 22
Seattle, WA 98124
(206) 358-6859
Contact: Cheryl DuBoise, President
Bellevue/Eastside Chapter
P.O. Box 93
Bellevue, WA 98104
(206) 788-3496
Contact: Fred Gallimore, Past President
Tacoma Chapter
c/o Weyerhaeuser Corp.

15716 13th Ave., Court E.
Tacoma, WA 98445
(206) 924-7715
Contact: Eric Scott, President
Chapters meet monthly and publish monthly newsletters and
annual member rosters. Member employment service.

National Association of Banking Women
PO Box 34030 C1-18
Seattle, WA 98124
(206) 433-7211
Contact: Karen Booth, President
Open to women and men bank officers and officers of other
financial service industries. Monthly meetings. Quarterly
newsletter.

National Association of Real Estate Executives
c/o Lane Premo, Southland Corp.
1035 Andover Park West
Seattle, WA 98188
(206) 575-6711
Meets monthly September to May.
National headquarters has job bank:
471 Spencer Drive South, Suite 8
West Palm Beach, FL 33409
(407) 683-8111
Monthly magazine, *Corporate Real Estate Executive;* quarterly
magazine, *NACOR News.*

**National Association of Social Workers, Washington
State Chapter**
2366 Eastlake Ave. E., Room 236
Seattle, WA 98102
(206) 325-9791
Contact: David E. Dickman, MSW, Executive Director
Local groups meet monthly and publish monthly newsletters.

**National Association of Women in Construction,
Seattle Chapter No. 60**
PO Box C-81435
Seattle, WA 98108
(206) 481-0919
Contact: Edna Green, President
Monthly newsletter, monthly meetings.

**National Electrical Contractors Association, Puget
Sound Chapter**
711 Sixth Ave. N., No. 100
Seattle, WA 98109
(206) 284-2150
Contact: Steve Washburn, Executive Director

Trade association for electrical contractors. Monthly board and membership meetings. Weekly newsletter includes job listings.

Northwest Culinary Alliance
Seattle First Bank Building, Suite 3811
Seattle, WA 98154
(206) 284-1780
Contact: Diane Hazen
Non-profit networking organization of chefs, caterers, food brokers, food and beverage producers, etc. Meets monthly. Yearly directory.

Northwest Fisheries Association
2208 N.W. Market St., No. 311
Seattle, WA 98107
(206) 789-6197
Contact: Greg Bloom, Executive Director
Trade association of processors, brokers, traders, suppliers, and shippers. Monthly membership meeting, bi-monthly newsletter. Membership directory published twice yearly.

Northwest Marine Trade Association
1900 N. Northlake Way, Suite 233
Seattle, WA 98103
(206) 634-0911
Contact: William West, Executive Director
Non-profit trade association for manufacturers, retailers, suppliers, and firms providing goods and services to the industry. Meets yearly and as needed. Monthly newsletter.

Northwest Translators and Interpreters Society (NOTIS)
PO Box 25301
Seattle, WA 98125
Contact: Judy Langley, President
Publishes *Directory of Translators and Interpreters*.

Olympia Business & Professional Women USA
PO Box 7841
Olympia, WA 98507
(206) 943-6153
Contact: Fran Raney

Olympia Master Builders
1211 State Ave. N.
Olympia, WA 98506
(206) 754-0912
Contact: Jan Teague
Non-profit trade organization affiliated with state and national organizations. Legislation, lobbying, evaluation, business enhancement. Monthly meetings, monthly newsletter.

Pacific Northwest Jewelers Association
PO Box 70526
Bellevue, WA 98007
(206) 885-7929
Contact: Sharron Nelson, Executive Director
Trade association to promote retail jewelers. Annual
convention. Quarterly newsletter.

Pacific Northwest Newspaper Association
PO Box 1128
Tacoma, WA 98411
(206) 272-3611
Contact: Jeff Marshall, Executive Director
Association for daily newspapers in six western states.
Educational workshops, monthly meetings. Bulletin published
every three weeks includes summaries of resumes, job
openings.

Pacific Northwest Personnel Management Association
3247 20th West
Seattle, WA 98199
(206) 283-0395
Organization for human resource management professionals.
Emphasis on continuing education. Monthly evening
meetings. Monthly newsletter.

Professional and Managerial Women's Network
217 Ninth Ave. N.
Seattle, WA 98109
(206) 623-8632
Contact: Ruth Easley, President
Provides career advancement opportunities and greater access
to information and resources for professional women.
"Celebrity Series" attracts top business women speakers three
times yearly. Monthly informal networking. Quarterly
newsletter includes job announcements.

**Professional Insurance Agents of Washington and
Alaska, Tacoma Chapter**
4117 Bridgeport Way West
Tacoma, WA 98466
(206) 694-5730
Periodic workshops and continuing education programs.
Monthly newsletter.

Professional Women's Fellowship
219 First Ave. N., No. 342
Seattle, WA 98109
(206) 382-7276
Contact: Lisa Clifton
Organization of professional Christian women emphasizes

spiritual growth in the workplace. Monthly breakfast meetings with speakers.

Public Relations Society of America
38 Irving Place, Third Floor
New York, NY 10008
(212) 995-2230
Professional society for individuals in public relations. Contact national office for names and phone numbers of local officers and activists. Networking meetings, programs, and newsletter.

Radio and Television News Directors Association
1717 K St. N.W., Suite 615
Washington, DC 20006
(202) 659-6510
Sponsors annual conference for young people interested in news careers. Call or write national office for local contact information.

Restaurant Association of Washington
722 Securities Building
1904 Third Ave.
Seattle, WA 98101
(206) 682-6174
Contact: Jack Gordon, General Manager
Trade association for owners and operators of food establishments in Washington. Monthly meetings and newsletter.

Seattle Advertising Federation
PO Box 4159
Seattle, WA 98104
(206) 623-8307
Organization for people involved in buying, selling, or producing advertising. Emphasis on legislation, education, and improving the image of the profession. Monthly "Get To Know" meetings and luncheon meetings. Monthly newsletter.

Seattle Design Association
PO Box 1097
Main Station
Seattle, WA 98111
(206) 448-4767
Contact: Cindy Hobbs
Non-profit professional association serving the graphic design industry and related businesses and professions.

Seattle Mortgage Bankers Association
1425 Fourth Ave., Suite 914
Seattle, WA 98101
(206) 358-3512
Contact: Jim Kirschbaum, President

Seattle Veterinary Medical Association
2050 112th Ave. N.E.
Bellevue, WA 98004
(206) 454-8381
Annual meeting and convention. Monthly newsletter for
members only includes help-wanted section.

Society for Marketing Professional Services
FORMA
1000 Lenora St.
Seattle, WA 98121
(206) 324-9530
Local job bank: 1-800-292-7677
Contact: Carla Thompson
Society of professionals who market for the architectural,
engineering, interior design, construction management, and
landscape architecture industries. Monthly meetings include
continuing education. Quarterly newsletter.

Society of Professional Journalists/Sigma Delta Chi
53 W. Jackson Blvd., Suite 731
Chicago, IL 60604
(312) 922-7424
Membership meetings, advocacy work, and continuing
education opportunities. Phone or write national office for
names of local contacts.

Society of Women Engineers
PO Box 31910
Seattle, WA 98103
(206) 655-9907
Contact: Suzanne Hakam
National non-profit organization promotes education,
participation of women in engineering. Monthly meetings.

Structural Engineers Association of Washington
PO Box 4250
Seattle, WA 98104
(206) 682-6026
Contact: Lynnell Brunswig, Business Manager
Professional organization emphasizes education and
maintaining industry standards. Seminars, workshops, and
refresher courses. Monthly newsletter in which member
companies may list job openings. Monthly dinner meetings.

Tacoma Mortgage Bankers Association
(206) 582-1252
Contact: Jim Cooper, President
Monthly membership meetings except in summer months.
Quarterly newsletter.

Washington Association of Legal Secretaries
c/o Shidler McBroom Gates and Lucas
999 Third Ave., Suite 3500
Seattle, WA 98104
(206) 223-4600
Contact: Virginia DeLay, President
Open to anyone in the legal profession (name change may be forthcoming). Chapters meet monthly. Monthly newsletter includes job announcements.

Washington Beer & Wine Wholesale Association
PO Box 1319
Olympia, WA 98507
(206) 352-5252
Contact: Phillip Wayt, Executive Director
Membership directory.

Washington Film and Video Association
PO Box 84588
Seattle, WA 98124
(206) 682-5495
Contact: David Franke, President
Monthly meetings open to non-members. *Monthly Point of View* includes classified section.

Washington Newspaper Publishers Association
3838 Stone Way N.
Seattle, WA 98103
(206) 634-3838
Contact: Miles Turnbull, Executive Director
Trade group for non-daily newspaper publishers. Bi-weekly bulletin includes job listings and resume summaries free of charge. Resume file.

Washington Retail Association
PO Box 2227
Olympia, WA 98507
(206) 943-9198
Contact: Janice L. Gee
Monthly newsletter to members. Lobbying at state level.

Washington Society for CPAs
902 140th Ave. N.E.
Bellevue, WA 98005
(206) 644-4800
Contact: John R. Plymer, Executive Director
Tacoma Chapter
c/o Phillips, Schmechel, and Gocke
625 Commercial St., Suite 370
Tacoma, WA 98402
(206) 572-6380
Contact: Ed Lord, President

Olympia Chapter
c/o St. Martin's College, Accounting Department
Lacey, WA 98503
(206) 438-4331
Contact: Wayne Borkowski, President
Chapters meet monthly. *The Washington CPA* comes out
monthly and includes job listings.

Washington Software Association
PO Box 8364
Kirkland, WA 98034
(206) 483-3323
Contact: Julie Schaefer, Executive Director
Open monthly dinner meetings with speakers. Subgroups
composed of programmers, managers, CEOs, etc., meet
periodically. Monthly *WSA Report*.

Washington State Association of Broadcasters
1001 Fourth Ave., Suite 3200
Seattle, WA 98154
(206) 448-9722
Contact: Karmi Speece, Executive Director
Trade group for general managers of commercial radio and TV
stations. Monthly newsletter. Legal and sales training seminars.
Callers may hear employment opportunities at radio and TV
stations statewide, updated weekly.

Washington State Bar Association
500 Westin Building
2001 Sixth Ave.
Seattle, WA 98121
(206) 448-0441
Seattle-King County Bar Association
320 Central Building
Seattle, WA 98104
(206) 624-9365
Tacoma-Pierce County Bar Association
930 Tacoma Ave. S.
Tacoma, WA 98402
(206) 383-3432
Non-profit organization, serving attorneys and the
community. King County chapter publishes monthly *Bar
Bulletin*, including job opportunity listings.

Washington State Dental Association
2033 Sixth Ave.
Seattle, WA 98121
(206) 448-1914
Seattle-King County Dental Society
720 Olive Way, Suite 918
Medical Dental Building
Seattle, WA 98101

(206) 624-4912
Pierce County Dental Society
PO Box 97351
Tacoma, WA 98497
(206) 584-4876

Washington State Master Builders Association
204 N. Quince
Olympia, WA 98507

Washington State Medical Association
2033 Sixth Ave., Suite 900
Seattle, WA 98121
(206) 441-9762
King County Medical Society
200 Broadway, No. 22
Seattle, WA 98122
(206) 621-9393
Pierce County Medical Society
705 S. Ninth Ave., Suite 203
Tacoma, WA 98405
(206) 572-3667
Thurston/Mason County Medical Society
PO Box 7279
Olympia, WA 98507
(206) 352-1417
Professional society for physicians.

Washington State Nurses Association
83 S. King St.
Seattle, WA 98104
(206) 622-3613
King County Nurses Association
8511 15th Ave. N.E.
Seattle, WA 98115
(206) 523-0997
Pierce County Nurses Association
5044 S. Yakima
Tacoma, WA 98408
(206) 472-4656
Professional organization for registered nurses.

Washington Vocational Association
PO Box 315
Olympia, WA 98507
(206) 786-9286
Contact: Kathleen Preston
Organization of vocational teachers meets monthly; subgroups
meet regularly. Yearly conference. Publications include
vocational update, newsletter, bulletin.

Washington Women Lawyers
Dexter Horton Building
710 Second Ave., Suite 618
Seattle, WA 98104
(206) 622-5585
Contact: Mary Fairhurst, President
Non-profit. Lawyers, judges, and law students promoting
interests of women in the legal profession. Monthly meetings
for networking, continuing education. Each of nine state
chapters publishes monthly newsletter with job listings.

**Women +
Business =
success**

Since **Women + Business** was
formed 11 years ago, this
Washington-based organization has
been very successful as a catalyst to:
1) develop conferences to provide
visibility for women, and 2) provide
educational programs on how to
achieve success and function
optimally in the business world.

Today, with women founding
their own companies at four times
the rate of men, **Women +
Business** is branching out to
conduct one or more special-issue
seminars throughout the year that
would 1) address technical and in-
depth topics, and 2) expand their
services for women who are starting
and operating their own businesses.

To learn more about what this
group has to offer, contact Donalee
Rutledge, President and CEO of
Market Street Computer Systems, at
(206) 783-2000.■

Women + Business
2033 Sixth Ave., Suite 804
Seattle, WA 98121
(206) 728-1744
Contact: Mag Mallory
Contact: Donalee Rutledge, (206) 783-2000
Sponsors executive women's forums and the annual Women +
Business Conference (see related sidebar in this section).

Women in Communications
610 Lloyd Building
Seattle, WA 98101
(206) 461-8550 or (206) 682-9424

How To Get a Job

Contact: Jane Kuechle
Nationwide non-profit organization for women in all branches of the communications industry. Monthly meetings.

Women in Graphic Arts
PO Box 61218
Seattle, WA 98121
(206) 283-2783
Contact: Caroline Layher
Organization serves the greater Puget Sound area. Members meet regularly.

Women in Trades
PO Box 3431
Seattle, WA 98144
(206) 723-9106
Contact: Hilary Emmer
Regional support and networking group for women in the building trades. Job referral service for members.

Women's Business Exchange
314 Lloyd Building
Seattle, WA 98101
(206) 382-1234
Contact: Megan Imre
This group of professional women networks at monthly breakfast gatherings. Training programs and classes held periodically.

Women's Fisheries Network
2442 N.W. Market, Box 199
Seattle, WA 98107
(206) 742-2810
Contact: Christy Suilzle
National non-profit organization for men and women in the fisheries and related businesses.

Executive networking

The higher your rung on the corporate ladder, the greater the chances that networking with executives outside your own field will pay off. If you're looking for a top spot in electronics, don't pass up a chance to discuss your credentials and employment needs with the recruiting executive of an advertising firm. He or she just might have the hidden connection that could land you a great job.

One hiring exec from a large corporation reports: "I network with recruiters from more industries than most people would think, both industries that are related to ours and those that are not. It helps to find out what talent is available. If one of my contacts has someone in a file they don't need and I do, they're happy to tell me about that person. And I work the same way." ■

PORTLAND AREA

American Association of Retired Persons, Chapter 158
The Galleria, Room 521
921 S.W. Tenth
Portland, OR 97205
(503) 227-5268
Maintains information and provides referrals to employment resources.

American Association of University Women
4050 S.E. Gladstone
Portland, OR 97202
(503) 777-7005

American Chemical Society, Portland Chapter
c/o Associated Chemists, Inc.
4401 S.E. Johnson Creek Blvd.
Portland, OR 97222
(503) 659-1708
Contact: Bob Henselman
Maintains small file of job listings. Monthly dinner meetings with speakers. Monthly newsletter.

American Handicapped Workers of the Northwest
1412 S.E. Morrison
Portland, OR 97214
(503) 235-3536

American Institute of Architects, Portland Chapter
215 S.W. First
Portland, OR 97204
(503) 223-8757
Monthly meetings. Publishes bi-monthly *Architalk* newsletter.

American Marketing Association, Oregon Chapter
PO Box 82, University Station
Portland, OR 97207
(503) 292-2260

How To Get a Job

American Society for Training and Development
200 S.W. Market, Suite 961
Portland, OR 97201
(503) 227-1151

American Society of Interior Designers, Oregon District Chapter
215 S.W. First
Portland, OR 97204
(503) 223-8231

American Society of Women Accountants
3516 S.E. Raymond
Portland, OR 97202
(503) 774-0964

Associated Builders and Contractors, Pacific Northwest Chapter
4815 S.W. Macadam
Portland, OR 97201
(503) 241-4921

Associated General Contractors of America
9450 S.W. Commerce Circle
Wilsonville, OR 97070
(503) 682-3363

Commercial Club of Portland
710 N.E. 21st
Portland, OR 97232
(503) 232-7155

Consulting Engineers Council of Oregon
5319 S.W. Westgate Drive
Portland, OR 97225
(503) 292-2348

Independent Insurance Agents of Oregon
4515 S.W. Corbett
Portland, OR 97201
(503) 222-4496

Institute of Electrical and Electronic Engineers
215 S.W. First
Portland, OR 97204
(503) 223-8231

Institute of Managerial and Professional Women
PO Box 40324
Portland, OR 97240
(503) 230-2129
Monthly meetings, monthly newsletter, annual conference.

International Association for Financial Planning, Oregon Chapter
3420 S.W. Macadam
Portland, OR 97201
(503) 295-2117

International Association of Business Communicators, Oregon Columbia Chapter
PO Box 292
Portland, OR 97207
(503) 239-8281
Monthly luncheon meetings, monthly newsletter.

Jewish Federation of Portland, Business and Professional Division
6651 S.W. Capitol Highway
Portland, OR 97219
(503) 245-6219

Metropolitan Business Association
621 S.W. Alder
Portland, OR 97205
(503) 223-6978

Multnomah County Medical Society
4540 S.W. Kelly
Portland, OR 97201
(503) 222-9977

National Association of Social Workers, Oregon Chapter
109 N.E. 50th
Portland, OR 97213
(503) 232-6003

**National Electrical Contractors Association
Northwest Line Constructors Chapter**
6162 N.E. 80th
Portland, OR 97218
(503) 255-4824
Oregon Columbia Chapter
601 N.E. Everett
Portland, OR 97232
(503) 233-5787

National Federation of Independent Business
6700 S.W. 105th, Suite 215
Beaverton, OR 97005
(503) 643-5301

Network for Executive Women
c/o National Association of Female Executives

127 W. 24th St.
New York, NY 10011
(212) 645-0770
Non-profit. Monthly meetings. Contact national association for local contacts and for monthly magazine, *Executive Female*.

Network of Business and Professional Women
5100 S.W. Macadam, Suite 290
Portland, OR 97201
(503) 295-1018
Non-profit. Monthly dinner networking meetings with speakers. Monthly newsletter.

North Clackamas Education Association
14741 S.E. 82nd Drive
Clackamas, OR 97015
(503) 655-2452

Northwest Food Processors Association
2300 S.W. First
Portland, OR 97201
(503) 226-2848

Northwest Society of Interior Designers
(503) 293-7709
No address or PO Box.

Oregon Association of Broadcasters
8383 N.E. Sandy Blvd., Room 460
PO Box 20037
Portland, OR 97220
(503) 257-3041
Contact: Vern Mueller, General Manager
Educational programs for members. Monthly *Broadcaster* newsletter includes job listings.

Oregon Association of Naturopathic Physicians
1920 N. Kilpatrick
Portland, OR 97217
(503) 285-3807

Oregon Association of Nurserymen
2780 S.E. Harrison, Suite 102
Milwaukee, OR 97222
(503) 653-8733
Contact: Clayton Hannon, Executive Director
Monthly magazine. Annual directory of members and services.

Oregon Association of Public Accountants
1804 N.E. 43rd
Portland, OR 97213
(503) 282-7247

Oregon Association of Tax Consultants
8325 S.W. Cirrus Drive, Building 18
Beaverton, OR 97005
(503) 643-1566
Chapters meet monthly. Monthly chapter newsletter. State
newsletter is bi-monthly.
Portland Chapter:
2410 N.E. Liberty St.
Portland, OR 97211
(503) 284-3702
Contact: Hazel Fulmore, Membership Chairwoman

Oregon Beer & Wine Distributors Association
111 S.W. Fifth, Suite 3200
Portland, OR 97204
(503) 228-2337

Oregon Cattlemen's Association
1000 N.E. Multnomah
Portland, OR 97232
(503) 281-3811

Oregon Computer Consultants Association
PO Box 5365
Portland, OR 97228
(503) 227-0791 (answering service)
Contact: Rubin Contrares, (503) 281-3551

Oregon Dental Association
17898 S.W. McEwan Road
Portland, OR 97224
(503) 620-3230
Referrals for Clackamas and Washington counties.
Multnomah Dental Society
2828 S.W. Corbett, Suite 210
Portland, OR 97201
(503) 223-4731
Referrals for Multnomah County.

Oregon Education Association
State Headquarters
6900 S.W. Haines Road
Tigard, OR 97223
(503) 684-3300
Teachers union. Newsletter and job listing service for teachers.

Oregon Energy Coordinators Association
3534 S.E. Main
Portland, OR 97214
(503) 235-0196

Oregon Executives Association
3505 S.E. Milwaukie
Portland, OR 97202
(503) 236-6973

Oregon Feed, Seed Grain and Suppliers Association
1725 N.W. 24th
Portland, OR 97210
(503) 226-2758

Oregon Financial Planners
9955 S.E. Washington
Portland, OR 97216
(503) 256-3963

Oregon Health Care Association
12200 N. Jantzen
Portland, OR 97217
(503) 285-9600

Oregon Independent Retail Grocers Association
310 S.W. Fourth
Portland, OR 97204
(503) 223-4185

Oregon Jewelers Association
919 S.W. Taylor
Portland, OR 97205
(503) 223-8772

Oregon Lodging Association
12724 S.E. Stark
Portland, OR 97233
(503) 255-5135

Oregon Medical Association
5210 S.W. Corbett Ave.
Portland, OR 97201
(503) 226-1555
Multnomah County Medical Society
4540 S.W. Kelly
Portland, OR 97201
(503) 227-2737
Placement Service:
(503) 222-9977

Oregon Mortgage Bankers Association
200 S.W. Market, Suite 961
Portland, OR 97201
(503) 295-6249

Oregon Newspaper Publishers Association
7150 S.W. Hampton, Suite 232
Portland, OR 97223
(503) 684-2874
Contact: Carol Dimich
Job placement service.

Oregon Nurses Association, State Headquarters
9700 S.W. Capitol Highway, Suite 200
Portland, OR 97219
(503) 293-0011

Oregon Restaurant Association
3724 N.E. Broadway
Portland, OR 97232
(503) 249-0974
Contact: Debby Wall Leahy
Non-profit. *Main Ingredient* newsletter published every six weeks. Seminars, quarterly chapter meetings.

Oregon Society of CPAs
10206 S.W. Laurel St.
Beaverton, OR 97005
(503) 641-7200
Contact: Rhonda Wolfenbarger, Membership Service Coordinator
Committees meet monthly. Monthly publication includes job listings.

Oregon State Association of Plumbing, Heating, and Cooling Contractors
8755 S.W. Citizens Drive
Wilsonville, OR 97070
(503) 682-7165

Oregon State Bar Association
5200 S.W. Meadows Road
Lake Oswego, OR 97035
(503) 620-0222
Both *Bar Bulletin* magazine and *For The Record* monthly tabloid newspaper have classified sections.
Multnomah Bar Association
711 S.W. Alder
Portland, OR 97205
(503) 222-3275

Oregon Trial Lawyers Association
1020 S.W. Taylor, Suite 750
Portland, OR 97205
(503) 223-5587
Contact: Carmel Lulay, Executive Director

Monthly board meeting; annual convention. Quarterly publication. Continuing legal education, legislative action.

Pacific Maritime Association
101 S.W. Main, Suite 330-B
Portland, OR 97204
(503) 227-3621
Contact: Roxa Bierman, Executive Secretary and Personnel Representative
Serves steamship companies, terminal operators. Annual membership meetings. Annual report.

Pacific Northwest Hardware and Implement Association
333 S.W. Fifth
Portland, OR 97204
(503) 226-1641

Pacific Northwest Newspaper Association
621 S.W. Morrison, Suite 1335
Portland, OR 97205
(503) 228-9831

Pacific Printing Industries
5319 S.W. Westgate Drive, Suite 117
Portland, OR 97221
(503) 297-3328
Non-profit affiliate of Printing Industries of America, serving commercial printers. Bi-weekly *Good Impressions* newsletter includes human resource listings.

Portland Advertising Federation
(503) 231-1777 or (503) 234-5800
Call after 6 p.m. or early morning.
Resume and job service.

Portland Association of Teachers
345 N.E. Eighth
Portland, OR 97232
(503) 233-5018
Representing only Portland teachers. Monthly meetings. Weekly newsletter for members.

Portland Executives Association
421 S.W. Sixth
Portland, OR 97204
(503) 227-6551

Portland Sales and Marketing Executives
140 S.W. Arthur
Portland, OR 97201
(503) 227-1900

Portland Women's Club
1220 S.W. Taylor
Portland, OR 97205
(503) 227-9201
Philanthropic pursuits, networking. Board meetings, public
meetings.

**Professional Insurance Agents of Washington and
Alaska**
1508 Broadway
Vancouver, WA 98663
(206) 694-5730
Contact: Michael Jans, Executive Director
Periodic workshops and continuing education programs.
Monthly newsletter.

United Metal Trades Association
906 N.E. 19th
Portland, OR 97232
(503) 235-8361

Women Entrepreneurs of Oregon, Portland Chapter
5100 S.W. Macadam, Suite 290
Portland, OR 97201
(503) 222-6011
Contact for Clackamas Chapter: Arlene Soto, (503) 632-7750
Non-profit, open to men. Monthly meetings, workshops,
annual conference. Monthly chapter newsletters, bi-monthly
statewide newsletter.

Women in Communications
PO Box 3924
Main Station
Portland, OR 97208
(503) 274-6215
Non-profit organization for women in all branches of the
communications industry.

**Small business is
big business in
Oregon**

Although layoffs of thousands by
Oregon timber and high-technology
industries hit by recession touched
off a massive exodus in the early
1980s, many Oregonians with no
place else to go started their own
businesses.

Today Oregon is a leader in the
creation of small-business jobs,
report two recent studies.

According to a survey by the
Oregon Economic Development

Department, 94 percent of the state's 83,000 registered businesses have fewer than 50 employees, and 49 percent employ 5 workers or less. The average number of employees for all Oregon businesses is 19.

When small businesses were asked to look to the next two years, an amazing 83 percent expected to hire an average of 1.7 new employees each and to experience 25 percent sales growth. One-fourth of the firms expected to add a new location within two years.

Economically, Oregon is "one of the West's most stable states," reports a U.S. West Communications survey of 800,000 small businesses in 14 states west of the Mississippi. The drop in lumber employment during the early 1980s has been offset by growth in the construction, high-technology, and service industries, according to the study.

Employment at Oregon small businesses grew 6 percent between 1986 and 1988 (Washington State small businesses came in second with a 5.6 percent increase), while the big business work force was up only 0.8 percent due to layoffs at some of the largest companies.■

6

Using Professional Employment Services

Conducting a job search is no easy task. When the pressure is on, many job seekers' first instinct is to turn to professional employment services for relief. "After all," he or she reasons, "everyone knows that professional services have all the job listings." Wrong!

It's smart to use every available resource to generate leads and interviews. But professional employment services vary from agencies that specialize in temporary clerical help to executive recruiters who deal primarily with top-management types. Employment agencies, career consultants, and executive recruitment firms differ greatly in the kinds of services they offer and in how—and by whom—they get paid. You can save yourself a lot of time, effort, and perhaps even money and anguish by informing yourself about the advantages and disadvantages of the various kinds of professional employment services. One handbook that might prove useful is the *Directory of Approved Counseling Services* (American Personnel and Guidance Association, 5201 Leesburg Pike 400, Falls Church, VA 22041).

Also, our advice in Chapter 2 (see the sidebar titled "Who's Good, Who's Not") bears repeating: as our listings do not constitute an endorsement of any consulting firm, search firm, or employment agency, try to get the opinion of one or more people who have already used the service you are considering, and check with consumer protection agencies such as those we have listed.

Employment Agencies

The thousands of employment agencies that have succeeded through the years have done so by acting as intermediaries in the job market between buyers (companies with jobs open) and sellers (people who want jobs). An employment agency obtains a fee when a person it refers to a company is hired by that company. The fee may be paid by the company, but in some cases it is paid by the worker. Agencies that specialize in restaurant and domestic help, for example, often charge the worker a fee. Usually the placement fee amounts to a certain percentage of the worker's annual salary.

Seldom will an employment agency place a candidate in a job that pays more than $30,000 a year. Most employment agencies concentrate on support jobs. Supervisory openings may be listed, too, but employment agencies usually don't handle middle- or upper-management positions. In the computer field, for example, computer operators, programmers, and perhaps systems analysts could find work through an agency. But directors of data processing or MIS (management information systems) would go to an executive search firm or would job-hunt on their own.

A company that's looking for a secretary gains certain advantages by going to a reputable agency. It doesn't have to advertise or screen the hundreds of resumes that would probably pour in from even a small want ad in the Sunday *Times*. A good employment agency will send over only qualified applicants for interviews. Referrals are made quickly, and there is no cost to the company until it hires the secretary. For many companies, it's worth it to pay an agency fee to avoid the hassle of prescreening dozens, if not hundreds, of applicants.

The advantage to the agency of a successful placement (besides the fee) is repeat business. After two or three referrals work out well, an employment agency can generally count on receiving future listings of company vacancies.

The value to the job seeker of using an employment agency depends on a number of factors, including the quality of the agency, the kind of work you're looking for, how much experience you have, and how broad your network of personal and business contacts is.

In general an agency's loyalty will be to its source of income. Agencies are more interested in making placements than in seeing to it that applicants land in jobs that are really fulfilling. An agency is likely to put pressure on its applicants to accept jobs that they don't really want, just so it can collect its fee. With certain exceptions, unless you're just starting out, new in town, or switching to a field in which you have no experience, an agency probably can't do much more for you than you could do for yourself in an imaginative and energetic job search. If a company has to pay a fee to hire you, you're at a disadvantage compared with applicants who are "free." Moreover, giving an employment agency your resume could be a serious mistake if you're trying to conduct a confidential job search.

On the other hand, a good agency can help its candidates develop a strategy and prepare for employment interviews. This training can be most valuable to people who are inexperienced in job-hunting techniques. Agency pros know the market, screen well, and provide sound advice. A secretary who tries to investigate the Seattle or Portland market on his or her own will take up to six times longer to get the "right" job than someone who uses a quality agency.

Historically, certain employment agencies have engaged in practices that can only be called questionable at best, and the field as a whole is trying to polish up a somewhat tarnished image. Today, all employment agencies in Washington and Oregon must be state licensed. Under state supervision, and the watchful eye of the Better Business Bureau, most questionable practices of disreputable agencies have been eliminated.

There are many highly respected, successful, excellent employment agencies able and willing to help qualified job seekers. But as in any profession, there are also crooks. It's still a practice in some agencies to advertise non-existent openings to attract applicants for other, less desirable positions.

So much for the pros and cons of employment agencies. If you decide to try one, be sure it's a reputable firm. Ask people in your field to recommend a quality agency, and consult the Better Business Bureau and other resources listed in Chapter 2 to see if there have been any complaints about the agency you're considering. Most important, *be sure to read the contract thoroughly, including all the fine print, before you sign it.* If you have any questions, or if there's something you don't understand, don't be afraid to ask. It's your right. Make sure you know who is responsible for paying the fee, and what the fee is. Remember that *in some cases, an agency's application form is also the contract.*

Here, then, is a selective listing of local employment agencies, including their areas of specialty.

EMPLOYMENT AGENCIES

SEATTLE/PUGET SOUND AREA

Accounting Personnel
1750 112th Ave. N.E., Suite E-163
Bellevue, WA 98004
(206) 454-5450
Accounting, engineering, insurance, bio-medical, data processing, computer programming.

Ace Employment Agency
1677-B Second Ave. S.
Tumwater, WA 98502
(206) 754-7755
All fields.

Aerospace Recruiters
PO Box 260
Mercer Island, WA 98040
(206) 641-3083
Aerospace administration, design, engineering, finance, marketing, operations.

Business Careers
1001 Fourth Ave., Suite 828
Seattle, WA 98154
(206) 447-4000 (clerical and administrative)

(206) 447-7474 (management and sales)
also:
1019 Pacific Ave., Suite 404
Tacoma, WA 98402
(206) 383-1881
Secretarial, reception, bookkeeping, word processing, office
support, sales.

Career Clinic
Northgate Executive Center II
9725 Third Ave. N.E., Suite 509
Seattle, WA 98115
(206) 524-9831
All fields.

Central Medical/Dental Agency
411 University, Suite 1200
Seattle, WA 98101
(206) 623-0061
Medical, dental.

Employment Northwest
4706 Lacey Blvd. S.E.
Lacey, WA 98503
(206) 491-4020
All fields.

Express Personnel Services
2627 Capital Mall Drive S.W.
Olympia, WA 98502
(206) 357-7195
All fields.

Faulk and Associates
6314 W. 19th W., Suite 5
Tacoma, WA 98466
(206) 565-9595
Banking, savings and loan.

General Employment Services
2525 One Union Square
Sixth and University
Seattle, WA 98101
(206) 623-1750
also:
11225 S.E. Sixth Ave., Suite 210
Bellevue, WA 98004
(206) 454 0718
Legal, mortgage banking, insurance, clerical, administration.
Publishes *Annual Salary Survey* and *Vacation/Holiday Survey*,
covering administrative and office personnel in Seattle and
the Eastside.

How To Get a Job

Heritage Restaurant and Hotel Employment Services
300 120th N.E., Building 2, Suite 215
Bellevue, WA 98005
(206) 453-2383
All positions in the restaurant and hotel industries.

Maritime Employment Services
1717 S. 341st Place
Federal Way, WA 98003
(206) 874-8374
All positions from captain to cook in the domestic and
international offshore maritime industry.

Medical-Dental Placement Service
705 S. Ninth Ave., Suite 301
Tacoma, WA 98405
(206) 572-3709

Northwest Professional Services
3010 Westin Building
2001 Sixth Ave.
Seattle, WA 98121
(206) 728-0728
Software, hardware, data processing, management, finance.

Pace Network
720 Third Ave.
Seattle, WA 98104
(206) 623-1050
Office professional placement, temporary staffing, specialized
management technical search.

Robert Half
600 University Way, Suite 2328
Seattle, WA 98101
(206) 624-9000
also:
1201 Pacific Ave., Suite 1780
Tacoma, WA 98402
(206) 272-1600
10900 N.E. Fourth Ave., Suite 1120
Bellevue, WA 98004
(206) 451-1000
Accounting, banking, bookkeeping, data processing.

Snelling and Snelling
131 S.W. 153rd
Burien, WA 98166
(206) 246-6610
also:
Tacoma Mall Office Building
Tacoma, WA 98409

(206) 473-1800
All fields.

PORTLAND AREA

Adams Personnel, Inc.
200 S.W. Market, Suite 1078
Portland, OR 97201
(503) 224-5870
Contact: Molly Sprague, Manager.
Office support staff.

Brown, D., and Associates
610 S.W. Alder, Suite 711
Portland, OR 97205
(503) 224-6860
Accounting and finance, computer hardware and software,
insurance, legal, sales, technical.

EDP Markets
610 S.W. Broadway
Portland, OR 97205
(503) 223-0470
DP and high-tech personnel.

Emerald Employment Agency
Kruse Woods One Building
5285 S.W. Meadows Road, Suite 281
Lake Oswego, OR 97035
(503) 684-8881
Sales, clerical, bookkeeping, insurance.

Legal Register, The
Rielly, Robert and Associates Personnel
620 S.W. Fifth, Suite 700
Portland, OR 97204
(503) 223-1122
All fees employer-paid.

Multnomah Bar Association Placement Service
711 S.W. Alder, Suite 311
Portland, OR 97205
(503) 227-0723
All fees employer-paid.

Robert Half
1 S.W. Columbia
Portland, OR 97201
(503) 222-9778
Accounting, financial, banking, data processing.

Snelling and Snelling Agency
711 S.W. Alder
Portland, OR 97205
(503) 243-2424

A cautionary tale on getting one's foot in the door

An employment agency referral wasn't exactly a step on the ladder to success for your friendly co-author, Sara Steinberg.

"When I was still looking for work about four months after graduating from college with a journalism degree," she says, "I registered with an employment agency. They urged me to take a secretarial position with a publishing company, assuring me that the company would put me into an editorial position as soon as one became available.

"When I went to the publishing company for an interview, I was surprised to recognize a familiar face—a former classmate who had graduated with me. She was cleaning out her desk, having quit the secretarial job that I was considering taking. She was quitting, she said, because she had not even been notified when an entry-level editorial job did open up at the company.

"I decided not to follow in her footsteps." ∎

Career Consultants

If you open the employment section of the Sunday *Oregonian*, the *Seattle Post-Intelligencer*, or the Northwest edition of the *Wall Street Journal*, you'll see several ads for career consultants (also known as career counselors or private outplacement consultants). The ads are generally directed to "executives" earning yearly salaries of anywhere between $20,000 and $300,000. Some ads suggest that the consultants have access to jobs that are not listed elsewhere. Others claim, "We do all the work." Most have branch offices throughout the country.

Career consultants vary greatly in the kind and quality of services they provide. Some may offer a single service, such as vocational testing or preparing resumes. Others coach every aspect of the job search and stay with you until you accept an offer. The fees vary just as broadly and range from $100 to several thousand dollars. You, not your potential employer, pay the fee.

A qualified career consultant can be a real asset to your job search. But *no consultant can get you a job.* Only you can do that. You are the one who will participate in the interview, and you are the one who must convince an employer to hire you. A consultant can help you focus on an objective, develop a resume, research the job market, decide on a strategy, and/or train you in interviewing techniques. But you can't send a consultant to interview in your place. It just doesn't work that way.

Don't retain a career consultant if you think that the fee will buy you a job. The only reason you should consider a consultant is that you've exhausted all the other resources we've suggested here and still feel you need expert and personalized help with one or more aspects of the job search. The key to choosing a career consultant is knowing what you need and verifying that the consultant can provide it.

Check references. A reputable firm will gladly provide them. Check the Better Business Bureau and other resources listed in this chapter and in Chapters 2 and 4. Has anyone lodged a complaint against the firm you're considering? Before you sign anything, ask to meet the consultant who will actually provide the services you want. What are his or her credentials? How long has the consultant been practicing? Who are the firm's corporate clients?

Read the contract carefully before you sign it. Does the contract put the consultant's promises in writing? Has the consultant told you about providing services that are not specified in the contract? What does the firm promise? What do *you* have to promise? Are all fees and costs spelled out? What provisions are made for refunds? For how long a time can you use the firm's or consultant's services?

Be sure to do some comparison shopping before you select a consultant. A list of Seattle/Puget Sound and Portland area consulting firms you may want to investigate is included in Chapter 2.

Executive Search Firms

An executive search firm is one that is compensated by a company to locate a person with specific qualifications that meet a precisely defined employment need. Most reputable executive search firms belong to an organization called the Association of Executive Recruiting Consultants (AERC). The association publishes a code of ethics for its membership.

A search firm never works on a contingency basis. Only employment agencies do that. The usual fee for a search assignment is 30 percent of the first year's salary of the person to be hired, plus out-of-pocket expenses. These are billed on a monthly basis. During hard times, most companies forgo retaining search firms because it's so expensive.

It's difficult to get an appointment to see a search specialist. Executive search consultants have only their time to sell. If a specialist spends time with you, he or she can't bill that time to a client. If you can use your personal contacts to meet a search professional, however, by all means do so. Executive specialists know the market and can be very helpful in providing advice and leads.

Search firms receive dozens of unsolicited resumes every day. They seldom acknowledge receipt and usually retain only a small portion for future search needs or business development. They really can't afford to file and store them all. Sending your resume to every search firm in the Portland or Seattle areas will be useful only if one firm coincidentally has a search assignment to find someone with exactly your background and qualifications. It's a long shot, similar to answering blind want ads.

The following is a selected list of executive search firms in the Portland and Seattle/Puget Sound areas.

EXECUTIVE SEARCH FIRMS

SEATTLE/PUGET SOUND AREA

Accounting Force
Plaza 600 Building, Suite 800
600 Stewart St.
Seattle, WA 98101
(206) 443-8840
Accounting, bookkeeping, finance.

Almond and Rogers
1101 Fawcett S., Suite 350
Tacoma, WA 98402
(206) 572-0300
Non-specialized.

Carroll Associates
11811 N.E. First, Suite 207
Bellevue, WA 98005
(206) 453-1318
High-tech, computer software, sales, systems engineering, and marketing.

Computer Professionals and Consultants
777 108th Ave. N.E., Suite 2350
Bellevue, WA 98004
(206) 637-8055
Full range in computer software industry.

Cox and Associates
740 14th Ave. W.
Kirkland, WA 98033
(206) 827-2230
High-tech, management, electrical engineering.

Execusearch
1800 112th Ave. N.E., Suite 250-E
Bellevue, WA 98009
(206) 454-3108
Non-specialized.

Executive Recruiters
600 108th N.E., Suite 242
Bellevue, WA 98004
(206) 447-7404
Non-specialized.

Houser Martin Morris and Associates
110 110th Ave. N.E., Suite 503
Bellevue, WA 98009
(206) 453-2700
Data processing, software, engineering, finance, health care.

HRA Insurance Staffing
Pacific First Plaza
155 108th Ave. N.E., Suite 510
Bellevue, WA 98004
(206) 451-4007
Insurance.

INTERACC
5310 12th St. E.

Tacoma, WA 98424
(206) 922-1300
Accounting, operations.

Kirkbride & Associates
405 114th Ave. S.E., Suite 300
Bellevue, WA 98004
(206) 453-5256
Sales, marketing, engineering.

Korn/Ferry International
1201 Third Ave., Suite 2120
Seattle, WA 98101
(206) 621-1834
World's largest executive recruiting firm.

Management Recruiters of Tacoma
1019 Pacific Ave., Suite 806
Tacoma, WA 98402
(206) 627-1972
Engineering, software, analogue and digital programming.

MRI Management Recruiters
2510 Fairview Ave. E.
Seattle, WA 98102
(206) 328-0936
Bellevue branch: (206) 646-7790
Engineering.

Pacific Law Recruiters
1424 Fourth Ave.
Seattle, WA 98101
(206) 625-0654
24-hour job hotline: (206) 625-0583
All positions in legal profession.

Prior, Harry J./Martech Associates
700 112th Ave. N.E., Suite 300
Bellevue, WA 98004
(206) 455-1774
Senior-level management.

Recruiters West
Columbia Center
701 Fifth Ave.
Seattle, WA 98104
(206) 628-0810
Management, engineering, insurance, sales, finance, banking,
MIS, data processing.

Sales Consultants and Management Recruiters of Seattle
11811 N.E. First, Suite 304
Bellevue, WA 98005
(206) 455-1805
Sales, technical, marketing.

Source Services
411 108th Ave. N.E., Suite 1740
Bellevue, WA 98004
(206) 454-6400
Finance, accounting, technical, data processing.

Thomas and Associates
PO Box 642
Issaquah, WA 98027
(206) 644-7072
Health care professionals.

PORTLAND AREA

Cole, John T., and Associates
4800 S.W. Griffith Drive
Beaverton, OR 97006
(503) 644-5133
Forest products industry.

EDP Markets/EDP Consultants
610 S.W. Broadway, Suite 308
Portland, OR 97205
(503) 223-0470
Full spectrum of data processing, including management; also high-technology, primarily hardware/software engineering. EDP Consultants provides contract services.

Elwood, C. R., and Associates
1020 S.W. Taylor
Portland, OR 97205
(503) 294-0242
Data processing, engineering, finance, and accounting.

Haldane, Bernard, Associates
1220 S.W. Morrison, Suite 800
Portland, OR 97205
(503) 295-5926
High-tech positions; career changes.

Koehn, Lee, Associates
4380 S.W. Macadam Ave., Suite 185
Portland, OR 97201
(503) 224-9067
Financial positions.

Management Careers
317 S.W. Alder, Suite 1235
Portland, OR 97204
(503) 299-6755

Management Recruiters of Portland
Lloyd Center, Suite 2324
Portland, OR 97232
(503) 287-8701
Non-specialized.

Management Search
806 S.W. Broadway, Suite 550
Portland, OR 97205
(503) 223-6211
Executive and technical positions in engineering, production, data processing, finance, marketing, and sales.

Murphy Symonds & Stowell
1001 S.W. Fifth, Suite 1210
Portland, OR 97204
(503) 242-0111
Non-specialized; includes outplacement services.

Peltz, Robert, & Associates
310 S.W. Fourth Ave., Suite 555
Portland, OR 97204
(503) 227-3131
Sales and sales management.

Personnel Specialists
8625 S.W. Cascade Ave., Suite 220
Beaverton, OR 97005
(503) 626-4078
Process controls, data processing.

Quest One
4500 S.W. Kruse Way, Suite 140
Lake Oswego, OR 97035
(503) 636-4541
Insurance.

Reiter Douglas Co., The
111 S.W. Fifth, Suite 1715
Portland, OR 97204
(503) 228-6916
Forest products industry, other diverse industries.

Sales Consultants of Portland
5901 S.W. Macadam Ave., Suite 208
Portland, OR 97201

(503) 241-1230
Sales, marketing.

Search North America
620 S.W. Fifth, Suite 925
Portland, OR 97204
(503) 222-6461

Social Service Agencies

Unlike professional employment agencies, career consultants, and executive search firms, social service agencies are not-for-profit. They offer a wide range of services, from counseling and vocational training to job placement and follow-up—and their services are either low-cost or free.

Be sure to check out the list of Social Service Agencies in Chapter 2 as well.

SEATTLE/PUGET SOUND AREA

AARP Senior Community Service Employment Program
1511 Third, Room 905
Seattle, WA 98101
(206) 526-7918
Federally funded employment program, serving persons 55 and older with yearly incomes under $6,000. Program offices throughout area, including Seattle, (206) 624-6698; Pacifica, (206) 859-1818; and Bellingham, (206) 733-1941.

Cascades Careers
841 N. Central Ave.
Kent, WA 98032
(206) 954-9163
Assists persons with disabilities in locating employment. No fee.

Center for Career Alternatives
3700 Rainier Ave. S., Suite C
Seattle, WA 98144
(206) 723-2286
Youth and adult programs, including job-search skills workshops and some counseling for income-eligible King County residents.

Centro Latino
1304 S. Yakima
Tacoma, WA 98405
(206) 383-3698

How To Get a Job

Refers Hispanics to English as a Second Language (ESL) classes, counseling, on-the-job training opportunities.

Chinese Information and Service Center
409 Maynard S., Suite 201
Seattle, WA 98104
(206) 624-4062
Also serves Vietnamese community. Agency provides English as a Second Language classes, job readiness evaluation, job matching with post-employment follow-up, as well as translation services. There is no fee.

Community Youth Social Service
824 Fifth Ave. S.E.
Olympia, WA 98501
(206) 943-0780
Contact: Paula Raven, Program Manager
On-the-job training for ages 16-21. Classroom vocational testing.

El Centro de la Raza
2524 16th Ave. S.
Seattle, WA 98144
(206) 323-6484
Services for low-income clients include nine-hour employment workshop, classes, Job Club, ESL, subsidized books and training, matching of clients to jobs.

Employment Opportunities Center
4726 Rainier Ave. S.
Seattle, WA 98118
Refugees: (206) 587-2828
All others: 725-8200
Private, non-profit agency offering typing, computer, ESL, and other classes. No fee.

Family Independence Program
1700 E. Cherry
Seattle, WA 98122
(206) 464-7338
Provides welfare recipients with vocational exploration, child care, job skills and on-the-job training, plus volunteer experience for clients with no work history.

Federal Way Senior Center
4016 S. 352nd St.
Auburn, WA 98001
(206) 927-9031
A Retired Senior Volunteer Employment program.

FOCUS
509 10th Ave. E.

Seattle, WA 98102
(206) 329-7918
Assists people seeking permanent part-time work. Monthly
workshops on such topics as resume writing, cover letters, and
interviewing. Assesses interests of paying members and mails
them appropriate job listings. Non-members may examine
listings at office.

Goodwill Industries
1400 S. Lane St.
Seattle, WA 98122
(206) 329-1000
Job training and placement in minimum-wage positions for
those who can read and speak English.

Millionair Club Charity Board
2515 Western
Seattle, WA 98121
(206) 728-5627
Non-profit private organization. Permanent and part-time
employment for men and women; counseling.

Operation Improvement
2932 Hoyt Ave.
Everett, WA 98201
(206) 258-2766
Serves low income, disabled, and clients over 55 in Snohomish
County. Vocational training, on-the-job training, job
placement. GED and summer youth program.

Opportunities
841 N. Central, Suite 201
Kent, WA 98032
(206) 872-6310
Serves individuals on public assistance whose youngest child is
over six years old. Vocational assessments and help to obtain
schooling and/or employment.

Retired Senior Volunteer Program
222 N. Columbia
Olympia, WA 98501
(206) 943-7787
Contact: Neil Stone
Hires persons 60 or older to work on various projects. No
income requirements to qualify.

Seattle Indian Center
611 12th Ave. S.
Seattle, WA 98144
(206) 329-8700
Multi-service center for homeless and Native Americans.

How To Get a Job

Employment training and referral, job development, GED preparation, school re-entry, food bank.

Seattle Urban League
105 14th Ave.
Seattle, WA 98122
(206) 461-3792
Computer-assisted learning center. Career planning, job readiness, counseling, placement. Regional and local job listings.

St. Louise Job Location Program
PO Box 6164
Bellevue, WA 98008
(206) 747-0509
Contact: Bruce Harding
Job placement for Eastside area of Seattle. Monthly newsletter lists Eastside job opportunities. Also assists refugees coming into the area.

Tacoma Community House
PO Box 5107
Tacoma, WA 98405
(206) 383-3951
ESL classes, employment training, and placement for Asian refugees and other immigrants.

Tacoma/Pierce County Employment and Training Consortium
747 Market St.
Tacoma, WA 98402
(206) 591-5450
Federally funded programs for economically disadvantaged residents of Tacoma/Pierce County. Targets youth and elderly but also helps administer programs for the handicapped and single women heads of households.

Tacoma Urban League
2550 S. Yakima
Tacoma, WA 98405
(206) 572-5002
Employment programs target low-income and/or disadvantaged Tacoma residents. Resume writing, cover letters, job-search skills, job listings. Job Club for those with college degree or at least three years experience in a given field; no economic eligibility requirements. No fees.

Tacoma YWCA Resource Center
405 Broadway
Tacoma, WA 98402
(206) 272-4181
Career counseling, job-search workshops, interest surveys. Job

Bank listings cover Puget Sound area. Displaced Homemaker Program (597-6427) offers preparation for non-traditional blue-collar jobs.

Thurston County Job Search Network
216 E. Tenth
Olympia, WA 98501
(206) 786-5416; 1-800-624-1234, Ext. 5416
Some counseling. Help writing resumes, cover letters. Access to typewriters, phones, newspapers, library, telephone answering service. Information and referral to other community resources. State and local job listings.

University YWCA
4057 Roosevelt Way
Seattle, WA 98105
(206) 632-4747
Workshops cover resume writing, resources, mock interviews. Employment counseling available on sliding scale, with maximum fee of $20 for a half-hour session. Job listings updated weekly.
also:
YWCA of Seattle/King County
1118 Fifth Ave.
Seattle, WA 98101
(206) 461-4851

Washington Human Development Corp.
4636 E. Marginal Way S., Suite 108
Seattle, WA 98134
(206) 762-5192
Contact: Jeanne Pratt, Director
Part of four-state organization, non-profit agency has sister agency in Oregon. Open-entry six-month program for King County low-income residents offers Office Occupations/Word Processing classes, Job Search Training. Youth services provide job counseling, educational training, part-time employment.

YMCA of Greater Seattle
909 Fourth Ave.
Seattle, WA 98104
Program information: (206) 382-5022
Youth employment programs, including GED and resume assistance, training, placement.
also:
YMCA
510 Franklin St. S.E.
Olympia, WA 98501
(206) 357-6609

How To Get a Job

PORTLAND AREA

Center for Urban Education
3835 S.W. Kelly
Portland, OR 97201
(503) 223-3444
Eight-week New Directions program for persons over 55
teaches computer and job-search skills through classroom time
and one-on-one counseling. Participants earn minimum wage
for every hour of classroom time. Job placement, six-month
follow-up.

Job Opportunity Bank
2710 N.E. 14th Ave.
Portland, WA 97212
(503) 288-1602
Job-hunt networking and resource center. Information, classes,
job lead postings, access to office equipment and phones.
Members pay $10 per year and perform eight hours per
month of volunteer work; fee can be waived.

Oregon Human Development Corp.
9620 S.W. Barbur Blvd., Suite 110
Portland, OR 97219
(503) 245-2600
Youth services include job readiness training, work
experience, permanent job placement help.

Urban League of Portland
10 N. Russell
Portland, WA 97227
(503) 280-2600
Employment services include applications for state and local
jobs and setting up interviews.

YWCA Downtown Center
Women's Resource Center
1111 S.W. Tenth
Portland, OR 97205
(503) 223-6281
Extensive state-wide job listings.

YWCA St. Johns Center
8010 N. Charleston
Portland, WA 97203
(503) 286-5748
Career counseling. Workshops in filling out applications,
writing resumes, mock interviews (with video critique), phone
skills. Some job listings.

Government Agencies

Most job seekers do not take advantage of the free employment listings available through the city and state because the caliber of jobs is often disappointing. The services of these government agencies are usually free, however, and if you are near one of the following offices, you may as well stop in and see what is available.

Included in this section are federally funded agencies and programs of special value to job seekers.

Don't forget also to check the listings of government resources in Chapter 2, including *Resources For Women*.

SEATTLE/PUGET SOUND AREA

Employment and Training Program
2001 Western Ave.
Market Place One, Room 250
Seattle, WA 98121
Contact: Alfred Star
Program handled through the Private Industry Council for the Seattle area, (206) 684-7390.

Job Corps
Regional Office, Employment and Training Administration, U.S. Department of Labor
909 First Ave.
Seattle, WA 98104
(206) 442-4696
Serves low-income youth ages 16-21 at training sites throughout state. GED preparation, hands-on vocational training.

JTPA Youth Program
428 W. Birch St.
Shelton, WA 98584
(206) 426-1200
Job training program for low-income youth.

Metropolitan Development Council
622 Tacoma Ave. S., Suite 6
Tacoma, WA 98402
(206) 383-3921
Street Outreach Services
201B South Broadway
Tacoma, WA 98402
(206) 627-8588
Contact: Doug Swanberg
Federally funded community action agency. Homeless

outreach and employment program, classroom training, job referrals.

Operation Improvement
2932 Hoyt Ave.
Everett, WA 98201
(206) 258-2766
Federally funded agency assists low income, disadvantaged, and clients over 55. GED, vocational training, job training. Summer youth employment program for Snohomish County.

Seattle Mayor's Office for Senior Citizens
Alaska Building
618 Second Ave., Room 250
Seattle, WA 98104
(206) 684-0500
Contact: John Peterson
Senior Job Hotline: (206) 684-0494
Operates Age 55 Plus Employment Resource Center. Workshops, job pre-screening, job clearinghouse, referrals. Information on Social Security, EEOC claims, related issues. No income restrictions.

Senior Community Service Employment Program/AARP
1511 Third Ave., Suite 905
Seattle, WA 98101
(206) 624-6698
Federally funded employment program for low-income persons 55 and over.

Tacoma/Pierce County Employment Training Consortium
747 Market St., Room 644
Tacoma, WA 98402
(206) 591-5450
Contact: Colin Conant
Federally funded programs, targeting youth and elderly; also serves handicapped, single women heads of households.

Thurston County Employment and Training
Pacific Mountain Consortium (Private Industry Council)
2617-A 12th Court S.W.
Olympia, WA 98502
(206) 754-4113
Contact: Michael Kennedy
Sole requirement to access this program is that client must be low-income. Provides counseling and job skills training.

Thurston County Job Search Network
Employee and Administrative Services
921 Lakeridge Drive, S.W., Room 202

Olympia, WA 985
(206) 786-5416

Veterans Reemployment Program
Mail Stop KG 11
212 Maple Park Drive
Olympia, WA 98504
Contact: Call your local employment security office.
Each office has a counselor to assist veterans. Counseling
includes pre-employment, training, employment problems,
unemployment, and upgrading of discharges.

Washington State Department of Labor & Industries
General Administration Building
HC154A
Olympia, WA 98504
(206) 586-0771

**Washington State Department of Personnel (for State
employment)**
600 S. Franklin
Olympia, WA 98504
(206) 753-5368
See sidebar at end of chapter entitled "Landing a job with the
State of Washington."

PORTLAND AREA

Employment Division, State of Oregon
Downtown Portland Office
1407 S.W. Fourth
Portland, OR 97201
(503) 229-5730
Daily one-hour orientation on employment service.
Counseling for veterans. Job referrals. Research Office at (503)
229-5746 provides labor market information. All offices
provide job listings on microfiche, updated daily. Listings
include State of Oregon and private employers in metropolitan
Portland, throughout Oregon, and from other states.
Other offices:
Beaverton Office
12901 S.W. Jenkins Road, Suite C
Beaverton, OR 97005
(503) 644-1229
East Multnomah Office
660 S.E. 160th
Portland, OR 97233
(503) 257-4249
Hillsboro Office
229 S. First
Hillsboro, OR 97123
(503) 681-0219

How To Get a Job

North Portland Office
5411 N.E. Union
Portland, OR 97211
(503) 280-6046
Northwest Office (temporary labor)
403 N.W. 11th
Portland, OR 97209
(503) 229-5936
Oregon City Office
506 High
Oregon City, OR 97045
(503) 657-2071

Job Corps
Apprenticeship and Training Program, State of Oregon Bureau
of Labor and Industries
1400 S.W. Fifth
Portland, OR 97201
(503) 229-6008
U.S. Department of Labor program serves low-income youth
ages 16-21 at training sites throughout state. GED preparation,
hands-on vocational training.

Private Industry Council (PIC)
520 S.W. Sixth Ave., Suite 400
Portland, OR 97204
(503) 241-4600
Recorded message: (503) 241-4620
also:
Employer Training and Business Services, Clackamas County
Marylhurst Campus
Highway 43
Marylhurst, OR 97036
(503) 635-1521
Federally funded private, non-profit employment and training
organization assists economically disadvantaged clients with
career assessment, job-search skills, Job Club, job listings and
referrals, use of office equipment.

Senior Community Service Employment Program/AARP
4520 S.E. Belmont
Portland, OR 97215
(503) 231-8078
Federally funded employment program for low-income
persons 55 or older.

172

Landing a job with the State of Washington

The Washington State Department of Personnel publishes a weekly listing of new positions. To learn the location nearest you where listings are displayed, stop in at 600 S. Franklin, Olympia, WA 98504 or call (206) 753-5368.

Many jobs require applicants to make an appointment to take a test. Other jobs include an application requesting detailed information on one's education, work history, and qualifications. Make sure the "objective" on your application or resume reflects the job title of the position you are seeking.

The application process can take four to six weeks. If you receive no response within that time period, call to check the status of your application. *Always keep a copy of anything you send* in case your documents get lost.

Every Wednesday an orientation session is held for those who want to apply for executive recruitment. You may also apply for temporary employment, by appointment.

Be advised that the State of Washington uses a "point" system for filling positions. You may score high on your qualifying examination yet not be called for employment because the system may be weighted in favor of veterans and minorities.■

How To Succeed In an Interview

If you've read straight through this book, you already know that networking (see Chapter 5) is one of the most important and useful job-hunting techniques around. Networking is nothing more or less than using personal contacts to research the job market and to generate both exploratory and formal job interviews.

Networking and interviewing go hand in hand; all the contacts in the world won't do you any good if you don't handle yourself well in an interview. No two interviews are ever identical, except that you always have the same goal in mind: to convince the person to whom you're talking that he or she should help you find a job or hire you personally. An interview is also an exchange of information. But you should never treat it as you would a casual conversation, even if the "interviewer" is an old friend.

Preparing for the Interview: The 5-Minute Resume

Whether you're talking to the housewife next door about her brother-in-law who knows someone you want to meet or going through a final, formal interview with a multinational corporation, you are essentially making a sales presentation—in this case, selling yourself. Your goal is to convince the interviewer that you have the ability, experience, personality, maturity, and other characteristics required to do a good job and to enlist the interviewer's help in getting you that job.

In an informal interview you'll be talking first to friends and acquaintances. Most of the people you'll be talking to will want to help you. But they need to know who you are, what you've done, what you want to do, and most important, *how they can help you.*

To prepare for any interview, first perfect what we like to call the five-minute resume. Start by giving a rough description, not too detailed, of what you're doing now (or did on your last job) so that when you're telling your story, the listener isn't distracted by wondering how it's going to end.

Then go all the way back to the beginning—not of your career, but of your life. Talk about where you were born, where you grew up, what your folks did, whether or not they're still living, what your brothers and sisters do, and so on. Then trace your educational background briefly and, finally, outline your work history from your first job to your latest.

"What!" say many of our clients. "Drag my PARENTS into this? Talk about my crazy BROTHER and the neighborhood where we grew up?"

Yes, indeed. You want to draw the listener into your story, to make him or her interested enough in you to work for you in your search. You want the interviewer to know not only who you are and what you have achieved but also what you are capable of. You also want to establish things in common with the listener. The more you have in common, the harder your listener will work for you.

Co-author Tom Camden, we are not ashamed to admit, is a master of the five-minute resume. Here's how he would begin a presentation to someone like the neighbor down the street:

"Would it be all right with you if I gave you a broadbrush review of my background? Let you know what I've done, what I'd like to do? That'll give us some time to talk about how I should go about this job search. Maybe I could pick your brain a little about how you can help me. OK?

"Currently, I'm an officer of EnterChange, a consulting firm specializing in corporate outplacement.

"Originally, I'm from Chicago. I'm 53 years old, married, with three kids.

"My father was a security guard at IIT Research Institute; my mother is retired. She used to work for Walgreens—made aspirins, vitamins, and other pills. I'm the oldest of four children. My brother John does the traffic 'copter reports for a Chicago radio station. My sister Connie is a consultant for an industrial relations firm.

"I went to parochial schools. When I was 14, I left home and went into a monastery. I stayed there until I was 19. Then I went to Loyola University, studied psychology, got my degree in '59. I was also commissioned in the infantry.

"I started my graduate work in Gestalt psychology. In 1960 Kennedy called up troops for the Berlin crisis. That included me, so I spent a year on active duty. Following that, I came back and continued my graduate work in industrial relations..."

Tom took exactly a minute and a half to make this part of his presentation, and he's already given his neighbor several areas in which they may have something in common. He's volunteered enough information not only to get the neighbor interested in his story but to let the neighbor form judgments about him. People don't like to play God, says Tom. Yet it's a fact of life that we constantly form judgments about each other. In an interview—even an exploratory, informal one—you may as well provide enough information to be judged on who you are rather than on what someone has to guess about your background. What does it mean to be the oldest of four kids? What can you deduce from Tom's middle-class background?

The typical personnel professional will tell you that the number of brothers and sisters you have has nothing to do with getting a job. Technically, that's true. The law says that an employer can't ask you how old you are, your marital status, and similar questions. Yet any one who's considering hiring you will want to know those things about you.

The typical applicant begins a presentation with something like, "I graduated from school in June, nineteen-whatever, and went to work for so-and-so." Our task in this book is to teach you how *not* to be typical. Our experience has convinced us that the way to get a job offer is to be *different* from the rest of the applicants. You shouldn't eliminate the first 20 years of your life when someone asks you about your background! That's the period that shaped your basic values and personality.

Neither should you spend too much time on your personal history. A minute or two is just about right. That gives you from three to eight minutes to narrate your work history. Most exploratory interviews, and many initial employment interviews, are limited to half an hour. If you can give an oral resume in 5 to 10 minutes, you have roughly 20 minutes left to find out what you want to know (more on that shortly).

The five-minute resume revisited

Psychologist and career expert Gayle Roberts has her own slant on the five-minute resume. She believes that "while nothing works every time, you should try to emphasize those aspects of your personal history that have a bearing on your current qualifications for the job you're seeking.

"For example, I am one of those rare creatures who always liked school. I got along fine with the teachers. I even liked studying and taking tests. I liked to learn, and I still do. That's part of why I choose to work in an academic setting. I think it's helpful to mention my long history as a book worm any time I'm applying for a position that requires research, writing, or critical thinking skills. I don't think I'd mention it if I were going for a sales position.

"I personally wouldn't recommend saying too much about your past unless you can connect it

to the present in a way that makes
you look like a better job candidate.
Everybody has a number of revealing
personal anecdotes. The trick is to
pick the right ones."■

A word about your work history. If you've done the
exercises in Chapter 2, or written your own resume, you
ought to be able to rattle off every job you've had, from
the first to the latest, pretty easily. In the oral resume
you want especially to *emphasize your successes and accomplishments* in each job. This will take some practice.
We are not accustomed to talking about ourselves posi-
tively. From childhood we're conditioned that it's not
nice to brag. Well, we are here to tell you that if you
don't do it in the interview, you *won't* get the offer.

We repeat: *the interview is a sales presentation.* It's the
heart of your job search, your effort to market yourself.
In an exploratory interview, the listener will be asking,
"Should I help this person?" In a formal interview, the
employer will be asking, "Should I hire this person?" In
either case, the answer will be "yes" only if you make a
successful presentation, only if you convince the interviewer that you're worth the effort.

So, the first step in preparing for any interview,
formal or informal, is to *practice your five-minute resume.*
Go through it out loud enough times so that you're
comfortable delivering it. Then work with a tape
recorder and critique yourself. Try it out on a couple of
friends.

When you're preparing for a formal employment interview, *do your homework* on the company. This advice
is merely common sense. But it's surprising how many
candidates will ask an interviewer, "What does this
company do?" Don't be one of them. Before you go in
for an employment interview, find out everything you
can about the company—its history, organization, products and services, and growth expectations. Get hold of
the company's annual report, catalogs, and brochures.
Consult your networking contacts, and use the resources
in Chapter 4.

Steps to a Successful Interview

Before the Interview
- Self-assessment: identify strengths, goals, skills, etc.
- Research the company.
- Rehearse what you plan to say. Practice answers to common questions.
- Prepare questions to ask employer.

During the Interview
- Make sure you arrive a few minutes early.
- Greet the interviewer by his/her last name; offer a firm handshake and a warm smile.
- Be aware of non-verbal communication. Wait to sit until you are offered a chair. Sit up straight, look alert, speak clearly and forcefully but stay relaxed. Make good eye contact, avoid nervous mannerisms, and try to be a good listener as well as a good talker. Smile.
- Follow the interviewer's lead, but try to get the interviewer to describe the position and duties to you fairly early in the interview so you can then relate your background and skills in context.
- Be specific, concrete, and detailed in your answers. The more information you volunteer, the better the employer gets to know you.
- Offer examples of your work that document your best qualities.
- Answer questions as truthfully and as frankly as you can. Do not appear to be "glossing over" anything. On the other hand, stick to the point and do not over-answer questions. The interviewer may steer the interview into ticklish political or social questions. Answer honestly, trying not to say more than is necessary.

Closing the Interview
- Don't be discouraged if no definite offer is made or specific salary discussed.
- If you get the impression that the interview is not going well and that you have already been rejected, do not let your discouragement show. Once in a while, an interviewer who is genuinely interested in you may seem to discourage you to test your reaction.

179

- A typical interviewer comment toward the close of an interview is to ask if you have any questions. Prepare several questions in advance, and ask those that weren't covered during the interview.
- At the conclusion of your interview, ask when a hiring decision will be made. Also thank your interviewer for his or her time and express your interest in the position.

After the interview

- Take notes on what you feel you could improve upon for your next interview.
- If you are interested in the position, type a brief thank-you letter to the interviewer, indicating your interest.
- If offered the position, one to two weeks is a reasonable amount of time to make a decision. All employment offers deserve a written reply whether or not you accept them.

How to dress

A young friend of ours who wanted to break into real estate finally landed her first big interview—with Coldwell Banker. It was fairly easy for her to do her homework on a company of that size. Two days before the interview, however, it suddenly dawned on her that she had no idea how to dress. How did she solve her problem?

"It was pretty easy, actually, and fun, too," says Susan. "All I did was go and hang around outside the office for 15 minutes at lunchtime to see what everyone else was wearing."

However, we recommend that even if the office attire is casual, one should still dress professionally. One career counselor recommends that one should "always dress one step above the attire of those in the office where you are interviewing."■

What Interviewers are Looking For

▌ General Personality: Ambition, poise, sincerity, trustworthiness, articulateness, analytical ability, initiative, interest in the firm. (General intelligence is assumed.) Different firms look for different kinds of people—personalities, style, appearance, abilities, and technical skills. Always check the job specifications. Don't waste time talking about a job you can't do or for which you do not have the minimum qualifications.

▌ Personal Appearance: A neat, attractive appearance makes a good impression and demonstrates professionalism.

▌ Work Experience: Again, this varies from job to job, so check job specifications. If you've had work experience, be able to articulate the importance of what you did in terms of the job for which you are interviewing and in terms of your own growth or learning. Even if the work experience is unrelated to your field, employers look upon knowledge of the work environment as an asset.

▌ Verbal Communication Skills: The ability to express yourself articulately is very important to most interviewers. This includes the ability to listen effectively, verbalize thoughts clearly, and express yourself confidently.

▌ Skills: The interviewer will evaluate your skills for the job, such as organization, analysis, and research. It is important to emphasize the skills that you feel the employer is seeking and to give specific examples of how you developed them. This is the main reason why it is important to engage in self-assessment prior to the interview.

▌ Goals/Motivation: Employers will assess your ability to articulate your short-term and long-term goals. You should seem ambitious, yet realistic about the training and qualifications needed to advance. You should demonstrate interest in the functional area or industry and a desire to succeed and work hard.

▌ Knowledge of the Interviewer's Company and Industry: At a minimum, you really are expected to have done some homework on the company. Don't waste interview time asking questions you could have found answers to in printed material. Know the firm's position and character relative to others in the same industry. General awareness of media coverage of a firm and its industry is usually expected.

Handling the Interview

In an exploratory, or informal, interview most of the people you'll talk with will want to help you. But they need to know *how*. After you've outlined your personal and work history, ask your contact how he or she thinks your experience fits into today's market. What companies should you visit? Specifically, what people should you contact?

When someone gives you advice or a recommendation to call someone else, do it! Few things can be more irritating than to provide free counsel to someone who then ignores it. If your contact suggests that you call Helen Smith, call her!

In a formal employment interview, there are several typical questions you can expect to encounter, though not necessarily in this order:

Tell me about yourself. (This is your cue for the five-minute resume.)

Why do you want to change jobs?

What kind of job are you looking for now?

What are your long-range objectives?

What are your salary requirements?

When could you be available to start here?

Tell me about your present company.

What kind of manager are you?

How would you describe yourself?

What are your strengths and weaknesses?

(In the course of his career, Tom Camden has posed this last question to untold numbers of applicants. "They'll list two or three strengths," he says, "and then can't wait to tell me about their weaknesses." Don't be one of those people! Accentuate the positive. Remember, this is a competitive interview.)

Describe your present boss.

To whom can I talk about your performance?

Are you open to relocation?

How long have you been looking for a new job?

Why are you interested in this company? (This is your golden opportunity to show the interviewer that you've done your homework on the company.)

Practice your answers to these questions *before* you go in for the interview. Anticipate other questions you might be asked, and develop answers for them. In general, keep your responses positive. Never volunteer a negative about yourself, another company, or a former employer. Even if you hate your present boss, describe your areas of disagreement in a calm, professional manner. You are selling *yourself,* not downgrading others. Even if you're not particularly interested in the company, always conduct the interview as if you were dead set on getting the job.

The interviewer will apply your responses to the questions he or she *really* wants answered:

Does the applicant have the ability to do the job?

Can he or she manage people?

How does he or she relate to people?

What kind of person is this? A leader? A follower?

What strengths does he or she have that we need?

Why the number of job changes so far?

Where is he or she weak?

How did the applicant contribute to present and past companies?

What are his or her ambitions? Are they realistic?

Is he or she too soft or too tough on subordinates?

What is this person's standard of values?

Does he or she have growth potential?

Is there a health problem anywhere?

What is the nature of the "chemistry" between us?

What will the department manager think of this applicant as opposed to the others?

Should this person get an offer?

The interview should not be a one-sided affair, however. Questions that you should ask the interviewer are equally important in this exchange of information. For example, you have to know about the job, the company, and the people in your future employment situation. It's necessary to use your judgment to determine how and when to ask questions in an interview. But without the answers, it will be next to impossible for you to make a sound decision if you receive an offer. Some of the questions you want answered are:

What are the job's responsibilities?

What is the company's recent history? Its current objectives? Its market position?

Where are its plants located? What distribution systems does it use?

To whom will I report? What's his or her background?

How much autonomy will I have to get the job done?

Why is the job available?

Where does the job lead?

What about travel requirements?

Where is the job located?

Are there any housing, school, or community problems that will develop as a result of this job?

What is the salary range? (Do not raise the question of explicit salary at this point.)

What is the detailed benefit picture?

What is the company's relocation policy?

When will an offer decision be made?

What references will be required?

When would I have to start?

What is the personality of the company?

Do the job and company fit my plan for what I want to do now?

What's the next step?

Career guides

Some companies administer standardized tests to see if applicants are qualified for certain kinds of work, such as secretarial, data processing, and the like.

Many of the libraries listed in Chapter 4 have an impressive number of workbooks to help you prepare for the most common tests. These include study guides for elevator operators, computer programmers, women in the armed forces, law and court stenographers, laboratory aides, supervisory engineers, even mortuary caretakers! Reviews for state board exams for nurses and certified public accountants are also available.■

Following the Interview

Many job seekers experience a kind of euphoria after a good interview. Under the impression that a job offer is imminent, a candidate may discontinue the search. This is a serious mistake. The decision may take weeks, or may not be made at all. On the average, about six weeks elapse between the time a person makes initial contact with a company and when he receives a final answer. If you let up on the search, you will prolong it. Maintain a constant sense of urgency. Get on with the next interview. Your search isn't over until an offer is accepted and you actually begin the new job.

Always follow up an interview with correspondence. The purpose of the letter is to supplement the sales presentation you made. Thank the interviewer for his or her time and hospitality. Express interest in the position (ask for the order). Then mention three additional points to sell yourself further. Highlight how your specific experience or knowledge is directly applicable to the company's immediate needs. Try to establish a date by which a decision will be made.

If you think you could benefit from professional counseling in interviewing skills, consider the resources suggested in Chapter 2 and in Chapter 6. You may also find it helpful to refer to some of the following books.

BOOKS ON INTERVIEWING

Allen, Jeffrey. *The Complete Q & A Interview Book*. New York: Wiley, 1988.

Biegelein, J.I. *Make Your Job Interview a Success*. New York: Arco, 1987.

Danna, Jo. *Winning the Job Interview Game: Tips for the High-Tech Era*. Briarwood, NY: Palamino Press, 1986.

Faux, Marian. *The Executive Interview*. New York: St. Martin's Press, 1985.

Goodale, James G. *The Fine Art of Interviewing*. Englewood Cliffs, NJ: Prentice-Hall, 1982.

Grice, Charles R. *Fifteen Tips on Handling Job Interviews*. Grange, CA: Career Publishers, 1987.

Medley, H. Anthony. *Sweaty Palms: The Neglected Art of Being Interviewed*. Berkeley, CA: Ten Speed Press, 1984.

Pell, Arthur R. *How to Sell Yourself in an Interview*. New York: Monarch Press, 1982.

Yate, Martin John. *Knock 'em Dead: With Great Answers to Tough Interview Questions*. Boston: Bob Adams, 1987.

How to get the most from your references

References should be kept confidential and never revealed until a company is close to making you an offer, and you want to receive one.

Always brief your references before you supply an interviewer with their names and numbers. Tell the references what company you're interviewing with and what the job is. Give them some background on the company and the responsibilities you'll be asked to handle. Your references will then be in a position to help sell your abilities. Finally, don't abuse your references. If you give their names too often, they may lose enthusiasm for your cause. ■

What To Do If Money Gets Tight

Any job search takes time. One particularly pessimistic career counselor we know suggests you plan to spend about two weeks of search time for every thousand dollars you want to earn per year. (Pity the poor soul who wants to make $60,000!) A more optimistic estimate for a job search is around three months, provided the search is conducted full time.

If you already have a full-time job, it will take you longer to find a new one. But at least you will be receiving a paycheck while you're looking. This chapter is intended for those who are unemployed and facing the prospect of little or no income during the search.

When the financial squeeze is on, the first thing to do is make a thorough review of your liquid assets and short-term liabilities. Ask yourself how much cash you can expect to receive during the next three months from the following sources, plus any others you might come up with:

Savings
Securities
Silver and gold
Insurance loan possibilities
Second mortgage possibilities
Unemployment compensation
Severance pay
Accrued vacation pay
Personal loan sources (relatives, friends)
Sale of personal property (car, boat, stamp collections, etc.)

Then you should consider exactly what bills absolutely *must* be paid. Don't worry about your total outstanding debt. Many creditors can be stalled or might be willing to make arrangements to forgo principal as long as interest payments are made. Talk to each of your creditors to see whether something can be worked out.

The final step is easy—if sometimes painful. You compare the amount of money you have on hand or expect to receive with the amount you know you'll have to spend. The difference tells you exactly what kind of financial shape you're in.

The old adage has it that it's better to be unemployed than underemployed. If you can afford it, it's wise not to take a part-time or temporary job. The more time you spend looking for a good full-time position, the sooner you're likely to succeed. But if the cupboard looks pretty bare, it may be necessary to supplement your income any way legally possible in order to eat during the search.

Try to find part-time or temporary work that leaves you as free as possible to interview during the day. For this reason, many people choose to drive a cab at night, or work in a bar or restaurant during the evenings. This kind of job gives you the advantage of flexible hours, but the pay is not always desirable. Commissioned sales positions abound in almost every industry. But if your personality isn't suited to sales work, don't pursue it. You'll find it very frustrating.

Good advice from a bartender

One of our friends, a successful freelance television producer, spent several years tending bar part-time in various popular saloons to support his television habit.

"The best places to look for part-time work," he says, "are those where you're already known. Bar owners will rarely hire a bartender who walks in off the street, or fresh out of Famous Bartending School's two-week course. That's because it's very easy for bartenders to steal. An owner wants to have a sense of a person's character before he hires a bartender.

"So if you're looking for part-time work—and this goes for waiters and waitresses, too—spend some time in the place for a couple of weeks. Get to know the people who work there and the regular customers, and become one of the regulars yourself. Learn how the place operates. Every bar or restaurant has its own way of doing things, from handling special orders to taking care of rowdy customers. The more you know about a place, the easier it is to step in when somebody calls in sick or quits."■

It's best if you can locate part-time work in your chosen field. The pay is usually more attractive, and you can continue to develop your network of contacts. Many professionals can freelance. An administrative assistant, for example, might be able to find part-time work at a law firm. An accountant might be able to do taxes on a part-time basis and still gain access to new referrals.

The following books explore part-time and flexible work options as permanent job opportunities but should be equally helpful in obtaining temporary part-time employment (several additional books on alternative work patterns are among those listed in Chapter 2).

SELECTED BOOKS ON PART-TIME AND FLEXIBLE EMPLOYMENT

Alter, Joanne. *A Part-Time Job for a Full-Time You*. Boston: Houghton Mifflin Co., 1982.

Anderson, Joan. *The Best of Both Worlds: A Guide to Home-Based Careers*. White Hall, VA: Betterway Publications, Inc., 1982.

Arden, Lynie. *The Work-at-Home Sourcebook*. Boulder, CO: Live Oak Publications, 1987.

Lowman, Kaye. *Of Cradles and Careers*. Franklin Park, IL: La Leche League, 1984.

Magid, Renee Y. *When Mothers and Fathers Work: Creative Strategies for Balancing Career and Family*. New York, NY: AMACOM, 1987.

O'Hara, Bruce. *Put Work in Its Place*. Victoria, BC, Canada: Work Well, 1988.

Olmsted and Smith. *The Job Sharing Handbook*. Walnut Creek, CA: Ten Speed Press, 1983.

Rothberg and Cook. *Part-Time Professional*. Washington, DC: Acropolis Books, 1985.

Sernaque, V. *Part-Time Jobs*. New York, NY: Ballantine Books, 1982.

New Ways to Work, a San Francisco-based work-resource center (149 Ninth St., San Francisco, CA 94103, (415) 552-1000) has also published a number of helpful booklets on job sharing, as well as *V-Time: A New Way to Work (A Resource Manual for Employers and Employees)*.

Here are some additional sources to consider when the money is really tight and you need part-time or temporary work.

SELECTED SOURCES FOR PART-TIME AND TEMPORARY WORK

SEATTLE/PUGET SOUND AREA

Accountemps
600 University, Suite 2328
Seattle, WA 98101
(206) 624-9000
also:
10900 N.E. Fourth, Suite 1120
Bellevue, WA 98004
(206) 451-1000
1201 Pacific Ave., Suite 1780
Tacoma, WA 98402
(206) 272-1700
Accounting. Part of Robert Half organization.

Adia Personnel Services
220 Blanchard, Suite C1
Seattle, WA 98121
(206) 448-2342
Clerical, accounting, legal.

At Your Fingertips
3131 Western, Suite 527
Seattle, WA 98121
(206) 281-7100
Desktop publishing. Graphics, design, electronic paste-up using Mac/PC.

Certified Resources Unlimited
603 Stewart St., Suite 715
Seattle, WA 98101
(206) 624-0940
Advertising, public relations, business, communications.

Conmarke USA
3213 151st S.W.
Lynwood, WA 98037
(206) 743-7259
Marine engineering, administration, drafting, technical.

Dean's Temporary Office Services (TOPS)
Securities Building
1904 Third Ave., Room 618
Seattle, WA 98101
(206) 623-8677
All fields.

Dental/Medical Fill-Ins
10 Harrison, Suite 300
Seattle, WA 98109
(206) 282-2911
Dental, medical.

Dunhill Temporary Systems
2001 Sixth Ave., Suite 3302
Westin Building
Seattle, WA 98121
(206) 448-0200
Clerical, marketing, data entry, data processing, word processing, industrial.

Employco Temps
1511 Third Ave.
Seattle, WA 98101
(206) 624-1700

Employers Overload
500 Union, Suite 435
Seattle, WA 98101
(206) 583-0808

Engineering Corp. of America
2705 California S.W.
Seattle, WA 98116
(206) 932-0654
Engineering, design, drafting, programming.

Evergreen Temporaries
31620 23rd Ave. S.
Federal Way, WA 98003
(206) 952-3000
All fields.

Express Temporary Services
Tacoma Mall Office Building, Suite 351
4301 S. Pine St.
Tacoma, WA 98409
(206) 475-6855

Focus Alternative Work Patterns
509 Tenth Ave. E.
Seattle, WA 98102
(206) 329-7918
Private, non-profit organization promotes part-time and flexible work options. Maintains job listings. Workshops, publications, reference library on alternative work options. Counseling and job search assistance.

Kelly Services
999 Third, Suite 2580
Seattle, WA 98104
(206) 382-7171
Branches throughout Puget Sound area.

Manpower Temporary Service
600 University, Suite 1710
Seattle, WA 98101
(206) 583-0880
24-hour job hotline: (206) 447-JOBS
also:
1148 Broadway Plaza, Suite 230
Tacoma, WA 98401
(206) 383-4338
905 24th Way S.W.
Olympia, WA 98502
(206) 357-5373
All fields.

Manus Temporary Services
1130 Rainier S.
Seattle, WA 98144
(206) 325-5666

Parker Personnel
450 Century Square
1501 Fourth Ave.
Seattle, WA 98101
(206) 447-9447
also:
340 Omni Building
400 112th N.E.
Bellevue, WA 98004
(206) 462-8050
All fields.

Professional Personnel Services
2608 Pacific Ave. S.E.
Olympia, WA 98501
(206) 786-8443
All fields.

VOLT Temporary Services
2200 Sixth Ave., Suite 104
Seattle, WA 98121
(206) 441-2929
also:
400 108th N.E., Suite 715
Bellevue, WA 98004
(206) 454-9451
Clerical, secretarial, word processing, accounting, bookkeeping, light industry.

Woods and Associates
1221 Second Ave., Suite 430
Seattle, WA 98101
(206) 623-2930
All fields.

PORTLAND AREA

Accountemps
1 S.W. Columbia
Portland, OR 97201
(503) 223-8369
Part of Robert Half organization.

Adia Personnel Services
1435 Jantzen Beach Center
Portland, OR 97217
(503) 283-1355

Clerical, accounting, legal. Three other branches in metropolitan Portland area.

Advanced Temporary Systems
506 S.W. Sixth
Portland, OR 97204
(503) 241-0800
Secretarial, bookkeeping, word processing, warehouse, other fields.

Amstaff—American Staff Management
1618 S.W. First Ave., Suite 415
Portland, OR 97201
(503) 241-8611
Employee leasing, temporary staffing.

Bridgeport Staffing
620 S.W. Fifth, Suite 1220
Portland, OR 97204
(503) 226-0060
Contact: Neen Fitzwalter, Office Manager
Clerical, industrial, technical.

Cascade Temporary Staffing
10700 S.W. Beaverton-Hillsdale Highway
Beaverton, OR 97005
(503) 643-6303
Exclusive electronics skilled personnel. No fees to applicants.

CDI Corporation West
10700 S.W. Beaverton-Hillsdale Highway
Beaverton, OR 97005
(503) 643-1825
Nationwide engineering contractors.

Kelly Services
1020 S.W. Taylor
Portland, OR 97205
(503) 227-1711
Branches throughout metropolitan Portland area.

Manpower Temporary Services
1211 S.W. Fifth Ave.
Portland, OR 97204
(503) 226-6281
also:
6700 S.W. 105th Ave., Suite 109
Beaverton, OR 97005
(503) 641-6992
Secretarial, word processing, data entry, electronic assembly, more.

Northwest Temporary Services
522 S.W. Fifth
Portland, OR 97204
(503) 242-0611
Secretarial, receptionist, technical, marketing, data entry, light industrial. Free word processing training.

VOLT Temporary Services
1020 S.W. Taylor, Suite 380
Portland, OR 97205
(503) 227-3332
Also has Beaverton branch.

Fast talk nets big part-time $$$

People who need to earn money while job hunting might consider the telemarketing, or telephone sales, field. Debbie Schwartz, who has worked as a telemarketing manager, feels the industry offers both challenges and rewards.

"Being a telemarketer is almost like acting in a radio play," says Debbie. "Your success depends on how well you control your voice. You must also be able to receive feedback from people without the benefit of eye contact or body language."

We asked Debbie what telemarketing managers look for in people they hire. "The crucial element is the person's voice. Telemarketers must speak clearly and have pleasing voices. They also must use standard English grammar. Previous sales experience is a plus, but not necessary. Managers also look for people who can handle rejection. A person might get rejected 25 or 30 times before making a sale."

According to Debbie, most telemarketers work in four-hour shifts. "You can't work on the phone longer than that without becoming ineffective. Also, many firms operate only in the afternoons and evenings. But some firms do have morning hours—those involved in corporate sales, for example."

How much can a telemarketer expect to make?

"Top people can make over $10 per hour," says Debbie. "The average telemarketer makes about $4-$8 per hour. The pay depends on whether you work on a straight commission basis or are paid a base hourly wage plus commissions."

Debbie suggests investigating a telemarketing firm carefully before accepting a job since there are quite a few fly-by-night operations. But she emphasizes the many benefits of working for a reputable firm: "Telemarketing is a great learning experience for job hunters. Many of its sales techniques are usable when promoting yourself to a potential employer."

Getting a part-time job in telemarketing requires persistence since managers receive hundreds of calls and applications. "Don't give up," advises Debbie. "Have your sales pitch ready when you call. Sell yourself on the phone in the same way you'd sell a product once you're hired." ▪

Unemployment Compensation

Every state has its own set of eligibility requirements for unemployment insurance. In general, your former employer must have paid unemployment tax, and you must have worked for a minimum number of hours (some states also have minimum earnings requirements) during the base period set by your state. Each state uses a different formula to determine this base period.

In Washington State, you must have worked a minimum of 680 hours during the year for which you are filing. To collect unemployment benefits in Oregon, you must have earned at least $1,000 and worked for 18 weeks during the base year.

`If you have been fired or you quit your job voluntarily, a determination of your eligibility for benefits will be based on your individual circumstances. If you recently moved to Washington or Oregon from another state, you may be able to collect unemployment benefits from that state by filing a claim through Washington or Oregon.

Contact the **Washington State Employment Security Department** to ask for the job service center closest to your home. In Oregon, call the **Oregon State Employment Division** for the office nearest you. They will tell you to bring verification of your social security number (your social security card, a pay stub, or an income tax return will do) as well as the name, address, and phone number of your last employer so you can file for benefits, which should begin arriving within two weeks.

You can reach the **Washington State Employment Security Department** in **Seattle** at (206) 464-6449, in **Tacoma** at (206) 593-2434, and in **Olympia** at (206) 438-7800.

In Oregon you can call the following offices of the **Oregon State Employment Division: Downtown Portland**, (503) 229-5645; **North Portland**, (503) 280-6046; **East Multnomah (Portland)**, (503) 257-

4291; **Beaverton,** (503) 644-7246; **Hillsboro,** (503) 640-6642; and **Oregon City,** (503) 657-2070.

Where To Turn If Your Confidence Wilts

Recently a bank fired a loan officer who had worked there for more than 10 years. The employee was 58 years old, about five feet, six inches tall, weighed almost 300 pounds, and did not have a college degree. His written communication skills were negligible. His poor attitude and appearance, lack of enthusiasm, and dismal self-esteem suggested he would be unemployed a long time.

The bank decided to use Tom Camden and Associates' outplacement service to help the person get another job. "There wasn't much we could do about changing his age, education, size, or communication skills," Tom recalls. "But we certainly could—and did—

work with him on improving his self-esteem and changing his attitude toward interviewing for new jobs."

After a four-month search, the loan officer succeeded in landing a position that exactly suited his needs. His new job even was located in the neighborhood where he lived. It seemed like a typical success story—until the bank informed Tom Camden about how dissatisfied that person was with the counsel he had received. The man told the bank that they would have been better off paying *him* the consulting fee instead of retaining outside help.

"He was really angry," Tom recalls. "And also full of stress, guilt, fear, anxiety, desire for vengeance, and a host of other emotions."

Such feelings, unfortunately, are not at all unusual. In fact, they're a *normal* part of any job search, particularly for those who have been laid off or fired. That's because rejection, unfortunately, is inevitable in any job search.

If you've read Chapter 5, you know that you may speak with up to 300 people on a formal or informal basis while you're looking for suitable work—and a healthy percentage of those people will be unable or unwilling to help you. Every job seeker must anticipate rejection—it comes with the territory. Being turned down in an interview is a painful experience, and it's normal to feel hurt. The trick is to keep those hurt and angry feelings from clouding your judgment or affecting your behavior.

What To Do If You Get Fired

Being fired ranks just after the death of someone you love or divorce when it comes to personal traumas. If it should happen to you, *take time to evaluate the bad news before accepting a settlement offer.* If you quickly accept what your employer has to offer, it will be much more difficult to change your situation later. Tell the boss you want some time to think about a settlement. Then go back in a day or two and negotiate.

Stay on the payroll as long as you can, even if your pride hurts. Find out if you are eligible for part-time work or consulting jobs to tide you over until you find your new job. You may be able to hang on to insurance and other benefits until you've found new employment.

Try to negotiate a generous severance payment. In the last five years, severance agreements have risen dramatically in some industries. What the company offers at first may not be their maximum. Negotiation doesn't always work, but you certainly ought to try to get the most for your years of service.

Check with your personnel office to make sure you're getting all the benefits to which you are entitled, such as vacation pay and profit sharing. Check your eligibility for unemployment compensation before you accept an offer to resign instead of being terminated.

Don't attack management during your termination interview. It may cost you good references and hurt your chances of finding a new job.

Take advantage of any placement assistance that is offered. Don't reject the company's offer to help even if your pride has been stung.

Dealing with Emotional Stress

If you're beginning to feel your confidence wilt, reread the tips in Chapter 5 for treating yourself well. Put yourself on a regular schedule. Make sure you're eating healthy foods and getting enough rest and exercise. Don't punish yourself for being unemployed or losing a job offer.

One of the worst things that can happen in any job search is to let rejection undermine your self-confidence. Like the little boy at the door who asks, "You don't want to buy a magazine, do you?" a person who doesn't feel good about himself will not easily convince an employer that he should be hired. Each new rejection further erodes self-esteem, and the job search stalls or takes a nose dive: "Maybe I *am* a loser. Perhaps I was lucky to have my old job as long as I did. Maybe my sights are set too high. I suppose I should look for something less responsible at a lower salary."

Thoughts such as these cross most people's minds at some time or other in the job search. As we've said, it's normal to feel hurt, angry, and depressed after a series of rejections. It's important, however, to recognize these feelings and learn to work them out in some nondestructive way. It is *not* normal to let such feelings sabotage your job search. Just because you're unemployed or looking for a new job doesn't mean you're a bad or worthless person. The only thing "wrong" with you is that you haven't found the offer that you want.

When your confidence starts to wilt, turn to a trusted friend or relative. Talk about your feelings frankly. Get mad or sad or vengeful. Then get back to work on your job search. Don't let fear of rejection keep you from making that next call. It may be just the lead you're looking for.

There are no hard and fast rules on when to seek professional counseling and support, but we can offer certain guidelines. If you seriously think you need professional help, you ought to investigate two or three sources. Besides the ones we've listed below, check with your minister, priest, or rabbi. Many clerics are trained counselors, and their help is free.

If you feel you have nowhere else to turn, or if you don't want to share your feelings with anyone you know, you should consider psychiatric or psychological counseling. If you're not making calls, not preparing for interviews, or not doing what you know you have to do to get the job you want, you could probably use some counseling.

Everybody feels bad about being rejected. But if you allow those feelings to overwhelm you, or if they're interfering with finding a job, it's probably time to talk with a professional. Another sure sign is if you're waking up most mornings too sick or lethargic from overeating, overdrinking, or abusing some other substance to do what you have to do.

Where To Find Help for Emotional Problems

A listing in this book does not constitute an endorsement of any institution, therapist, or school of therapy. Therapy depends a great deal on the "chemistry" between therapist and patient—something only you can evaluate. A basic rule of thumb is that if you're not comfortable with or confident in a particular therapist, it may not be wise to continue seeing him or her.

Therapy is offered by quite a variety of people, from psychiatrists and psychologists with years of postgraduate training to those with considerably lower levels of education and experience. Before engaging a therapist, check his or her credentials. Where was the therapist trained? What degrees does the therapist hold? How long has the therapist been practicing? Does he or she belong to any professional associations?

WASHINGTON STATE

Psychologists are licensed in the State of Washington by **Health Care Unit No.1** of the **Washington State Department of Health,** PO Box 1099, Olympia, WA 98507. Requirements include a doctoral degree from an institution approved by the American Psychological Association, 1,500 hours of postdoctoral experience, satisfactory scoring on national examinations, and completion of a course on AIDS. To inquire whether any complaints have been proven against a psychologist, call either **(206) 753-3095** or **(206) 753-2147.** This agency does not do referrals. Check with the **Washington State Psychological Association** at **(206) 363-9772** for more information.

Psychiatrists practicing in Washington State are licensed by the **Washington State Board of Medical Examiners** through the Washington State Department of Health. Requirements vary depending on whether the psychiatrist's medical degree was obtained in the United States or in a foreign country. To verify a psychiatrist's credentials or inquire whether he or she has had any disciplinary action taken against them, call **(206) 753-2205.** This agency does not do referrals.

Counselors in the State of Washington are licensed by the **Washington State Department of Health, Professional Licensing Division,** PO Box 1099, Olympia, WA 98507. Their number for counselor licensing is **(206) 753-6936.** The state licenses counselors who complete a course on AIDS and file an application. For **certification**—which is strictly voluntary—a counselor must have a Master of Social Work (MSW) degree plus two years of postgraduate supervision, and take an examination.

To be a **family and marriage and/or mental health counselor,** one must have a Master's degree in a behavioral science plus two years postgraduate supervision, and take an examination. This agency does not do referrals but will handle client complaints. The number to call is **(206) 753-6936.**

Social workers in the State of Washington can be either certified or registered. Both procedures are handled by the **Department of Licensing, Professional Licensing Regulation,** at **(206) 586-4561.**

OREGON

Both **counselors** and **marriage and family therapists** are licensed by the **Oregon Board** of **Licensed Professional Counselors and Therapists.** Their number is **(503) 378-5499.** To check the credentials for either type of professional, ask for a copy of their professional disclosure statement. This statement, which should indicate approval by the licensing board, includes the person's philosophy and approach to counseling or therapy, their formal education and training, continuing education and supervision, and fee schedule.

To be licensed, **counselors** must have a graduate degree in counseling, pass an examination, and have three years of full-time supervised experience. **Marriage and family therapists** must have a graduate degree in marriage and family therapy or an equivalent, pass an examination, and have three years of full-time clinical experience with supervision. You can also call the **Oregon Association for Marriage and Family Therapy** at **(503) 227-1330** for information.

Clinical social workers are licensed in the State of Oregon by the **Board of Clinical Social Workers** at **(503) 378-5735.** Minimum requirements are a Master of Social Work (MSW) degree, passage of a written exam, two years of experience, and 3,000 hours of postgraduate clinical practice and 100 hours of supervised experience.

Psychologists are licensed in Oregon by the **Board of Psychologist Examiners** at **(503) 378-4154.** You can also call the **Oregon Psychological Association** at **(503) 292-4914** for more information.

Psychiatrists in the State of Oregon are licensed by the **Board of Medical Examiners** at **(503) 229-5027.** This agency can conduct a malpractice search for a small fee. Referrals are not provided.

The **Mental Health Association, Portland Chapter** at **(503) 228-6571** is another source for information and referrals.

Self-Help Groups: A Directory of Family Resources can guide you to some 280 self-help and social service organizations in the Portland area. To obtain a copy, call the United Way of the Columbia-Willamette at (503) 226-9630.

SELECTED CRISIS CENTERS AND INSTITUTIONS

In addition to the resources described below, don't overlook the social service agencies listed in Chapter 6.

SEATTLE/PUGET SOUND AREA

Asian Counseling and Referral Service
1032 S. Jackson, Second Floor
Seattle, WA 98104
(206) 461-3606
Mental health and career counseling, serving the Asian community.

Catholic Community Services
100 23rd Ave. S.
Seattle, WA 98144
(206) 325-5162
Contact: Candy Adams
Mental health counseling on a sliding-fee basis. Callers are referred to a counselor, who contacts them within 24 hours. Central number above applies to Auburn, Bellevue, Bethel, Federal Way, Kent, Kirkland, Redmond, Renton, and Seattle.
also:
Thurston County: (206) 352-2559
Pierce County: (206) 752-2455

Community Mental Health
4422 Sixth Ave. S.E.
Lacey, WA 98503
(206) 438-1900
also:
1800 Olympic Highway
South Shelton, WA 98584
(206) 426-1696
Counseling services.

Counseling Referral Services
(206) 322-2873
The address is not divulged, but this agency provides free referrals to an appropriate counselor. Fees are charged for counselors' services.

Crisis Clinic of King County
Emotional support (24-hour, accessible to TDD/TTY): (206) 461-3222, also 1-800-621-6040
Community information: (206) 461-3200
The address is not divulged, but this group assists callers, lending an ear if a caller needs someone to talk to and providing services or referrals to meet a variety of needs.

Crisis Clinic of Thurston and Mason Counties
PO Box 2463
Olympia, WA 98507
(206) 352-2211
Provides referrals for counseling, emergency needs, food,
housing, health services, legal assistance, minority information,
substance abuse, and other needs. Publishes community
services lists.

Crisis Line for Tacoma/Pierce County
Information and referrals: (206) 756-0744
Emotional support (24-hour): (206) 759-6700

Everett Crisis Line
(206) 258-4357
Crisis services and counseling.

Korean Community Counseling Center
302 N. Seventh St.
Seattle, WA 98103
(206) 784-5691
Provides information, counseling, and some job-hunting
assistance.

Lewis County Mental Health
135 W. Main St.
Chehalis, WA 98532
(206) 748-6696
Counseling services.

Listening Post Counseling
107 N. Eighth St.
Shelton, WA 98584
(206) 426-9717
also:
Allyn: (206) 427-0442
North Mason: (206) 275-4213 or (206) 876-3935
Mental health counseling, drug and alcohol rehabilitation.

Open Quest Institute
1-800-992-9239
Non-profit mental health agency provides referrals and
outpatient counseling.

Presbyterian Counseling Services
564 N.E. Ravenna Blvd.
Seattle, WA 98115
(206) 527-2266
Staff of 23 counselors. Sliding-scale fee. Service area includes
Bellevue, Redmond, Renton, Lake Burien, Lake Sammamish,
Steel Lake, and Kent.

Seattle Mental Health Institute
1600 E. Olive
Seattle, WA 98122
(206) 281-4300
Counseling, vocational rehabilitation.

Seattle Psychological Services
216 First Ave., Suite 333
Seattle, WA 98104
(206) 621-7007
Contact: Catherine Knowlton or Steven Feldman
Services include counseling for job hunters experiencing
stress.

Sound Therapy Institute
600 Stewart St.
Seattle, WA 78101
(206) 628-4600
A division of the Washington Mental Health Council. Provides
counseling for individuals with depression. Sliding fee.

State of Washington Psychological Association
13500 Lake City Way N.E., Room 208
Seattle, WA 98125
(206) 363-9772
Does not do referrals, but if asked whether any complaints
have been lodged against a specific doctor, will answer with a
yes or no. No offices in other cities.

Washington Mental Health Council
600 Stewart St., Suite 520
Seattle, WA 98101
(206) 628-4608
One of the few mental health agencies that will counsel
private individuals on a sliding-fee basis.

PORTLAND AREA

Delaunay Mental Health Center
5215 N. Lombard
Portland, OR 97203
(503) 285-9871
Minimum fee $40 to $70, with sliding fee based on gross
monthly income.

Good Samaritan Ministries
7929 S.W. Cirrus Drive
Beaverton, OR 97005
(503) 644-2339
Group reality therapy counseling; donations accepted.

National Association of Social Workers
109 N.E. 50th
Portland, OR 97213
(503) 232-6003

Rebound
2310 S.E. Bertha Blvd.
Portland, OR 97201
(503) 244-4611
Contact: Violet Eaton (evenings)
Support group for people who have been out of work for a long period of time.

United Way Information and Referral Services
(503) 222-5555
Known for its caring and sensitivity, this agency can refer you to the program that can give you the most assistance, whether you need counseling, food, transportation, or any other services.

Risk and Opportunity: Career Transition Issues

Any job search is going to involve risk and opportunity, according to a notable career counselor. If you are autonomous, you are able to view the risk as opportunity and to come up with creative ideas for changing jobs. However, many job searchers begin to lose their sense of independence and control after some setbacks. They start believing that nothing they do will help lift them out of their situation.

An autonomous person is "self-governing" and believes that his actions will have a definite effect on his or her life. One of the most important aspects of finding or changing a job is to keep believing that you can control your life. When this belief begins to falter, many people slip into some of the traps of self-doubt and loss of independence.

Seven key issues that most people confront during a job hunt are:

Self-esteem: Do you feel good about yourself, your daily life, and your future? Are you self-accepting? Do you have a positive self-image?

Self-validation: Do you validate yourself both from without and within? Do you have an inner sense of your own worth? Are you able to learn from the feedback you get from others during the job hunt?

Risk-taking: Are you willing to take the risks needed to get what you want? Are you willing to reveal yourself even in a situation such as a job interview when you're not completely in control?

Sadness or depression: Can you feel sad about loss but still bounce back? Can you learn from failure even as you feel good about success?

Internalized anger: Can you recognize when you feel angry? If you are angry, can you identify which of your needs are not being met? Can you discover effective and appropriate ways to express anger?

Goal setting: Are your goals appropriate to who you are and what you need? Are your goals and expectations realistic in terms of the current job market and your own training and expertise?

Phase of life issues: How have your goals changed over time? Has your self-image changed as you have changed and grown? Are you flexible enough to change as your life changes?

Beating the Job-Hunt Blues

Although it's not easy to relax when you're worried about dwindling savings, professional identity, and an uncertain future, even the most dedicated job hunter sometimes needs to take a breather. An afternoon off the beaten job-search path can help clear your head of the job-hunt blues. Giving yourself a vacation day in the midst of your job search can revive flagging confidence. Imagine that you already have a great job and that this is your day off. Following are some suggestions for free or inexpensive diversions.

SEATTLE AREA

If you don't mind getting your feet wet, Seattle is a recreational smorgasbord. Washington State has more than five million acres of national parks and forests. Climbers, hikers, skiers, and bikers flee to the mountains, the largest being the majestic **Mount Rainier,** flanked by **Mounts Baker and Olympus.**

Lose yourself in the kaleidoscopic environment of the famous **Pike Place Market** near the Seattle waterfront. It costs nothing to browse the craft tables, take in the sights, sounds, and tantalizing aromas as farmers and fishermen call out their wares, or enjoy the street musicians.

From there, stroll down to the waterfront. For $3.30, you can be a foot passenger on the round-trip **ferry**

from Seattle to Bremerton. This breezy joyride can be enhanced if you have a few crumbs to feed the sea gulls that follow the boat.

Discover at close hand the beauty and diversity of the region's marine life with a visit to the **Aquarium,** also on the Seattle waterfront.

To top off a trip to explore the **Woodland Park Zoo,** north of Lake Union, you can enjoy a relaxing stroll around nearby **Green Lake** (in summer, take along your swimsuit for a refreshing plunge).

If you prefer some night life, try the **Blue Banjo** in Pioneer Square, where you can enjoy hours of great fun and music for the price of a beer.

OLYMPIA

In front of the **State Capitol** is an information center with guides to free or inexpensive diversions throughout the region. Around the Capitol grounds is a lot of free entertainment. You can pack a lunch and be treated to musicians, acrobats, and other surprises in the park just four blocks south of the Capitol.

You can catch a matinee or evening movie for only $1.50 at the four-screen **State Theatre** at 204 E. Fourth Ave. Call (206) 357-4010 for times and shows.

BELLEVUE

If you enjoy art, the **Bellevue Art Museum,** at the top of the largest covered shopping center in the state, Bellevue Square, is a world unto itself. You can also kick back and let go at the popular beachfront park, **Chism Beach.**

TACOMA

A ramble along the **waterfront on Rustin Way** can soothe a troubled soul, as the waters lap along the shore and the Olympic Mountains come into full view. If you have a few shekels, you can stop in **Old Town** at **Grazie,** an espresso bar, delicatessen, and restaurant rolled into one.

Tacoma has many beautiful parks. Best of all is **Point Defiance.** In this 700-acre park, you'll find a peaceful forest, a zoo, an aquarium, hiking trails, gardens, and seashell-strewn beaches.

PORTLAND AREA

If you are feeling adventurous, you can take an **all-day sightseeing tour** for only 85 cents. Just catch the Line 63 MAX (lightrail system), leaving from S.W. Washington Street and Fifth Avenue. This tour includes **Washington Park,** home of the **International Rose Gardens,** a spectacular view of Mt. Hood, and the **Washington Park Zoo.** You'll also visit the **Oregon Museum of Science and Industry (OMSI)** and **Hoyt Arboretum.** Some of these attractions charge admission fees; call (503) 233-3511 for details.

Check out the arts and crafts, ethnic food, and music at the **Saturday Market** in **McCall Waterfront Park** along the Willamette River in the northern end of downtown Portland.

In northeast Portland, there are 64 lush acres to roam at the **Grotto.** Its chapel and wildflower-lined Stations of the Cross offer a serene setting for a moment of quiet reflection.

If you have a car and enough money for gasoline, you might take a trip along the **Columbia River Gorge.** Its breathtaking beauty any time of the year includes the waterfront, miles of forest, waterfalls, and hiking trails. It is also the premier windsurfing spot in the continental U.S.

Drive northwest along Highway 26 to **Cannon Beach,** a quaint seaside town where you can go whale watching, fly a kite, or enjoy charming shops, eateries, and theaters.

From Portland, a short drive southwest on the way to Newberg will take you past a number of **wineries** that offer tours and a taste of their product.

Selecting the Right
Job for You

Welcome to the most pleasant chapter of this book—and the one that's the most fun. You've figured out what you want to do, developed an acceptable resume, and used your contacts and other resources to research the job market and generate all sorts of interviews. At this point in the process you've probably received or are pretty close to landing at least a couple of offers that come fairly close to your objective.

You have a problem if one of your possibilities becomes a firm offer that demands an immediate response while you're still investigating other promising leads. The employer making this offer is essentially telling you, "We think you have everything we're looking for, and we want you to start as soon as possible." It is difficult to stall or delay your acceptance just because other promising leads still haven't yielded firm offers. You have to use your best judgment in such a case, but try to delay a final decision until all likely offers are in. Unless you're absolutely desperate, there's no reason to jump at the first offer you receive.

You owe it both to yourself and the people who interviewed you to consider all outstanding possibilities and *then* make your decision. Tell the employer who gave you the offer the truth—that you need more time to review the offer against all the situations that are outstanding and pending—that a decision can't be made for at least two weeks. If the offering company refuses to wait, that tells you a great deal about the atmosphere in which you'd be working.

If a company wants you badly enough, they'll wait a reasonable length of time for you to decide. In the meantime, use your offer to "encourage" other companies to reach a decision about your candidacy. We're not suggesting that you play hardball. That probably won't work and might even work against you. But it makes perfect sense to inform other companies who are interested in you that you have an offer. If you're sure you'd rather work for them, say so. But also say that you'll have to accept the first offer if you don't hear from them within the allotted time. Don't lie about your intentions. If you don't intend to accept the first offer, don't say that you do. Otherwise, the second (and perhaps better) company might write you off, assuming that you won't be available by the time they're ready to decide.

A job involves much more than a title and base salary. For any firm offer, be sure you understand what your responsibilities will be, what benefits you'll receive besides salary (insurance, vacation, profit sharing, training, tuition reimbursement, and the like), how much overtime is required (and whether you'll be paid for it), how much travel is involved in the job, who your superior will be, how many people you'll be supervising, and where the position might lead. (Is it a dead-end job or are people in this slot often promoted?) In short, find out anything and everything you need to know to evaluate the offer.

For many positions, especially those requiring several years' experience, it's appropriate to ask for an offer in writing. Such a document would specify the position's title, responsibilities, reporting relationship, and compensation and include a statement of company benefits.

At the very least, before you make a firm decision, be sure to obtain a copy of the company's personnel policy. It will fill you in on such details as the number of paid sick days, overtime and vacation policy, insurance benefits, and profit sharing. These so-called fringe benefits can really add up. It's not a bad idea to try to assign a dollar value to them to help you evaluate the financial pros and cons of each offer.

It seems obvious to us that it's unwise to choose a job exclusively on the basis of salary and benefits. Don't condemn yourself to working with people you can't stand, doing work you find boring, to accomplish goals you don't believe in.

Finding the Right Culture

Career counselors often warn that you ignore a company's "culture" at your own peril. You can find a position that suits you to a "T" but still be unhappy if you don't fit the culture of the company that hires you. It takes some doing to assess an organization's culture, but it's worth your while.

Some signs are fairly obvious: What do people wear? What is the furniture like? Are office doors kept open or closed? Are there any minorities or women in positions of power? How friendly are people to you? To each other? Does anybody laugh? A very important question to ask—Do I feel comfortable here?

There are five aspects of an organization's culture to consider. Try to find out as much as you can about each.

1. What is the relationship between a company and its environment? Does it control its own destiny or must it depend on the mood of an adversarial home office? You probably wouldn't be wise to work for the Department of Defense under a pacifist administration.

2. How does a company view human nature? Good or evil? Changeable or immutable? Answers to these questions determine how employees are treated, how much supervision and control is exerted. How openly will employees communicate? Will there be opportunities for training and development?

3. What are the philosophy and mission of a company? Printed brochures are often good indicators. A good company is clear on what business it's in.

4. How do people relate to each other in a company? Is there a formal flow chart? Are there many vertical levels (the military)? Or is power more evenly and horizontally spread out (some new high-tech firms)? The more horizontal, the more informal and the easier it is to get things done, generally through relationships.

5. How are decisions made, who makes them, and upon what basis? Facts and reason? Politics? Ideology? Good-old-boy network? The whims of an autocrat at the top?

The answers to these questions will determine the working atmosphere for most companies.

Salary Strategy

Before you accept an offer—or bicker about salary—you need to know what other people who fill similar positions are making. The *Occupational Outlook Handbook,* put out by the U.S. Department of Labor every two years, cites salary statistics by field. Probably a better source of information is *The American Almanac of Jobs and Salaries* by John Wright, published by Avon. What you really need to know is what other people with your qualifications and experience are making in the Seattle/Portland area for working the job you're considering. Professional societies and associations frequently provide this sort of information. It's one more good reason to belong to one. Probably the best source of all for salary orientation is—you guessed it—your network of contacts.

For advice on how to get the salary you want, we recommend two books:

Cohen, Herb. *You Can Negotiate Anything.* New York: Bantam Publishing Co., 1982.
Kennedy, Marilyn Moats. *Salary Strategies: Everything You Need to Know to Get the Salary You Want.* New York: Rawson Wade, 1982.

Compare the Offers on Paper

You've talked with each employer and taken notes about the responsibilities and compensation being offered. Where possible, you've obtained a job offer in writing. You have also read through the company's personnel policy. Next, draw up a checklist for comparing the relative merits of each offer. We've provided a sample here, but if another format suits your purposes better, use it. The idea is to list the factors that you consider important in any job and then assign a rating for how well each offer fills the bill in each particular area.

We've listed some of the factors that we think ought to be considered before you accept any offer. Some may not be relevant to your situation. Others that we've left out may be of great importance to you. So feel free to make any additions, deletions, or changes you want.

Once you've listed your factors, make a column for each job offer you're considering. Assign a rating (say, 1 to 5, with 1 the lowest and 5 the highest) for each factor and each offer. Then, total the scores for each offer.

The offer with the most points is not necessarily the one to accept. The chart doesn't take into account the fact that "responsibilities" may be more important to you than "career path," or that you promised yourself you'd never punch a time clock again. Nevertheless, looking at the pros and cons of each offer in black and white should help you make a much more methodical and logical decision.

Factor	Offer A	Offer B	Offer C
Responsibilities	___	___	___
Company reputation	___	___	___
Salary	___	___	___
Insurance	___	___	___
Paid vacation	___	___	___
Pension	___	___	___
Profit sharing	___	___	___
Tuition reimbursement	___	___	___
On-the-job training	___	___	___
Career path (where can you go from this job?)	___	___	___
Company future	___	___	___
Quality of product or service	___	___	___

Location (housing market, schools, transportation)	_____	_____	_____
Boss(es)	_____	_____	_____
Other workers	_____	_____	_____
Travel	_____	_____	_____
Overtime	_____	_____	_____
Other	_____	_____	_____
_____	_____	_____	_____
_____	_____	_____	_____
TOTAL POINTS	_____	_____	_____

A Final Word

Once you have accepted a job, it's important that you notify each of the people in your log of your new position, company, address, and phone number. Be sure to thank these people; let them know you appreciated their assistance. After all, you never know when you may need to ask them to help you again. *Keep your network alive!*

On each anniversary date of your new job, take the time to run through the self-appraisal process to evaluate your situation and the progress you are making (as measured by increased responsibilities, salary, and abilities). Compare your progress against the objectives you set at the start of your search. Although you may be completely satisfied in your new assignment, remember that circumstances can change overnight, and you must always be prepared for the unexpected. So make an employment "New Year's resolution" to weigh every aspect of your job annually and compare the result with what you want and expect from your life's work.

We hope that you have made good use of the job-search techniques outlined in this book. Indeed, we hope that the resulting experiences not only have won you the job you want but—equally important—also have made you a better person. Perhaps the next time you talk to an unemployed person or someone who is employed but seeking a new job, you will look at that person with new insight gained from your own search experiences. We hope you'll gladly share what you've learned about how to get a job in the Seattle or Portland areas.

Where
Seattle/Portland
Works

This chapter contains the names, addresses, and phone numbers of the Seattle/Puget Sound and Portland areas' top 1,900 employers of white-collar workers. The companies are arranged in categories according to the major products and services they manufacture or provide. Where appropriate, entries contain a brief description of the company's business and the name of the personnel director or other contact.

This listing is intended to help you survey the major potential employers in fields that interest you. It is *selective*, not exhaustive. We have not, for example, listed *all* the advertising agencies in the area, as you can find that information in the Yellow Pages. We have simply listed the top 25 or so—that is, the ones with the most jobs.

The purpose of this chapter is to get you started, both looking and thinking. This is the kickoff, not the final gun. Browse through the whole chapter, and take some time to check out areas that are unfamiliar to you. Many white-collar skills are transferable. People with marketing, management, data processing, accounting, administrative, secretarial, and other talents are needed in a huge variety of businesses.

Ask yourself in what areas your skills could be marketed. Use your imagination, especially if you're in a so-called specialized field. A dietician, for instance, might look first under Health Care, or perhaps Hotels/Motels. But what about Insurance, Cultural Institutions, Banks, or the scores of other places that run their own dining rooms for employees or the public? What about Food or Media? Who invents all those recipes and tests those products?

The tips and insider interviews that are scattered throughout this chapter are designed to nudge your creativity and suggest additional ideas for your job search. Much more detailed information on the area's top employers and other, smaller companies can be found in the directories and other resources suggested in Chapter 4. We can't stress strongly enough that *you have to do your homework when you're looking for a job,* both to unearth places that might need a person with your particular talents and to succeed in the interview once you've lined up a meeting with the hiring authority.

A word about hiring authorities: If you've read Chapter 5, you know that the name of the game is to meet the person with the power to hire you, or to get as close to that person as you can. You don't want to go to the chairman or the personnel director if the person who actually makes the decision is the marketing manager or customer service director.

Obviously, we can't list every possible hiring authority in the area's "Top 1,900." If we tried, you'd need a wagon to haul this book around. Besides, printed directories go out of date—even those that are regularly and conscientiously revised. So always double-check a contact whose name you get from a book or magazine, including this one. If necessary, call the company's switchboard to confirm who heads a particular department or division.

Here, then, are the Seattle/Puget Sound and the Portland areas' greatest opportunities. Happy hunting!

The Seattle/Puget Sound and Portland areas' top 1,900 employers are arranged in the following categories:

Accounting/Auditing
Advertising/Public Relations
Aircraft and Aerospace
Apparel and Textiles
Architecture/Interior Design
Auto/Truck/Marine/Transportation Equipment
Banks/Savings and Loans
Chemicals
Computers: Data Processing
Computers: Hardware/Software
Contractors/Construction
Cultural Institutions
Drugs/Cosmetics/Biological Products
Educational Institutions
Electronics/Telecommunications
Energy and Oil Companies
Engineering Firms
Film, Video, and Related Fields
Food/Beverage Producers and Distributors
Government
Health Care
Hotels/Motels
Human Services
Instruments and Related Products
Insurance
Investment Bankers/Stock Brokers
Law Firms
Management Consultants
Manufacturers
Media: Broadcasting and Cable TV
Media: Print
Metal Products
Office Supplies
Paper/Packaging/Forest Products
Plastics/Rubber
Printers/Graphic Design
Real Estate Developers and Brokers
Recreation/Sports/Fitness

Restaurants
Retailers/Wholesalers
Transportation/Shipping
Travel
Utilities

Accounting/Auditing Firms and Services

You may also want to check the sections on **Banks** and **Investment Bankers/Stock Brokers**

For networking in **accounting** and related fields, check out these professional organizations listed in Chapter 5:

PROFESSIONAL ORGANIZATIONS:

American Society of Women Accountants, Seattle and Portland Chapters
American Women's Society of Certified Public Accounting, Seattle Chapter
National Association of Accountants, Seattle Chapter
Washington Society for CPAs
Oregon Association of Public Accountants
Oregon Society of CPAs

For additional information, you can write to:

American Institute of CPAs
1211 Ave. of Americas
New York, NY 10036

American Society of Women Accountants
35 E. Wacker Drive
Chicago, IL 60601

National Association of Accountants
10 Paragon Drive
Montvale, NJ 07645

National Association of Minority CPAs
1625 I Street N. W.
Washington, DC 20006

National Society of Public Accountants
1010 Vermont Ave. N.W.
Washington, DC 20005

PROFESSIONAL PUBLICATIONS:

The CPA Journal
Journal of Accountancy
Management Accounting
National Public Accountant

DIRECTORIES:

Who Audits America (Data Financial Press, Menlo Park, CA)
National Directory of Certified Public Accountants (Peter Norback
   Publishing Co., Princeton, NJ)

EMPLOYERS Seattle/Puget Sound Area:

Arthur Andersen & Co.
801 Second Ave., Suite 900
Seattle, WA 98104
(206) 623-8023

Benson & McLaughlin, P.S.
2201 Sixth Ave., Suite 1400
Seattle, WA 98121
(206) 441-3500
National headquarters.

Clark, Nuber & Co., P.S.
320 108th Ave. N.E., Suite 600
Bellevue, WA 98004
(206) 454-4919

Coopers & Lybrand
999 Third Ave., Suite 1800
Seattle, WA 98104
(206) 622-8700

Deloitte & Touche
1111 Third Ave., Suite 3000
Seattle, WA 98101
(206) 292-1800

Ernst & Young
999 Third Ave., Suite 3300
Seattle, WA 98104
(206) 621-1800

Knight Vale & Gregory
1145 Broadway, Suite 900
Tacoma, WA 98402
(206) 572-7111

How To Get a Job

KPMG Peat Marwick
1301 Fifth Ave., Suite 2600
Seattle, WA 98102
(206) 292-1500

Laventhol & Horwath
701 Fifth Ave., Suite 2100
Seattle, WA 98104
(206) 621-1900

Moss Adams
1001 Fourth Ave., Suite 2830
Seattle, WA 98154
(206) 223-1820
National headquarters.

Peterson Sullivan & Co.
601 Union, Suite 2300
Seattle, WA 98161
(206) 382-7777

Price Waterhouse
1001 Fourth Ave., Suite 4200
Seattle, WA 98154
(206) 622-1505

EMPLOYERS Portland Area:

Arthur Andersen & Co.
111 S.W. Columbia St.
Portland, OR 97201
(503) 226-1331

Coopers & Lybrand
1300 S.W. Fifth Ave.
Portland, OR 97201
(503) 227-8600

Deloitte & Touche
3900 U.S. Bancorp Tower
Portland, OR 97204
(503) 222-1341

Ernst & Young
101 S.W. Fifth Ave., Suite 2000
Portland, OR 97204
(503) 225-1700

Grant Thornton
111 S.W. Columbia St.
Portland, OR 97201
(503) 222-3562

Isler & Co.
1300 S.W. Fifth Ave.
Portland, OR 97201
(503) 224-5321

Laventhol & Horwath
111 S.W. Fifth Ave.
Portland, OR 97204
(503) 221-0141

Moss Adams
1001 S.W. Fifth Ave.
Portland, OR 97204
(503) 242-1447

Niemi, Holland & Scott
111 S.W. Fifth Ave.
Portland, OR 97204
(503) 226-6681

Peat Marwick Main & Co.
1211 S.W. Fifth Ave.
Portland, OR 97204
(503) 221-6500

Price Waterhouse
101 S.W. Main St.
Portland, OR 97204
(503) 224-9040

Sander Perkins & Co.
111 S.W. Fifth Ave.
Portland, OR 97204
(503) 221-0336

Yergen & Meyer
4640 S.W. Macadam Ave.
Portland, OR 97202
(503) 295-1288

Advertising Agencies/Public Relations

For Networking in **advertising/public relations** and related fields, check out the following professional organizations, some of which are listed in Chapter 5:

PROFESSIONAL ORGANIZATIONS

Advertising Production Association, Seattle Chapter
American Marketing Association, Seattle and Oregon Chapters
International Association of Business Communicators, Seattle and Oregon Columbia Chapters
Portland AD2 (membership all under age of 31)
Portland Advertising Federation
Professional Photographers of Washington
Public Relations Society of America, Washington Chapter and Columbia River Chapter, Oregon
Sales and Marketing Executives, Seattle and Portland Chapters
Seattle Advertising Federation
Seattle Direct Marketing Association
Women in Communications, Seattle and Portland Chapters

For additional information, you can write to:

The Advertising Council
825 Third Ave.
New York, NY 10022

American Association of Advertising Agencies
666 Third Ave.
New York, NY 10017

Direct Marketing Association
6 E. 43rd St.
New York, NY 10017

Public Relations Society of America
33 Irving Place
New York, NY 10001

PROFESSIONAL PUBLICATIONS:

Advertising Age
Adweek
Direct Marketing Magazine
Journal of Advertising Research
Madison Avenue
Marketing Communications
O'Dwyer's Newsletter
PR Reporter
Public Relations Journal
Public Relations Review

DIRECTORIES:

Bradford's Directory of Marketing Research (Bradford's, Fairfax, VA)

O'Dwyer's Directory of Public Relations Firms (J.R. O'Dwyer Co., New York, NY)

Public Relations Journal—Register Issue (Public Relations Society of America, New York, NY)

Standard Directory of Advertising Agencies (National Register Publishing Co., Skokie, IL)

EMPLOYERS Seattle/Puget Sound Area:

Arst Public Relations
411 108th Ave. N.E., Suite 520
Bellevue, WA 98004
(206) 455-9055
Public relations.

Borders Perrin & Norrander
1115 First Ave.
Seattle, WA 98101
(206) 343-7741
Advertising.

Brems Eastman Glade
3131 Elliott Ave., Suite 280
Seattle, WA 98121
(206) 284-9400
Advertising.

Cole & Weber
308 Occidental Ave. S.
Seattle, WA 98104
(206) 447-9595
Advertising.

Ehrig & Associates
Fourth & Vine Building, Eighth Floor
Seattle, WA 98121
(206) 441-6666
Advertising.

Elgin Syferd
1008 Western Ave., Suite 601
Seattle, WA 98104
(206) 442-9900
Advertising, public relations.

Evans/Kraft
190 Queen Anne Ave. N.

Seattle, WA 98109
(206) 285-2222
Advertising, public relations.

Fearey Group
Tower Building
1807 Seventh Ave., Suite 1111
Seattle, WA 98101
(206) 343-1543
Public relations.

Floathe & Associates
12011 N.E. First
Bellevue, WA 98005
(206) 462-8400
High-tech advertising and public relations. Also has small office
in Beaverton, Oregon.

Herring/Newman Direct Response Advertising
101 Yesler Way, Fourth Floor
Seattle, WA 98104
(206) 343-9654
Advertising.

Hill and Knowlton
520 Pike Tower, Suite 1301
Seattle, WA 98101
(206) 682-6944
Public relations.

Livingston & Co.
800 Fifth Ave., Suite 3800
Seattle, WA 98104
(206) 382-5500
Advertising, public relations.

Manus Direct Response Marketing
1130 Rainier Ave. S.
Seattle, WA 98144
(206) 325-2200
Advertising.

McCann-Erickson Seattle
1011 Western Ave., Suite 600
Seattle, WA 98104
(206) 682-6360
Advertising, marketing.

Mogelgaard & Associates
2025 First Ave. S., Suite 600
Seattle, WA 98121

(206) 448-6303
Advertising.

Molin/Cutler Telemarketing Services
83 S. King, Suite 804
Seattle, WA 98104
(206) 622-4707

Ogilvy & Mather/West
316 Occidental Ave. S.
Seattle, WA 98104
(206) 447-0505
Public relations.

**Pacific Affairs Group/Fisher Brady & La Brue
Advertising and Public Relations**
2033 Sixth Ave., Suite 717
Seattle, WA 98121
(206) 448-3456
Advertising, public relations.

Rockey Co.
2121 Fifth Ave.
Seattle, WA 98121
(206) 728-1100
Public relations.

Sharp Hartwig
100 West Harrison Plaza
Seattle, WA 98119
(206) 282-6242
Advertising, public relations.

Stimpson-Clarke Advertising
83 S. King St., Suite 800
Seattle, WA 98104
(206) 583-8110
Advertising.

TFB/BBDO
1100 Olive Way, Suite 1600
Seattle, WA 98101
(206) 287-0200
High-tech advertising and public relations.

EMPLOYERS Portland Area:

Al Bauer Advertising Co., Inc.
2470 N.W. Westover Road
Portland, OR 97210
(503) 295-2955
Advertising.

Borders, Perrin & Norrander
111 S.W. Oak St.
Portland, OR 97204
(503) 227-2506
Advertising.

CB&S Advertising
1314 N.W. Northrup St.
Portland, OR 97209
(503) 225-1200
Advertising.
In-house agency for Fred Meyer, Inc.

Cole & Weber
55 S.W. Yamhill St.
Portland, OR 97204
(503) 226-2821
Advertising.

Davis, Johnson, Mogul & Colombatto Advertising (DJMC)
101 S.W. Main St.
Portland, OR 97204
(503) 241-7781
Advertising.

Gerber Advertising Agency
209 S.W. Oak St.
Portland, OR 97204
(503) 221-0100
Advertising.

Karakas, VanSickle, Ouellette
15220 N.W. Greenbrier Parkway
Beaverton, OR 97006
(503) 645-1551
Advertising.

Kobasic, Harris & Savage Advertising and Public Relations
2020 S.W. Fourth Ave.
Portland, OR 97201
(503) 295-1922
Advertising, public relations.

Marx/Knoll, Denight & Dodge
1230 S.W. First Ave.
Portland, OR 97204
(503) 226-2867
Advertising.

McDonald, Babb & Clarkson
315 S.W. Fifth Ave.
Portland, OR 97204
(503) 223-8309
Advertising.

Pihas, Schmidt, Westerdahl Co.
319 S.W. Washington St.
Portland, OR 97204
(503) 279-4000
Advertising.

Richardson Strang Engel
829 N.W. 19th Ave.
Portland, OR 97209
(503) 226-2721
Advertising.

Ryan Communications
1201 S.W. 12th Ave.
Portland, OR 97205
(503) 227-5547
Advertising.

Treasure Chest Advertising
6031 N.E. 92nd Drive
Portland, OR 97220
(503) 257-0383
Newspaper inserts.

Turtledove Clemens
111 S.W. Front Ave.
Portland, OR 97204
(503) 226-3581
Advertising.

Whitman Advertising & Public Relations
111 S.W. First Ave.
Portland, OR 97204
(503) 242-0070
Advertising, public relations.

Wieden & Kennedy
320 S.W. Washington St.
Portland, OR 97204
(503) 228-4381
Advertising.

Young & Roehr
6415 S.W. Canyon Court
Portland, OR 97221

(503) 297-4501
Ranked Portland's second largest advertising agency in 1989.

Aircraft and Aerospace

You may also want to check out the sections on **Computers and Electronics.**

For networking in **aeronautics** and related fields, you might want to contact the following professional organization listed in Chapter 5:

PROFESSIONAL ORGANIZATIONS:

American Institute of Aeronautics and Astronautics, Pacific Northwest Section

For additional information, you can write to:

Aerospace Industries Association of America
1250 I St. N.W.
Washington, DC 20005

American Institute of Aeronautics and Astronautics
370 L'Enfant Plaza S.W.
Washington DC 20024

PROFESSIONAL PUBLICATIONS:

Aviation Week & Space Technology
Business & Commercial Aviation

DIRECTORIES:

Aviation Telephone Directory: Pacific and Western States
(Directional Media Systems, Brea, CA 92621)
Aviation Week & Space Technology, Buyer's Guide (McGraw-Hill,
New York, NY)

EMPLOYERS Seattle/Puget Sound Area:

All Fab Corp.
Building C19, Paine Field
Everett, WA 98204
(206) 743-2700
Fabricator of aluminum aerospace parts.

Bell Industries Illuminated Displays Division
18225 N.E. 76th St.
Redmond, WA 98052
(206) 885-4353

Boeing Co., The
7755 E. Marginal Way
Seattle, WA 98109
(206) 655-2121
Commercial and military aircraft, missile and space systems,
computer and other information systems.

Criton Technologies
10800 N.E. Eighth
Bellevue, WA 98004
(206) 453-9400

Eldec Corp.
16700 13th Ave. W.
Lynnwood, WA 98036
(206) 743-8206
Electronic and electromechanical products for aerospace use.

Exotic Metals Forming Co.
5411 S. 226th St.
Kent, WA 98032
(206) 395-3710

Heath Tecna Aerospace Co.
19819 84th Ave. S.
Kent, WA 98032
(206) 872-7500
Aircraft interiors, composite parts, and air-frame structural
components.

Mamco Manufacturing Co.
1411 N.W. 50th St.
Seattle, WA 98107
(206) 789-1111

Modern Manufacturing
2900 Lind Ave. S.W.
Renton, WA 98055
(206) 251-1515

Olin Defense Systems, Aerospace Division
11441 Willows Road
Redmond, WA 98052
(206) 885-5000
Rocket propulsion systems and aviation electronics.

Precision Machine Works
2024 Puyallup Ave. E.
Tacoma, WA 98421
(206) 272-5119 or (206) 584-3632
Air frame parts.

Spectra-Lux Corp.
11825 120th Ave. N.E.
Kirkland, WA 98034
(206) 747-0560 or (206) 823-6857
Instumentation and lighting panels for aviation industry.

Spencer Aircraft Industries
8410 Dallas Ave. S.
Seattle, WA 98108
(206) 763-0210
Industrial aircraft equipment.

Sundstrand Data Control
15001 N.E. 36th St.
Redmond, WA 98073
(206) 885-3711
Avionic systems for commercial and military aircraft.

EMPLOYERS Portland Area:

Boeing Portland/Commercial Airplane Division
19000 N.E. Sandy Blvd.
Gresham, OR 97030
(503) 667-8000
Fabrication of airplane parts, including landing gear beams, flap tracks, and control stands.

Flight Dynamics
16600 S.W. 72nd Ave.
Portland, OR 97224
(503) 684-5384
Aircraft navigation equipment.

Peco, Inc.
4707 S.E. 17th Ave.
Portland, OR 97202
(503) 233-6401
Custom components for aircraft, missiles, ships; electronic, test, and measurement equipment; die casting; machining; assembly.

Precision Castparts Corp.
4600 S.E. Harney Drive
Portland, OR 97206
(503) 777-3881
Components for commercial and military jet aircraft engines.

Apparel and Textiles

You may also want to check the **Retailers/Wholesalers** section.

For networking in the **apparel** and **textile industries** and related fields, check out the following professional organizations:

PROFESSIONAL ORGANIZATIONS:

Fashion Group of Seattle
Pacific Northwest Apparel, Association, Seattle

For additional information, you can write to:

Educational Foundation for the Fashion Industries
227 W. 27th St.
New York, NY 10001

Federation of Apparel Manufacturers
450 Seventh Ave.
New York, NY 10001

National Association of Textile and Apparel Distributors
401 Seventh Ave.
New York, NY 10001

Textile Research Institute
Box 625
Princeton, NJ 08540

PROFESSIONAL PUBLICATIONS:

Textile Products
Textile Research Journal
Textile World
Women's Wear Daily

DIRECTORIES:

Apparel Industry Sourcebook (Denyse & Co., Inc., North Hollywood, CA)
Apparel Trades Book (Dun & Bradstreet, Inc., New York, NY)

How To Get a Job

Models Mart Directory (Peter Glenn Publications, New York, NY)
Textile Blue Book (Davison Publishing Co., Glen Rock, NJ)

EMPLOYERS Seattle/Puget Sound Area:

BRB Manufacturing
320 Spring St.
Puyallup, WA 98372
(206) 845-6074
Garment manufacturing.

Calvert Manufacturing Co.
1964 Fourth Ave. S.
Seattle, WA 98134
(206) 467-1003
Apparel and accessories.

Eddie Bauer
15010 N.E. 36th St.
Redmond, WA 98052
(206) 882-6100
Outdoor apparel.

Farwest Garments
1051 First Ave. S.
Seattle, WA 98134
(206) 622-3065

Fisher Bag Co.
1560 First Ave. S.
Seattle, WA 98134
(206) 623-1966

Generra Sportswear Co.
278 Broad St.
Seattle, WA 98121
(206) 282-6888
Designer and importer.

Gerry Sportswear Corp.
1051 First Ave. S.
Seattle, WA 98134
(206) 623-4194

Helly-Hanson USA
17275 N.E. 67th Court
Redmond, WA 98052
(206) 883-8823
Men's and boy's underwear.

J. Marcel Enterprises
2650 Rainier Ave. S.
Seattle, WA 98144
(206) 722-1412
Outer wear, law enforcement uniforms.

Jay Jacobs
1530 Fifth Ave.
Seattle, WA 98101
(206) 622-5400
Specialty retail chain and wholesale apparel manufacturer,
primarily of junior women's clothing.

Marontate-Jones
320 Terry Ave. N.
Seattle, WA 98109
(206) 623-4310
Women's outerwear.

Overall Laundry Services
222 Yale N.
Seattle, WA 981
(206) 682-6666
Uniform rental. Planning move in early 1990s to Paine Field,
Everett. Also has plants in Tacoma, WA, and Corvallis, OR.

Pacific Trail Sportswear
1310 Mercer St.
Seattle, WA 98109
(206) 622-8730
Active outerwear.

Seattle Fur Exchange
240 Andover Park W.
Seattle, WA 98198
(206) 246-7611
Auction house.

Seattle Pacific Industries
1700 Westlake Ave. N.
Seattle, WA 98109
(206) 282-8889
Fashion sportswear.

Simon Golub & Sons
5506 Sixth Ave. S.
Seattle, WA 98108
(206) 762-4800
Jewelry manufacture and distribution.

Sun Sportswear
101 Andover Park E.

Seattle, WA 98188
(206) 248-2789
National screen printer of casual sportswear.

Topline Inports
3625 132nd Ave. S.E., Fourth Floor
Bellevue, WA 98006
(206) 643-3003
Importer and wholesaler of shoes.

EMPLOYERS Portland Area:

Avia Group International
16160 S.W. Upper Boones Ferry Road
Portland, OR 97224
(503) 684-0490
Athletic shoes.

Dennis Uniform Manufacturing Co.
135 S.E. Hawthorne Blvd.
Portland, OR 97214
(503) 238-7123

Fabric Wholesalers
2035 N.E. 181st Ave.
Portland, OR 97230
(503) 666-4511

Jantzen, Inc.
411 N.E. 19th Ave.
Portland, OR 97232
(503) 238-5000
Sportswear and swimwear.

Nike, Inc.
3900 S.W. Murray Blvd.
Beaverton, OR 97005
(503) 641-6453
Athletic footwear, apparel.

Pendleton Woolen Mills
Mitchell Building
220 N.W. Broadway
Portland, OR 97208
(203) 226-4801
Contact: Lila Wilson, Assistant Manager, Personnel
Sportswear, blankets, area rugs, specialty robes, throws.

Architecture/Interior Design

You may also want to check the sections on
Contractors/Construction, Engineering, and **Real
Estate.**

To network in **architecture** and related fields, check out the
following professional organizations, some of which are listed
in Chapter 5:

PROFESSIONAL ORGANIZATIONS:

**American Institute of Architects, Portland Chapter
and Southwest Washington Chapter, Tacoma**
**American Society of Interior Designers, Seattle
Chapter and Oregon District Chapter**
Northwest Society of Interior Designers
**American Society of Landscape Architects,
Washington Chapter**
Society for Marketing Professional Services, Seattle

For additional information, you can write to:

American Institute of Building Design
1412 19th St.
Sacramento, CA 95814

Association of Women in Architecture
7440 University Drive
St. Louis, MO 63130

Society of American Registered Architects
600 S. Michigan Ave.
Chicago, IL 60601

PROFESSIONAL PUBLICATIONS:

AIA Journal
Architectural Forum
Architectural Record
Building Design and Construction
Progressive Architecture

DIRECTORIES:

Design Center Northwest Directory (Design Center Northwest, Seattle, WA)
PRO FILE/ The Official Directory of the American Institute of Architects (Archimedia, Topeka, KS)

EMPLOYERS Seattle/Puget Sound Area:

Architectural Alliance
1218 Third Ave., Suite 1900
Seattle, WA 98101
(206) 467-9341
Commercial interior design.

Bassetti/Norton/Metler/Rekevics Architects
2021 Third Ave.
Seattle, WA 98121
(206) 448-8668

BJSS Group, The
320 West Bay Drive
Olympia, WA 98502
(206) 943-4650

Bumgardner Architects, The
101 Stewart St., Suite 200
Seattle, WA 98101
(206) 223-1361
Architecture and commercial interior design.

Burr Lawrence Rising + Bates
1111 Fawcett, Suite 201
Tacoma, WA 98402
(206) 627-5599

Business Space Design
111 S. Jackson
Seattle, WA 98104
(206) 223-5000
Commercial interior design.

Callison Partnership Ltd.
1423 Third Ave.
Seattle, WA 98101
(206) 623-4646
Architecture and commercial interior design.

Commercial Design Architects
4230 198th St., S.W.

Lynnwood, WA 98036
(206) 771-2300

Dykeman Architects, The
1602 Hewitt Ave., Suite 400
Everett, WA 98201
(206) 259-3161

FORMA
1000 Lenora, Suite 600
Seattle, WA 98121
(206) 628-8900
Commercial interior design.

John Graham Associates/DLR Group
520 Pike St.
Seattle, WA 98101
(206) 461-6000

Kober/Sclater Architects
1100 Olive Way, Suite 200
Seattle, WA 98101
(206) 624-8682

Loschky Marquardt & Nesholm
801 Second Ave., Suite 501
Seattle, WA 98104
(206) 682-3460
Architecture and commercial interior design.

Louis Owen
419 Occidental Ave. S., Suite 404
Seattle, WA 98104
(206) 622-3265
Commercial interior design.

Mahlum & Nordfors
2505 Third Ave., Suite 219
Seattle, WA 98121
(206) 441-4151

Marvin Stein & Associates
2221 Fifth Ave.
Seattle, WA 98121
(206) 441-1449
Commercial interior design.

McKinley Architects, PSC, The
1201 Third Ave., Suite 1000
Seattle, WA 98101
(206) 464-1880
Architecture and commercial interior design.

Mithun Partners
2000 112th Ave. N.E.
Bellevue, WA 98004
(206) 454-3344

NBBJ Group, The
111 S. Jackson St.
Seattle, WA 98104
(206) 223-5555

Paul Seibert and Associates
1932 First Ave.
Seattle, WA 98101
(206) 448-8873
Commercial interior design.

Schemmer Associates, Inc., The
1601 114th Ave. S.E., Suite 110
Bellevue, WA 98004
(206) 453-8901

TRA Architecture, Engineering, Planning, Interiors
215 Columbia St.
Seattle, WA 98104
(206) 682-1133
Architecture and commercial interior design.

Tsang Partnership, The
1221 Second Ave., Suite 300
Seattle, WA 98101
(206) 343-3044
Second office in Tacoma.

Wyatt Stapper Architects
88 Spring St.
Seattle, WA 98104
(206) 587-5340
Architecture and commercial interior design.

EMPLOYERS Portland Area:

Ankrom Moisan Associated Architects
3223 S.W. Front St.
Portland, OR 97201
(503) 224-7117

Broome Oringdulph O'Toole
Rudolf Boles & Associates
733 N.W. 20th Ave.
Portland, OR 97209
(503) 226-1575
Architecture.

GBD Architects/GBD Interiors
920 S.W. Third Ave.
Portland, OR 97204
(503) 224-9656

Ingrim/Mills
One Centerpointe Drive
Lake Oswego, OR 97035
(503) 620-2025
Interior design.

Jensen Krause Schoenleber Associates
1962 N.W. Kearney St.
Portland, OR 97209
(503) 227-5616
Architecture.

Karol Niemi Associates
1800 S.W. First Ave.
Portland, OR 97201
(503) 222-3426
Interior design.

Mackenzie/Saito & Associates
0690 S.W. Bancroft St.
Portland, OR 97201
(503) 224-9570
Architecture.

Soderstrom Architects
320 S.W. Stark St.
Portland, OR 97204
(503) 228-5617

SRG Partnership
520 S.W. Yamhill St.
Portland, OR 97204
(503) 222-1917
Architecture.

Thompson Valvoda & Associates
1010 S.W. 11th Ave.
Portland, OR 97205
(503) 220-0668
Architecture.

Yost Grube Hall
1211 S.W. Fifth Ave.
Portland, OR 97204
(503) 221-0150
Architecture.

ZGF Interiors
320 S.W. Oak St.
Portland, OR 97204
(503) 224-3860
Interior design.

Zimmer Gunsul Frasca Partnership
320 S.W. Oak St.
Portland, OR 97204
(503) 224-3860
Architecture.

Auto/Truck/Marine/Transportation Equipment

For networking in the **auto, truck, and transportation equipment industry** and related fields, check out the following professional organizations, some of which are listed in Chapter 5.

PROFESSIONAL ORGANIZATIONS:

**Autobody Craftsman Association, Seattle and
    Portland Chapters
Automotive Service Association, Greater Seattle and
    Milwaukie, OR Chapters
Oregon Automotive Parts Association
Oregon Trucking Associations
Portland Auto Dealers Association
Portland Automotive Trades Association
Washington Automotive Wholesalers Association
Washington State Automobile Dealers Association
Washington Trucking Associations
Western Washington Sports Car Council**

You might also want to contact the following organizations for additional information:

Automotive Service Industry Association
444 N. Michigan Ave.
Chicago, IL 60611

National Marine Manufacturers Association
401 N. Michigan Ave., Suite 1150
Chicago, IL 60611

Society of Automotive Engineers
400 Commonwealth Drive
Warrendale, PA 15096

PROFESSIONAL PUBLICATIONS:

Automotive Age
Automotive Industries
Automotive News
Jobber Topics
Motor
Motor Age
Truck & Off Highway Industries

DIRECTORIES:

ASIA Membership Directory (Automotive Service Industries
    Association, Chicago, IL)
Automotive Age, Buyers Guide issue (Freed-Crown Publishing
    Co., Van Nuys, CA)
Automotive News, Market Data Book issue (Crain Automotive
    Group, Detroit, MI)

EMPLOYERS Seattle/Puget Sound Area:

Delta Marine Industries
1608 S. 96th
Seattle, WA 98108
(206) 763-2383
Ship building, repairing.

Duwamish Shipyard
5658 W. Marginal Way S.W.
Seattle, WA 98106
(206) 767-4880
Ship building, repairing.

Kenworth Truck Co.
10630 N.E. 38th Place
Kirkland, WA 98033
(206) 828-5000

Lake Union Dry Dock Co.
1515 Fairview Ave. E.
Seattle, WA 98102
(206) 323-6400
Ship building, repairing.

PACCAR, Inc.
777 106th Ave. N.E.

Bellevue, WA 98004
(206) 455-7400
Manufacturer of trucks, truck parts, railcars, military
equipment.

Schuck's Auto Supply
15395 S.E. 30th Place
Bellevue, WA 98008
(206) 644-2002
Auto parts and accessories. Over 44 locations.

Tacoma Boatbuilding Co.
1840 Marine View Drive
Tacoma, WA 98422
(206) 572-3600
Boat construction and repair.

Todd Pacific Shipyards Corp.
1801 16th Ave. S.W.
Seattle, WA 98134
(206) 623-1635

United Marine Shipbuilding
1441 N. Northlake Way
Seattle, WA 98103
(206) 632-1441

EMPLOYERS Portland Area:

Burns Brothers
621 S.E. Union Ave.
Portland, OR 97214
(503) 238-7393
Automobile components, diesel fuels, related products.

Freightliner Corp.
4747 N. Channel Ave.
Portland, OR 97217
(503) 283-8000
Produces and markets medium- and heavy-duty trucks.

Gunderson, Inc., a Greenbrier Co.
4350 N.W. Front Ave.
Portland, OR 97210
(503) 228-9281
Railroad freight cars, marine barges.

Hanna Carwash International
2000 S.E. Hanna Drive
Milwaukie, OR 97222
(503) 659-0361

Car washes, car wash equipment and supplies; world's largest car wash manufacturer.

Northwest Marine Iron Works
5555 N. Channel Ave., Building 2
PO Box 3109
Portland, OR 97208
(503) 285-7557
Ship conversion and repair, machine shop.

West State
5555 N. Channel Ave., Building 72
PO Box 4768
Portland, OR 97208
(503) 285-9706
Marine, industrial repairs, conversions.

Banks/Savings and Loans

You may also want to check out the sections on **Accounting** and **Investment Banking.**

For networking in the **banking industry** and related fields, check out the following professional organizations listed in Chapter 5:

PROFESSIONAL ORGANIZATIONS:

Financial Women International, Seattle
Oregon Mortgage Bankers Association
Seattle Mortgage Bankers Association
Tacoma Mortgage Bankers Association

For additional information, you can write to:

American Bankers Association
1120 Connecticut Ave., NW
Washington, DC 20036

Bank Marketing Association
309 W. Washington Blvd.
Chicago, IL 60606

Mortgage Bankers Association of America
1125 15th St., NW
Washington, DC 20005

National Council of Savings Institutions
1101 15th St., NW
Washington, DC 20005

United States League of Savings Institutions
111 E. Wacker Drive
Chicago, IL 60601

PROFESSIONAL PUBLICATIONS:

American Banker
Bank Administration
Bank Marketing Magazine
Bankers Magazine
Bankers Monthly
Savings Institutions

DIRECTORIES:

American Bank Directory (McFadden Business Publications,
    Norcross, GA)
American Banker's Guides (American Banker, New York, NY)
Money Market Directory (Money Market Directories,
    Charlottesville, VA)
Moody's Bank & Finance Manual (Moody's Investor Services,
    New York, NY)
Polk's Bank Directory (R.L. Polk, Nashville, TN)
Rand McNally Bankers Directory (Rand McNally, Chicago, IL)
Shesunoff 1,000 Largest U.S. Banks (Shesunoff, Austin, TX)

EMPLOYERS Seattle/Puget Sound Area:

American Marine Bank
PO Box 10788
Bainbridge Island, WA 98110
(206) 842-5651
Three branches in Puget Sound area.

American Savings Bank
820 A St.
Tacoma, WA 98402
(206) 272-8305
Seventeen full-service branches, most in southern King and
northern Pierce counties.

Bank of Tacoma
1160 Broadway Plaza
Tacoma, WA 98401
(206) 593-5150
Five area branches.

Cascade Savings & Loan Association
2828 Colby Ave.
Everett, WA 98201
(206) 339-5500
Eight branches in Puget Sound area.

Citybank
14807 Highway 99
Lynnwood, WA 98037
(206) 745-5933
Seven branches in Puget Sound area.

Evergreen Bank
301 Eastlake Ave.
Seattle, WA 98111
(206) 628-4250

First Interstate Bank of Washington
999 Third Ave.
Seattle, WA 98111
(206) 292-3111
Branches statewide total 106.

First Mutual Savings Bank
400 108th N.E.
Bellevue, WA 98004
(206) 455-7300
Five branches in the Puget Sound area.

First National Bank of Enumclaw
1212 Cole St.
Enumclaw, WA 98022
(206) 825-1651
Five branches in the Puget Sound area.

Frontier Bank
6623 Evergreen Way
Everett, WA 98023
(206) 347-0600
Seven branches in Puget Sound area.

Gibralter Savings Bank
11000 N.E. 33rd. Place
Bellevue, WA 98004
(206) 828-0404
Two branches in Bellevue, four in Seattle.

Great Northwest Federal Savings & Loan Association
500 Pacific Ave.
Bremerton, WA 98310
(206) 479-1551
Seventeen branches statewide.

Great Western Savings Bank
11201 S.E. Eighth St.
Bellevue, WA 98004
(206) 451-2000
Twelve branches in Puget Sound area, 19 statewide.

Heritage Federal Savings & Loan Association
201 W. Fifth Ave.
Olympia, WA 98507
(206) 943-1500
Seven branches in Washington.

InterWest Savings Bank
1259 W. Pioneer Way
Oak Harbor, WA 98277
(206) 679-4181
Twenty-two branches in western Washington, 26 statewide.

Key Bank of Puget Sound
1000 Second Ave.
Seattle, WA 98104
(206) 684-6000
Thirty-one branches in Puget Sound area.

Kitsap Bank
619 Bay St.
Port Orchard, WA 98366
(206) 876-7820
Ten branches in Puget Sound area.

Metropolitan Federal Savings & Loan Association of Seattle
1100 Olive Way
Seattle, WA 98101
(206) 625-1818
Seven branches in Puget Sound area.

North Pacific Bank
5448 S. Tacoma Way
Tacoma, WA 98409
(206) 472-3333
Two area branches.

Olympic Savings Bank
217 Pine
Seattle, WA 98101
(206) 382-4900
Twenty branches in western Washington, some located in Safeway stores.

Pacific First Federal Savings Bank
1420 Fifth Ave., Suite 4200

Seattle, WA 98101
(206) 224-3000
Twenty-four branches in Puget Sound area, 32 statewide.

Pioneer Federal Savings Bank
4111 200th S.W.
Lynnwood, WA 98036
(206) 771-2525
Seventeen branches in Snohomish and King counties.

Puget Sound Bancorp
1119 Pacific Ave.
Tacoma, WA 98402
(206) 593-3600
Branches in Puget Sound area total 94.

Puget Sound Savings Bank
1325 Fourth Ave., Suite 412
Seattle, WA 98101
(206) 447-5700
Wholly owned by Puget Sound Bancorp. Eighty-five branches
in Puget Sound area.

Seafirst Corp.
Columbia Seafirst Center
Seattle, WA 98124
(206) 358-3000
Bank branches statewide total 157.

Seattle First National Bank
701 Fifth Ave.
Seattle, WA 98104
(206) 358-5222

Security Pacific Bancorporation Northwest
1301 Fifth Ave.
Seattle, WA 98124
(206) 621-4111
Eighty-four branches in Puget Sound area.

Security Pacific Savings Bank
1102 Commerce
Tacoma, WA 98402
(206) 572-5220
Thirteen branches statewide.

University Savings Bank
6400 Roosevelt Way N.E.
Seattle, WA 98115
(206) 526-1000
Twenty-two branches in Puget Sound area.

U.S. Bank of Washington
1414 Fourth Ave.
Seattle, WA 98111
(206) 344-2300
Seventy-four branches in Puget Sound area.

U.S. Savings Bank of Washington
220 Unity St.
Bellingham, WA 98225
(206) 676-2300

Washington Federal Savings & Loan Association
425 Pike St.
Seattle, WA 98101
(206) 624-7930
Thirteen branches in Puget Sound area, 23 statewide.

Washington Mutual Savings Bank
1201 Third Ave.
Seattle, WA 98101
(206) 461-2000
Forty-seven Puget Sound branches.

Western Community Bank
1375 Regents Blvd.
Fircrest, WA 98466
(206) 564-0100
Nine branches in Puget Sound area.

EMPLOYERS Portland Area:

Bank of California, The
407 S.W. Broadway
Portland, OR 97205
(503) 225-3636

Bank of Tokyo
411 S.W. Sixth Ave.
Portland, OR 97204
(503) 222-3661

Benjamin Franklin Federal Savings & Loan Association
501 S.E. Hawthorne Blvd.
Portland, OR 97214
(503) 275-1234
Headquarters for Oregon's largest thrift, with 29 metropolitan branches.

Clackamas County Bank
38975 Proctor Blvd.

Sandy, OR 97055
(503) 668-5501

CrossLand Savings, FSB Utah
4333 N.E. Sandy Blvd.
Portland, OR 97213
(503) 249-2111
Ten metropolitan branches.

Far West Federal Bank
421 S.W. Sixth Ave.
Portland, OR 97204
(503) 224-4444
Headquarters for Oregon's second largest thrift, with 32
metropolitan branches.

First Independent Bank
1313 Main St.
Vancouver, WA 98660
(206) 699-4242
Fifteen local branches.

First Interstate Bank of Oregon
1300 S.W. Fifth Ave.
Portland, OR 97201
(503) 225-2111
Seventy-seven local branches.

First Interstate Bank of Washington
1800 Main St.
Vancouver, WA 98660
(206) 695-7190

Key Bank of Oregon
1211 S.W. Fifth Ave.
Portland, OR 97204
(503) 790-7500
Thirty-seven local branches.

Northwest National Bank
1607 Main St.
Vancouver, WA 98663
(206) 695-1311
Nine branches.

Pacific First Bank
12th & Washington Streets
Vancouver, WA 98660
(206) 694-1553
Sixteen branches in the metropolitan area.

Pacific First Federal Savings Bank
811 S.W. Sixth Ave.
Portland, OR 97204
(503) 275-9300
Eight branches in the metropolitan area.

Riverview Savings Bank
700 N.E. Fourth Ave.
Camas, WA 98607
(206) 834-2231

Seafirst Bank
805 Broadway
Vancouver, WA 98660
(206) 696-5670

Security Pacific Bank Washington
801 Main St.
Vancouver, WA 98666
(206) 696-8500

Security Pacific Oregon Bancorp
1001 S.W. Fifth Ave.
Portland, OR 97204
(503) 222-7777
Metropolitan branches total 31.

U.S. Bank of Oregon
Employment Office
555 S.W. Oak
Portland, OR 97204
(503) 275-6111
Eighty-seven local branches.

Vancouver Federal Savings Bank
1205 Broadway
Vancouver, WA 98660
(206) 694-1234
Headquarters with six branches.

Washington Federal Savings Bank
314 E. Main St.
Hillsboro, OR 98123
(503) 648-4131
Headquarters for this savings and loan with 17 metropolitan branches.

West One Bank
234 S.W. Broadway
Portland, OR 97205
(503) 248-6672
Eleven local branches.

Willamette Savings & Loan Association
100 S.W. Market St.
Portland, OR 97201
(503) 220-8300
Third largest Oregon thrift in 1989, with 25 metropolitan
branches, most at Fred Meyer, Inc., stores.

Chemicals

You may also want to look at the section on **Drugs.**

To network in the **chemical industry,** check out the
following professional organization listed in Chapter 5:

PROFESSIONAL ORGANIZATIONS:

American Chemical Society, Portland Chapter

For additional information, you can write to:

American Chemical Society
1155 16th St., N.W.
Washington, DC 20036

Chemical Specialties Manufacturers Association
1001 Connecticut Ave.
Washington, DC 20036

PROFESSIONAL PUBLICATIONS:

Chemical and Engineering News
Chemical Week

DIRECTORIES:

Chemical and Engineering News Facts and Figures Issue (American
Chemical Society, Washington, DC)
Chemical Week: Buyer's Guide issue (McGraw Hill, New York, NY)
Chemical Week: Financial Survey of the 300 Largest Companies
(McGraw Hill, New York, NY)
OPD Chemical Buyers Directory: The Green Book (Schnell
Publishing, New York, NY)

EMPLOYERS Seattle/Puget Sound Area:

All-World Scientific & Chemical
5515 186th Place S.W.
Lynnwood, WA 98037
(206) 282-2133
Chemicals, solvents, acids.

Argent Chemical Laboratories
8702 152nd Ave. N.E.
Redmond, WA 98052
(206) 885-3777
Fine and industrial chemicals, solvents, acids, inorganics, testing solutions.

Auto-Chlor System of Washington
4315 Seventh Ave. S.
Seattle, WA 98108
(206) 622-0900
Wholesale, retail of chemicals.

Bardahl Manufacturing Corp.
1400 N.W. 52nd
Seattle, WA 98107
(206) 783-4851
Additives, lubricants.

Borden Chemical Division of Borden
520 112th Ave. N.E.
Bellevue, WA 98004
(206) 455-4400

Discovery Chemical Corp.
49 37th St. N.W.
Auburn, WA 98001
(206) 939-6269
Institutional, janitorial, industrial chemicals.

Emerald City Chemical
1409 E. Madison St.
Seattle, WA 98122
(206) 328-2040
Chemicals for industrial, laboratory, home use.

Fiberchem, Inc.
1120 Andover Park E.
Seattle, WA 98188
(206) 575-0270
Fiberglass.

Gaco Western
18700 Southcenter Parkway

Tukwila, WA 98188
(206) 575-0450
Elastomeric coatings.

Great Western Chemical Co./McCall Lubricants
6900 Fox Ave. S.
Seattle, WA 98108
(206) 763-2350

Inland Chemical Co.
1918 Milwaukee Way
Tacoma, WA 98421
(206) 383-3692
Chemicals for industrial, transportation, institutional uses.

Jones Chemicals
1919 Marine View Drive N.E.
Tacoma, WA 98422
(206) 572-9030
Ammonia, bleach, chlorine, industrial chemicals.

Occidental Chemical Corp.
605 Alexander Ave.
Tacoma, WA 98421
(206) 593-1345
Chlorine used in pulp and paper industry, caustic sodas, other saltwater byproducts.

Olympic Homecare Products Co.
2233 112th Ave. N.E.
Bellevue, WA 98004
(206) 453-1700
Paint products.

Pennwalt Corp., Agchem Division
2901 Taylor Way
Tacoma, WA 98421
(206) 627-9101
Saltwater byproducts.

Preservative Paint Co.
5410 Airport Way S.
Seattle, WA 98108
(206) 763-0300
Consumer maintenance and industrial paint coatings.

Univar Corp./Van Waters & Rogers
1600 Norton Building
801 Second Ave.
Seattle, WA 98104
(206) 447-5911
also:

8201 S. 212th St.
Kent, WA 98032
(206) 623-6151
Largest distributor of industrial chemicals in North America.

EMPLOYERS Portland Area:

Atlas Chemical
1922 N. Vancouver Ave.
Portland, OR 97227
(503) 284-4125
Chemicals for pool and spa, cleaning, water treatment, acids, solvents, degreasers.

Cascade Chemicals
16081 S.E. Evelyn
Clackamas, OR 97015
(503) 656-1899
Solvents, surfactants.

Great Western Chemical Co.
808 S.W. 15th Ave.
Portland, OR 97205
(503) 228-2600
Mold release, antifoams, chemical specialties, paints and coatings.

High-Purity Chemical
2730 N.E. Riverside Way
Portland, OR 97211
(503) 249-2985
Distributes chemicals and laboratory supplies.

Little Chemical Co.
12304 N.E. Whitaker Way
Portland, OR 97230
(503) 255-7652
Chemical commodities, swimming pool chemicals, detergents, boiler treatment products.

McCall Oil & Chemical Corp.
808 S.W. 15th Ave.
Portland, OR 97205
(503) 228-2600

Nurnberg Scientific
6310 S.W. Virginia Ave.
Portland, OR 97201
(503) 246-8297
Stocking laboratory supply house.

Owens-Corning Fiberglas Corp.
14101 S.W. 72nd Ave.
Tigard, OR 97224
(503) 620-1014
Glass fiber products, wood fiberboard, polyurethane foam,
polyester resins.

Pennwalt Corp., Indchem Division
Inorganic Chemical Plant
6400 N.W. Front St.
Portland, OR 97201
(503) 228-7655

Tex Chemical
3805 N. Mississippi Ave.
Portland, OR 97227
(503) 288-6058
Industrial cleaning compounds.

Computers: Data Processing

You may also want to check out the sections on **Electronics**
and **Computers: Hardware/Software.**

For networking in the **data processing industry** and related
fields, you can contact the following professional organizations,
some of which are listed in Chapter 5:

PROFESSIONAL ORGANIZATIONS:

Association for Women in Computing, Seattle Chapter
Data Processing Management Association
Independent Computer Consultants Association
Oregon Computer Consultants Association
Professional and Technical Consultants Association

For more information about the data processing industry, you
can write to:

Association of Data Center Owners & Managers
PO Box 7623
Van Nuys, CA 91049

Data Processing Management Association
505 Busse Highway
Park Ridge, IL 60068
(708) 825-8124

PROFESSIONAL PUBLICATIONS:

Data Communications
Datamation

DIRECTORIES:

Data Communications Buyers Guide (McGraw-Hill, New York, NY)
Data Processing Equipment Directory (American Business
    Directories, Omaha, NE)
Data Processing Services Directory (American Business Directories,
    Omaha, NE)
Data Sources (Ziff-Davis, Cherry Hill, NY)
Engineering, Science and Computer Jobs (Peterson's Guides,
    Princeton, NJ)
Greater Seattle Area Computer Directory (The Data Center,
    Seattle, WA)
Portland Area Computer Directory (The Data Center, Seattle, WA)

EMPLOYERS Seattle/Puget Sound Area:

ADP-Automatic Data Processing
5000 148th Ave. N.E.
Redmond, WA 98052
(206) 867-1275

Boeing Computer Services Co.
2800 160th Ave. S.E.
Bellevue, WA 98008
(206) 865-6360
Time sales, financial services, data base services, programming,
consulting.

Brost Data Input
2722 Eastlake E.
Seattle, WA 98102
(206) 325-2635

Calma Co.
11808 Northup Way
Bellevue, WA 98005
(206) 828-3643
Computer-aided design.

Control Data
2308 Sixth Ave.
Seattle, WA 98121
(206) 728-4000
Business management services.

Data Force
Sixth & Stewart Plaza, 600 Building
Seattle, WA 98101
(206) 443-8840
Analysis, programming, conversions.

Infotech Corp.
1511 Sixth Ave.
Seattle, WA 98101
(206) 621-6600

Input Factory, The
1800 N.E. 44th St., Suite 200
Renton, WA 98056
(206) 228-1733
Data processing, computer entry.

Labels & Lists
2500 116th Ave. N.E.
Bellevue, WA 98004
(206) 822-1984

LaserPrint Communications
19026 72nd Ave. S.
Kent, WA 98032
(206) 251-6688

McDonnell Douglas
15660 N.E. 36th St.
Redmond, WA 98052
(206) 885-3205

National Business Systems
13256 Northup Way
Bellevue, WA 98005
(206) 641-8100

Professional Business Services
AGC Building
1200 Westlake Ave. N., No. 414
Seattle, WA 98109
(206) 285-3375
Custom data processing, time sharing.

Programming Resource Organization
10900 N.E. Eighth St.
Bellevue, WA 98004
(206) 462-0033
Data processing, consulting, programming.

Weyerhaeuser Information Systems
1-800-654-9347

World's largest private owner of timber and one of the largest employers in the Puget Sound area.

EMPLOYERS Portland Area:

ADP-Automatic Data Processing
2525 S.W. First Ave.
Portland, OR 97201
(503) 294-4200
Payroll Services:
10155 S.E. Sunnyside Rd.
Clackamas, OR 97015
(503) 654-6800

AKA Business Services
1515 E. Burnside St.
Portland, OR 97214
(503) 235-2524

Cascade Information Resources
111 S.W. Columbia, Suite 1250
Portland, OR 97201
(503) 796-6300

Control Data
10200 S.W. Eastridge St.
Portland, OR 97225
(503) 297-4841
Business management services.

McDonnell Douglas/Health Systems Co.
500 N.E. Multnomah St.
Portland, OR 97232
(503) 239-5915

Poorman-Douglas Corp.
1325 S.W. Custer Drive
Portland, OR 97219
(503) 245-5555
Full service data processing.

Computers: Hardware/Software

Be sure to also take a look at the section on **Electronics**.

For networking in the **computer and electronics industries,** check out the following trade and professional organizations, some of which are listed in Chapter 5:

PROFESSIONAL ORGANIZATIONS:

American Electronics Association
Association for Computing Machinery/Creative
  Graphics, Seattle
Association for Women In Computing, Seattle
Independent Computer Consultants Association
Oregon Computer Consultants Association
Semiconductor Industry Association
Semiconductor Equipment & Materials Institute
Washington Software Association

For more information, you can write:

ADAPSO—The Computer Software and Services
Association
1300 N. 17th St.
Arlington, VA 22209

Association for Computing Machinery
11 W. 42nd St.
New York, NY 10036

IEEE Computer Society
1730 Massachusetts Ave. N.W.
Washington, DC 20036

Semiconductor Industry Association
10201 Torre Ave.
Cupertino, CA 95014

PROFESSIONAL PUBLICATIONS:

Byte
Computerworld
Electronic Business
Electronic News
MIS Week
PC Magazine
Personal Computing

DIRECTORIES:

Advanced Technology in the Pacific Northwest (Quamtix Data
  Services, West Linn, OR)
Data Sources: v.1 Hardware, v.2 Software (Ziff-Davis Publishing,
  Cherry Hill, NJ)
Directory of Computer Software and Services Companies (ADAPSO,
  Arlington, VA)
Engineering, Science and Computer Jobs (Peterson's Guides,
  Princeton, NJ)

How To Get a Job

ICP Software Directory (International Computer Programs, Indianapolis, IN)
Washington State Software Industry Directory (Washington State Software Assoc., Kirkland, WA)
Yearbook/Directory (Semiconductor Industry Association, Cupertino, CA)

EMPLOYERS Seattle/Puget Sound Area:

Accountants Microsystems
3633 136th Place S.E.
Bellevue, WA 98006
(206) 643-2050
Accounting and financial software.

Agena Corp.
9709 Third Ave. N.E., Suite 500
Seattle, WA 98115
(206) 525-0005
Insurance software.

Aldus Corp.
411 First Ave. S.
Seattle, WA 98104
(206) 622-5500
Graphics and layout software.

Applied Microsystems Corp.
5020 148th Ave. N.E.
Redmond, WA 98073
(206) 882-2000
Engineering software.

Attachmate Corp.
13231 S.E. 36th St.
Bellevue, WA 98006
(206) 644-4010
Software.

Care Computer Systems
636 120th N.E.
Bellevue, WA 98005
(206) 451-8272
Software for nursing homes.

Custom Software Services
10900 N.E. Fourth St., Suite 900
Bellevue, WA 98004
(206) 455-3507
Software for legal and professional services.

Data I/O Corp.
10525 Willows Road N.E.
Redmond, WA 98073
(206) 881-6444
Hardware and software for users of programmable integrated
circuits (PICs).

DP Enterprises
1300 Dexter Ave. N.
Seattle, WA 98109
(206) 283-1300
Computer sales, leasing, service, support.

Emerald Technology
18912 North Creek Parkway
Bothell, WA 98011
(206) 485-8200
Communications software.

ESCA Corp.
11120 N.E. 33rd Place
Bellevue, WA 98004
(206) 822-6800
Software.

FOURGEN Software
7620 242nd St. S.W.
Edmonds, WA 98020
(206) 776-5088
Commercial accounting software.

Generic Software
11911 North Creek Parkway S.
Bothell, WA 98011
(206) 487-2233
Software.

IBM Corp.
Central Employment
600 University St.
Seattle, WA 98101
(206) 587-3192

Interlinq Software Corp.
10700 Northup Way, Suite 110
Bellevue, WA 98004
(206) 827-1112
Residential mortgage loan software.

Ioline Corp.
12020 113th Ave. N.E.
Kirkland, WA 98034

(206) 821-2140
Computer-aided design products.

Mannesmann Tally Corp.
8301 S. 180th St.
Kent, WA 98032
(206) 251-5500
Computer peripherals, including printers, teleprinters, data
communication systems.

Microrim, Inc.
3925 159th Ave. N.E.
Redmond, WA 98052
(206) 885-2000
Information management software.

Microsoft Corp.
16011 N.E. 36th Way
Redmond, WA 98073
(206) 882-8080
Languages, microcomputer applications software, operating
systems.

NCR Corp.
15400 S.E. 30th Place
Bellevue, WA 98007
(206) 643-4150
Business information processing systems.

Nintendo, Inc., of America
4820 150th Ave. N.E.
Redmond, WA 98052
(206) 882-2040
Electronic media computer games.

Revelation Technologies
3633 136th Place S.E.
Bellevue, WA 98006
(206) 643-9898
Database applications development software.

Sierra Geophysics
11255 Kirkland Way
Kirkland, WA 98033
(206) 822-5200
Software.

Software Research Northwest
17710 100th Ave. S.W.
Vashon Island, WA 98070
(206) 463-3030
Administrative systems software.

Timeline, Inc.
3055 112th Ave. N.E., Suite 106
Bellevue, WA 98004
(206) 822-3140
Financial accounting software.

TOM Software
127 S.W. 156th St.
Seattle, WA 98166
(206) 246-7022
Accounting software.

Traveling Software
18702 North Creek Parkway
Bothell, WA 98011
(206) 483-8088
Connectivity and accessibility software.

Walker, Richer & Quinn
2825 Eastlake Ave. E.
Seattle, WA 98102
(206) 324-0350
Communications software.

Weyerhaeuser Information Systems
Park Center II
Tacoma, WA 98477
(206) 924-4200
Software.

EMPLOYERS Portland Area:

Apple Computer
Regional Sales Office
4000 S.W. Kruse Way Place
Building One, Suite 100
Lake Oswego, OR 97034
(503) 635-7711
Contact: Personnel Department, 20525 Mariani, Cupertino, CA
95014, (408) 996-1010.
Personal computers; systems for business, scientific,
educational, and home applications; disk drives; applications
software.

ADP Dealer Services
2525 S.W. First Ave., No. 450
Portland, OR 97201
(503) 294-4200
Turnkey systems and software for vehicle dealerships.

Central Point Software
15220 N.W. Greenbriar Parkway, Suite 200

Beaverton, OR 97006
(503) 690-8090 (recorded message)
Utility software.

Concept Technologies
6950 S.W. Hampton
Tigard, OR 97223
(503) 684-3314
PC expansion boards, software products for high-tech market.

Data General Corp.
8600 S.W. Salish Lane
Wilsonville, OR 97070
(503) 682-7267
Computer systems, including peripherals, software services.

Epson Portland
3950 N.W. Aloclek Place
Hillsboro, OR 97124
(503) 645-1118
Computers, printing terminals, accessories.

FPS Computing
3601 S.W. Murray Blvd.
Beaverton, OR 97005
PO Box 23489
Portland, OR 97223
(503) 641-3151
Computer processing units.

Fujitsu America
7300 N.E. Evergreen Parkway
Hillsboro, OR 97124
(503) 681-7300
Computer peripherals.

Hewlett-Packard Co.
18110 S.E. 34th St.
Camas, WA 98607
PO Box C006
Vancouver, WA 98668
(206) 254-8110
Workstation and personal computer printers, including
Wilsonville plant.

IBM Corp.
1211 S.W. Fifth Ave., Suite 300
Portland, OR 97204
(503) 294-6500

Intel Corp.
5200 N.E. Elam Young Parkway

Hillsboro, OR 97214
(503) 696-8080
Microcomputer components and systems; OEM platforms.
Most products manufactured overseas. Hillsboro houses
engineering and administration, also manufactures pilot and
testing products. Personal Computer Enhancement Operation
is Beaverton Division.

Lattice Semiconductor Corp.
5555 N.E. Moore Court
Hillsboro, OR 97124
(503) 681-0118
Programmable logic devices for high-tech electronics industry.

Logiplex Corp.
2045 N.E. Union Ave.
Portland, OR 97212
(503) 249-7224
Support equipment for computer, high-tech industries.

Mentor Graphics Corp.
8500 S.W. Creekside Place
Beaverton, OR 97005
(503) 626-7000
Manufactures electronic design software; will move
headquarters to Boeckman Road and Parkway Ave. in
Wilsonville toward end of 1990.

Metheus Corp.
PO Box 1049
Hillsboro, OR 97123
(503) 640-8000
Corporate headquarters. High-tech graphics equipment;
software and related products.

Radix Microsystems
Oregon Graduate Center Science Park
19545 N.E. Von Neumann Drive
Beaverton, OR 97006
(503) 690-1229
Embedded personal computers for industrial automation
market.

Sage Polytron
1700 N.W. 167th Place
Beaverton, OR 97006
(503) 645-1150
Software for IBM-compatible personal computers; some
software for mainframes.

Sequent Computer Systems
15450 S.W. Koll Parkway

Beaverton, OR 97006
(503) 626-5700
Parallel architecture computer systems, many designed for
database management market.

Sidereal Corp.
9600 S.W. Barnes Road
Portland, OR 97225
(503) 297-5531
Corporate headquarters. Computer-based message
communications terminals, office automation systems, related
products.

Wang Laboratories
9500 S.W. Barbur Blvd.
Portland, OR 97219
(503) 245-5586
Office automation systems.

Wyatt Software Services
5335 S.W. Meadows Road
Lake Oswego, OR 97035
(503) 620-9800
Software for insurance and finance applications, including
benefit and compensation management and investment
management.

In computers, not just a job, a career

"When we hire someone at Hewlett-Packard, we're hiring for a career rather than simply for a single project," states one research and development manager for Hewlett-Packard Laboratories.

"We hire both hackers and theorists, but our primary criterion is that the people will contribute ideas. We look for a strong technical degree, at least a B.S. in computer science or electrical or mechanical engineering. But because we're dealing with artificial intelligence, we also hire philosophers, anthropologists, and people from the humanities and business. We're interested in the interface between people and machines."

HP recruits at colleges, through conferences and other networks, and through newspaper ads.

"Hiring is a group decision. Two or three people review a resume. We do a phone screening and a day-and-a-half interview. We look for a strong background in the area we're working in, plus proof of good original work—a Ph.D. thesis or master's project and, of course, previous experience. Because projects include only three to ten people, we want to be sure of a good fit.

"After the interview, we have a postmortem, and the hiring decision is made by consensus. If one person is strongly opposed, it will be a 'no' decision. We may interview three or four people, but we make the decision person-by-person rather than competitively. You see, if a person looks exceptionally strong, we can find opportunities for her or him.

"Because HP is such a big company, there is tremendous job stability. You know that the company is not going to be bought out. Within the company, projects are still cancelled and departments are phased out, but once you're in, you're in. There are a lot of resources, and you have an opportunity to really learn. The industrial blends with the academic. You have access to the experts in your field.

"The corporate culture is informal, with a live-and-let-live attitude. People can work the hours they want if they get results. You can wear whatever you want.

"The downside is that you'll never become a millionaire working here. To do that, you have to take the risk at a start-up company." ■

Contractors/Construction

You may also want to look at the sections on **Architecture, Engineering,** and **Real Estate.**

For networking in the **construction** industry and related fields, check out the following trade and professional organizations, some of which are listed in Chapter 5:

PROFESSIONAL ORGANIZATIONS:

American Institute of Steel Construction
American Plywood Association
American Society of Landscape Architects
Associated Builders and Contractors of Western Washington
Associated Builders and Contractors, Inc., Pacific Northwest Chapter (Portland)
Associated General Contractors of America (Wilsonville, OR)
Associated General Contractors of Washington
Associated Women Contractors, Suppliers, and Design Professionals
Building Industry Association of Washington
National Association of Women in Construction, Seattle Chapter
National Electrical Contractors Association, Portland Chapter, Puget Sound Chapter
Olympia Master Builders, Olympia, WA
Oregon State Association of Plumbing, Heating, and Cooling Contractors
Seattle Master Builders Association
Washington State Master Builders Association
Women in Trades (Seattle)

For additional information, you can write to:

National Association of Home Builders
15th & M Sts., N.W.
Washington, DC 20005

National Construction Industry Council
2000 L. St., N.W., Suite 612
Washington, DC 20036

PROFESSIONAL PUBLICATIONS:

Building Design & Construction
Construction Review
Engineering News-Record
Pacific Builder & Engineer
Pit and Quarry

DIRECTORIES:

Blue Book of Major Homebuilders, West Edition (LSI Systems, Crofton, MD)
Construction Equipment Buyers Guide (Cahners Publishing, Des Plaines, IL)
Construction Equipment: Construction Giants (Cahners Publishing, Des Plaines, IL)
Washington Construction Industry Directory (National Electrical Contractors Assoc., Seattle, WA)

EMPLOYERS Seattle/Puget Sound Area:

Absher Construction Co.
PO Box 280
Puyallup, WA 98371
(206) 845-9544
Commercial contractor.

Artistic Drywall
3500 Sylvana Terrace
Stanwood, WA 98292
(206) 652-6727
Drywall, steel framing, plaster and stucco, grid system ceilings.

Ballard Construction
8220 Seventh Ave. S.
Seattle, WA 98108
(206) 764-1313
Public works, general construction.

Bartells, E.J. Co.
700 Powell S.W.
Renton, WA 98057
(206) 228-4111
Refractory supply.

Baugh Enterprises
900 Poplar Place S.
Seattle, WA 98144
(206) 447-2000
Holding company for commercial and industrial construction operations.

Bayley, Robert E., Construction
One Union Square Building, Suite 1601
Seattle, WA 98101
(206) 621-8884
General contractor, commercial.

Bayliner Marine Corp.
PO Box 24467
Seattle, WA 98124
(206) 435-5571
Boat building.

Berkley Engineering and Construction
2203 Airport Way S., Suite 200
Seattle, WA 98134
(206) 628-3000
Commercial contractor.

Brower Co., The
7043 S. 190th
Kent, WA 98032
(206) 251-6750
General contracting, materials distribution.

Buchan, John F. Construction
11555 Northup Way
Bellevue, WA 98004
(206) 827-2266
Subdivisions.
also:
Buchan, William E.
(206) 828-6424
Executive homes.

Burnstead Construction Co.
1215 120th N.E.
Bellevue, WA 98005
(206) 454-1900
Home construction.

Centex Homes
2223 112th Ave. N.E.
Bellevue, WA 98004
(206) 455-2858
Home construction.

Chaffey Corp.
205 Lake St. S.
Kirkland, WA 98083
(206) 822-5981
Home construction.

Clark, W.G., Construction Co.
408 Aurora Ave. N.
Seattle, WA 98109
(206) 624-5244
Commercial contractor.

Close, D.W., Co.
3317 Third Ave. S.
Seattle, WA 98134
(206) 623-8960
Contracting. Electrical, heavy construction, industrial, service, data cabling.

Cochran Electric Co.
12500 Aurora Ave. N.
Seattle, WA 98133
(206) 367-1900.

Conner Development Co.
846 108th Ave. N.E., Suite 202
Bellevue, WA 98004
(206) 455-9280
Home construction.

Danmor Co., The
110 110th Ave. N.E.
Bellevue, WA 98004
(206) 454-3331
Nonresidential.

Ferguson Construction
7433 Fifth Ave. S.
Seattle, WA 98108
(206) 767-3810
Commercial contractor.

Foushee & Associates
3260 118th Ave. S.E.
Bellevue, WA 98009
(206) 746-1000
Commercial contractor.

Gall Landau Young Construction Co.
100 116th S.E.
Bellevue, WA 98108
(206) 451-8877
Commercial contractor.

General Construction Co.
3840 W. Marginal Way S.W.
Seattle, WA 98106
(206) 938-6200

Halvorson Osborne Construction Co.
10628 N.E. 38th Place, Suite 110
Kirkland, WA 98033
(206) 827-4221
Commercial contractor.

Henderson Homes
2223 112th Ave. N.E.
Bellevue, WA 98004
(206) 453-0496
Home construction.

Lakeside Industries
7735 178th Place N.E.
Redmond, WA 98052
(206) 641-4600
Asphalt paving contractor.

Lease Crutcher Lewis
4330 148th Ave. N.E.
Redmond, WA 98052
(206) 455-2480
General contractors, commercial.

Lockheed Shipbuilding Co.
2929 16th Ave. S.W.
Seattle, WA 98134
(206) 292-5945

Lozier Homes Corp.
12443 Bel-Red Road, Suite H
Bellevue, WA 98005
(206) 454-8690
Home construction.

Murphy, Donald B. Contractors
PO Box 6139
Federal Way, WA 98063
(206) 838-1402
Commercial contractor.

Murray Franklyn Group
14410 Bel-Red Road
Bellevue, WA 98007
(206) 644-2323
Home construction.

Newhall Jones
12515 Bel-Red Road
Bellevue, WA 98005
(206) 462-8200
Home construction, light commercial.

Parkwood Homes
8920 152nd Ave. N.E.
Redmond, WA 98052
(206) 881-6600
Home construction.

Rafn, J.M., Co.
PO Box 4229
Bellevue, WA 90009
(206) 455-3331
Commercial contractor.

Rector Construction
975 John St., Suite 108
Seattle, WA 98101
(206) 343-7504
Hoisting and concrete work.

Schneider Homes
6510 Southcenter Blvd.
Tukwila, WA 98188
(206) 248-2471
Home construction.

SDL Corp.
2100 112th N.E.
Bellevue, WA 98009
(206) 455-2101
Commercial contractor.

Sellen Construction Co.
228 Ninth Ave. N.
Seattle, WA 98109
(206) 682-7770
General building contractor, especially in commercial and
medical fields.

Stafford Homes, Inc.
16016 188th Place N.E.
Bothell, WA 98011
(206) 488-2222
Home construction.

Stewart Greacen
1160 140th N.E.
Bellevue, WA 98005
(206) 641-6110
Home construction.

Tucci & Sons
4224 Waller Road
Tacoma, WA 98443

(206) 922-6676
Commercial contractor.

Turner Construction Co.
2033 Sixth Ave., Suite 450
Seattle, WA 98121
(206) 728-7101
Commercial contractor.

Wick Construction Co.
720 N. 35th
Seattle, WA 98103
(206) 634-1550
Commercial contractor.

Woodworth & Co.
1200 East D St.
Tacoma, WA 98421
(206) 383-3585
Commercial contractor.

Wright Schuchart
PO Box 3764
Seattle, WA 98124
(206) 447-7545
Commercial contractor.

EMPLOYERS Portland Area:

Andersen Construction Co.
6712 N. Cutter Circle
Portland, OR 97217
(503) 283-6712
Commercial contractor.

Baugh Industrial Contractors/Baugh Construction Co.
15500 S.W. Jay St.
Beaverton, OR 97006
(503) 641-2500

Contractors, Inc.
11965 S.W. Herman Road
Tualatin, OR 97062
(503) 692-0100
Commercial contractor.

Drake, Donald M. Co.
1740 N.W. Flanders St.
Portland, OR 97209
(503) 226-3991
Commercial contractor.

Emerick Construction Co.
8850 S.E. Otty Road
Portland, OR 97266
(503) 777-5531
Commercial contractor.

Gray, R.A., & Co.
11445 S.W. Tiedeman Road
Tigard, OR 97223
(503) 639-6127
Commercial contractor.

Grigsby Construction Co.
8114 S.W. Nimbus Ave.
Beaverton, OR 97005
(503) 641-7343
Commercial contractor.

Harder Mechanical Contractors
2148 N.E. Union Ave.
Portland, OR 97212
(503) 281-1112
Construction, fabrication, piping, instrumentation.

Hoffman Construction Co.
1300 S.W. Sixth Ave.
Portland, OR 97201
(503) 221-8811
Commercial contractor.

Hyland & Sons
8885 S.W. Canyon Road
Portland, OR 97225
(503) 297-5622
Commercial contractor.

John, James E. Construction Co.
7223 N.E. Hazel Dell Ave.
Vancouver, WA 98665
(206) 696-0837
Commercial contractor.

Lonigan, William L. Contractors
4000 S.W. 114th St.
Beaverton, OR 97005
(503) 641-6727
Commercial contractor.

Lorentz Bruun Co.
3636 S.E. 20th Ave.
Portland, OR 97242

(503) 232-7106
Commercial contractor.

McCormack, W.L., & Co.
500 S.E. 25th Ave.
Portland, OR 97202
(503) 232-4157
Commercial contractor.

P & C Construction Co.
390 N.E. Ninth St.
Gresham, OR 97030
(503) 665-0165
Commercial contractor.

R & H Construction Co.
338 N.W. Fifth Ave.
Portland, OR 97208
(503) 228-7177
Commercial contractor.

Riedel Resources
4555 N. Channel Ave.
Portland, OR 97217
(503) 285-9111
Heavy construction, marine construction, related services.

Robinson Construction Co.
7320 S.W. Hunziker Road
Tigard, OR 97223
(503) 639-8021
Commercial contractor.

Westwood Corp. Developers and Contractors
3030 S.W. Moody St.
Portland, OR 97201
(503) 222-2000
Commercial contractor.

Cultural Institutions

For networking among **cultural institutions, museums, and the arts,** check out the following professional organizations, many of which are listed in Chapter 5:

PROFESSIONAL ORGANIZATIONS:

Allied Arts of Seattle
Allied Arts, Tacoma

Chamber Music Society of Oregon
Music & Art Foundation, Seattle
Northwest Area Music Association
Pacific Northwest Black Community Festival
Association
Portland Music Association
Washington Commission for the Humanities
Portland Area Theatre Alliance
Oregon Arts Commission
Seattle Artist's Guild

For more information, you can write to:

American Association of Museums
1225 I St., N.W.
Washington, DC 20005

American Federation of Arts
41 E. 65th St.
New York, NY 10021

Arts and Business Council
130 E. 40th St.
New York, NY 10016

PROFESSIONAL PUBLICATIONS:

Art World
Museum News
Symphony Magazine

DIRECTORIES:

Oregon Arts Index (Portland Metropolitan Chamber of
    Commerce, Portland, OR)
Official Museum Directory (National Register Publishing Co.,
    Wilmette, IL)
Symphony Magazine's North American Orchestra Directory Issue
    (American Symphony Orchestra League, Washington, DC)

EMPLOYERS Seattle/Puget Sound Area:

A Contemporary Theatre
100 W. Roy St.
Seattle, WA 98119
(206) 285-3220

Bathhouse Theatre
7312 W. Greenlake Drive N.

Seattle, WA 98103
(206) 524-9108

Bellevue Art Museum
301 Bellevue Square
10310 N.E. Fourth St.
Bellevue, WA 98004
(206) 454-3322

Bellevue Philharmonic Orchestra
400 108th N.E.
Bellevue, WA 98004
(206) 455-4171

Burke Memorial Washington State Museum
17th N.E. and N.E. 45th
Seattle, WA 98105
(206) 543-5590

Empty Space Theatre, The
95 S. Jackson St.
Seattle, WA 98104
(206) 587-3737

Fifth Avenue Theatre
1308 Fifth Ave.
Seattle, WA 98101
(206) 625-1468

Frontier Museum
2301 23rd Ave. S.E.
Puyallup, WA 98372
(206) 845-4402

Frye Art Museum
704 Terry Ave.
Seattle, WA 98101
(206) 622-9250

Henry Art Gallery
University of Washington Campus
41st St. N.E. and 15th Ave. N.E.
Seattle, WA 98105
(206) 543-2280

Intiman Theatre
Playhouse, Seattle Center
305 Harrison St.
Seattle, WA 98109
(206) 626-0775

Meany Hall for the Performing Arts
University of Washington
Seattle, WA 98195
(206) 543-4880

Museum Of Flight
9404 E. Marginal Way S.
Seattle, WA 98108
(206) 764-5700

Museum Of History & Industry
2700 24th Ave. E.
Seattle, WA 98112
(206) 324-1125

Northwest Chamber Orchestra
1305 Fourth Ave., Suite 522
Seattle, WA 98101
(206) 343-0445

On the Boards
153 14th Ave.
Seattle, WA 98122
(206) 325-7901

Pacific Northwest Ballet
4649 Sunnyside Ave. N.
Seattle, WA 98103
(206) 547-5900

Pacific Science Center
Seattle Center
200 Second Ave. N.
Seattle, WA 98109
(206) 443-2001

Pantages Centre
901 Broadway
Tacoma, WA 98402
(206) 591-5890

Seattle Art Museum
Volunteer Park
14th Ave. E. and E. Prospect
Seattle, WA 98112
(206) 625-8900

Seattle Children's Museum
305 Harrison, Seattle Center
Seattle, WA 98109
(206) 441-1767 (recording)

Seattle Children's Theatre
Seattle Center
Seattle, WA 98109
(206) 443-0807

Seattle Group Theatre
3940 Brooklyn Ave. N.E.
Seattle, WA 98105
(206) 545-4969

Seattle Opera Association
Seattle Center House, Fourth Floor
Seattle, WA 98109
(206) 443-4700

Seattle Repertory Theatre Company
Bagley Wright Theatre, Seattle Center
155 Mercer St.
Seattle, WA 98109
(206) 443-2210

Seattle Symphony Orchestra
305 Harrison St., Seattle Center
Seattle, WA 98109
(206) 443-4740

State Capitol Museum
211 W. 21st St.
Olympia, WA 98501
(206) 753-2580

Tacoma Actors Guild
1323 S. Yakima Ave.
Tacoma, WA 98405
(206) 272-3107

Tacoma Art Museum
1123 Pacific Ave.
Tacoma, WA 98402
(206) 272-4258

Village Theatre
120 Font St. N.
Issaquah, WA 98027
(206) 392-1942

Washington State Historical Society Museum
315 N. Stadium Way
Tacoma, WA 98403
(206) 593-2830

Whatcom Museum of History and Art
21 Prospect St.
Bellingham, WA 98225
(206) 676-6981

Wing Luke Asian Museum
407 Seventh Ave. S.
Seattle, WA 98104
(206) 623-5124

EMPLOYERS Portland Area:

Children's Museum
3037 S.W. Second
Portland, OR 97204
(503) 248-4587

Clackamas County Historical Society
Mertie Stevens House
603 Sixth
Oregon City, OR 97045
(503) 655-2866

Gresham Historical Museum
55 S. Main
Gresham, OR 97080
(503) 661-8839

Historic Preservation League Of Oregon
26 N.W. Second
Portland, OR 97209
(503) 243-1923

McLoughlin House
Seventh & Center
Oregon City, OR 97045
(503) 656-5146

Milwaukie Museum
3737 S.E. Adams
Portland, OR 97222
(503) 659-5780

Oregon Art Institute/Portland Art Museum
1219 S.W. Park Ave.
Portland, OR 97205
(503) 226-2811

Oregon Historical Society
1230 S.W. Park Ave.
Portland, OR 97205
(503) 222-1741

Oregon Maritime Center & Museum
113 S.W. Front
Portland, OR 97204
(503) 224-7724

Oregon Museum of Science and Industry
4015 S.W. Canyon Rd.
Portland, OR 97221
(503) 222-2828

Oregon Symphony Orchestra
813 S.W. Alder St.
Portland, OR 97205
(503) 228-4294

Portland Ballet/Portland Opera Association
Portland Civic Auditorium
222 S.W. Clay St.
Portland, OR 97201

Portland Black Repertory Theatre
PO Box 8655
Portland, OR 97207
(503) 287-3959

Portland Carousel Museum
630 N.E. Pacific St.
Portland, OR 97232
(503) 235-2252

Portland Center for the Performing Arts
1111 S.W. Broadway
Portland, OR 97205
(503) 248-4335

Portland Civic Theatre
1530 S.W. Yamhill St.
Portland, OR 97205
(503) 226-3048

Portland Youth Philharmonic
1119 S.W. Park
Portland, OR 97205
(503) 223-5939

Jobs for artists

We asked the director of a West Coast fine arts college what jobs were available to those with a fine arts degree.

"Few people realize it," he says, "but times are very good for fine artists.

"Fine artists make less than the average for other graduates. However, for artists who remain serious, practicing their art, at 40 their average income surpasses the average for all others. The point is, you can't initially support yourself through art—at least not for the first 10 years.

"If you're serious and productive, you can turn the first 10 years around. I tell graduates, 'You should be planning a dual path. Don't plan your art career without planning your other career as well.' If you're driving a cab, being a waiter, or working in an office, I don't think you have the energy to do your art after work. Instead, if you pursue a related and parallel course, you still remain in the energy of the arts, and you're more likely to make important contacts.

"For example, a textile artist might go into textile conservation at a museum working with tapestries, fifties clothes, and renaissance lace. Or that artist could work in the costume shop of one of the local theaters. The sculptor or ceramicist might take advantage of industrial applications, making dental molds or molds for plastics.

"Americans are spending an ever increasing percentage of their income on art. Corporations are also buying art as never before. In 1987, for the first time corporations bought more art than individual

Americans. Corporate art consultants act as brokers between the artist and the company. It's a growing field.

"There are jobs, too, in galleries and other arts institutions. As government funding of non-profit institutions falls, staffing becomes critical. Every cultural institution is looking for sharp, culturally aware staff to serve as grantwriters, fund raisers, publicists, program staff, volunteer coordinators, and graphic designers.

"For years the fall-back career for fine artists was teaching. The bad news is that teaching positions at all levels are shrinking, and there is no indication that is going to change. Every academic department is inundated with resumes for jobs they don't have." ■

Drugs/Cosmetics/Biological Products

You may also want to want to check out the sections on **Chemicals** and **Instruments**.

For networking in the **drug industry** and related fields, contact the following professional organizations, some of which are listed in Chapter 5:

PROFESSIONAL ORGANIZATIONS:

American Chemical Society, Portland Chapter
Oregon Society of Hospital Pharmacists
Washington Association for Biomedical Research
Washington State Pharmacists Association

For more information, you can write:

American Pharmaceutical Association
2215 Constitution Ave., N.W.
Washington, DC 20037

Association of Biotechnology Companies
1220 L St., N.W.
Washington, DC 20005

National Association of Chain Drugstores
PO Box 1417
Arlington, VA 22313

National Association of Retail Druggists
205 Daingerfield Road
Alexandria, VA 22314

Pharmaceutical Manufacturers Association
1155 15th St., N.W.
Washington, DC 20005

PROFESSIONAL PUBLICATIONS:

American Druggist
Biotechnology
Biotechnology Business
Cosmetics and Toiletries
Drug Topics
Drugstore News
Soap/Cosmetics/Chemical Specialties

DIRECTORIES:

*Biotechnology Directory: Products, Companies, Research &
    Organizations* (The Nature Press, New York, NY)
Drug Topics Red Book (Litton Publications, Oradell, NJ)
*Genetic Engineering & Biotechnology Related Firms Worldwide
    Directory* (Sittig & Noyes, Kingston, NY)
NACDS Membership Directory (National Association of Chain
    Drugstores, Arlington, VA)

EMPLOYERS Seattle/Puget Sound Area:

Apex Wholesale
521-A First Ave. N.
Seattle, WA 98109
(206) 285-2639
Non-prescription drugs, cosmetics.

Drug and Sundry Supply Co.
3201 First Ave. S.
Seattle, WA 98134
(206) 622-0234
Drug wholesaler.

Evergreen Pharmaceutical Service
402 Sixth S.
Kirkland, WA 98033
(206) 827-0416

Everylife Nutritionals
2021 15th Ave. W.
Seattle, WA 98119
(206) 285-3800
Manufactures vitamins, OTC pharmaceuticals.

Immunex Corp.
51 University St.
Seattle, WA 98101
(206) 587-0430
Develops pharmaceuticals, including cancer-fighting drugs.

Lanz International Laboratories
18930 59th Ave. N.E.
Arlington, WA 98223
(206) 435-6677
Hair and skin care products.

Lilly, Eli, and Co.
11811 Willows Rd. N.E.
Redmond, WA 98052
(206) 867-4800

Merck Sharp & Dohme
Regional Sales Office
3015 112th Ave. N.E.
Bellevue, WA 98004
(206) 822-4300

Merrell-Dow Pharmaceuticals
14042 N.E. Eighth St.
Bellevue, WA 98007
(206) 641-7087

Northwest Biotech International
5909 138th Place S.E.
Bellevue, WA 98006
(206) 644-2262
Pharmaceutical products.

Northwestern Drug Co.
801 C St. N.W.
Auburn, WA 98002
(206) 939-5550
Distributes drugs and non-drug items to independent
pharmacies, medical facilities.

Panlabs, Inc.
11804 N. Creek Parkway W.
Bothell, WA 98011
(206) 487-8200
Biological products.

Whitehall Laboratories/Division of American Home Products Corp.
915 Houser Way N.
Renton, WA 98055
(206) 255-6330
Drug wholesaler.

Wyeth-Ayerst Laboratories/Division of American Home Products Corp.
19255 80th S.
Kent, WA 98032
(206) 872-8790

EMPLOYERS Portland Area:

BioPharmaceuticals Corp.
8280 S.W. Nimbus
Beaverton, OR 97005
(503) 643-4322

Cache Cosmetic Co.
9725 S.W. Commerce Circle
Wilsonville, OR 97070
(503) 682-3426

Classi Color Studios
1934 N.E. 45th Ave.
Portland, OR 97213
(503) 281-5303

Columbia Cosmetics Manufacturers
2701 N.W. Vaughn St., Suite 416
Portland, OR 97210
(503) 295-1233

Dermacare Pharmaceutical
495 N.E. Beech Ave.
Gresham, OR 97030
(503) 669-8845

Diabetes Supply Club
3510 N.E. 57th Ave.
Portland, OR 97213
(503) 287-9303
Wholesale diabetes supplies.

Haba Supply Co.
7235 S.E. Foster Rd.
Portland, OR 97206
(503) 657-5001
Health and beauty aids wholesaler.

Markron Cosmetics
8325 S.W. Mohawk
Tualatin, OR 97062
(503) 692-6455

Option Care
8715 St. Helens Ave.
Vancouver, WA 98664
1-800-824-1990
Health and beauty aids wholesaler.

Educational Institutions

For networking in **education** and related fields, check out the following professional organizations, some of which are listed in Chapter 5:

PROFESSIONAL ORGANIZATIONS:

Educators for Social Responsibility, Portland
Health and Safety Through Education, Seattle
Independent Colleges of Washington
Medical and Health Education Association
Oregon Education Association
Oregon Music Teachers Association
Pacific Northwest Association of Independent Schools
Portland Association of Teachers
Public School Employees of Washington
Seattle Education Association
Washington Education Association
Washington Library Association

For additional information, you can write to:

American Association of School Administrators
1801 N. Moore St.
Arlington, VA 22209

American Association of University Women
2401 Virginia Ave. N.W.
Washington, DC 20037

Association of School Business Officials
11401 N. Shore Drive
Reston, VA 22090

**National Association of College and University
Business Officials**
1 Dupont Circle N.W.
Washington, DC 20036

National Education Association
1201 16th St. N.W.
Washington, DC 20036

PROFESSIONAL PUBLICATIONS:

Chronicle of Higher Education
Instructor
School Administrator
Teaching K-8
Today's Catholic Teacher

DIRECTORIES:

Guide to Secondary Schools (College Board, New York, NY)
Oregon School Directory (Oregon Dept. of Education, Salem, OR)
Pacific Northwest Assoc. of Independent Schools Directory (Pacific
    Northwest Assoc. of Independent Schools, Seattle, WA)
Paterson's American Education (Educational Directories, Mt.
    Prospect, IL)
Peterson's Guide to Independent Secondary Schools (Peterson's
    Guides, Princeton, NJ)
Public Schools USA (Williamson Publications, Charlotte, NC)
QED's School Guide (Quality Education Data, Denver, CO)
Washington Education Directory (Barbara Krohn and Assoc.,
    Seattle, WA)

EMPLOYERS Seattle/Puget Sound Area:

HIGHER EDUCATION:

Bellevue Community College
3000 Landerholm Circle S.E.
Bellevue, WA 98007
(206) 641-0111

City University
16661 Northup Way
Bellevue, WA 98008
(206) 643-2000

How To Get a Job

Clark College
1800 E. McLoughlin Blvd.
Vancouver, WA 98663
(206) 694-6521

Cornish College of the Arts
710 E. Roy St.
Seattle, WA 98102
(206) 323-1400

Edmonds Community College
20000 68th Ave. W.
Lynnwood, WA 98036
(206) 771-1500

Everett Community College
801 Wetmore Ave.
Everett, WA 98201
(206) 259-7151

Evergreen State College
Olympia, WA 98501
(206) 866-6000

Green River Community College
12401 S.E. 320th St.
Auburn, WA 98002
(206) 833-9111

Highline Community College
2400 S. 240th St.
Des Moines, WA 98198
(206) 878-3710

John Bastyr College of Naturopathic Medicine
144 N.E. 54th St.
Seattle, WA 98105
(206) 523-9585
The only accredited naturopathic college in the U.S.

Lake Washington Vocational Technical Institute
11605 132nd Ave. N.E.
Kirkland, WA 98034
206) 828-3220

North Seattle Community College
9600 College Way N.
Seattle, WA 98103
(206) 527-3600

Olympic College
16th and Chester

Bremerton, WA 98310
(206) 478-4506

Pacific Lutheran University
121st S. and Park S.
Tacoma, WA 98444
(206) 535-7185

Pierce College
9401 Far West Dr. S.W.
Tacoma, WA 98499
(206) 964-6500

Seattle Central Community College
1701 Broadway
Seattle, WA 98122
(206) 587-3800

Seattle Pacific University
Third W. and W. Nickerson
Seattle, WA 98119
(206) 281-2065

Seattle University
Broadway and Madison
Seattle, WA 98122
(206) 296-5870

Shoreline Community College
16101 Greenwood Ave. N.
Seattle, WA 98133
(206) 546-4717

Skagit Valley College
2405 College Way
Mount Vernon, WA 98273
(206) 428-1261

South Puget Sound Community College
2011 Mottman Rd. S.W.
Tumwater, WA 98502
(206) 754-7711

South Seattle Community College
6000 16th Ave. S.W.
Seattle, WA 98106
(206) 764-5300

Tacoma Community College
5900 S. 12th St.
Tacoma, WA 98465
(206) 566-5000

University of Washington
Seattle, WA 98195
(206) 543-2100

Western Washington University
Bellingham, WA 98225
(206) 676-3000

ELEMENTARY AND HIGH SCHOOLS:

Auburn School District No. 408
915 Fourth N.E.
Auburn, WA 98002
(206) 931-4916

Bellevue Public Schools District No. 405
12111 N.E. First
Bellevue, WA 98005
(206) 455-6096

Bethel School District No. 403
516 E. 176th
Spanaway, WA 98387
Personnel: (206) 536-7272
Job Information: (206) 536-7270

Bush School
405 36th Ave. E.
Seattle, WA 98112
(206) 322-7978
Private college prep; K through 12.

Centralia Public Schools District No. 401
2320 Borst
Centralia, WA 98531
(206) 736-9387

Clover Park School District No. 400
10020 Gravelly Lake Dr. S.W.
Tacoma, WA 98499
Personnel: (206) 756-8296
Job Line Personnel: (206) 756-8506

Edmonds School District No. 15
3800 196th S.W.
Lynnwood, WA 98036
Personnel Employment Inquiries: (206) 670-7021
Personnel General Information: (206) 670-7020

Enumclaw Public Schools
1221 Myrtle

Enumclaw, WA 98022
(206) 825-0070

Federal Way Public Schools
31405 18th S.
Federal Way, WA 98003
(206) 941-0100

Franklin Pierce School District No. 402
315 129th S.
Tacoma, WA 98444
(206) 537-0211

Highline Public Schools District 401
15675 Ambaum Blvd. S.W.
Seattle, WA 98166
(206) 433-2281

Issaquah School District No. 411
565 N.W. Holly
Issaquah, WA 98027
Personnel: (206) 392-0717
Job Information: (206) 392-0707

Kent School District No. 415
12033 S.E. 256th
Kent, WA 98031
Employment Applications: (206) 859-7209
Classified Job Line: (206) 859-7508

Lake Washington School District No. 414
10903 N.E. 53rd
Kirkland, WA 98033
(206) 828-3220

Lakeside School
14050 First N.E.
Seattle, WA 98125
(206) 368-3600
Private college prep; Grades 5 through 12.

Mercer Island School District No. 400
4160 86th Ave. S.E.
Mercer Island, WA 98040
(206) 236-3302

North Thurston District No. 3
305 College St. N.E.
Lacey, WA 98506
(206) 456-7641

Northshore School District No. 417
18315 Bothell Way N.E.
Bothell, WA 98011
(206) 485-0417

Olympia School District No. 111
1113 Legion Way S.E.
Olympia, WA 98501
General Information: (206) 753-8827
Personnel Cooperative—Public Schools
601 McPhee Rd. S.W.
Olympia, WA 98502
(206) 753-2855

Renton School District No. 403
435 Main Ave. S.
Renton, WA 98055
Personnel: (206) 235-2385
Employment Jobline: (206) 235-5826

Seattle School District No. 1
815 Fourth Ave. N.
Seattle, WA 98109
(206) 281-6000

Steilacoom Historical School District No. 1
510 Chambers
Steilacoom, WA 98388
(206) 588-1772

Tacoma School District No. 10
601 S. Eighth
Tacoma, WA 98405
Job Line (Certificated): (206) 596-1300
Job Line (Classified): (206) 596-1265

University Place School District No. 83
8805 40th St. W.
Tacoma, WA 98466
(206) 564-1400

Yelm Community Schools
404 Yelm Ave. W.
Yelm, WA 98597
(206) 458-1900

EMPLOYERS Portland Area:

HIGHER EDUCATION:

City University
12600 S.W. 72nd Ave.

Tigard, OR 97223
(503) 620-2900
Private university.

Clackamas Community College
19600 S. Molalla Ave.
Oregon City, OR 97045
(503) 657-8400

Clark College
1800 E. McLoughlin Blvd.
Vancouver, WA 98663
(206) 694-6521
Community college.

Columbia Christian College
9101 E. Burnside St.
Portland, OR 97216
(503) 255-7060
Liberal arts.

Concordia College/Portland
2811 N.E. Holman St.
Portland, OR 97221
(503) 288-9371
Lutheran professional/liberal arts college.

Lewis and Clark College
0615 S.W. Palatine Hill Road
Portland, OR 97219
(503) 244-6161
Independent college of liberal arts and sciences.

Linfield College
900 S. Baker St.
McMinnville, OR 97128
(503) 472-4121

Marylhurst College
Highway 43
Marylhurst, OR 97036
(503) 636-8141
Private liberal arts college.

Mount Hood Community College
26000 S.E. Stark St.
Gresham, OR 97030
(503) 667-6422

Multnomah School of the Bible
8435 N.E. Glisan St.
Portland, OR 97220

(503) 255-0332
Interdenominational evangelical bible college.

Oregon Graduate Institute
19600 N.W. Von Neumann Ave.
Beaverton, OR 97006
(503) 690-1028
Private graduate school of sciences and technology. Graduate Center houses OCATE, the Oregon Center for Advanced Technology Education, a cooperative education organization.

Oregon Health Sciences University
3181 S.W. Sam Jackson Park Road
Portland, OR 97201
(503) 279-8311

Oregon Institute of Technology, Metro Campus
1912 S.W. Sixth Ave.
Portland, OR 97207
(503) 464-3066
Public technical college.

Pacific University
2043 College Way
Forest Grove, OR 97116
(503) 357-6151
Private university.

Portland Community College
12000 S.W. 49th Ave.
Portland, OR 97219
(503) 244-6111

Portland State University
1633 S.W. Park Ave.
Portland, OR 97207
(503) 464-3000

Reed College
3203 S.E. Woodstock Blvd.
Portland, OR 97202
(503) 771-1112
Private undergraduate college.

Trend College
3209 N.E. 78th St.
Vancouver, WA 98665
(503) 283-4121
Headquarters for vocational school with 14 campuses in Oregon, Washington, and British Columbia.

University of Oregon, Portland Center
720 S.W. Second Ave.
Portland, OR 97201
(503) 464-3055
Continuing education, offering bachelor's, master's, doctorate;
all students part-time.

University of Portland
5000 N. Willamette Blvd.
Portland, OR 97203
(503) 283-7911
Private university.

Warner Pacific College
2219 S.E. 68th Ave.
Portland, OR 97215
(503) 775-4366
Christian liberal arts college.

Western Business College
505 S.W. Sixth Ave.
Portland, OR 97204
(503) 222-3225
Vocational school with campuses at Portland and Vancouver;
also operates Portland Fashion Center.

Western States Chiropractic College
2900 N.E. 132nd Ave.
Portland, OR 97230
(503) 327-3180

ELEMENTARY AND HIGH SCHOOLS:

Beaverton School District No. 48J
16550 S.W. Merlo
Beaverton, OR 97006
(503) 591-8000

Belmont School
3841 S.E. Belmont St.
Portland, OR 97214
(503) 232-8985
Private elementary school and day care center.

Centennial School District No. 28J
18135 S.E. Brooklyn
Portland, OR 97236
(503) 760-7990

David Douglas School District No. 40
1500 S.E. 130th

Portland, OR 97236
(503) 252-2900

Gladstone School District No. 115
17789 Webster Road
Gladstone, OR 97027
(503) 655-2777

Gresham Grade School District No. 4
1331 N.W. Eastman Parkway
Gresham, OR 97030
(503) 661-3000

Gresham Union High School District No. U2-20 JT
1331 N.W. Eastman Parkway
Gresham, OR 97030
(503) 661-3000

Lake Oswego School District No. 7
2455 S.W. Country Club Road
Lake Oswego, OR 97034
(503) 636-7691

Multnomah Education Service District
220 S.E. 102nd
Portland, OR 97216
(503) 255-1841

North Clackamas School District No. 12
4444 S.E. Lake Road
Milwaukie, OR 97222
(503) 653-3607

Oregon City School District No. 62
1417 12th
Oregon City, OR 97045
Job Information: (503) 657-2465

Parkrose School District No. 3
10636 N.E. Prescott
Portland, OR 97220
(503) 257-5200

Portland School District No. 1J
501 N. Dixon
Portland, OR 97227
Employment Information: (503) 280-5156
Personnel Services: (503) 249-2000

Reynolds School District No. 7
1424 N.E. 201st

Troutdale, OR 97060
(503) 661-7200

Riverdale School District No. 51J
11733 S.W. Breyman
Portland, OR 97219
(503) 636-4511

Sauvie Island School District No. 19
14445 N.W. Charlton Road
Portland, OR 97231
(503) 621-3426

Tigard School District No. 23J
13137 S.W. Pacific Highway
Tigard, OR 97223
(503) 620-1620

West Linn School District No. 3 JT
22210 S.W. Stafford Road
West Linn, OR 97068
(503) 638-9869

Electronics/Telecommunications

Be sure also to check out the sections on **Aircraft and Aerospace** and **Computers: Hardware/Software.**

For networking in the **electronics** industry and related fields, check out the following organizations, some of which are listed in Chapter 5:

PROFESSIONAL ORGANIZATIONS:

American Electronics Association
Electronic Representatives Association, Cascade Chapter, Seattle
Electronics Industry Secretaries Association (EISA)
Institute of Electrical & Electronic Engineers (IEEE), Portland and Seattle Chapters
Professionals in Telecommunications (ProTel)

For additional information, you can write to:

Electronics Industry Association
1722 I St. N.W.
Washington, DC 20006

How To Get a Job

Institute of Electrical & Electronics Engineers (IEEE)
345 E. 47th St.
New York, NY 10017

North American Telecommunications Association
2000 M St. N.W.
Washington, DC 20036

PROFESSIONAL PUBLICATIONS:

Communications Week
Electronic Business
Electronic News
Telecommunications Reports
Telephone Engineer & Management
Telephony

DIRECTORIES:

Advanced Technology in the Pacific Northwest (Quantix Data
    Services, West Linn, OR)
Directory & Buyers Guide (Telephony, Chicago,IL)
EIA Trade Directory & Membership List (Electronics Industry
    Association, Washington, DC)
Telephone Engineer & Management Directory (Edsgell, Cleveland,
    OH)
Who's Who in Technology (Gale Research, Detroit, MI)

EMPLOYERS Seattle/Puget Sound Area:

Advanced Technology Laboratories
22100 Bothell Highway S.E.
Bothell, WA 980
(206) 487-7416
Electronic diagnostic equipment for use in health care.

AT&T Business Markets Group
2901 Third Ave.
Seattle, WA 98121
(206) 443-7054
Telecommunications equipment.

Bell Industries/Farwest Manufacturing Division
18225 N.E. 76th
Redmond, WA 98052
(206) 885-4353
Electronic components.

Business Telephone Systems
19426 68th Ave. S.

Kent, WA 98032
(206) 575-1520
Telecommunications equipment.

Comtel, Inc.
1000 S.W. Seventh St.
Renton, WA 98055
(206) 228-7000
Telecommunications equipment.

Criton Technologies
10800 N.E. Eighth St.
Bellevue, WA 90004
(206) 453-9400
Aerospace and defense electronics.

Eldec Corp.
16700 13th Ave. W.
Lynnwood, WA 98046
(206) 743-1313
Electronic and electromechanical products for aerospace,
defense, and industrial applications.

Esterline Corp.
10800 N.E. Eighth St., Suite 600
Bellevue, WA 98004
(206) 453-6001
Printed circuit board drilling machinery, production machinery
for electronics and semiconductor industries.

Executone Information Systems
421 Tukwila Parkway
Seattle, WA 98188
(206) 248-6100
Telecommunications equipment.

Fluke, John Manufacturing Co.
6920 Seaway Blvd.
Everett, WA 98203
(206) 347-6100
Electronic test and measurement equipment.

GTE Northwest
1629 220th St. S.E.
Bothell, WA 98021
1-800-235-3663
Telecommunications equipment.

Interpoint Corp.
10301 Willows Road
Redmond, WA 98073
(206) 882-3100

Proprietary and custom hybrid microcircuit products for electronics industry.

Korry Electronics Co.
901 Dexter Ave. N.
Seattle, WA 98109
(206) 281-1300
Mailed inquiries only. Electronic switching equipment and related products; aircraft equipment.

Matrix Telecommunications
17533 15th Ave. N.E.
Seattle, WA 98155
(206) 362-1000

McCaw Cellular Communications
5400 Carillon Point
Kirkland, WA 98033
(206) 827-4500
Largest mobile phone company in U.S.

Memorex Telex
11000 N.E. 33rd Place, Suite 210
Bellevue, WA 98004
(206) 827-9600
Telecommunications equipment.

Northern Telecom Meridian Systems
11400 S.E. Eighth, Suite 400
Bellevue, WA 98004
(206) 453-5090
Telecommunications equipment.

Opcon, Inc.
720 80th St. S.W.
Everett, WA 98203
(206) 353-0900
Electronics and communication equipment.

Pacific Electro Dynamics
11465 Willows Rd. N.E.
Redmond, WA 98052
(206) 881-1700
Electronics components and systems, including industrial measurement devices.

Ratelco, Inc.
1260 Mercer St.
Seattle, WA 98109
(206) 624-7770
Electronics equipment, components, systems. Several radio service centers.

Stusser Electric Co.
660 S. Andover
Seattle, WA 98108
(206) 624-8770
Electrical supply distributor.

Tel Plus
401 Second Ave. S., Suite 101
Seattle, WA 98104
(206) 682-2900
Telecommunications equipment.

TIE Systems
14001 57th Ave. S.
Seattle, WA 98168
(206) 242-1224
Telecommunications equipment.

United Communications Systems
11911 N.E. First St., Suite 103
Bellevue, WA 98004
(206) 455-2800
Telecommunications equipment.

US West Information Systems
15395 S.E. 30th Place, Suite 200
Bellevue, WA 98007
(206) 747-7444
Telecommunications equipment.

US West NewVector Group
3350 161st Ave. S.E.
Bellevue, WA 98008
(206) 747-4900
Diversified cellular telephone and mobile communications
systems.

Western Marine Electronics
18500 68th Ave. N.E.
Seattle, WA 98115
(206) 481-2296
Equipment for diverse uses, including scanning and sonar
equipment, industrial measurement machinery.

EMPLOYERS Portland Area:

ACT, Inc.
7741 S.W. Cirrus Drive
Beaverton, OR 97005
(503) 796-9124
Telephone interconnect.

AT&T
2125 S.W. Fourth Ave.
Portland, OR 97201
(503) 295-5000
Telephone interconnect.

Communication Services & Engineering
3488 S.W. Cedar Hills Blvd.
Beaverton, OR 90005
(503) 626-8908
Telephone interconnect.

Electro Scientific Industries
13900 N.W. Science Park Drive
Portland, OR 97229
(503) 641-4141
Laser trimming/processing equipment for microelectronic
circuitry, electronic test equipment.

Executone Information Systems
1400 S.W Marlow St.
Portland, OR 97225
(503) 297-8471
Telephone interconnect.

GTE West
8625 S.W. Cascade Blvd.
Beaverton, OR 97005
(503) 626-6000
Telephone interconnect.

Hewlett-Packard Co.
PO Box C-006
Vancouver, WA 98668
(206) 254-8110
Precision electronics instruments.

Kentrox Industries
14375 N.W. Science Park Drive
Portland, OR 97229
(503) 643-1681
Telephone equipment.

Lanier Voice Products Division
7165 S.W. Fir Loop Drive
Tigard, OR 97223
(503) 620-9821
Telephone interconnect.

NEC America
3100 N.E. Shute Rd.
Hillsboro, OR 97124

(503) 648-5000
Fiber optics transmission equipment, microwave equipment, data modems, cellular phones, facsimiles, mini earth stations.

Northwest Information Services (NIS)
Lincoln Center, Suite 109B
10250 S.W. Greenburg Road
Portland, OR 97223
(503) 246-8585
Telecommunications consulting, data processing.

OECO Corp.
4607 S.E. International Way
Milwaukie, OR 97222
(503) 659-5999
Power supplies, transformers, and related power conversion products for electronics and aerospace industries.

Pacific Telecom
805 Broadway
Vancouver, WA 98668
(206) 696-0983
Local, national, and international telecommunications service.

Portland Paging
5901 S.W. Macadam Ave.
Portland, OR 97201
(503) 228-2255
Portland's largest paging and signaling equipment company.

Selectron, Inc.
7401 S.W. Capitol Highway
Portland, OR 97219
(503) 245-9988
Telephone interconnect.

Tektronix, Inc.
14150 S.W. Karl Braun Drive
Beaverton, OR 97077
(503) 627-7111
Electronic equipment for testing, measurement and communications; graphics workstations, computer printers.

Telepage Northwest
9620 S.W. Barbur Blvd.
Portland, OR 97219
1-800-537-2800
Paging and signaling equipment.

TIE Systems, Northwest
9130 S.W. Pioneer Court
Wilsonville, OR 97070

(503) 682-2008
Telephone interconnect.

US West
421 S.W. Oak St.
Portland, OR 97204
(503) 242-8593
Telecommunications.

US West Communications Systems
14255 S.W. Brigadoon Court
Beaverton, OR 97005
(503) 626-4778
Telephone interconnect.

Western Telephone
7600 S.W. Bridgeport Road
Durham, OR 97224
(503) 624-7600
Telephone interconnect.

Energy and Oil Companies

For networking in the **energy** industry and its related fields, check out the following organizations, some of which are listed in Chapter 5:

PROFESSIONAL ORGANIZATIONS:

Mining & Metallurgical Society of America
Oil Heat Institute of Washington
Oregon Energy Coordinators Association
Pacific Coast Gas Association
Washington Oil Marketers Association
Washington Wood Energy Association
Western States Petroleum Association

For more information, you can write to:

American Association of Petroleum Geologists
1444 S. Boulder
Tulsa, OK 74119
(918) 584-2555

American Gas Association
1515 Wilson Blvd.
Arlington, VA 22209

American Nuclear Society
555 N. Kensington Ave.
La Grange Park, IL 60525
(312) 352-6611

American Petroleum Institute
211 N. Ervay St.
Dallas, TX 75201

Clean Energy Research Institute
PO Box 248294
Coral Gables, FL 33124
(305) 284-4666

PROFESSIONAL PUBLICATIONS:

Drilling
Engineering & Mining Journal
Mining Journal
National Petroleum News
Oil and Gas Journal
Public Power
Solar Age

DIRECTORIES:

Mining Annual Review (Mining Journal, Ltd., London, England)
National Petroleum News Factbook (Hunter Publishing, Des Plaines, IL)
Oil and Gas Directory (Geophysical Directory, Houston, TX)
The Oil and Gas Journal 400 (Penwell Publishing, Tulsa, OK)
Pacific Coast Oil Directory (Petroleum Publishers, Brea, CA)
Solar Census (Aatec Publications, Ann Arbor, MI)
US Oil Industry Directory (Penwell Publishing, Tulsa, OK)
Western Mining Directory (Howell Publishing, Denver, CO)
Western Petroleum Register (Chapman Publications, Glendale, CA)
Whole World Oil Directory (National Register Publishing Company, Wilmette, IL)

EMPLOYERS Seattle/Puget Sound Area:

Arco Petroleum Products/Atlantic Richfield
7901 168th Ave. N.E.
Redmond, WA 98052
(206) 881-2113
Exploration and production of crude oil and natural gas; petroleum products, petrochemical feed stocks.

Atlantic Richfield Co.
PO Box 1127
Cherry Point
Ferndale, WA 98248
(206) 384-1500
Production of diesel and jet fuel, gasoline, other petroleum products.

Burlington Resources
999 Third Ave.
Seattle, WA 98104
(206) 467-3838
Holding company for energy and resource operations.

Cascade Natural Gas Co.
222 Fairview Ave. N.
Seattle, WA 98109
(206) 624-3900
Distribution and transport.

Mobil Oil Corp.
PO Box 8
Ferndale, WA 98248
(206) 384-1011
Area refiner of petroleum and related products.

Pacific Northern Oil Corp.
100 W. Harrison
Seattle, WA 98119
(206) 282-4421
Marketer of petroleum, gas station retailer, seller of industrial fuels.

Texaco Refining and Marketing
10602 N.E. 38th Place
Kirkland, WA 98033
(206) 827-0761

Time Oil Co.
2737 W. Commodore Way
Seattle, WA 98199
(206) 285-4400
Independent gas retailer; marketing and petroleum storage.

U.S. Oil & Refining
3001 Marshall Ave.
Tacoma, WA 98421
(206) 383-1651
Petroleum refinery.

Washington Energy Co.
815 Mercer St.

Seattle, WA 98109
(206) 622-6767
Diversified holding firm. Supplies natural gas to Puget Sound region, markets energy-saving products and systems, and develops oil and gas reserves nationwide through its subsidiaries: Washington Natural Gas Co.; Thermal Exploration, Inc.; Thermal Efficiency, Inc.; Thermal Energy, Inc., and ThermRail, Inc.

EMPLOYERS Portland Area:

McCall Oil Co./Division, McCall Oil and Chemical Corp.
808 S.W. 15th
Portland, OR 97205
(503) 228-2600
Markets petroleum products.

NERCO, Inc.
111 S.W. Columbia St.
Portland, OR 97201
(503) 797-6208
Coal mining, gas, oil development.

Northwest Natural Gas Co.
220 N.W. Second Ave.
Portland, OR 97209
(503) 220-2434
Distributor serving Portland, Willamette Valley, and northern Oregon coast.

Pacificorp
920 S.W. Sixth Ave.
Portland, OR 97204
(503) 243-5190
Diversified; provides electric power to area customers; natural resource development including coal mining.

U.S. Natural Resources
4800 S.W. Macadam Ave.
Portland, OR 97201
(503) 223-7586
Coal development, mining activities, forestry equipment.

Engineering Firms

You may also want to look at the sections on **Architecture** and **Contractors/Construction.**

For networking in **engineering** and related fields, check out the following professional organizations, some of which are listed in Chapter 5:

PROFESSIONAL ORGANIZATIONS:

American Society of Mechanical Engineers
Consulting Engineers Council of Oregon
Consulting Engineers Council of Washington
Society of Women Engineers

For additional information, you can write to:

American Institute of Plant Engineers
3975 Erie Ave.
Cincinnati, OH 45208

American Society of Civil Engineers
345 E. 47th St.
New York, NY 10017

National Society of Professional Engineers
1420 King St.
Alexandria, VA 22314

PROFESSIONAL PUBLICATIONS:

Building Design and Construction
Chemical Engineering Progress
Civil Engineering
Engineering News Record

DIRECTORIES:

American Consulting Engineers Council Directory (American Consulting Engineers Council, Washington, DC)
Directory of Contract Service Firms (C.E. Publications, Kirkland, WA)
Hi-Tech Buyers Guide: The Western States (Directories of Industry, Westminster, CA)

Official Register (American Society of Civil Engineers, New York, NY)

Who's Who in Engineering (American Association of Engineering Societies, New York, NY)

Who's Who in Technology Today (Research Publications, Woodbridge, CT)

EMPLOYERS Seattle/Puget Sound Area:

ABAM Engineers, a member of The Berger Group
33301 Ninth Ave. S.
Federal Way, WA 98003
(206) 952-6100
Civil, consulting, environmental, industrial, structural, transit engineering.

Andersen Bjornstad Kane Jacobs
220 W. Harrison
Seattle, WA 98119
(206) 285-1185
Civil, structural, industrial, transportation engineering.

Beck, R.W., and Associates
2121 Fourth Ave., Suite 600
Seattle, WA 98121
(206) 441-7500
Civil, consulting, electrical, environmental, mechanical, water resources, waste management, construction management engineering.

Brown and Caldwell
100 W. Harrison St., Suite 205
South Tower
Seattle, WA 98119
(206) 281-4000
Civil, consulting, environmental, sanitary, electrical, mechanical, hazardous materials, waste management engineering.

CH2M Hill Northwest
777 108th Ave. N.E.
Bellevue, WA 98004
(206) 453-5000
Consulting, industrial, traffic and transportation, environmental, waste management engineering.

Coffman Engineers
1601 Fifth Ave., Suite 900
Seattle, WA 98101
(206) 623-0717
Civil, consulting, electrical, energy, mechanical, structural engineering.

Ebasco Services
10900 N.E. Eighth St.
Bellevue, WA 98004
(206) 451-4500
Civil, mechanical, instrumentation/control, electrical, structural, geotechnical, chemical, transportation, environmental, construction management, consulting engineering.

Entranco Engineers
5808 Lake Washington Blvd. N.E., Suite 200
Kirkland, WA 98033
(206) 827-1300
Civil, environmental, structural, traffic and transportation engineering.

Golder Associates
4101 148th N.E.
Redmond, WA 98052
(206) 883-0777
Geotechnical, hydrogeology, environmental, waste management, foundation, consulting engineers.

Harris Group
425 Pontius Ave. N.
Seattle, WA 98109
(206) 382-7410
All major engineering disciplines.

Hart Crowser
1910 Fairview Ave. E.
Seattle, WA 98102
(206) 324-9530
Consulting, environmental, foundation, geotechnical engineering. Waste and water resources management.

HDR Engineering
11225 S.E. Sixth, Building C
Suite 200
Bellevue, WA 98004
(206) 453-1523
Civil, consulting, environmental, transportation, electrical, structural, mechanical, water and waste management engineering.

Howard Needles Tammen and Bergendoff
600 108th Ave. N.E., Suite 405
Bellevue, WA 98004
(206) 455-3555
Consulting, civil, transportation, environmental, electrical, mechanical, structural, industrial, institutional engineering.

Kramer, Chin & Mayo
1917 First Ave.
Seattle, WA 98101
(206) 443-5300
Civil, consulting, environmental, mechanical, sanitary,
structural, commercial, industrial, traffic and transportation,
waste management engineering.

Shannon & Wilson
400 N. 34th St., Suite 100
Seattle, WA 98103
(206) 632-8020
Civil, consulting, environmental, foundation, geotechnical,
waste management, structural, transportation engineering.

Skilling Ward Magnusson Barkshire
1215 Fourth Ave., Suite 2200
Seattle, WA 98161
(206) 292-1200
Civil, consulting, commercial, institutional, industrial, structural
engineering.

Sverdrup Corp.
1200 112th Ave. N.E., Suite 143-C
Bellevue, WA 98004
(206) 454-9562
Civil, consulting, electrical, mechanical, structural,
architectural, construction management, transportation
engineering.

URS Consultants
3131 Elliott Ave., Suite 300
Seattle, WA 98121
(206) 284-3131
Hazardous waste, waste and water management; civil,
industrial, environmental, sanitary, structural, traffic and
transportation engineering.

EMPLOYERS Portland Area:

CH2M Hill Northwest
2020 S.W. Fourth Ave.
Portland, OR 97201
(503) 224-9190
Civil, environmental, electrical, energy, waste management
engineering.

CRS Sirrine
4380 S.W. Macadam Ave.
Portland, OR 97201
(503) 226-2777
All major engineering disciplines.

Engineering & Design Associates, Inc.
6900 S.W. Haines Road
Tigard, OR 97223
(503) 639-8215
Electrical, mapping, computer software.

Harris Group, Inc.
1750 N.W. Front Ave.
Portland, OR 97228
(503) 228-7200
All major engineering disciplines.

Jeddeloh, Hays
3420 S.W. Macadam Ave.
Portland, OR 97201
(503) 223-7799
Mechanical, chemical, electrical, civil, structural engineering.

KPFF Consulting Engineers
421 S.W. Sixth Ave.
Portland, OR 97204
(503) 227-3251
Structural, civil engineering.

Lattice Semiconductor Corp.
5555 N.E. Moore Court
Hillsboro, OR 97124
(503) 681-0118

Mentor Graphics Corp.
8500 S.W. Creekside Place
Beaverton, OR 97005
(503) 626-7000
Computer-aided engineering systems.

Moffatt, Nichol & Bonney
1845 N.E. Couch St.
Portland, OR 97232
(503) 232-2117
Structural, planning, civil, waterfront, industrial engineering.

Otak, Inc.
17355 S.W. Boones Ferry Road
Lake Oswego, OR 97034
(503) 635-3618
Civil, environmental, highway, municipal engineering.

Pacific Engineering Corp.
9400 S.W. Barnes Road
Portland, OR 97225
(503) 297-1631

Electrical, heavy industrial, mechanical, design, nuclear, utilities engineering.

Rust International
15400 N.W. Greenbriar Parkway
Beaverton, OR 97006
(503) 645-5022
All major engineering disciplines.

SJO Consulting Engineers
1500 S.W. 12th Ave.
Portland, OR 97201
(503) 226-3921
All major engineering disciplines.

Wilsey & Ham Pacific
1099 S.W. Columbia St.
Portland, OR 97201
(503) 227-0455
Civil, transportation, landscape architecture, construction management, surveying engineering.

Film, Video, and Related Fields

You may also want to check out the section on **Media: Broadcasting/Cable TV.**

For networking in **film, videotape,** and related fields, check out these professional organizations, some of which are listed in Chapter 5:

PROFESSIONAL ORGANIZATIONS:

Film Arts Foundation
International Animated Film Association
Media Alliance
National Academy of Television Arts and Sciences, Washington Chapter
National Asian American Telecommunications Association
Washington Film and Video Association
Washington State Film and Video Office

For additional information, you can write to:

Academy of Motion Picture Arts & Sciences
8949 Wilshire Blvd.
Beverly Hills, CA 90211

American Film Institute
6430 Sunset Blvd.
Hollywood, CA 90028

International Television Association (ITVA)
6311 N. O'Connor Road, LB-51
Irving, TX 75039

PROFESSIONAL PUBLICATIONS:

American Film
Corporate Television
Film Comment
InView
Millimeter
Variety
Videography

DIRECTORIES:

Audio-Visual Communications: Who's Who (Media Horizons, New York, NY)
Audio-Visual Marketplace (R.R. Bowker, New York, NY)
Back Stage Film/Tape Syndication Directory (Back Stage Publications, New York, NY)
Bill Board International Buyers Guide (Billboard Publishers, New York, NY)
Puget Sound Finderbinder Media Directory (The McConnell Co., Seattle, WA)

EMPLOYERS Seattle/Puget Sound Area:

Aircastle Media Productions
25670 74th Ave. S.
Kent, WA 98032
(206) 854-7596
Film, video, photographic productions.

American Motion Pictures
7023 15th Ave. N.W.
Seattle, WA 98117
(206) 789-1011
Video duplication, production, post-production, audio services.

Bristol Productions, Ltd.
2401 Bristol Court S.W.
Olympia, WA 98502
(206) 754-4260
Video production, post-production.

Cameron Productions
222 Minor Ave. N.
Seattle, WA 98109
(206) 623-4103
Film, video production.

High Sierra Video Productions
7220 40th Ave. N.E.
Gig Harbor, WA 98335
(206) 265-6800

Kramer Video
2719 E. Madison St.
Seattle, WA 98112
(206) 322-6555
Video editing services.

Northwest Transforms
25670 74th Ave. S.
Kent, WA 98032
(206) 854-7596
Video services, including duplication, conversion, graphics, dubbing, subtitling, color correction.

Pacific Communications (PACCOM)
1801 E. Fourth
Olympia, WA 98506
(206) 754-7081
Full-service video production.

Royal Video Productions
3515 S.W. Alaska St.
Seattle, WA 98126
(206) 935-3563
Film, video production.

Synergy Video Productions
1201 First S.
Seattle, WA 98134
(206) 467-9436
Training, marketing, high-tech scriptwriting and production.

Telemation Productions
1200 Stewart
Seattle, WA 98101
(206) 623-5934
Full-service video production, post-production.

Third Avenue Productions
2707 Third Ave.
Seattle, WA 98121

How To Get a Job

(206) 728-8290
Video production, post-production.

Video Presentations
2326 Sixth Ave., Suite 230
Seattle, WA 98121
(206) 728-9241
Video production, editing services.

Vision Productions
3717 128th Ave. S.E.
Bellevue, WA 98006
(206) 644-0093

Western Video Services
1331 120th Ave. N.E.
Bellevue, WA 98005
(206) 454-5253
Full-service production, post-production.

EMPLOYERS Portland Area:

Aurion Video Productions
PO Box 22412
Milwaukie Branch, OR 97222
(503) 653-2927
Full-service production support.

Delta Video Productions
5215 N.E. Sandy Blvd.
Portland, OR 97213
(503) 287-1917
Pre and post-production services.

Insight Productions
17575 S.W. TV Highway, Suite 202
Beaverton, OR 97006
(503) 642-7419

Media West
10255 S.W. Arctic Drive
Beaverton, OR 97005
(503) 626-7002
Video production, editing.

Mira Film and Video
116 N. Page
Portland, OR 97227
(503) 464-0630
Full-service film and video production.

Odyssey Productions
122 N.W. Third
Portland, OR 97231
(503) 223-3480
Video and film production.

Official Productions
5755 S.W. Jean Rd.
Lake Oswego, OR 97035
(503) 697-8032
Video production.

Teknifilm Video
909 N.W. 19th Ave.
Portland, OR 97209
(503) 224-3835
Video, audio, and film laboratory.

Tyee Productions
1815 S.E. Seventh
Portland, OR 97214
(503) 231-1641
Film and video production.

Video Professionals Production Co.
630 S.E. Powell Blvd.
Portland, OR 97202
(503) 233-2141

Food/Beverage Producers and Distributors

You may also want to check out the sections on **Restaurants** and **Retailers/Wholesalers.**

For networking in the **food industry** and related fields, check out the following professional organizations, some of which are listed in Chapter 5:

PROFESSIONAL ORGANIZATIONS:

American Frozen Food Institute
National Food Processors Association, Seattle
Northwest Fisheries Association, Seattle
Northwest Food Processors Association, Seattle and Portland Chapters
Northwest Meat Processors Association, Portland
Oregon Beer and Wine Distributors Association

Oregon Brewers Association
Oregon Independent Retail Grocers Association
Pacific Seafood Processors Association, Seattle
Washington Beer and Wine Wholesale Association, Olympia
Washington Fish Growers Association
Washington State Food Dealers Association
Wine Institute
Women's Fisheries Network

For additional information, you can write to:

Dairy and Food Industries Supply Association
6245 Executive Blvd.
Rockville, MD 20852

Distilled Spirits Council
1250 I St., N.W.
Washington, DC 20005

Food Marketing Institute
1750 K St., N.W.
Washington, DC 20006

National Dairy Council
6300 N. River Rd.
Rosemont, IL 60018

National Food Distributors Association
111 E. Wacker Drive
Chicago, IL 60601

National Frozen Food Association
PO Box 398
Hershey, PA 17033

National Soft Drink Association
1101 16th St., N.W.
Washington, DC 20036

Wine & Spirits Wholesalers of America
1025 15th St. N.W.
Washington, DC 20005

PROFESSIONAL PUBLICATIONS:

Bakery Production and Marketing
Beverage World
Food and Beverage Marketing
Food Management
Foodservice Product News
Institutional Distribution

Progressive Grocer
Wines and Vines

DIRECTORIES:

Directory of the Canning, Freezing, Preserving Industry (James J.
  Judge, Westminster, MD)
Foodservice/West—Manufacturers, Brands & Sources (Harlequin
  Publications, Palos Verdes, CA)
Frozen Food Fact Book & Directory (National Frozen Food
  Association, Hershey, PA)
Grocers/West—Manufacturers, Brands & Sources (Harlequin
  Publications, Palos Verdes, CA)
Impact Yearbook: A Directory of the Wine and Spirits Industry (M.
  Shanken Communications, New York, NY)
National Beverage Marketing Directory (Beverage Marketing
  Corp., New York, NY)
NFBA Directory (National Food Brokers Association,
  Washington, DC)
Washington Food Dealer—Grocery Industry Directory (Washington
  State Food Dealers Assoc., Seattle WA)
*Wines & Vines Buyers Guide: Directory of the Wine Industry in
  North America* (The Hiaring Co., San Rafael, CA)

EMPLOYERS Seattle/Puget Sound Area:

Acme Poultry Co.
2001 21st Ave. S.
Seattle, WA 98144
(206) 324-8992

Alpac Corp.
2300 26th Ave. S.
Seattle, WA 98144
(206) 323-2932
Soft drinks.

Archway Cookies
810 N. Washington
Kent, WA 98032
(206) 852-6312

Arctic Alaska Fisheries Corp.
4250 24th W.
Seattle, WA 98199
(206) 282-3445
Bottomfish and crab; nation's largest fishing and at-sea
processing company.

Arctic Ice Cream Novelties of Seattle
1901 23rd S.

Seattle, WA 98144
(206) 324-0414

Arrowac Fisheries
4039 21st Ave. W., Suite 200
Seattle, WA 98199
(206) 282-5655

Carnation Co.
2746 N.E. 45th
Seattle, WA 98105
(206) 527-7400
Food products, pet foods.

Chateau Ste. Michelle
One Stimson Lane
Woodinville, WA 98072
(206) 488-1133
Winery.

Coast Oyster Co./Hilton Seafoods Co.
1437 Elliott Ave. W.
Seattle, WA 98119
(206) 281-4010

Columbia Winery
1445 120th Ave. N.E.
Bellevue, WA 98005
(206) 453-1977

Continental Baking Co.
1805 S. Main St.
PO Box 3226
Seattle, WA 98114
(206) 322-4242
Part of nation's largest wholesale bakery operation.

Continental Mills
7851 S. 192nd St.
Kent, WA 98032
(206) 872-8400
Prepared flour mixes, frozen products.

Crescent Foods
25 S. Hanford St.
Seattle, WA 98134
(206) 461-1400
Nuts, spices, extracts, seasoning mixes.

Darigold, Inc.
635 Elliott Ave. W.
Seattle, WA 98119

(206) 284-7220
Dairy products.

Famous Pacific Dessert Co., The
420 E. Denny Way
Seattle, WA 98122
(206) 328-1950
Wholesale and retail desserts; full-service catering.

Food Services of America
18430 E. Valley Highway
Kent, WA 98031
(206) 251-9100
Distributes food and serving equipment.

Gai's Seattle French Baking Co.
2006 S. Weller St.
Seattle, WA 98144
(206) 322-0931
Produces variety of bakery products.

Glacier Fish Co.
4601 11th Ave. N.W.
Seattle, WA 98107
(206) 782-0118

Golden Age Fisheries
111 Queen Anne Ave. N., Suite 201
Seattle, WA 98109
(206) 285-2815

Hygrade Food Products Corp.
1623 E. J St.
Tacoma, WA 98421
(206) 627-8121
Produces meat products.

Icicle Seafoods
4019 21st Ave. W.
Seattle, WA 98199
(206) 282-0988

Johnny's Food Centers
11120 Kent-Kangley Road
Kent, WA 98031
(206) 854-7500
Retail grocer.

Keeners Inc. dba K & N Meats
2900 Fourth Ave. S.
Seattle, WA 98134

(206) 628-4811
Wholesale fish, meat, poultry, and frozen foods.

Kemp Pacific Fisheries
121 S. River St. S.
Seattle, WA 98108
(206) 764-3151

Langendorf Baking Co. of Seattle
2901 Sixth Ave. S.
Seattle, WA 98124
(206) 682-2244

Lee Grocery Co.
3210 Hewitt Ave.
Everett, WA 98206
(206) 259-2145
Wholesale grocer.

Nalley's Fine Foods
3303 S. 35th
Tacoma, WA 98409
(206) 383-1621
Food products, including chili, salad dressings, soups, peanut butter, snack foods.

National Frozen Foods Corp.
2371 Eastlake Ave. E.
Seattle, WA 98102
(206) 322-8900
Frozen fruits and vegetables.

North Pacific Processors
2155 N. Northlake Way
Seattle, WA 98103
(206) 632-9900
Seafood.   -

Ocean Beauty Seafoods
1100 W. Ewing St.
Seattle, WA 98107
(206) 285-6800

Odom Corp.
26 S. Hanford
Seattle, WA 98134
(206) 623-3256
Holding company for wholesale beverage and food distribution company.

Olson's Food Stores
17525 Highway 99

Lynnwood, WA 98046
(206) 745-1266
Retail grocer.

Oroweat Foods Co.
1604 N. 34th St.
Seattle, WA 98103
(206) 634-2700
Baked goods for commercial distribution.

Pabst Brewing Co.
100 Custer Way
Tumwater, WA 98501
(206) 754-5000
Beer and malt beverages.

Pasta and Co.
2640 N.E. University Village Mall
Seattle, WA 98105
(206) 523-8594
Take-home food, specialty groceries.

Penwest, Ltd.
777 108th Ave. N.E., Suite 2390
Bellevue, WA 98004
(206) 462-6000
Produces value-added specialty carbohydrate products for use
in paper coatings, food and flavor ingredients, and agricultural
nutrition supplements.

Peter Pan Seafoods
1000 Denny Building
Sixth Ave. and Blanchard St.
Seattle, WA 98121
(206) 728-6000

Port Chatham Packing Co.
632 N.W. 46th St.
Seattle, WA 98107
(206) 783-8200
Smoked fish.

Queen Fisheries
Fishermen's Terminal
Seattle, WA 98119
(206) 284-7571
Fishery, seafood processor.

Raden, G., & Sons
18289 Olympic S.
Seattle, WA 98188

(206) 251-9300
Wine and beer wholesaler.

Rainier Brewing Co.
3100 Airport Way S.
Seattle, WA 98134
(206) 622-2600

Red Hook Brewery
3400 Phinney Ave. N.
Seattle, WA 98103
(206) 548-8000

Roman Meal Co.
2101 S. Tacoma Way
Tacoma, WA 98409
(206) 475-0964
Bread mixes, specialty bread products, cereal and grain
products.

Snoqualmie Winery
1000 Winery Road
Snoqualmie, WA 98065
(206) 888-4000

Southland Corp., North Pacific Division
1035 Andover Park W.
Tukwila, WA 98188
(206) 575-6711
Major processor of dairy products; also operates Seven-Eleven
Food Stores and other retail outlets.

Trident Seafood Corp.
5303 Shilshole Ave. N.W.
Seattle, WA 98107
(206) 783-3818

Twin City Foods
10120 269th Place N.W.
Stanwood, WA 98292
(206) 629-2111
Frozen vegetables.

Unisea, Inc.
15110 N.E. 90th St.
Redmond, WA 98073
(206) 881-8181
Seafood processor.

Vernell's Fine Candies
11959 Northup Way

Bellevue, WA 98004
(206) 455-8400

Ward's Cove Packing Co.
88 E. Hamlin St.
Seattle, WA 98105
(206) 323-3200
Seafood processor.

Western Alaska Fisheries
1111 Third Ave., Suite 1210
Seattle, WA 98101
(206) 382-0640

EMPLOYERS Portland Area:

**Blitz-Weinhard Brewing Co., a Division of G.
Heileman Brewing**
1133 W. Burnside St.
Portland, OR 97209
(503) 222-4351
Malt beverages.

Flavorland Foods
2329 Yew St.
PO Box 157
Forest Grove, OR 97116
(503) 357-7124
Processing of frozen fruits, vegetables.

Frito Lay
4808 N.W. Fruit Valley Road
Vancouver, WA 98660
(206) 694-8478
Cookies, snack items.

Gray and Co./Portland Foods
2331 23rd Ave.
PO Box 218
Forest Grove, OR 97116
(503) 357-3141
Processes maraschino cherries.

Heikes Produce Co.
535 N.W. Fourth Ave.
PO Box 471
Cornelius, OR 97113
(503) 357-7777
Frozen fruit, nuts, dried fruit, grain.

Knudsen Erath Winery
17000 N.E. Knudsen Lane

Dundee, OR 97115
(503) 538-3318

Lewis Packing Co.
PO Box 431
Gresham, OR 97030
(503) 665-8139
Frozen berries.

Nabisco Brands
100 N.E. Columbia Blvd.
Portland, OR 97211
(503) 240-7600
Cookies, snack items.

Norpac Foods (Dayton Plant No. 3)
14425 S.E. Wallace Rd.
Dayton, OR 97114
(503) 868-7204
Frozen fruits and vegetables.

Northwest Packing Co.
16 Simpson Ave.
Vancouver, WA 98660
(206) 696-4356
Cannery, primarily for fruit.

Oak Knoll Winery
Route 6, Box 184
Hillsboro, OR 97123
(503) 648-8198

Pepsi-Cola Bottling Co.
2505 N.E. Pacific St.
Portland, OR 97232
(503) 238-7000
Bottled soft drinks, beverage dispensing equipment.

Portland Bottling Co.
1321 N.E. Couch St.
Portland, OR 97232
(503) 230-7777
Bottles and distributes wholesale soft drinks and juice
products.

Reser's Fine Foods
15570 S.W. Jenkins Rd.
PO Box 8
Beaverton, OR 97075
(503) 643-6431
Salads, Mexican food, sausages, chip dip; distributes specialty
foods.

Scenic Fruit Co.
7510 S.E. Altman Rd.
Gresham, OR 97080
(503) 663-3434
Berry processing.

Sokol Blosser Winery
PO Box 399
Dundee, OR 97115
(503) 864-2282

Sysco/Continental-Portland
1750 S.E. Ochoco St.
PO Box 02179
Portland, OR 97222
(503) 652-2210
Food service distribution.

Tualatin Vineyards Winery
Route 1, Box 339
Forest Grove, OR 97116
(503) 357-5005

United Beer Distributors Co.
2615 N.W. Industrial St.
Portland, OR 97210
(503) 274-9999

United States Bakery
340 N.E. 11th Ave.
Portland, OR 97232
(503) 232-2191
Wholesale bakery.

Government

You will find some listings for individual government departments in Chapters 6 and 8.

For networking in **government** and related fields, check out the following organizations:

PROFESSIONAL ORGANIZATIONS:

Municipal League of Seattle and King County
Oregon Public Employees Union

How To Get a Job

For additional information, you can also contact:

American Society for Public Administration
1120 G St., N.W., Suite 500
Washington, DC 20036

PROFESSIONAL PUBLICATIONS:

Government Executive
Public Employee
Public Management
Public Works Magazine
Western City

DIRECTORIES:

Directory of Economic Development Organizations in Oregon
(Council for Economic Development in Oregon, Portland, OR
Directory of Planning and Community Development Agencies
(Washington State Department of Community Development, Olympia, WA)

EMPLOYERS Seattle/Puget Sound Area:

CITY GOVERNMENT:

Auburn, City of
25 W. Main
Auburn, WA 98001
Jobline: (206) 931-3077
Personnel: 931-3040

Bellevue, City of
11511 Main
Bellevue, WA 98004
Job information: (206) 455-7822
Personnel: (206) 455-6838

Bothell, City of
18305 101st N.E.
Bothell, WA 98011
(206) 486-3256

Enumclaw, City of
1339 Griffin
Enumclaw, WA 98022
(206) 825-3591

Kent, City of
220 Fourth Ave. S.
Kent, WA 98032
Job opportunities (recording): (206) 859-3375
Personnel: (206) 859-3328

Kirkland, City of
123 Fifth Ave.
Kirkland, WA 98033
Personnel: (206) 828-1113

Lacey, City of
420 College S.E.
Lacey, WA 98506
Personnel: 491-3214

Mercer Island, City of
9611 36th S.E.
Mercer Island, WA 98040
Personnel: (206) 236-3650

Olympia, City of
900 Plum, S.E.
Olympia, WA 98501
Personnel: (206) 753-8383

Puyallup, City of
218 W. Pioneer
Puyallup, WA 98371
Jobline: (206) 841-5596
Personnel: (206) 841-5551

Redmond, City of
15670 N.E. 85th
Redmond, WA 98052
Personnel: (206) 882-6479
Job information: (206) 882-6474

Renton, City of
200 Mill S.
Renton, WA 98055
Job opportunities (recording): (206) 235-2514
Personnel: (206) 235-2556

Seattle, City of
Dexter Horton Building, Floor 4
710 Second Ave.
Seattle, WA 98104
Job openings (recording): (206) 684-7999
Fire and police employment: (206) 386-1303
Fire Department personnel: (206) 386-1470
Police Department employment: (206) 684-5464

How To Get a Job

Public Library job openings: (206) 386-4120
Public Library personnel: (206) 386-4121
Municipal Court personnel: (206) 684-5652
Parks and Recreation Department personnel: (206) 684-7063
Seattle Center personnel/job openings: (206) 684-7218
Water Department personnel: (206) 684-5822

Tacoma, City of
Personnel Department
747 Market St.
Tacoma, WA 98402
Jobline: (206) 591-7466
Personnel/City Civil Service Board: (206) 591-5400

Tumwater, City of
555 Israel Road S.E.
Tumwater, WA 98501
(206) 754-5855

COUNTY GOVERNMENT:

King County Personnel Division
King County Administration Building
500 Fourth Ave.
Seattle, WA 98104
Classification and testing: (206) 296-7586
Employment openings (recording): (206) 296-5209
Personnel information: (206) 296-7340

Pierce County Personnel Department
930 Tacoma Ave. S.
Tacoma, WA 98402
Job Service Line: (206) 591-7466
Personnel: (206) 591-7480

Snohomish County
3000 Rockefeller
Everett, WA 98201
(206) 259-9411

Thurston County, Employee and Administrative Services
921 Lakeridge Drive S.W.
Olympia, WA 98502
Civil Service: (206) 786-5498
Employment and training: (206) 786-5586
Job search network: (206) 786-5416
Personnel: (206) 786-5498
Personnel jobline: (206) 786-5499

STATE OF WASHINGTON:

Information
1-800-321-2808

Personnel Department
600 Franklin S.E.
Olympia, WA 98501
Administration/information: (206) 753-5368

U.S. GOVERNMENT:

Army Corps of Engineers, Seattle District Office
4735 E. Marginal Way S.
Seattle, WA 98134
Personnel: (206) 764-3739

Central Intelligence Agency
Employment: (206) 623-6114

Coast Guard, 13th District
915 Second
Seattle, WA 98104
Civilian Personnel: (206) 442-5155

Customs Service
909 First
Seattle, WA 98104
Personnel: (206) 442-8274

Department of the Air Force
McChord Air Force Base
McChord AFB, WA 98438
(206) 948-5630

Department of the Army
Fort Lewis
Fort Lewis, WA 98433
(206) 967-5014

Department of Commerce
Western Administrative Service Center
7600 Sand Point Way N.E.
Seattle, WA 98115
Personnel: 526-6053

Department of Education
915 Second
Seattle, WA 98104
(206) 442-0460

Department of Health and Human Services
Office of the Secretary, Region X
2201 Sixth
Seattle, WA 98121
Personnel: (206) 442-0566

Department of Housing and Urban Development
1321 Second
Seattle, WA 98101
Personnel: 442-7581

Department of the Interior
Pacific Northwest Regional Office
83 S. King
Seattle, WA 98104
Personnel: (206) 442-4409

Department of the Navy
Naval Station Puget Sound
7500 Sand Point Way N.E.
Seattle, WA 98115
Civilian Personnel Division: (206) 526-3598

District Court
1010 Fifth
Seattle, WA 98104
Office of Clerk: (206) 442-5598

Environmental Protection Agency
1200 Sixth
Seattle, WA 98101
Personnel: (206) 442-1240

Federal Aviation Administration
Northwest Mountain Regional Headquarters
17900 Pacific Highway S., C68966
Seattle, WA 98168
Employment inquiries: 431-2350

General Services Administration (GSA) Regional Office
15th and C St. S.W.
Auburn, WA 98001
(206) 931-7000
Property procurement and management center.

Internal Revenue Service
915 Second Ave. M/S 630
Seattle, WA 98174
Job Vacancy Hotline: (206) 442-2639
Personnel: 442-4774

Office of Personnel Management
Federal Job Information
915 Second
Seattle, WA 98104
(206) 442-4365

Postal Service
Personnel/Employment
415 First N.
Seattle, WA 98109
(206) 442-6240

Puget Sound Naval Shipyard
Bremerton, WA 98314
(206) 476-3711

Small Business Administration
2615 Fourth Ave.
Seattle, WA 98121
Personnel/Administration: (206) 442-7646

Veterans Administration
915 Second
Seattle, WA 98104
Personnel/job inquiries: (206) 764-2135

EMPLOYERS Portland Area:

CITY GOVERNMENT:

Beaverton, City of
4755 S.W. Griffith Drive
Beaverton, OR 97005
Personnel: (503) 526-2200
Job Information: (503) 526-2299

Forest Grove, City of
1924 Council St.
Forest Grove, OR 97116
Personnel: (503) 359-3200

Gresham, City of
1333 N.W. Eastman Parkway
Gresham, OR 97030
Personnel: (503) 669-2309

Hillsboro, City of
205 S.E. Second
Hillsboro, OR 97123
Personnel: (503) 681-6100

How To Get a Job

Lake Oswego, City of
380 S.W. A St.
Lake Oswego, OR 97034
Personnel: (503) 635-0220

Milwaukie, City of
10722 S.E. Main
Milwaukie, OR 97222
(503) 659-5171

Oregon City, City of
320 Warner Milne Road
Oregon City, OR 97045
Personnel: (503) 657-0891

Portland, City of
1120 S.W. Fifth
Portland, OR 97204
Employment with city: (503) 248-4352
Employment/job recording: (503) 248-4573
Personnel: (503) 248-4352

Tigard, City of
13125 S.W. Hall Blvd.
Tigard, OR 97223
Personnel: (503) 639-4171

Tualatin, City of
18880 S.W. Martinazzi Ave.
Tualatin, OR 97062
(503) 692-2000

Vancouver, City of
210 E. 13th St.
Vancouver, WA 98660
(206) 696-8200

Wilsonville, City of
30000 Town Center Loop E.
Wilsonville, OR 97070
(503) 682-1011

COUNTY GOVERNMENT:

Clackamas, County of
Personnel-Civil Service
904 Main
Oregon City, OR 97045
Job information: (503) 655-8894

Multnomah, County of
Employee Services Division

1120 S.W. Fifth
Portland, OR 97204
Job recording: (503) 248-5035
Personnel: (503) 248-5015

Washington, County of
Personnel-Civil Service
150 N. First Ave.
Hillsboro, OR 97124
Courthouse B-2: (503) 648-8606
Job hotline: (503) 648-8607

U.S. GOVERNMENT:

Army Corps of Engineers
319 S.W. Pine
Portland, OR 97204
Recruitment/employment: (503) 221-6976
also:
North Pacific Division
220 N.W. Eighth
Portland, OR 97209
Personnel: (503) 221-3788

Department of Agriculture
Farmers Home Administration
1220 S.W. Third
Portland, OR 97204
Personnel: (503) 221-2733
also:
Forest Service, Pacific Northwest Region
319 S.W. Pine
Portland, OR 97204
Job Corps information: (503) 221-3223
Job information (recording): (503) 221-2200
Personnel: (503) 221-3651
also:
Soil Conservation Service, State Office
1220 S.W. Third
Portland, OR 97204
Personnel: (503) 221-2783

Department of Commerce
National Oceanic and Atmospheric Administration
Western Administrative Service Center
Job hotline (Seattle): (206) 526-6294

Department of Energy
Bonneville Power Administration
905 N.E. 11th
Portland, OR 97232

How To Get a Job

Portland employment information: (503) 230-3055
Vancouver, WA employment information: (206) 690-2091

Department of Health and Human Services
Indian Health Service
1220 S.W. Third
Portland, OR 97204
Personnel: (503) 221-2015

Department of Housing and Urban Development
520 S.W. Sixth
Portland, OR 97204
Personnel: (503) 221-2567

Department of the Interior
Bureau of Land Management
825 N.E. Multnomah
Portland, OR 97232
Personnel: 231-6288
also:
Fish and Wildlife Service, Regional Office
2501 S.W. First Ave.
Portland, OR 97201
Personnel: (503) 231-6136
Bureau of Indian Affairs
1425 N.E. Irving
Portland, OR 97232
Personnel: (503) 231-6708

Department of Transportation
U.S. Coast Guard
6767 N. Basin
Portland, OR 97217
Personnel: (503) 240-9335
also:
Federal Highway Administration Region 10
708 S.W. Third
Portland, OR 97204
Personnel: (503) 221-2044

District Court
620 S.W. Main
Portland, OR 97205
Office of Clerk: (503) 221-2202

Federal Reserve Bank of San Francisco, Portland Branch
915 S.W. Stark
PO Box 3436
Portland, OR 97208
Personnel: (503) 221-5926

Internal Revenue Service
Personnel: (503) 221-3688

Office of Personnel Management
Federal Job Information Center
1220 S.W. Third
Portland, OR 97204
(503) 221-3141

U.S. Postal Service
715 N.W. Hoyt St.
Portland, OR 97209
Personnel: (503) 294-2277

Veterans Administration
Medical Center, Portland Division
3710 S.W. U.S. Veterans Hospital Road
Portland, OR 97201
General employment information: (503) 273-5236
Personnel: 273-5235

Health Care

For networking in **health care** and related fields, check out
the following organizations, some of which are listed in
Chapter 5:

PROFESSIONAL ORGANIZATIONS:

Association of Washington Chiropractors, Seattle
Medical and Health Education Association, Bellevue, WA
Oregon Association of Hospitals
Oregon Association of Naturopathic Physicians
Oregon Chiropractic Physicians Association
Oregon Dental Association
Oregon Health Care Association
Oregon Medical Association
Oregon Nurses Association, Portland
Oregon Optometric Association
Oregon Psychiatric Association
Oregon Psychological Association
Washington Community Mental Health Council, Seattle
Washington State Dental Association, Seattle
Washington State Hospital Association, Seattle
Washington State Medical Association, Seattle
Washington State Pharmacists Association, Renton
Washington State Psychiatric Association, Seattle

How To Get a Job

Washington State Psychological Association, Seattle
Washington State, King County, and Pierce County
 Nurses Associations

For additional information, you can write to:

American Health Care Association
1201 L St. N.W.
Washington, DC 20005

American Hospital Association
840 N. Lake Shore Drive
Chicago, IL 60611

American Psychiatric Association
1400 K St. N.W.
Washington, DC 20005

American Public Health Association
1015 15th St. N.W.
Washington, DC 20005

National Association of Social Workers
7981 Eastern Ave.
Silver Spring, MD 20901

PROFESSIONAL PUBLICATIONS:

American Journal of Nursing
Health Care Systems
Healthcare Financial Management
Hospitals
Modern Healthcare
Modern Hospital

DIRECTORIES:

American Hospital Association Guide to the Healthcare Field
 (American Hospital Association, Chicago, IL)
Medical & Health Information Directory (Gale Research Co.,
 Detroit, MI)
Washington Health Care Assoc. Directory (Washington Health Car
 Assoc., Olympia, WA)

EMPLOYERS Seattle/Puget Sound Area:

Allenmore Hospital
South 19th and Union
Tacoma, WA 98405
(206) 572-2323

Auburn General Hospital
20 Second St. N.E.
Auburn, WA 98002
(206) 833-7711

Ballard Community Hospital
N.W. Market and Barnes
Seattle, WA 98107
(206) 782-2700

Ballard Convalescent Center
820 N.W. 95th St.
Seattle, WA 98117
(206) 782-0100
For-profit nursing home.

Bethany of the Northwest
3322 Broadway
Everett, WA 98201
(206) 259-5508
Non-profit nursing home.

Blue Cross of Washington and Alaska Prudent Buyer Plan
15700 Dayton Ave. N.
Seattle, WA 98111
(206) 361-3000
Preferred provider organization.

Children's Hospital and Medical Center
4800 Sand Point Way N.E.
Seattle, WA 98105
(206) 526-2000

CIGNA HealthPlan of Washington
701 Fifth Ave., Suite 2940
Seattle, WA 98104
(206) 625-8800
Health maintenance organization.

CRISTA Senior Community
19303 Fremont Ave. N.
Seattle, WA 98133
(206) 546-7400
Non-profit nursing home.

Equicor Preferred
520 Pike St., Suite 1515
Seattle, WA 98101
(206) 621-1090
Preferred provider organization.

Family Health Plan
11400 S.E. Eighth St., Suite 265
Bellevue, WA 98004
(206) 455-9936
Preferred provider organization.

First Choice Health Network
1100 Olive Way, Suite 1480
Seattle, WA 98101
(206) 292-8255
Preferred provider organization.

Foss Home
13023 Greenwood Ave. N.
Seattle, WA 98133
(206) 364-1300
Non-profit nursing home.

Fred Hutchinson Cancer Research Center
1124 Columbia
Seattle, WA 98104
(206) 467-5000

General Hospital Medical Center
14th and Colby
Everett, WA 98201
(206) 258-6300

Good Health Plan of Washington
1501 Fourth Ave., Fifth Floor
Seattle, WA 98101
(206) 622-6111
Health maintenance organization.

Good Samaritan Hospital
407 14th Ave. S.E.
Puyallup, WA 98372
(206) 848-6661

Group Health Cooperative Central Hospital
200 15th Ave. E.
Seattle, WA 98112
(206) 326-3434

Group Health Cooperative Eastside Hospital
2700 152nd Ave. N.E.
Redmond, WA 98052
(206) 883-5181

Group Health Cooperative of Puget Sound
521 Wall St.
Seattle, WA 98121

(206) 448-6565
Health maintenance organization.

Harborview Medical Center
325 Ninth Ave.
Seattle, WA 98104
(206) 223-3000

Harrison Memorial
2520 Cherry Ave.
Bremerton, WA 98310
(206) 377-3911

HealthPlus
7007 220th S.W.
Mountlake Terrace, WA 98043
(206) 670-4700
Health maintenance organization.

Highline Community Hospital
16251 Sylvester Road S.W.
Seattle, WA 98166
(206) 244-9970

Hillhaven Corp.
1148 Broadway
Tacoma, WA 98402
(206) 572-4901
Nursing home operator.

HMO Washington
1800 Terry Ave.
Seattle, WA 98101
(206) 340-6600
Health maintenance organization.

King County Medical Preferred Plan
1800 Terry Ave.
Seattle, WA 98101
(206) 464-3600
Preferred provider organization.

Lake-Vue Gardens Convalescent Center
10101 N.E. 120th
Kirkland, WA 98033
(206) 823-2323
For-profit nursing home.

Laurelwood Care Center
150 102nd Ave. S.E.
Bellevue, WA 98004

(206) 454-6166
For-profit nursing home.

Madigan Army Medical Center
Civilian Personnel
ICORPS, Fort Lewis
PO Box 33128
Fort Lewis, WA 98433
(206) 967-2131

Martha and Mary Nursing Home
19160 Front St. N.E.
PO Box 127
Poulsbo, WA 98370
(206) 779-4517
Non-profit nursing home.

Mount St. Vincent Nursing Center
4831 35th Ave. S.W.
Seattle, WA 98126
(206) 937-3700
Non-profit nursing home.

MultiCare Medical Center
315 S. K St.
Tacoma, WA 98405
(206) 594-1000

National Health Laboratories
21903 68th Ave. S.
Kent, WA 98032
(206) 395-4000
Medical testing laboratory.

Network Management
7525 S.E. 24th, Suite 200
Mercer Island, WA 98040
(206) 236-2500
Preferred provider organization.

Northwest Hospital
1550 N. 115th St.
Seattle, WA 98133
(206) 364-0500

Overlake Hospital Medical Center
1035 116th Ave. N.E.
Bellevue, WA 98004
(206) 454-4011

Pacific Health
401 Second Ave. S., Suite 300

Seattle, WA 98104
(206) 326-4645
Health maintenance organization.

Park Rose Care Center
3919 S. 19th
Tacoma, WA 98405
(206) 752-5677
For-profit nursing home.

Pierce County Medical Preferred Plan
1114 Broadway Plaza
Tacoma, WA 98402
(206) 597-6520
Preferred provider organization.

Puget Sound Hospital
215 S. 36th St.
Tacoma, WA 98408
(206) 474-0561

Qual-Med Health Plan
10700 Northup Way, Suite 280
Bellevue, WA 98009
(206) 889-3000
Health maintenance organization.

Restorative Care Center
2821 S. Walden
Seattle, WA 98144
(206) 725-2800
For-profit nursing home.

Saint Cabrini Hospital of Seattle
Madison and Terry Aves.
Seattle, WA 98014
(206) 682-0500

Seatoma Convalescent Center
2800 S. 224th St.
Des Moines, WA 98198
(206) 824-0600
For-profit nursing home.

Sherwood Terrace
2102 S. 96th St.
Tacoma, WA 98444
(206) 582-4141
For-profit nursing home.

Sisters of Providence of Washington
520 Pike

Seattle, WA 98111
(206) 464-3355
Among subsidiaries are:
Providence Hospital
916 Pacific Ave.
Everett, WA 98201
(206) 258-7123
Providence Medical Center
500 17th Ave.
Seattle, WA 98122
(206) 326-5555

SmithKline Bio-Science Laboratories
1737 Airport Way S.
Seattle, WA 98134
(206) 623-8100
Medical testing.

St. Joseph Hospital and Health Care Center
1718 S. I St.
P.O. Box 2197
Tacoma, WA 98401
(206) 627-4101

Stevens Memorial Hospital
21600 76th Ave. W.
Edmonds, WA 98202
(206) 774-0555

Swedish Hospital Medical Center
747 Summit
Seattle, WA 98104
(206) 386-6000

Tacoma Lutheran Home
1301 Highlands Parkway N.
Tacoma, WA 98407
(206) 752-7112
Non-profit nursing home.

University of Washington Medical Center
1959 N.E. Pacific St.
Seattle, WA 98195
(206) 548-3300

Valley Medical Center
400 S. 43rd St.
Renton, WA 98055
(206) 228-3430

Virginia Manor Convalescent Center
3515 Hoyt Ave.

Everett, WA 98201
(206) 259-0242
For-profit nursing home.

Virginia Mason Health Plan
1200 Fifth Ave., Suite 1919
Seattle, WA 98101
(206) 223-8844
Health maintenance organization.

Virginia Mason Hospital
1100 Ninth Ave.
Seattle, WA 98111
(206) 583-6082

Wesley Homes
816 S. 216th St.
Des Moines, WA 98198
(206) 824-5000
Non-profit nursing home.

Whatcom Medical Bureau Alternative Choice Plan
3000 Northwest Ave., CS 9953
Bellingham, WA 98227
(206) 734-8000
Preferred provider organization.

EMPLOYERS Portland Area:

Bess Kaiser Medical Center
5055 N. Greeley Ave.
Portland, OR 97217
(503) 285-9321

Blue Cross/Blue Shield of Oregon Preferred Option Plan
100 S.W. Market St.
Portland, OR 97201
(503) 225-5406
Preferred provider organization.

CareNet
PO Box 1600
Vancouver, WA 98668
(206) 256-2299
Preferred provider organization.

CODA, Inc.
210 N.E. 20th Ave.
Portland, OR 97232
(503) 239-8400
Chemical dependency treatment provider.

CPC Cedar Hills Hospital & Mental Health Clinic
10300 S.W. Eastridge St.
Portland, OR 97225
(503) 297-2252

Dammasch State Hospital
28801 S.W. 110th Ave.
Wilsonville, OR 97070
(503) 682-3111

DePaul Treatment Centers
1306 S.W. Washington St.
Portland, OR 97205
(503) 294-1449
Chemical dependency treatment provider.

Eastmoreland Hospital
2900 S.E. Steele St.
Portland, OR 97202
(503) 234-0411

Emanuel Hospital & Health Center/Healthlink
2801 N. Gantenbein Ave.
Portland, OR 97227
(503) 280-3200

Emerald Terrace
1015 N. Garrison St.
Vancouver, WA 98664
(503) 694-7501
Nursing home.

Family Health Plan
1815 S.W. Marlow St.
Portland, OR 97225
(503) 297-3806
Preferred provider organization.

Forest Grove Community Hospital
1809 Maple St.
Forest Grove, OR 97116
(503) 357-2173

Good Samaritan Hospital and Medical Center/Legacy Health Systems
1015 N.W. 22nd Ave.
Portland, OR 97210
(503) 229-7711

Health Maintenance of Oregon
1800 S.W. First Ave.
Portland, OR 97201

(503) 274-0755
Health maintenance organization.

HealthGuard Services
dba SelectCare
PO Box 10106
Eugene, OR 97440
1-800-421-0544
Health maintenance organization.

Holladay Park Medical Center/Legacy Health System
1225 N.E. Second Ave.
Portland, OR 97232
(503) 233-4567

Hooper Memorial Center
20 N.E. Union Ave.
Portland, OR 97232
(503) 238-2067
Chemical dependency treatment provider.

Kaiser Permanente
3600 N. Interstate Ave.
Portland, OR 97227
(503) 280-2050
Regional office for organization of hospitals, medical and
dental offices, chemical dependency treatment providers,
health maintenance organization, other health-related
services.

Kaiser Sunnyside Medical Center
10180 S.E. Sunnyside Road
Clackamas, OR 97015
(503) 652-2880

Legacy Health Systems
500 N.E. Multnomah St.
Portland, OR 97232
(503) 234-4500
Corporate offices for health care chain.

Mainstream Youth Program
5311 S.E. Powell Blvd.
Portland, OR 97206
(503) 777-4141
Chemical dependency treatment provider.

Managed Health Care Northwest d/b/a Caremark
2701 N.W. Vaughn St.
Portland, OR 97210
(503) 224-0409
Preferred provider organization.

Maryville Nursing Home
14645 S.W. Farmington Road
Beaverton, OR 97007
(503) 643-8626

Meridian Park Hospital/Legacy Health System
19300 S.W. 65th Ave.
Tualatin, OR 97062
(503) 692-1212

Mount Hood Medical Center/Legacy Health System
24800 S.E. Stark St.
Gresham, OR 97030
(503) 667-1122

Mount St. Joseph's Residence and Extended Care Center
3060 S.E. Stark St.
Portland, OR 97214
(503) 232-6193
Nursing home.

Native American Rehabilitation Association of the Northwest
2022 N.W. Division St.
Gresham, OR 97030
(503) 669-7889
Chemical dependency treatment provider.

Oregon Health Sciences University Hospital
3181 S.W. Sam Jackson Park Road
Portland, OR 97201
(503) 279-8311

PACC Health Plan
12901 S.E. 97th Ave.
Clackamas, OR 97015
(503) 659-4212
Health maintenance organization.
also:
PACC Preferred
Preferred provider organization at same address.

Pacific Gateway Hospital
1400 S.E. Umatilla St.
Portland, OR 97202
(503) 234-5353

PacifiCare of Oregon
7360 S.W. Hunziker Road
Tigard, OR 97223

(503) 620-9324
Health maintenance organization.

Partners National Health Plans
200 S.W. Market St.
Portland, OR 97201
(503) 221-5434
Preferred provider organization.

Physicians MedLab
6600 S.W. Hampton St.
Portland, OR 97223
(503) 284-4316
Medical testing laboratory.

Portland Adventist Convalescent Center
6040 S.E. Belmont St.
Portland, OR 97215
(503) 231-7166
Nursing home affiliated with Portland Adventist Medical
Center.

Portland Adventist Medical Center
10123 S.E. Market St.
Portland, OR 97216
(503) 257-2500

Portland Veterans Administration Medical Center
3710 S.W. U.S. Veterans Hospital Road
Portland, OR 97207
(503) 220-8262

**Portland Veterans Administration Nursing Home
Care Unit**
Fourth Plain Blvd. and O St.
Vancouver, WA 98661
(206) 696-4061

Providence Medical Center
4805 N.E. Glisan St.
Portland, OR 97213
(503) 230-1111

Providence Milwaukie Hospital
10150 S.E. 32nd Ave.
Milwaukie, OR 97222
(503) 652-8300

Rest Harbor Extended Care Center
5905 E. Powell Valley Road
Gresham, OR 97030

(503) 665-1151
Nursing home.

Rose Vista Nursing Center
5001 Columbia View Drive
Vancouver, WA 98661
(206) 696-0161

Shriners Hospital for Crippled Children
3101 S.W. Sam Jackson Park Road
Portland, OR 97201
(503) 241-5090

Sisters of Providence Good Health Plan of Oregon
1235 N.E. 47th Ave.
Portland, OR 97214
(503) 249-2981
Health maintenance organization; chemical dependency
treatment provider.

Southwest Washington Hospitals
PO Box 1600
Vancouver, WA 98668
(206) 256-2000

St. Joseph Community Hospital
600 N.E. 92nd Ave.
Vancouver, WA 98664
(206) 256-2000

St. Vincent Hospital and Medical Center
9205 S.W. Barnes Road
Portland, OR 97225
(503) 297-4411

Travelers Preferred
1211 S.W. Fifth Ave.
Portland, OR 97204
(503) 248-2000
Preferred provider organization.

Tuality Community Hospital
335 S.E. Eighth Ave.
Hillsboro, OR 97123
(503) 681-1111

Turn Around At Vancouver
600 N.E. 92nd Ave.
Vancouver, WA 98668
(206) 256-2170
Chemical dependency treatment provider.

Vancouver Memorial Hospital
3400 Main St.
Vancouver, WA 98660
(206) 696-5000

Vantage
1235 N.E. 47th Ave.
Portland, OR 97213
(503) 288-0115
Preferred provider organization.

Visiting Nurse Association/Legacy Health System
2701 N.W. Vaughn St.
PO Box 3426
Portland, OR 97208

Western Health Clinics
3777 S.E. Milwaukie Ave.
Portland, OR 97202
(503) 234-1777
Chemical dependency treatment provider.

Willamette Falls Hospital
1500 Division St.
Oregon City, OR 97045
(503) 656-1631

Willamette View Convalescent Center
13021 S.E. River Road
Milwaukie, OR 97222
(503) 652-6200

Woodland Park Hospital
10300 N.E. Hancock St.
Portland, OR 97220
(503) 257-5500

Hotels/Motels

For networking in the **hospitality** industry and related fields, you can contact the following professional organizations:

PROFESSIONAL ORGANIZATIONS:

Hotel Employees and Restaurant Employees Local 8, Seattle
Oregon Lodging Association, Portland
Oregon Restaurant and Hospitality Association, Portland

How To Get a Job

For more information, you can write to:

American Hotel and Motel Association
1201 New York Ave. N.W.
Washington, DC 20005

Hotel Sales Marketing Association International
1300 L St. N.W.
Washington, DC 20005

PROFESSIONAL PUBLICATIONS:

Hotel Management
Hotel & Motel Management
Hotels & Restaurants
Lodging Magazine
Meetings & Conventions

DIRECTORIES:

Directory of Hotel and Motel Systems (American Hotel & Motel Association,Washington, DC)
Directory Meetings & Conventions Magazine (Murdoch Magazines, New York, NY)
Hotel & Motel Red Book (American Hotel & Motel Association, Washington, DC)
Hotel/Facilities Directory (Western Assoc. News, Los Angeles, CA)

EMPLOYERS Seattle/Puget Sound Area:

Bellevue Hilton
100 112th Ave. N.E.
Bellevue, WA 98004
(206) 455-3330

Best Western Greenwood Inn
625 116th Ave. N.E.
Bellevue, WA 98004
(206) 455-9444

Doubletree Inn at Southcenter
205 Strander Blvd.
Seattle, WA 98188
(206) 246-8220

Doubletree Suites Hotel
16500 Southcenter Parkway
Seattle, WA 98188
(206) 575-8220

Edgewater Inn
2411 Alaskan Way, Pier 67
Seattle, WA 98121
(206) 728-7000

Everett Pacific Hotel
3105 Pine St.
Everett, WA 98201
(206) 339-3333

Four Seasons Olympic Hotel
411 University St.
Seattle, WA 98101
(206) 464-170

Hilton Downtown
Sixth and University
Seattle, WA 98111
(206) 624-0500

Holiday Inn Crowne Plaza
Sixth and Seneca St.
Seattle, WA 98101
(206) 464-1980

Holiday Inn of Bellevue
11211 Main St.
Bellevue, WA 98004
(206) 455-5240

Holiday Inn/Sea-Tac
17338 Pacific Highway S.
Seattle, WA 98188
(206) 248-1000

Marriott Corp.
3201 S. 176th St.
Seattle, WA 98188
(206) 241-2000
Hotel operator; restaurant and airline food-service distributor.

Mayflower Park Hotel
405 Olive Way
Seattle, WA 98101
(206) 623-8700

Radisson Hotel
17001 Pacific Highway S.
Seattle, WA 98188
(206) 244-6000

Red Lion Inn/Bellevue
300 112th Ave. S.E.
Bellevue, WA 98004
(206) 455-1300

Red Lion Inn/Sea-Tac
18740 Pacific Highway S.
Seattle, WA 98188
(206) 433-1881

Renton Inn
800 Rainier Ave. S.
Renton, WA 98057
(206) 226-7700

Sea-Tac Marriott Hotel
3201 S. 176th St.
Seattle, WA 98188
(206) 241-2000

Seattle Downtown Hilton
Sixth and University
Seattle, WA 98111
(206) 624-0500

Seattle Sheraton
1400 Sixth Ave.
Seattle, WA 98101
(206) 621-9000

Sheraton Tacoma Hotel
1320 Broadway Plaza
Tacoma, WA 98402
(206) 572-3200

Stouffer Madison Hotel
515 Madison
Seattle, WA 98104
(206) 583-0300

Warwick Hotel
Fourth and Lenora
Seattle, WA 98121
(206) 443-4300

Westin Hotel
1900 Fifth Ave.
Seattle, WA 98181
(206) 728-1000

EMPLOYERS Portland Area:

Embassy Suites Hotel
9000 S.W. Washington Square Road
Tigard, OR 97223
(503) 644-4000
Contact: Roger Bennett, General Manager

Execulodge/Portland Airport
6221 N.E. 82nd Ave.
Portland, OR 97220
(503) 255-6511
Contact: Ron Mead, General Manager

Greenwood Inn, The
10700 S.W. Allen Blvd.
Beaverton, OR 97005
(503) 643-7444
Contact by letter: Dave Murray, General Manager

Heathman Hotel, The
S.W. Broadway and Salmon St.
Portland, OR 97205
(503) 241-4100
Contact: Beverly Beam, Personnel Director

Holiday Inn Portland South
25425 S.W. Boones Ferry Road
Wilsonville, OR 97070
(503) 682-2211

**Holiday Inn/Portland Airport Hotel and Trade
Center**
8439 N.E. Columbia Blvd.
Portland, OR 97220
(503) 256-5000
Contact: Teri Swarnner, Director of Personnel

Monarch Motor Hotel and Convention Center
12566 S.E. 93rd Ave.
Clackamas, OR 97015
(503) 652-1515
Contact: Lennea Cordray, Director of Personnel

Nendels Corp.
12725 S.W. 66th Ave., Suite 100
Portland, OR 97223
(503) 684-7201
Corporate office for regional chain of mid-priced hotels with
franchising headquarters in Seattle.

Portland Hilton Hotel
921 S.W. Sixth Ave.
Portland, OR 97204
(503) 226-1611
Contact: Debra Carus, Director of Human Resources

Portland Inn
1414 S.W. Sixth Ave.
Portland, OR 97201
(503) 221-1611
Contact: Betty Smith, Hotel Manager

Portland Marriott Hotel
1401 S.W. Front Ave.
Portland, OR 97201
(503) 226-7600
Contact: Betty Ederer, Director of Human Resources

Red Lion Hotel/Columbia River
1401 N. Hayden Island Drive
Portland, OR 97217
(503) 283-2111
Contact: Mark Englizian, Director of Human Resources

Red Lion Hotel/Downtown
310 S.W. Lincoln St.
Portland, OR 97201
(503) 221-0450
Contact: Mary Raglan, Director of Personnel

Red Lion Hotel/Jantzen Beach
909 N. Hayden Island Drive
Portland, OR 97217
(503) 283-4466
Contact: Mark Brigham, Director of Human Resources

Red Lion Inn/Lloyd Center
1000 N.E. Multnomah St.
Portland, OR 97232
(503) 281-6111
Contact: Tamara Deoca, Director of Human Resources

Red Lion Hotels and Inns
4001 Main St.
Vancouver, WA 98663
(206) 696-0001
Hotel chain owner/operator.

Red Lion/Inn at the Quay
100 Columbia St.
Vancouver, WA 98660

(206) 694-8341
Contact: Cerise Jolliver, Director of Human Resources

Rippling River Resort and Conference Center
68010 E. Fairway Ave.
Welches, OR 97067
(503) 622-3101
Contact: Margie O'Cain, Director of Personnel

Sheraton Portland Airport Hotel
8235 N.E. Airport Way
Portland, OR 97220
(503) 281-2500
Contact: Patrice Staley, Director of Personnel

Westin Benson, The
309 S.W. Broadway
Portland, OR 97205
(503) 228-2000
Contact: Diana Ronk, Director of Human Resources

Human Services

For networking in **human services** and related fields, check out the following organizations, some of which are listed in Chapter 5:

PROFESSIONAL ORGANIZATIONS:

National Association of Social Workers, Oregon and Washington State Chapters
Oregon Society of Association Executives
Washington Society of Association Executives

For more information, you can write to:

National Association of Social Workers
7981 Eastern Ave.
Silver Spring, MD 20910

PROFESSIONAL PUBLICATIONS:

Children and Youth Services
The Nonprofit Times
Society

DIRECTORIES:

Directory of Human Services (United Way of the Columbia-
Willamette, Portland, OR)
National Directory of Children and Youth Services (Marion
Peterson, Longmont, CO)
National Directory of Private Social Agencies (Croner Publications,
Queens, NY)

EMPLOYERS Seattle/Puget Sound Area:

American Cancer Society, Local and State Office
2120 First Ave. N.
Seattle, WA 98109
(206) 283-1152

American Diabetes Association
3201 Fremont N.
Seattle, WA 98103
(206) 632-4576

American Heart Association
4414 Woodland Park N.
Seattle, WA 98103
(206) 632-6881

American Red Cross, Seattle/King County Chapter
1900 25th Ave. S.
Seattle, WA 98144
(206) 323-2345

Association for Retarded Citizens/National Employment Training Program
1305 Fourth
Seattle, WA 98101
(206) 622-2075

Attitudinal Healing, Northwest Center
11700 First N.E.
Seattle, WA 98125
(206) 362-3897

Autism Society of America
15230 15th N.E.
Seattle, WA 98125
(206) 368-0997

Big Brothers of King County
8511 15th N.E.
Seattle, WA 98115
(206) 461-3630

also:
Eastside Branch
257 100th N.E.
Bellevue, WA 98004
(206) 462-1514
South King Branch
525 Fourth Ave. N.
Kent, WA 98032
(206) 852-1344

Boy Scouts of America, Chief Seattle Council
3120 Rainier Ave. S.
Seattle, WA 98144
(206) 725-5200

Boys and Girls Clubs of King County
107 Cherry St., Room 200
Seattle, WA 98104
(206) 461-3890

Camp Fire, Seattle/King County Council
8511 15th Ave. N.E.
Seattle, WA 98115
(206) 461-8550
also:
East King County Office
257 100th N.E.
Bellevue, WA 98004
(206) 453-7020
South King County Office
329 S. Washington
Kent, WA 98032
(206) 854-3676

Catholic Community Services, Seattle/King County
100 23rd Ave. S.
Seattle, WA 98144
(206) 323-6336
Eastside Office: (206) 643-1937
South King County: (206) 854-0077
Kent Office: (206) 854-5157
Tacoma (Seattle Tel No.): (206) 838-2073
Everett (Seattle Tel No.): (206) 622-8905

Center for Human Services
17011 Meridian Ave. N.
Seattle, WA 98133
(206) 546-2411

Childhaven
316 Broadway
Seattle, WA 98122

(206) 624-6477
Therapeutic day care for abused and neglected children, parent counseling, other related services.

Children's Home Society of Washington
3300 N.E. 65th
Seattle, WA 98115
(206) 524-6020
Auburn: (206) 854-0700
Bellevue: (206) 453-5698
Prevention and crisis intervention services for families in distress.

Crisis Clinic
1515 Dexter Ave. N.
Seattle, WA 98109
(206) 461-3210
Hotline, community information line, day care referral service.

Easter Seal Society for Crippled Children and Adults
521 Second W.
Seattle, WA 98119
(206) 281-5700

Eastside Mental Health
2840 Northup Way
Bellevue, WA 98004
(Bellevue Tel No.): (206) 455-4801/9233 or (206) 641-2999
Bothell/Northshore: (206) 486-7181

El Centro de la Raza
2524 16th S.
Seattle, WA 98144
(206) 329-9442

Family Services
107 Cherry St., Suite 500
Seattle, WA 98104
(206) 461-3883

Foundation for the Handicapped
1550 W. Armory Way, Suite 205
Seattle, WA 98119
(206) 283-4520

Girl Scouts, Totem Council
3611 Woodland Park Ave. N.
Seattle, WA 98103
(206) 633-5600

Goodwill Industries
Rainier S. and S. Dearborn

Seattle, WA 98144
(206) 329-1000
Everett: (206) 743-6470
Federal Way: (206) 941-4754

Japanese Community Service
1414 S. Weller
Seattle, WA 98144
(206) 323-0250

Jewish Federation of Greater Seattle
2031 Third
Seattle, WA 98121
(206) 622-8211

Kirkland Multi-Service Center
10021 N.E. 124th
Kirkland, WA 98033
(206) 821-7150

Leukemia Society of America
Joseph Vance Building
1402 Third Ave.
Seattle, WA 98101
(206) 628-0777

Lutheran Social Services of Washington
19230 Forest Park Drive N.E.
Seattle, WA 98155
(206) 365-2700

March of Dimes Birth Defects, Puget Sound Chapter
Securities Building
1904 Third Ave.
Seattle, WA 98101
(206) 624-1373

Medina Children's Service
123 16th Ave.
Seattle, WA 98122
(206) 461-4520
Adoption services, counseling for unplanned pregnancy,
services for pregnant teens and teen parents.

Multi-Service Centers of North and East King County
18220 96th N.E.
Bothell, WA 98011
(Seattle Tel No.): (206) 382-9704

Muscular Dystrophy Association
215 Sixth N.

Seattle, WA 98109
(206) 728-1255

National Pacific Asian Resource Center on Aging
410 United Airlines Building
2033 Sixth Ave.
Seattle, WA 98121
(206) 448-0313

Neighborhood House
905 Spruce St.
Seattle, WA 98104
(206) 461-8430
Varied services for low-income persons and families, Southeast
Asian refugees, seniors, and disabled persons.

Ruth Dykeman Children's Center
1033 S.W. 152nd St.
Seattle, WA 98166
(206) 242-1698
In-home crisis counseling for dysfunctional youth and families,
parenting classes, special education day treatment, residential
treatment, after care.

Ryther Child Center
2400 N.E. 95th St.
Seattle, WA 98115
(206) 525-5050
Variety of alcohol and substance abuse treatment programs.

Salvation Army
Northwest Divisional Headquarters
233 First Ave. W.
Seattle, WA 98119
(206) 281-4600

Seattle Children's Home
2142 Tenth Ave. W.
Seattle, WA 98119
(206) 283-3300
Rehabilitative and educational programs for mentally ill
children, teens, and young adults.

Seattle Indian Center
611 12th S.
Seattle, WA 98144
(206) 329-8700

Seattle Urban League
105 14th Ave.
Seattle, WA 98122
(206) 461-3792

Social service and job-related programs, housing counseling, educational advocacy, learning center.

Senior Services of Seattle/King County
1601 Second Ave., Suite 800
Seattle, WA 98101
(206) 448-5757

South King County Multi-Service Center
1505 S. 356th
Federal Way, WA 98003
(206) 838-6810
Renton: (206) 226-6969

TASH, The Association for People With Severe Handicaps
7010 Roosevelt Way N.E.
Seattle, WA 98115
(206) 523-8446

Travelers Aid Society
909 Fourth Ave., Room 630
Seattle, WA 98104
(206) 461-3888
Emergency and transitional services to mobile homeless persons, children, seniors, and disabled or ill persons.

United Cerebral Palsy Association of King-Snohomish Counties
4409 Interlake N.
Seattle, WA 98103
(206) 632-2827

United Indians of All Tribes Foundation
1945 Yale Place E.
Seattle, WA 98102
(206) 325-0070
Educational and social services.

United Way of King County
107 Cherry
Seattle, WA 98104
(206) 461-3700
also:
Pierce County
734 Broadway
Tacoma, WA 98402
(206) 272-4263
Snohomish County
4526 Federal Ave.
Everett, WA 98203
(206) 742-5911

How To Get a Job

Thurston County
Security Building
203 E. Fourth
Olympia, WA 98501
(206) 943-2773

Visiting Nurse Services of Seattle/King County
400 N. 34th St.
Seattle, WA 98103
(206) 548-2340

Volunteers of America
6559 35th N.E.
Seattle, WA 98115
(206) 523-3565

YMCA of Greater Seattle
909 Fourth Ave.
Seattle, WA 98104
(206) 382-5003

YWCA of Seattle/King County
1118 Fifth Ave.
Seattle, WA 98101
(206) 461-4851

EMPLOYERS Portland Area:

American Cancer Society, Oregon Division
0330 S.W. Curry
Portland, OR 97201
(503) 295-6422

American Red Cross
3131 N. Vancouver Ave.
PO Box 3200
Portland, OR 97208
(503) 284-1234

Association for Retarded Citizens
Clackamas County Office
Marylhurst Campus
Marylhurst, OR 97036
(503) 635-4318
also:
Multnomah County Office
718 W. Burnside
Portland, OR 97209
(503) 223-7279

Boys Clubs of Portland
9204 S.E. Harold

Portland, OR 97266
(503) 777-5806

Burnside Community Council
313 E. Burnside
Portland, OR 97214
(503) 231-7158
also:
Burnside Projects
435 N.W. Glisan
Portland, OR 97209
(503) 222-9362
Emergency shelter, alcohol detoxification, energy assistance, other services.

Camp Fire
718 W. Burnside
Portland, OR 97209
(503) 224-7800

Catholic Services for Children
319 S.W. Washington
Portland, OR 97204
(503) 228-6531

Christian Women Against Crime
120 N.E. Ivy
Portland, OR 97212
(503) 282-1316

Ecumenical Ministries of Oregon
0245 S.W. Bancroft St.
Portland, OR 97201
(503) 221-1054
Organization of 17 denominations conducts wide variety of social service projects.

Friendly House
1819 N.W. Everett
Portland, OR 97209
(503) 228-4335
Emergency services, senior center, community center.

Goodwill Industries of the Columbia Willamette
1831 S.E. Sixth Ave.
Portland, OR 97214
(503) 238-6100

Harry's Mother Runaway Youth Agency
2710 N.E. 14th
Portland, OR 97212
(503) 281-9900

How To Get a Job

March of Dimes
1220 S.W. Morrison
Portland, OR 97205
(503) 222-9434

Portland Impact
3534 S.E. Main
Portland, OR 97214
(503) 233-8491
Operates family resource center, senior resource and social center, youth service center.

Salvation Army, Cascade Division
1785 N.E. Sandy Blvd.
Portland, OR 97232
(503) 234-0825

United Way of the Columbia Willamette
718 W. Burnside
Portland, OR 97209
(503) 228-9131
Statewide: (503) 224-1760

YMCA of the Columbia Willamette
Metropolitan Corporate Offices
621 S.W. Alder
Portland, OR 97205
(503) 223-9622
also:
Clark County
6810 E. Fourth Plain Blvd.
Vancouver, WA 98661
(206) 695-3414

YWCA Downtown Center
1111 S.W. 10th
Portland, OR 97205
(503) 223-6281

Success in human services

One career consultant we know had nine years of experience in human services before she started her own company. Her background included work in a reform school, in a transitional home for boys leaving detention centers, and with heroin addicts, disadvantaged youths, and women in transition. Here she shares her thoughts on career opportunities in the human services and, in particular, with non-profits.

"People are successful in non-profits when they feel their work reflects their values. Non-profit professionals tend to be extroverted, intuitive, feeling types. In the human services, people must be patient, with a concern for process as much as a simple focus on results. The concern must be for the community, the environment, people, or animals.

"You must understand that you'll never be compensated in the same way you would be if you did equivalent work in the private sector. Of course, in the bigger non-profits you will be paid more. And those in management, administration, and fund raising are likely to be paid more appropriately."

When looking for human service and/or non-profit jobs, she says, "Choose your resources carefully because some of the best agencies tend to push people toward corporate work. Target your area of interest—youth, for example—and go to those agencies for informational interviews. You'll learn more than you thought you could.

"Your resume ought to begin with a summary of qualifications and then a work history. Your cover letter is even more important. Use it to pique the reader's attention and show how your unique qualifications and skills will directly benefit the organization.

"Don't forget the professional associations. I know a woman who was working for a small non-profit and began volunteering and getting very involved with professional associations. When a job as Development Director opened at the

Public Broadcasting Station, she applied. The job was a big jump for her. But because of her volunteering and range of contacts, she got the job and it's a plum."■

Instruments and Related Products

For more information about the **instrument** industry, you may want to write to the following organization:

PROFESSIONAL ORGANIZATIONS:

Instrument Society of America
67 Alexandria Drive
Research Triangle Park, NC 27709

DIRECTORIES:

Analytical Chemistry Lab Guide (American Chemical Society, Washington, DC)
Corporate Technology Directory (Corporate Technologies Information Services, Woburn, MA)
ISA Directory of Instrumentation (Instrument Society of America, Research Triangle Park, NC)
Optical Industry & Systems Purchasing Directory (Laurin Publishing, Pittsfield, MA)

EMPLOYERS Seattle/Puget Sound Area:

Advanced Technology Laboratories
22100 Bothell Highway S.E.
Bothell, WA 98021
(206) 487-7000
Surgical and medical instruments.

Cooper Vision, IOL
3190 160th Ave. S.E.
Bellevue, WA 98008
(206) 644-2400
Vision related instruments, lenses.

Eldec Corp.
16700 13th Ave. W.
Lynnwood, WA 98037
(206) 743-1313

Precision aerospace electronics, including sensing systems, monitor and control systems.

Fluke, John Manufacturing Co.
6920 Seaway Blvd.
Everett, WA 98206
(206) 347-6100
Electronic, test measurement, and calibration equipment.

Hewlett-Packard, Lake Stevens Instrument Division
8600 Soper Hill Road
Everett, WA 98205
Personnel: (206) 335-2424
also:
Hewlett-Packard Electronic Instruments
15815 S.E. 37th
Bellevue, WA 98006
(206) 643-4000
Electronic products for measurement and computation. Also has manufacturing operation in Vancouver, WA.

IDEA, Inc.
4611 S. 134th Place
Tukwila, WA 98168
(206) 244-6100
Electronic scales and testing equipment. Tukwila headquarters manufactures electronic, on-board weighing systems for trucks.

Instrumed, Inc.
12911 N.E. 126th Place
Kirkland, WA 98034
(206) 821-7377

Instrument Sales and Service
18814 72nd Ave. S.
Kent, WA 98032
(206) 251-9092

Instrumentation Northwest
14972 N.E. 31st Circle
Redmond, WA 98052
(206) 885-3729

International Biomedics
1631 220th Ave. S.E.
Bothell, WA 98021
(206) 485-2200
Surgical, medical instruments.

Kistler-Morse Corp.
10201 Willows Road N.E.
Redmond, WA 98052

(503) 881-8000
Weighing systems.

Physio-Control Corp.
11811 Willows Road N.E.
Redmond, WA 98052
(206) 867-4000
Cardiac care and related medical instruments and equipment, including defibrillators and monitors.

Quinton Instruments Co.
2121 Terry Ave.
Seattle, WA 98121
(206) 223-7373
Electronic medical instruments.

Spacelabs, Inc.
4200 150th Ave. N.E.
Redmond, WA 98052
(206) 882-3700
Medical monitoring equipment, clinical information systems.

EMPLOYERS Portland Area:

Al Smith Co.
3422 N.E. Halsey
Portland, OR 97232
(503) 234-7877
Distributes electronic test instruments, electronic components.

Branom Instrument Co.
8435 N. Interstate Place
Portland, OR 97217
(503) 283-2555
Distributors.

Eicher-Richards Co.
10180 S.W. Laurel St.
Beaverton, OR 97005
(503) 641-3300
Sales and service of electronic instruments.

Electro Scientific Industries
13900 N.W. Science Park Dr.
Portland, OR 97229
(503) 641-4141
Medical diagnostic measurement instruments, including handling, processing, and testing equipment for passive electronic components, and laser trimming systems for semiconductor and hybrid circuits industries.

Hewlett-Packard Co., Sales Office
9255 S.W. Pioneer Court
Wilsonville, OR 97070
(503) 682-8000

Instromedix, Inc.
One Technology Center
7431 N.E. Evergreen Parkway, Suite 120
Hillsboro, OR 97124
(503) 648-4576
Electronic equipment, including medical engineering and
diagnostic machinery.

Instrument Sales and Service
33 N.E. Sixth
Portland, OR 97232
(503) 239-0754

Instruments for Cardiac Research
5215 N.E. Elam Young Parkway
Hillsboro, OR 97124
(503) 640-3344

ISSPRO/Instrument Sales and Service
315 S.E. Seventh
Portland, OR 97214
(503) 232-0134

Johnson Controls
PO Box 840
Canby, OR 97013
(503) 266-2051
Batteries, air temperature control systems.

Leupold and Stevens
600 N.W. Meadow Drive
Beaverton, OR 97006
(503) 646-9171
Measurement and control equipment for varied industrial
applications.

Magni Systems
9500 S.W. Gemini Drive
Beaverton, OR 97005
(503) 626-8400
Video test and measurement products, and some personal
computer graphics products.

Northwest Test and Measurement
17200 N.W. Corridor Court
Beaverton, OR 97006
(503) 645-9000

Prescription Instrument Corp./EPIC
8052 N.E. Couch St.
Portland, OR 97213
(503) 230-1011
Medical equipment.

Rodgers Instrument Corp.
1300 N.E. 25th Ave.
Hillsboro, OR 97124
(503) 648-4181

Speedometer Service and Instrument Co.
530 N.W. 11th Ave.
Portland, OR 97209
(503) 227-5567

Tektronix, Inc.
14150 S.W. Karl Braun Drive
PO Box 500
Beaverton, OR 97077
(503) 627-7111
Test and measurement group incorporates Tek's former
instruments group; designs oscilloscopes and other electronic
test instruments.

Tempress Measurement and Control Corp.
8235 S.W. Cirrus Drive
Beaverton, OR 97005
(503) 641-1014

United Instrument
11943 N.E. Sumner St.
Portland, OR 97220
(503) 256-4243

Westcon, Inc.
5101 N. Interstate Ave.
Portland, OR 97217
(503) 283-0132
Distributes test equipment and instruments.

Insurance

For information on HMOs and PPOs, refer to the section on
Health Care.

For networking in **insurance** and related fields, check out the
following professional organizations, some of which are listed
in Chapter 5:

PROFESSIONAL ORGANIZATIONS:

Independent Insurance Agents and Brokers of King County Association
Independent Insurance Agents of Oregon
Independent Insurance Agents of Washington
Insurance Information Institute
Insurance Women of Puget Sound
Oregon Life Underwriters Association
Portland Life Underwriters Association
Professional Insurance Agents of Washington and Alaska, Tacoma and Vancouver, WA Chapters
Washington State Association of Life Underwriters, Inc.

For additional information, you can write to:

American Council of Life Insurance
1001 Pennsylvania Ave. N.W.
Washington, DC 20004

American Insurance Association
1130 Connnecticut Ave. N.W.
Washington, DC 20036

National Association of Independent Insurers
2600 River Road
Des Plaines, IL 60018

National Association of Life Underwriters
1922 F St. N.W.
Washington, DC 20006

PROFESSIONAL PUBLICATIONS:

Best's Review
Business Insurance
National Underwriter

DIRECTORIES:

Best's Directory of Recommended Insurance Adjusters (A.M. Best Co., Oldwick, NJ)
Best's Insurance Reports (A.M. Best Co., Oldwick, NJ)
Insurance Almanac (Underwriter Publishing Co., Englewood, NJ)
Underwriters' Handbook (National Underwriter Co., Cincinnati, OH)

EMPLOYERS Seattle/Puget Sound Area:

Aetna Casualty and Surety Co.
1501 Fourth Ave.
Seattle, WA 98101
(206) 467-2409
Contact: Shelly Jacobson, Human Resource Coordinator
Liability, workmen's compensation. Underwriters, claims, and
clerical only. They don't hire agents; you must contact each
individual agency, listed in the phone book.

Allstate Insurance Co.
Regional Office
3400 188th S.W., Suite 500
Lynnwood, WA 98037
(206) 778-0655
Contact: Human Resource Service
Northgate Claims Department
PO Box 24107-TAS
Seattle, WA 98124
(206) 361-1600
Life, casualty, property, home owner's, automobile, many
others.

American States Insurance Co./American Economy
Insurance Co.
115 N.E. 100th
Seattle, WA 98125
(206) 527-6400
All types of insurance; Washington branches in Bellingham and
Tacoma.

Blue Cross of Washington and Alaska
15700 Dayton Ave. N.
Seattle, WA 98133
(206) 361-3000
Jobline: (206) 361-3820

Farmers New World Life Insurance Co.
3003 77th Ave. S.E.
Mercer Island, WA 98040
(206) 232-8400

Manufacturers Life Insurance Co. of Canada
720 Olive Way, Suite 1010
Seattle, WA 98101
(206) 623-3992
Contact: Dave Bryant, Manager of Marketing and
Administrative Services

Marsh & McLennan
720 Olive Way

Seattle, WA 98101
(206) 223-1240
Local office of world's largest insurance brokerage.

Metropolitan Life Insurance Co., Evergreen Branch
9725 Third Ave. N.E., Suite 505
Seattle, WA 98115
(206) 524-4000
Numerous branch offices; each does its own hiring of sales and
clerical personnel. Company's underwriters are in another
state. Contact local branch manager for hiring information.

Milliman & Robertson
1301 Fifth Ave., Suite 3600
Seattle, WA 98101
(206) 624-7940
One of the nation's largest independent consulting actuarial
firms.

MONY Financial Services, Seattle Office
600 108th N.E., Suite 805
Bellevue, WA 98004
(206) 462-8006
Life insurance.

Mutual of Enumclaw Insurance Co.
1460 Wells Street
Enumclaw, WA 98022
(206) 825-2591
Property and casualty.

New York Life Insurance Co.
2100 Century Square
1501 Fourth Ave.
Seattle, WA 98101
(206) 682-4574
Contact for agents: Rod Oakley
Contact for clerical: Bill Mayer

SAFECO Insurance Co. of America
SAFECO Plaza
Seattle, WA 98185
(206) 545-5000
Contact: Employment Center O-2
Life, health, casualty, property, surety, auto, homeowner's,
mutual funds, real estate.

Transamerica Insurance Group, Main Office
PO Box 681
Seattle, WA 98111
1-800-262-9441
Casualty and property.

United Pacific Insurance Co.
Regional Office
33405 Eighth Ave. South, C-3000
Federal Way, WA 98003
(206) 952-7880
Life, property, and casualty.

Washington Physicians Service
Fourth and Battery, Suite 600
Seattle, WA 98121
(206) 441-9370
Contact: Ms. Chris Baruso, Vice President of Administrative
Services
Health insurance.

EMPLOYERS Portland Area:

Aetna Life Insurance Co.
PO Box 180
Portland, OR 97207
(503) 221-5580
Contact: Kathy Whitted
Group claims, government-wide claims, annuities, pensions.

American States Insurance Co./American Economy
Insurance Co.
PO Box 2100
Lake Oswego, OR 97035
(503) 684-4200
All types of insurance.

Blue Cross and Blue Shield of Oregon
100 S.W. Market St.
PO Box 1271
Portland, OR 97207
(503) 225-5402
Medical, life, and disability. Clerical only. Agents contact
marketing department.

Columbia Health Service
PO Box 2989
Vancouver, WA 98668
Portland Tel No.: (503) 283-3187
Health and accident insurance.

Farmers Insurance Group
Washington Home Office:
5306 N.E. Gher Road
Vancouver, WA 98682
(206) 253-7200
Property and casualty.
Contact for clerical and underwriting: Doug Ashbridge,

Manager of Human Resources Department
Contact for agents: John Mitchell, Sales Manager
Regional Office:
13333 S.W. 68th Parkway
Tigard, OR 97223
(503) 620-6200
Contact for clerical and underwriting: Jerry Roth, Manager of
Human Resources Department
Contact for agents: Charlie Snyder, Manager of Sales

Fred S. James and Co. of Oregon
111 S.W. Columbia St.
Portland, OR 97201
(503) 248-6400
Insurance brokerage, risk management, claims management,
employee benefit consultant, actuarial services.

Liberty Northwest Insurance Corp.
825 N.E. Multnomah St.
Portland, OR 97232
(503) 239-1391
Business and personal; property and casualty.

Manufacturers Life Insurance Co. of Canada
PO Box 3425
Portland, OR 97208
(503) 246-6789
Contact: Ron Robb, Administrative Manager

Metropolitan Life Insurance Co., Portland Branch
5335 S.W. Meadows Rd., Suite 355
Lake Oswego, OR 97035
(503) 624-7310
Numerous branch offices; each does its own hiring of sales and
clerical personnel. Company's underwriters are in another
state. Contact local branch manager for hiring information.

MONY Financial Services
210 S.W. Morrison
Portland, OR 97204
(503) 222-7100
Contact: Karelyn Backstrom, Administrative Manager
Life insurance.

Mutual Life Insurance Co. of New York
210 S.W. Morrison St.
Portland, OR 97204
(503) 222-7100

Nationwide Insurance
919 N.E. 19th Ave.
PO Box 4114

Portland, OR 97208
(503) 238-4100
Insurance sales and service.

New York Life Insurance Co.
2020 S.W. Fourth
Portland, OR 97201
(503) 226-1376
Contact for agents and clerical: Tom Teeley
North Pacific Pension Regional Office
700 N.E. Multnomah St.
Portland, OR 97232
(503) 234-0344

North Pacific Insurance Co.
1675 S.W. Marlow Ave.
PO Box 74
Portland, OR 97207
(503) 643-7661
Property and casualty insurance.

Northwestern Mutual Life Insurance Co.
1221 S.W. Yamhill St., Suite 400
Portland, OR 97205
(503) 223-7335
Contact: Debbie Powell

Oregon Dental Service
315 S.W. Fifth Ave.
Portland, OR 97204
(503) 228-6554
Second largest area health insurer.

Pacific Heritage Assurance Co.
PO Box 1020
Portland, OR 97207
(503) 221-6700
Contact: Maryann O'Connell
Health and accident insurance.

Pacific Mutual Life Insurance Co.
500 N.E. Multnomah
Portland, OR 97232
(503) 234-9631
Contact: Debra Meyer
Health and accident insurance.

Prudential Insurance Co. of America, Oregon Agency
4380 S.W. Macadam
Portland, OR 97201
(503) 266-7777
Contact: Jeff Meloy

Portland East District:
909 N. Tomahawk Island Dr.
Portland, OR 97217
(503) 283-1212
Portland West District:
10220 S.W. Greenburg Rd.
Portland, OR 97223
(503) 245-8033
Contact: Patti O'Grady
Life insurance.

Safeco Insurance Co.
4101 S.W. Kruse Way
Lake Oswego, OR 97035
(503) 635-9111
Marketing insurance to independent agents.

Standard Insurance Co.
1100 S.W. Sixth
PO Box 711
Portland, OR 97207
(503) 248-2700
Job openings: (503) 248-2884
Oregon's largest life insurance company. Home office. Does
not accept unsolicited resumes; only those for positions that
are open. Has job hotline, updated every Thursday: (503) 248-
2884

State Farm Insurance Co.
4600 25th Ave. N.E.
Salem, OR 97313
(503) 463-3000
Contact: Ivan Bullock, Personnel Manager
Life, casualty, property, homeowner's, automobile, many
others. Regional office for Washington and Oregon. There are
many claims offices and agents throughout the two states, and
they do some of their own hiring.

Transamerica Insurance Group
825 N.E. Multnomah
Portland, OR 97232
(503) 233-6571
Casualty and property.

Transamerica Occidental Life Insurance Co.
825 N.E. Multnomah, Suite 540
Portland, OR 97232
(503) 233-8661
Life insurance. Sales, clerical only. No underwriting.

Investment Bankers/Stock Brokers

You may also want to look at the sections on **Accounting** and **Banking**.

For networking in **finance** and related fields, check out the following professional organizations, some of which are listed in Chapter 5:

PROFESSIONAL ORGANIZATIONS:

Commercial Investment Brokers Association, Seattle
Institute for Certified Financial Planners (ICFP)
International Association for Financial Planning,
  Oregon and Washington Chapters
Oregon Financial Planners
Washington State Association of Certified Financial
  Planners

For additional information, you can write to:

Financial Analysts Federation
5 Boar's Head Lane
Charlottesville, VA 22903

National Association of Securities Dealers
1735 K St. N.W.
Washington, DC 20006

PROFESSIONAL PUBLICATIONS:

Corporate Financing Week
Finance
Financial Analysts Journal
Financial Executive
Financial World
Institutional Investor
Investment Dealers Digest
Securities Week
Wall Street Transcript

DIRECTORIES:

Corporate Finance Sourcebook (National Register, WIlmette, IL)
Money Market Directory (Money Market Directories,
  Charlottesville, VA)

Security Dealers of North America (Standard & Poor's, New York, NY)

EMPLOYERS Seattle/Puget Sound Area:

Bateman Eichler Hill Richards
600 University St., Suite 2010
Seattle, WA 98101
(206) 587-5775
Contact: Frank Quaney, Operations Manager

Dain Bosworth
1201 Third Avenue, Suite 2500
Seattle, WA 98101
(206) 621-3200
Contact: Doris Lattin, Associate Vice President of Human Resources

Dean Witter Reynolds
1301 Fifth Ave.
Seattle, WA 98101
(206) 464-4098
Five offices in the Puget Sound area.

Edwards, A.G. & Sons
520 Pike Tower, Suite 2420
Seattle, WA 98101
(206) 622-4451
Contact for broker positions: Robert Herrin, Vice President and Branch Manager, Seattle
Contact for other positions: Karen Sturm, Operations Manager

Harper McLean & Co.
500 Union Street, Suite 730
Seattle, WA 98101
(206) 628-3951
Contact: Cathy Shea, Office Manager

Kidder Peabody & Co., Inc.
1001 Fourth Avenue Plaza Building, Suite 2600
Seattle, WA 98154
(206) 628-8511
Contact: Sheryl Archer, Branch Administrator

Merrill Lynch, Pierce, Fenner & Smith, Inc.
1215 Fourth Ave.
Seattle, WA 98161
(206) 464-3500
Contact: Marilynne Brown, Personnel
Seven offices in the Puget Sound area.

Murphey Favre
1000 Second Ave., Suite 2700
Seattle, WA 98104
(206) 461-8900
Contact: Pam Paris, Manager of Recruiting and Employment

National Securities Corp.
500 Union St.
Seattle, WA 98101
(206) 622-7200

Oppenheimer & Co.
4000 Columbia Center
Seattle, WA 98104
(206) 447-2100
Contact: Sherri Corcoron, Personnel Administrator

Pacific First Securities Limited
1135 Broadway
Tacoma, WA 98402
(206) 383-1860
Contact: Ken Wagner, President
Located at most Pacific First Federal branches.

Paine Webber
1111 Third Ave., Suite 2300
Seattle, WA 98101
(206) 447-2400

Piper, Jaffray & Hopwood
1600 IBM Building
PO Box 34930
Seattle, WA 98124
(206) 223-3800
Contact: Annamarie Hidell, Assistant Managing Director

Prudential-Bache Securities
2400 One Union Square Building
Seattle, WA 98101
(206) 223-2500

Ragen MacKenzie
999 Third Ave., Suite 4300
Seattle, WA 98104
(206) 343-5000
Contact: Judi Sterling, Vice President
Privately held. Six western Washington offices.

Safeco Securities
Safeco Plaza
Seattle, WA 98185

(206) 545-5269
Contact: Personnel Department, 545-5000

Seattle Northwest Securities Corp.
800 Fifth Ave., Suite 3400
Seattle, WA 98104
(206) 628-2882
Contact: Shandra Tietze, Assistant Vice President
Securities, investment banking.

Shearson Lehman Hutton
999 Third Ave., 40th Floor
Seattle, WA 98104
(206) 344-3500
Contact: Karen Bowles, Administrative Manager
Several offices in the Puget Sound area.

Smith Barney, Harris Upham & Co.
1301 Fifth Ave., Suite 3229
Seattle, WA 98101
(206) 628-4400
Contact for broker positions: Gary Hirata, Senior Vice President
and Resident Manager
Contact for other positions: Sherri Calkins, Administrative
Assistant

SunAmerica Securities
425 Pike St., Suite 505
Seattle, WA 98101
(206) 622-7660
Independent contractors with six offices in the Puget Sound
area.

EMPLOYERS Portland Area:

Black & Co.
1 S.W. Columbia St.
Portland, OR 97258
(503) 248-9600
Stock brokerage.

Dean Witter Reynolds
1100 S.W. Sixth Ave.
Portland, OR 97204
(503) 221-8600
also:
10300 S.W. Greenburg Road
Portland, OR 97223
(503) 293-0411
8101 N.E. Parkway Drive
Vancouver, WA 98660

(206) 253-3161
Nationwide stock brokerage.

Edwards, A.G., & Son
4412 S.W. Barbur Blvd.
Portland, OR 97201
(503) 248-9544
also:
825 N.E. Multnomah St.
Portland, OR 97232
(503) 232-6020
1104 Main St.
Vancouver, WA 98660
(206) 693-1225
Nationwide stock brokerage.

Livingston Securities
4380 S.W. Macadam Ave.
Portland, OR 97201
(503) 294-6000
Stock brokerage.

Merrill Lynch, Pierce, Fenner & Smith
1211 S.W. Fifth Ave.
Portland, OR 97204
(503) 221-4600
Nationwide stock brokerage.

Murphey Favre
900 S.W. Fifth Ave.
Portland, OR 97204
(503) 224-2711
also:
2005 Broadway
Vancouver, WA 98663
(206) 693-3606
Stock brokerage.

Paine Webber
111 S.W. Fifth Ave.
Portland, OR 97204
(503) 226-1800
also:
700 S.W. Taylor St.
Portland, OR 97205
(503) 221-5800
Nationwide stock brokerage.

Paulson Investment Co.
811 S.W. Front St.
Portland, OR 97204

(503) 243-6000
Stock brokerage.

Piper Jaffray & Hopwood
101 S.W. Main St.
Portland, OR 97204
(503) 224-9020
also:
5285 S.W. Meadows Road
Lake Oswego, OR 97035
(503) 620-4208
Nationwide stock brokerage.

Prudential Bache Securities
2020 S.W. Fourth Ave.
Portland, OR 97201
(503) 222-9900
Nationwide stock brokerage.

Shearson Lehman Hutton
222 S.W. Columbia St.
Portland, OR 97201
(503) 243-6900
also:
1001 S.W. Fifth Ave.
Portland, OR 97204
(503) 221-6600
Nationwide stock brokerage.

Smith Barney Harris Upham & Co.
200 S.W. Market St.
Portland, OR 97201
(503) 221-7600
Nationwide stock brokerage.

U.S. Securities Clearing Corp.
10550 S.W. Allen Blvd.
Beaverton, OR 97005
(503) 626-1053
Stock brokerage.

Law Firms

For networking in **law** and related fields, check out the
following professional organizations, some of which are listed
in Chapter 5:

PROFESSIONAL ORGANIZATIONS:

Multnomah Bar Association
National Lawyers Guild, Seattle
Oregon State Bar Association
Oregon Trial Lawyers Association
Oregon Women Lawyers
Seattle/King County Bar Association
Tacoma/Pierce County Bar Association
Washington Association of Legal Secretaries
Washington State Bar Association
Washington State Trial Lawyers Association
Washington Women Lawyers

For more information, you can write to:

American Bar Association
750 N. Lake Shore Drive
Chicago, IL 60611

National Association of Bar Executives
750 N. Lake Shore Drive
Chicago, IL 60611

PROFESSIONAL PUBLICATIONS:

ABA Journal
American Lawyer
Banking Law Journal
Criminal Law Bulletin
Legal Times

DIRECTORIES:

ABA Directory (American Bar Association, Chicago, IL)
Directory of Attorneys of King County (Daily Journal of
    Commerce, Seattle, WA)
Martindale-Hubbell Law Directory (Martindale-Hubbell, Summit,
    NJ)

EMPLOYERS Seattle/Puget Sound Area:

Betts, Patterson & Mines
800 Financial Center
1215 Fourth Ave.
Seattle, WA 98161
(206) 292-9988
Contact: Lynn Frink, Personnel Manager

Bogle & Gates
Bank of California Center
900 Fourth Ave.
Seattle, WA 98164
(206) 682-5151
Contact: John Cykler, Human Resources
Seattle's second largest law firm includes consulting affiliate.

Carney Stephenson
2300 Columbia Center
701 Fifth Ave.
Seattle, WA 98104
(206) 622-8020
Contact: Carole Hammond, Personnel Director

Culp, Guterson & Grader
One Union Square, 27th Floor
600 University St.
Seattle, WA 98101
(206) 624-7141
Contact for staff positions: Gerald Ainsworth, Executive
Director
Contact for legal positions: Nancy Noble, Recruiting
Coordinator

Davis Wright Tremaine
2600 Century Square Building
1501 Fourth Ave.
Seattle, WA 98101
(206) 622-3150
Contact for staff positions: Janize Rose, Administrative
Assistant to Director of Personnel
Contact for legal positions: Carol Yuly, Employment Recruiter
Second largest law firm in Pacific Northwest includes
consulting affiliate.

Ferguson & Burdell
2900 One Union Square
Seattle, WA 98101
(206) 622-7141
Contact for staff positions: Susan Smith, Assistant Administrator
Contact for legal positions: Sue Scott, Hiring Coordinator

Foster, Pepper & Shefelman
1111 Third Ave., Suite 3400
Seattle, WA 98101
(206) 447-4400
Contact: Lee Kowbel, Personnel Manager
Firm includes consulting affiliate.

Garvey, Schubert & Barer
1011 Western Ave., 10th Floor

Seattle, WA 98104
(206) 464-3939
Contact: Diane Ball, Personnel Manager

**Gordon, Thomas, Honeywell, Malanca, Peterson &
Daheim**
1201 Pacific Ave., Suite 2200
Tacoma, WA 98402
(206) 572-5050
Contact: Mary Phelps, Personnel Coordinator

Graham & Dunn
Rainier Bank Tower, Suite 3400
1301 Fifth Ave.
Seattle, WA 98101
(206) 624-8300
Contact for staff positions: Libby Matheny, Personnel Manager
Contact for legal positions: Carmen Smith, Hiring Coordinator
Formal association with Jones, Day, Reavis & Pogue of
Cleveland, nation's second-largest law firm.

Helsell, Fetterman, Martin, Todd & Hokanson
1325 Fourth Ave., Suite 1500
Seattle, WA 98101
(206) 292-1144
Contact: Win DeForest, Business Manager

Karr Tuttle Campbell
1201 Third, Suite 2900
Seattle, WA 98101
(206) 223-1313
Also has Bellevue office.

Lane, Powell, Moss & Miller
Pacific First Centre
1420 Fifth Ave., Suite 4100
Seattle, WA 98101
(206) 223-7000
Contact: Personnel

Oles, Morrison & Rinker
3300 Columbia Center
701 Fifth Ave.
Seattle, WA 98104
(206) 623-3427
Contact for staff positions: Jeanne Wells, Business Manager
Contact for legal positions: Robert Burke, Hiring Coordinator

Perkins Coie
1201 Third Ave., Suite 4000
Seattle, WA 98101
(206) 682-8770

Contact: Ann Mary Oylear, Director of Personnel
Northwest's largest law firm; has consulting affiliate.

Preston, Thorgrimson, Shidler, Gates & Ellis
5400 Columbia Seafirst Center
701 Fifth Ave.
Seattle, WA 98104
(206) 623-7580
Contact for staff positions: Nancy Sullivan, Assistant
Employment Coordinator
Contact for legal positions: Janet Walker, Hiring Coordinator
One specialty is high-tech.

Reed, McClure, Moceri, Thonn & Moriarty
3600 Columbia Center
701 Fifth Ave.
Seattle, WA 98104
(206) 292-4900
Contact: Joni Jabker, Personnel Manager

Riddell, Williams, Bullitt & Walkinshaw
1001 Fourth Ave. Plaza, Suite 4400
Seattle, WA 98154
(206) 624-3600
Contact: Maryellen Johnson, Hiring Coordinator

Short, Cressman & Burgess
First Interstate Building, Suite 3000
999 Third Ave., 30th Floor
Seattle, WA 98104
(206) 682-3333
Contact for all positions: Christopher Soeling, Hiring
Coordinator

Stoel, Rives, Boley, Jones & Grey
Union Square Building
600 University St., Suite 3600
Seattle, WA 98101
(206) 624-0900
Contact for staff positions: Donna Baker, Records Supervisor
Contact for legal positions: Joan Watson, Hiring Coordinator

Williams, Kastner & Gibbs
1400 Washington Building
Seattle, WA 98111
(206) 461-6600
Contact: Peggy Shanahan, Personnel Manager

EMPLOYERS Portland Area:

Bullivant, Houser, Bailey, Pendergrass & Hoffman
1211 S.W. Fifth Ave.

How To Get a Job

Portland, OR 97204
(503) 228-6351

Davis Wright Tremaine
2300 First Interstate Tower
1300 S.W. Fifth Ave.
Portland, OR 97201
(503) 241-2300

Dunn, Carney, Allen, Higgins & Tongue
851 S.W. Sixth Ave.
Portland, OR 97204
(503) 224-6440

Hanna, Murphy, Jensen & Holloway
1211 S.W. Fifth Ave.
Portland, OR 97204
(503) 273-2300

Lindsay, Hart, Neil & Weigler
222 S.W. Columbia St.
Portland, OR 97201
(503) 226-1191

Miller, Nash, Wiener, Hager & Carlsen
111 S.W. Fifth Ave.
Portland, OR 97204
(503) 224-5858

Mitchell, Lang & Smith
101 S.W. Main St.
Portland, OR 97204
(503) 221-1011

Perkins Coie
111 S.W. Fifth Ave.
Portland, OR 97204
(503) 295-4400

Ragen, Tremaine, Krieger, Schmeer & Neill
1300 S.W. Fifth Ave.
Portland, OR 97201
(503) 241-2300

Rappleyea, Beck, Heiterline, Spencer & Roskie
707 S.W. Washington St.
Portland, OR 97205
(503) 224-5560

Schwabe, Williamson & Wyatt
1211 S.W. Fifth Ave.
Portland, OR 97204

(503) 222-9981
Portland's second-largest law firm.

Stoel Rives Boley Jones & Grey
900 S.W. Fifth Ave., Suite 2300
Portland, OR 97204
(503) 224-3380
Portland's largest law firm.

Tonkon, Torp, Galen, Marmaduke & Booth
1001 S.W. Fifth Ave.
Portland, OR 97204
(503) 221-1440

Management Consultants

For networking in **management consulting** and related
fields, check out the following professional organizations, some
of which are listed in Chapter 5:

PROFESSIONAL ORGANIZATIONS:

Administrative Management Society
American Management Association
American Society for Training and Development,
    Puget Sound Chapter, Seattle, and Portland
    Chapter
Association for the Integration of Management
Association of Management Consultants
Association of Management Consulting Firms
Institute of Personal Image Consultants
Pacific Northwest Personnel Management
    Association, Seattle
Society of Professional Management Consultants

For more information, you can write to:

Association of Management Consultants
331 Madison Ave.
New York, NY 10017

National Management Association
2210 Arbor Blvd.
Dayton, OH 45439

PROFESSIONAL PUBLICATIONS:

Academy of Management Journal
Academy of Management Review
Business Quarterly
Harvard Business Review
Management Review
Management Today

DIRECTORIES:

AMC Directory (Association of Management Consultants, New
   York, NY)
Directory of Management Consultants (Kennedy & Kennedy,
   Fitzwilliam, NH)
IMC Directory (Institute of Management Consultants, New
   York, NY)

EMPLOYERS Seattle/Puget Sound Area:

Alston-Kline
9336 232nd St. S.W.
Edmonds, WA 98020
(206) 546-8911

Arthur Young and Co.
One Union Square Building
600 University St., Suite 2200
Seattle, WA 98101
(206) 623-9000

Cook Newhouse and Associates
3050 152nd Ave. N.E.
Redmond, WA 98052
(206) 882-6060

Drake Beam Morin
10900 N.E. Fourth St.
Bellevue, WA 98004
(206) 454-7284

Harry J. Prior/Martech Associates
700 112th St. N.E.
Seattle, WA 98125
(206) 455-1774
Offices in Bellevue and Portland.

KPMG Peat Marwick
1301 Fifth Ave., Suite 2600
Seattle, WA 98101

(206) 292-1500
Offices also in Bellevue.

MacDonald and Wolff
7655 N.E. 205th
Bothell, WA 98011
(206) 481-8700

Management Advisory Services
2401 Fourth Ave.
Seattle, WA 98121
(206) 441-0500

Myriad Systems and Services
4900 Ninth Ave. N.W.
Seattle, WA 98107
(206) 783-6246

Pacific Coast Concepts
1516 Second Ave., Suite 300
Seattle, WA 98101
(206) 624-6024

Potentials Development
1223 N.E. Ballinger Place
Seattle, WA 98155
(206) 364-0737

Training Consultants Co.
600 Stewart St., Suite 1320
Seattle, WA 98101
(206) 441-9163

Washington Employers
2940 Fairview Ave. E.
Seattle, WA 98102
(206) 329-1120

EMPLOYERS Portland Area:

Arthur Young and Co.
1001 S.W. Fifth Ave.
Portland, OR 97204
(503) 225-1700

Attitudes For Selling
700 S.W. Taylor St., Suite 302
Portland, OR 97205
(503) 241-1988

Cascade Center for Training and Development
7180 S.W. Fir Loop

Tigard, OR 97223
(503) 639-3009

Day-Floren Associates
1020 S.W. Taylor St., Suite 400
Portland, OR 97205
(503) 226-4184

Drake Beam Morin
1001 S.W. Fifth Ave.
Portland, OR 97204
(503) 224-1321

Executive Forum
404 E. 15th St.
Vancouver, WA 98663
Portland Tel No.: (503) 283-0004

J.C. Thomas and Associates
8383 N.E. Sandy Blvd., Suite 140
Portland, OR 97229
(503) 255-4168

JIM Enterprises
1809 N.W. Johnson St., Suite 14
Portland, OR 97209
(503) 248-9477

Management/Marketing Associates
Bank of California Tower
707 S.W. Washington St.
Portland, OR 97205
(503) 228-9327

Martech Associates
Bank of California Tower
707 S.W. Washington St.
Portland, OR 97205
(503) 226-4985

McCutcheon Associates Northwest
10700 S.W. Beaverton Highway
Beaverton, OR 97005
(503) 644-1104

Northwest Career and Organizational Consulting
3815 S.W. Hall Blvd., Suite C
Beaverton, OR 97005
(503) 644-0526

Manufacturers

For networking in **manufacturing,** check out the following trade and professional organizations:

PROFESSIONAL ORGANIZATIONS:

Central Eastside Industrial Council, Portland
Industrial Designers Society of America, Northwest Chapter, Seattle
Industrial Workers District Council, Pacific Northwest, Tacoma, WA

You may also want to write to:

National Association of Manufacturers
1331 Pennsylvania Ave.
Washington, DC 20004

Other organizations representing specific types of manufacturers are listed in the *Encyclopedia of Associations* under **Directories** in Chapter 4.

PROFESSIONAL PUBLICATIONS:

Assembly Engineering
Design News
Iron Age
Manufacturing Engineering
Manufacturing Systems
Manufacturing Week
Metal Working Digest

DIRECTORIES:

Directory of Major Manufacturers—Central Puget Sound Region (Greater Seattle Chamber of Commerce, Seattle, WA)
Directory of Oregon Manufacturers (Oregon Economic Development Department, Portland, OR)
Manufacturers Directory for the Portland Metropolitan Area (Portland Chamber of Commerce, Portland, OR
Thomas Register of Manufacturers (Thomas Publishing, New York, NY)
US Industrial Directory (Cahners Publications, Stamford, CT)

EMPLOYERS Seattle/Puget Sound Area:

Ace Novelty Co.
13434 N.E. 16th St.
Bellevue, WA 98005
(206) 644-1820

Admac, Inc.
21440 68th Ave. S.
Kent, WA 98032
(206) 395-4040
Ultra-high-pressure jetting systems for industrial cleaning and
construction applications.

Ball-Incon Glass Packaging Corp.
5801 E. Marginal Way S.
Seattle, WA 98134
(206) 762-0660
Glassware.

Bayliner Marine Corp.
17825 59th Ave. N.E.
Arlington, WA 98223
(206) 435-5571
Fiberglass pleasure boats.

Carver Corp.
20121 48th Ave. W.
Lynnwood, WA 98046
(206) 775-1202
High-fidelity audio components for consumer, professional
use.

Cascade Business Forms, Division of Vanier Graphics
1545 134th N.E.
Bellevue, WA 98005
(206) 641-5800
Regional business forms manufacturer, emphasizing medical
market.

Enterprises International
Blaine and Firman Streets
Hoquiam, WA 98550
(206) 533-6222
Forest products industry machinery.

Esterline Corp.
10800 N.E. Eighth St.
Bellevue, WA 98004
(206) 453-6001
Diversified manufacturing, including printed circuit automation
and measurement instruments.

Flow International Corp.
21440 68th Ave. S.
Kent, WA 98032
(206) 872-4900
Cutting devices based on ultra-high-pressure water jets.

Genie Industries
18340 N.E. 76th
Redmond, WA 98052
(206) 881-1800
Hoists, cranes, monorail systems.

Hewlett Packard Co., Lake Stevens Division
8600 Soper Hill Road
Everett, WA 98205
(206) 335-2000
Electrical test and measurement equipment.

Honeywell, Marine Systems Division
6500 Harbour Heights Parkway
Everett, WA 98204
(206) 356-3000
Underwater acoustic equipment, including weapons and sonar systems.

Intermec Corp.
4405 Russell Road
Lynnwood, WA 98046
(206) 348-2600
Bar code data collection systems.

Interpoint Corp.
10301 Willows Road
Redmond, WA 98073
(206) 882-3100
Proprietary power converters and custom hybrid microcircuits for aerospace and industrial use.

JanSport, Inc.
2201 West Valley Highway N.
Auburn, WA 98001
(206) 735-2211
Backpacks, other outdoor equipment and clothing.

K2 Corp.
19215 99th Ave. S.W.
Vashon Island, WA 98070
(206) 463-3631
Camping and skiing equipment, other athletic, sporting goods.

Lindal Cedar Homes
4300 S. 104th Place

Seattle, WA 98178
(206) 725-0900
Custom cedar homes and sunrooms; windows, hardwood
flooring.

Marco Seattle
2300 W. Commodore Way
Seattle, WA 98199
(206) 285-3200
Commercial marine machinery, fishing equipment and vessels,
oil spill management systems, and other pollution control
products.

Milgard Manufacturing
1010 54th Ave. E.
Tacoma, WA 98411
(206) 922-6030
Windows, doors, and glass products.

Muzak
915 Yale Ave. N.
Seattle, WA 98109
(206) 682-3737
Music services delivered via satellite or on premises to
commercial and retail firms and through franchised dealers.

Nintendo of America
4820 150th Ave. N.E.
Redmond, WA 98052
(206) 882-2040
Electronic games, home video games and systems, watches.

Olympic HomeCare Products Co.
2233 112th N.E.
Bellevue, WA 98004
(206) 453-1700
Stains and paints.

PACCAR, Inc.
777 106th Ave. N.E.
Bellevue, WA 98004
(206) 455-7400
Heavy-duty trucks, truck parts, mining equipment.

Precor U.S.A.
20001 North Creek Parkway
Bothell, WA 98052
(206) 486-9292
Exercise equipment.

Preservative Paint Co.
5410 Airport Way S.

Seattle, WA 98108
(206) 763-0300

Robbins Co., The
22445 76th S.
Kent, WA 98031
(206) 872-0500
Mechanical excavation equipment for the mining and
construction industries.

Westmark International
701 Fifth Ave., Suite 6800
Seattle, WA 98104
(206) 682-6800
Advanced medical technologies.

EMPLOYERS Portland Area:

A/DEC Inc.
2601 Crestview Dr.
Newberg, OR 97132
(503) 538-9471
Dental equipment, industrial components.

Bemis Co.
1401 W. Fourth Plain Blvd.
Vancouver, WA 98660
(206) 695-1251 or (503) 285-5207
Multi-wall bags.

Blount Oregon Cutting Systems
4909 S.E. International Way
Portland, OR 97222
(503) 653-8881
Cutting chains, chain saw accessories.

Brod & McClung-Pace Co.
9800 S.E. McBrod Ave.
Portland, OR 97222
(503) 659-5880
Heating, ventilation, and air conditioning equipment.

Burns Brothers
516 S.E. Morrison St., Suite 1200
Portland, OR 97214
(503) 238-7393
Automotive/truck service stations, automotive supplies, tire
chains, flashlights.

Cascade Corp.
2020 S.W. Fourth Ave., Suite 600
Portland, OR 97201

(503) 227-0024
Material handling attachments, hydraulic cylinders.

Coe Manufacturing Co.
7930 S.W. Hunziker Road
Portland, OR 97223
(503) 639-3121
Lumber equipment, electrical sawmill equipment.

Columbia Machine
107 Grand Blvd.
Vancouver, WA 98661
(206) 694-1501 or (503) 283-5290
Concrete block plant equipment, palletizing and depalletizing
equipment.

Freightliner Corp.
4747 N. Channel Ave.
Portland, OR 97217
(503) 283-8000
Class Eight heavy-duty trucks.

Fujitsu Microelectronics
21968 N.E. Glisan
Troutdale, OR 97060
(503) 667-4032

Gerber Legendary Blades
14200 S.W. 72nd Ave.
Portland, OR 97223
(503) 639-6161
Cutlery.

Gunderson, Inc.
4350 N.W. Front Ave.
Portland, OR 97210
(503) 228-9281
Railroad freight cars.

Hyster Co., Headquarters Unit
2701 N.W. Vaughn St., Suite 900
Portland, OR 97208
(503) 721-6000
Industrial lift trucks, trailers, winches, compaction equipment,
research and development.

Kyocera Northwest
5701 E. Fourth Plain Blvd.
Vancouver, WA 98661
(206) 696-2840
Multi-layered chip capacitors.

Leupold & Stevens
600 N.W. Meadow Drive
Beaverton, OR 97075
(503) 646-9171
Rifle scopes, water record flow meters, Nosler bullets.

Mercer Industries
2636 N.W. 26th Ave.
Portland, OR 97210
(503) 226-2511
Aluminum windows and doors, insulating glass, wood millwork.

Omark Industries
5550 S.W. Macadam Blvd.
Portland, OR 97201
(503) 796-1400
Sawchains and accessories.

Owens-Illinois Glass Container
5850 N.E. 92nd Drive
Portland, OR 97220
(503) 254-7331
Glass containers.

Precision Castparts Corp.
4600 S.E. Harney Drive
Portland, OR 97206
(503) 777-3881
Aerospace components; impellers for pumps, compressors; industrial gas turbine castings; medical prosthetic castings.

Purdy Corp.
13201 N. Lombard St.
Portland, OR 97203
(503) 286-8217
Paint brushes, rollers.

Rundel Products
1100 N.E. 28th Ave.
Portland, OR 97232
(503) 284-5511
Custom vinyl products, computer software packaging, custom indexes.

SEH America
4111 N.E. 112th Ave.
Vancouver, WA 98682
(206) 254-3030
Silicon wafers.

Sulzer Bingham Pumps, Division of Guy F. Atkinson Co.
2800 N.W. Front Ave.
Portland, OR 97210
(503) 226-5200
Industrial pumps, specialty machining, and fabrication.

View-Master Ideal Group
8585 S.W. Hall Blvd.
Portland, OR 97207
(503) 644-1181
Viewers, toy products.

Viking Industries
18600 N.E. Wilkes Rd.
Portland, OR 97220
(503) 667-6030
Aluminum windows, patio doors, insulating glass.

Wacker Siltronic Corp.
7200 N.W. Front Ave.
Portland, OR 97210
(503) 243-2020
Silicon wafers.

Wagner Mining Equipment Co.
4424 N.E. 158th Ave.
Portland, OR 97220
(503) 255-2863
Underground mining equipment and vehicles.

Warn Industries
13270 S.E. Pheasant Court
Milwaukie, OR 97222
(503) 659-8750
Automatic overdrive electric winches, locking automatic hubs.

Media: Broadcasting and Cable TV

You may also want to look at the section on **Film, Video, and Related Fields.**

For networking in **TV, radio, cable TV,** and related fields, check out the following professional organizations, some of which are listed in Chapter 5:

PROFESSIONAL ORGANIZATIONS:

American Federation of TV & Radio Artists, Portland and Seattle Chapters
International Association of Business Communicators, Oregon/Columbia and Seattle Chapters
National Academy of Television Arts and Sciences, Washington Chapter, Seattle
National Asian American Telecommunications Associations
Oregon Association of Broadcasters
Pacific Northwest Cable Communications Association
Radio and Television News Directors Association
Society of Broadcast Engineers, Seattle Chapter 16
Washington State Association of Broadcasters
Women In Cable
Women in Communications, Portland and Seattle Chapters

For additional information, you can write to:

National Academy of Television Arts & Sciences
111 W. 57th St.
New York, NY 10019

National Association of Broadcasters
1771 N St. N.W.
Washington, DC 20036

National Cable Television Association
1724 Massachusetts Ave. N.W.
Washington, DC 20036

Radio-Television News Directors Association
1717 K St. N.W.
Washington, DC 20006

PROFESSIONAL PUBLICATIONS:

Billboard
Broadcast Communications
Broadcasting
Cable Age
Communications News
TV/Radio Age
Variety

DIRECTORIES:

Broadcasting / Cablecasting Yearbook (Broadcasting Publishing
Co., Washington, DC)
Greater Seattle Radio Guide (Radio Guide, Seattle, WA)
Oregon Media Guide (Center for Urban Education, Portland, OR)
Television and Cable Fact Book (Television Digest, Washington,
DC)
TV/Radio Age Twelve City Directory (TV Editorial Corp., New
York, NY)
Washington State Broadcasters Directory (Washington State Assoc.
of Broadcasters, Seattle, WA)

EMPLOYERS Seattle/Puget Sound Area:

**American Cable &
Communications**
4700 42nd Ave. S.W.
Seattle, WA 98116
(206) 937-2340
Design and engineering of
alternative cable systems
for hotels, motels, multi-
family residences.

KBRD FM
PO Box 11335
Tacoma, WA 98411
(206) 838-1000

KBSG AM & FM
1730 Minor Ave., 20th
Floor
Seattle, WA 98101
(206) 343-9700

**KCPQ-TV/Kelly
Television Co.**
Studio
4400 Steilacoom Blvd.
Tacoma, WA 98388
Seattle Tel No.: (206) 625-
1313

KCTS-TV
401 Mercer St. N.E.
Seattle, WA 98109
(206) 728-6463

KEZX FM
3876 Bridge Way N.
Seattle, WA 98101
(206) 633-5590

KING
333 Dexter Ave. N.
Seattle, WA 98109
AM: (206) 448-3666
FM: (206) 448-3981

King Broadcasting Co.
333 Dexter N.
Seattle, WA 98109
(206) 448-5555
Employment line: (206) 448-
3915
Television, cable, radio, mobile
production.

KIRO AM and KIRO-TV
2807 Third Ave.
Seattle, WA 98121
(206) 728-7777

KISW FM
712 Aurora Ave. N.
Seattle, WA 98109
(206) 285-7625

KIXI AM/KMGI FM
1100 Olive Way, Suite 1550
Seattle, WA 98101
(206) 622-3251

KLDY AM
South Sound Center
PO Box 3487
Lacey, WA 98503
(206) 438-1366

KLSY AM & FM
12011 N.E. First, Suite 206
Bellevue, WA 98005
(206) 454-1540

KLTX FM
190 Queen Anne Ave. N.
Seattle, WA 98109
(206) 285-2295

KMAS AM
2608 Pacific Ave. S.E.
Olympia, WA 98501
(206) 754-6341

KMPS AM & FM
113 Dexter Ave. N.
Seattle, WA 98109
(206) 443-9400

KNUA FM
1109 First Ave.
Seattle, WA 98101
(206) 292-8600

KOMO AM
100 Fourth Ave. N.
Seattle, WA 98109
(206) 443-4010

KOMO-TV/Fisher Broadcasting
100 Fourth Ave. N.
Seattle, WA 98109
(206) 443-4000
KOMO Job Line: (206) 443-6444

KPLZ FM/KVI AM
1809 Seventh Ave., Suite 200
Seattle, WA 98101
(206) 223-5700

KQEU
2914 Yelm Highway S.E.
Olympia, WA 98501
(206) 491-9200

KRPM AM & FM
22220 Marine View Drive
Seattle, WA 98198
(206) 343-9145

KSEA FM
2807 Third Ave.
Seattle, WA 98121
(206) 728-5732

KSTW-TV
2033 Sixth Ave.
Seattle, WA 98121
(206) 441-1111
also:
2320 S. 19th St.
Tacoma, WA 98405
(206) 572-KSTW
Broadcast television.

KTOL AM
4414 Pacific S.E.
Lacey, WA 98503
(206) 438-1280

KTZZ-TV
945 Dexter Ave. N.
Seattle, WA 98109
(206) 282-2202

KUBE FM
120 Lakeside Ave., Suite 310
Seattle, WA 98122
(206) 322-1622

KVOS-TV
1151 Ellis St.
Bellingham, WA 98225
(206) 671-1212

KXRX FM
3131 Elliott Ave., Seventh Floor
Seattle, WA 98121
(206) 283-5979

How To Get a Job

KZOK FM
200 W. Mercer, Suite 304
Seattle, WA 98119
(206) 281-5600

**Northwest Cable
Advertising**
401 Second Ave. S.
Seattle, WA 98104
(206) 624-6464

Northwest Cable TV
3013 Third Ave. N.
Seattle, WA 98109
(206) 285-6323

**TCI Cablevision
West Coast
Administrative
Offices:**
13343 Bellevue-Redmond
Road
Bellevue, WA 98005
(206) 747-9830
Personnel (Seattle Tel
No.): Angie Granberry,
Human Resources Officer,
(206) 433-3434, Ext. 3054

also:
Studio (Seattle Tel No.): (206)
522-6672
South End Office:
15241 Pacific Highway S.
Seattle, WA 98188
(206) 433-3401
North End Office
1140 N. 94th
Seattle, WA 98103
(206) 527-7545

Viacom Cablevision
8914 Roosevelt Way N.E.
Seattle, WA 98115
(206) 527-4555

EMPLOYERS Portland Area:

Cable Northwest
1318 S.W. 12th Ave.
Portland, OR 97201
(503) 222-6403

KATU-TV/ABC
2153 N.E. Sandy Blvd.
Portland, OR 97232
(503) 231-4222

KEX
4949 S.W. Macadam
Portland, OR 97201
(503) 225-1190
Radio.

KGON FM
4614 S.W. Kelly Ave.
Portland, OR 97201
(503) 223-1441

**KGW AM/King
Broadcasting**
1501 S.W. Jefferson St.
Portland, OR 97201
(503) 226-5055

KGW-TV/NBC
1501 S.W. Jefferson St.
Portland, OR 97201
(503) 226-5000

King Broadcasting Co.
1501 S.W. Jefferson St.
Portland, OR 97201
(503) 226-5055
Communications organization
(KINK-FM, KGW-AM, KGW TV)

KINK FM
1501 S.W. Jefferson St.
Portland, OR 97201
(503) 226-5080

KKCW FM
12655 S.W. Center, Suite 500
Beaverton, OR 97005
(503) 643-5103

KKEY
1223 S.W. Stark St.
Portland, OR 97205
(503) 222-1150

KKRZ FM
4949 S.W. Macadam
Portland, OR 97201
(503) 226-0100

KMJK AM & FM
9500 S.W. Barbur Blvd.
Portland, OR 97219
(503) 245-1433

KOAP FM
2828 S.W. Front Ave.
Portland, OR 97201
(503) 293-1905

KOAP-TV
7140 S.W. Macadam Ave.
Portland, OR 97219
(503) 244-9900
Broadcast television.

KOIN-TV/CBS
222 S.W. Columbia
Portland, OR 97201
(503) 464-0600

KPDX-TV
910 N.E. Union Ave.
Portland, OR 97232
(503) 239-4949

KSGO AM
4614 S.W. Kelly Ave.
Portland, OR 97201
(503) 223-1441

KUIK
Route 2, Box 21
Hillsboro, OR 97123
(503) 640-1360

KUPL AM & FM
6400 S.W. Canyon Court
Portland, OR 97221
(503) 297-3311

KWJJ AM & FM
931 S.W. King Ave.
Portland, OR 97205
(503) 228-4393

KXL AM & FM
PO Box 14957
East Portland Station, OR 97214
(503) 231-0750

Metropolitan Area Communications Commission
Cable Television Regulation and Access Programming
1815 N.W. 169th Place
Beaverton, OR 97006
Portland Tel No.: (503) 220-0689

Multnomah Cable Access-Community Television
26000 S.E. Stark St.
Gresham, OR 97030
(503) 667-7636

North Willamette Telecom
150 S.E. Second Ave.
Canby, OR 97013
(503) 656-8343

Oregon Public Broadcasting
7140 S.W. Macadam Ave.
Portland, OR 97219
(503) 244-9900

Portland Cable Access
2766 N.E. Union
Portland, OR 97212
(503) 288-1515

Rogers Cable TV
3075 N.E. Sandy Blvd.
Portland, OR 97232
Portland: (503) 230-2099
East County: (503) 667-3055

TCI Cablevision of Oregon, Inc.
6327 S.W. Capitol Highway #B
Portland, OR 97201
(503) 243-7426

Media: Print

For networking in the **book, magazine and newspaper publishing** business, check out the following professional organizations, some of which are listed in Chapter 5:

PROFESSIONAL ORGANIZATIONS:

Oregon Newspaper Publishers Association
Pacific Northwest Newspaper Association, Portland OR and Tacoma, WA
Society of Professional Journalists/Sigma Delta Chi, Portland and Seattle Chapters
Washington Newspaper Publishers Association
Women in Communications, Portland and Seattle Chapters

For additional information, you can write to:

American Booksellers Association
122 E. 42nd St.
New York, NY 10017

American Newspaper Publishers Association
11600 Sunrise Valley Drive
Reston, VA 22091

Audit Bureau of Circulations
900 Meacham Road
Schaumburg, IL 60195

Magazine Publishers Association
575 Lexington Ave.
New York, NY 10022

National Press Club
529 14th St. N.W.
Washington, DC 20045

West Writers Guild of America
8955 Beverly Blvd.
Los Angeles, CA 90048

412

PROFESSIONAL PUBLICATIONS

The Columbia Journalism Review
Editor and Publisher
Folio
Oregon Publisher
Publishers Weekly
Western Publisher
The Writer
Writer's Digest

DIRECTORIES:

American Book Trade Directory (R. R. Bowker, New York, NY)
Directory of Western Book Publishers and Production Services
    (Bookbuilders West, San Francisco, CA)
Editor and Publisher International Yearbook (Editor and Publisher,
    New York, NY)
Literary Market Place (R. R. Bowker, New York, NY)
Magazine Industry Market Place (R. R. Bowker, New York, NY)
Metro Washington Media (Public Relations Plus, New Milford,
    CT)
National Directory of Magazines (Oxbridge Communications, Inc.,
    New York, NY)
Oregon Media Guide (Center for Urban Education, Portland, OR)
Pacific Northwest Publishers Directory (Pacific Northwest
    Publishers Directory, Seattle, WA)
Puget Sound Finderbinder Media Directory (The McConnell Co.,
    Seattle, WA)
Western Media Contacts (Bulldog Reporter, Berkeley, CA)
Writer's Guide to Publishing in the West (Pinnacle Books, New
    York, NY)

EMPLOYERS Seattle/Puget Sound Area:

For an extensive listing of the Seattle/Puget Sound and
Portland areas' key print media outlets, see Chapter 4. What
follows supplements those lists.

AAA Washington Motorist
330 Sixth Ave. N.
Seattle, WA 98109
(206) 448-5353
Contact: Janet E. Ray, Editor and Advertising Manager
Monthly tabloid for auto club members.

Adventure Northwest Magazine/Leisure Publications
2521 A Pacific Highway E.
Tacoma, WA 98424-1007
(206) 922-2080

413

Contact: Cary Ordway, Editor and Publisher
Tabloid magazine published nine times per year.

Alaska Airlines Magazine
1932 First Ave., Suite 403
Seattle, WA 98101
(206) 441-5871
Contact: Candace Dempsey, Editor
Monthly.

Argus Weekend
14900 Interurban Ave. S., Suite 290
Seattle, WA 98168
(206) 243-7510
Contact: Sherri L. Handley, Editor
Weekly tabloid shopper.

Back Door Travel
120 Fourth Ave. N.
Edmonds, WA 98020
(206) 771-8303
Quarterly newsletter covering budget travel in Europe.

Bellowing Ark/Bellowing Ark Society
PO Box 45637
Seattle, WA 98145
(206) 545-8302
Contact: Robert R. Ward, Editor
Literary magazine, featuring modern poetry in the American
Romantic tradition for a general audience, published six times
yearly.

Bicycle Paper
7901 168th Ave. N.E., Suite 103
Redmond, WA 98052
(206) 882-0706
Contact: Barclay Kruse, Editor and Publisher
Monthly, covering bicycling in Pacific Northwest.

Blacksmith's Gazette
PO Box 1268
Mount Vernon, WA 98273
(206) 336-2969
Contact: Fred Holder, Editor and Advertising Manager
Bimonthly metalworking magazine.

Boatracing Magazine/Muncey Productions
PO Box 2936
Redmond, WA 98073
(206) 868-8411
Contact: Andrew J. Muntz, Editor
Bimonthly covering power boating.

Call A.P.P.L.E./Apple Pugetsound Program Library Exchange
290 S.W. 43rd
Renton, WA 98055
(206) 251-5222
Contact: Kathryn Hallgrimson Suther, Editor
Monthly technical journal on inner workings of Apple machines and programming.

Canoe/Canoe America Association
PO Box 3146
Kirkland, WA 98083
(206) 827-6363
Contact: George Thomas, Editor
Bimonthly on canoeing, kayaking, other outdoor activities.

Condominium News
2620 Alki Ave. S.W.
Seattle, WA 98116
(206) 932-6010
Contact: D. W. Hellriegel, Director
Monthly.

Fishing and Hunting News
PO Box C-19000
Seattle, WA 98109
(206) 624-3845
Contact: Vince Malernee, Editor
Weekly magazine.

Freedom Socialist/Freedom Socialist Party
5018 Rainier Ave. S.
Seattle, WA 98118
(206) 722-2453
Contact: Robert Crisman, Editor
Quarterly political newspaper.

Grange News
3104 Western Ave.
Seattle, WA 9812
(206) 284-1750
Contact: David Howard, Editor
Monthly newspaper, covering agricultural and legislative issues and Grange activities.

Heritage Music Review
4217 Fremont Ave. N.
Seattle, WA 98103
(206) 632-4389
Contact: Doug Bright, Editor
Monthly music guide.

Issue Watch/Municipal League of Seattle
414 Central Building
Seattle, WA 98104
(206) 622-8333
Contact: Steve Forman, Editor
Non-partisan tabloid on city, county, and state government,
published 10 times yearly.

Jewish Transcript, The/Jewish Federation
510 Securities Building
Seattle, WA 98101
(206) 624-0136
Contact: Craig Degginger, Editor
Jewish interest newspaper published twice monthly.

Journal of the Association for Persons With Severe Handicaps
7010 Roosevelt Way N.E.
Seattle, WA 98115
(206) 523-8446
Quarterly journal.

Mainline Modeler/Hundman Publishing Co.
5115 Monticello Drive
Edmonds, WA 98020
(206) 743-2607
Contact: Robert L. Hundman, Editor
Monthly magazine on railroad modeling.

National Boycott News/Institute for Consumer Responsibility
6506 28th Ave. N.E.
Seattle, WA 98115
(206) 523-0421
Contact: Todd Putman, Editor
Quarterly.

New Times
PO Box 51186
Seattle, WA 98115
(206) 524-9071
Monthly newspaper on New Age topics.

North American Post
661-1/2 S. Jackson St.
Seattle, WA 98144
(206) 623-0100
Contact: Akiku Kusunose, Editor
North American and Japanese news, published three times a
week.

416

Northwest Skier
PO Box 95229
Seattle, WA 98145
(206) 634-3620
Contact: Ian F. Brown, Editor and Publisher
Monthly sports magazine.

Northwest Technocrat/Technocracy
7513 Greenwood Ave. N.
Seattle, WA 98103
(206) 784-2111
Contact: John Berge, Editor
Quarterly aimed at preparing readers for social change.

OP/Lost Music Network
PO Box 2391
Olympia, WA 98507
(206) 352-9735
Contact: John Foster, Editor
Bimonthly music review sourcebook.

Parsley Sage & Time/Pike Market Senior Center
1931 First Ave.
Seattle, WA 98101
(206) 728-2773
Contact: Karen Kaushansky, Editor
Monthly senior citizens newsletter.

Passages/Horizons Publishing
1110 Tower Building
Seattle, WA 98101
(206) 467-1149
Contact: Patricia C. Glenham, Editor and Publisher
Travel magazine published six times yearly.

Permaculture Activist, The/Permaculture Institute of North America
4649 Sunnyside Ave. N.
Seattle, WA 98103
(206) 221-3979
Contact: Guy Baldwin, Editor and Advertising Manager
Quarterly newsletter.

Pesca Y Marina
2464 33rd Ave. W., Suite 221
Seattle, WA 98199
(206) 285-3200
Contact: G. Fisch, Editor
Magazine for commercial fisheries of Latin America (Spanish), published six times yearly.

The Progress
910 Marion
Seattle, WA 98104
(206) 382-4850
Weekly newspaper serving Roman Catholic community in
western Washington.

**Puget Sound Council of Governments (PSCOG)
Newsletter**
216 First Ave. S.
Seattle, WA 98104
(206) 464-7090
Monthly newsletter, covering government news in four-
county area.

Seattle Storytellers Guild
1921 Taylor Ave. N., #5
Seattle, WA 98109
(206) 328-1328
Quarterly newsletter.

Seattle's Child
PO Box 22578
Seattle, WA 98122
(206) 322-2594
Contact: Ann Bergman, Editor and Publisher
Monthly regional magazine for parents of children under 12.

**Senior Scene/Council on Aging, Lutheran Social
Services of Washington**
223 N. Yakina
Tacoma, WA 98403
(206) 272-2278
Contact: Harold L. Reinhardt, Managing Editor
Monthly tabloid.

Sew It Seams
PO Box 2698
Kirkland, WA 98083
(206) 822-6700
Contact: Christopher Lewis, Editor
Sewing magazine, published six times yearly.

Signpost/Washington Trails Association
1305 Fourth Ave., Suite 518
Seattle, WA 98101
(206) 625-1367
Contact: Ann Marshall, Editor and Advertising Manager
Monthly magazine on the outdoors.

Spiritual Women's Times/Silver Owl Publications
PO Box 51186

Seattle, WA 98115
(206) 524-9071
Contact: Krysta Gibson, Editor and Publisher
Quarterly tabloid.

Sports Northwest Magazine
4556 University Way N.E., Suite 203
Seattle, WA 98105
(206) 547-9709
Contact: John Erben, Editor
Monthly magazine.

Then and Now
PO Box 842
Mount Vernon, WA 98273
(206) 336-2969
Contact: Fred and Arlene Holder, Publishers
Bimonthly muzzle-loading shooting sport magazine.

Thurston-Mason Senior News
529 W. Fourth Ave.
Olympia, WA 98501
(206) 786-5595
Contact: Hugh Park, Editor
Monthly tabloid.

Trailblazer
15325 S.E. 30th Place
Bellevue, WA 98007
(206) 644-1100
Contact: Gregg D. Olsen, Editor
Monthly RV camping magazine for members of Thousand
Trails, Inc.

Video Librarian
PO Box 2725
Bremerton, WA 98310
(206) 377-2231
Contact: Randy Pitman, Editor and Publisher
Monthly newsletter.

Waves/Northwest Passage
PO Box 47111
Seattle, WA 98146
(206) 325-8037
Contact: Edited by the Staff Collective
Monthly alternative/anarchist newspaper.

WEA Action
33434 Eighth Ave. S.
Federal Way, WA 98003
(206) 941-6700

How To Get a Job

Contact: Jeanne Giardina, Editor
Labor union and educational organization interests; published monthly.

Western Flyer
PO Box 98786
Tacoma, WA 98498
(206) 584-7737
Contact: Dane S. Claussen, Editor and Publisher
Tabloid on general aviation, published 26 times yearly.

Western Viking
2040 N.W. Market St.
Seattle, WA 98107
(206) 784-4617
Contact: Henning C. Boe, Editor and Publisher
Weekly Norwegian community newspaper.

EMPLOYERS Portland Area:

American Indian Basketry Magazine
PO Box 66124
Portland, OR 97266
(503) 233-8131
Quarterly magazine, featuring basketry and other native arts.

Book Buyer
PO Box 02112
Portland, OR 97202
(800) 541-9498
Bimonthly magazine, containing lists of newly-published books.

Church and Synagogue Libraries
PO Box 19357
Portland, OR 97219
(503) 244-6919
Bimonthly magazine, featuring religious books and equipment.

Encore Arts in Performance Magazine
1410 S.W. Morrison St.
Portland, OR 97205
(503) 226-1468
Sixty-six publications, featuring performance programs for cultural events in the Puget Sound and Portland areas.

Flyfishing
PO Box 02112
Portland, OR 97202
(503) 653-8151
Flyfishing magazine, published five times yearly.

Geological Newsletter
PO Box 8579
Portland, OR 97207
(503) 284-4320
Monthly earth sciences newsletter.

Gleaner
PO Box 16677
Portland, OR 97216
(503) 255-7300
Semi-monthly general news magazine for Seventh-Day
Adventist Church members in Alaska, Washington, Oregon,
Idaho, and Montana.

Injury and Illness Incidence
Yeon Building
522 S.W. Fifth Ave.
Portland, OR 97204
(503) 224-3930
Quarterly publication, listing statistical reports on injury
experience for lumber manufacturing in the Western Woods
Region.

Lariat, The
12675 S.W. First St.
Beaverton, OR 97005
(503) 644-2233
Monthly magazine for equine enthusiasts.

Last Day Messenger
PO Box 17406
Portland, OR 97217
(503) 283-5985
Quarterly religious magazine for Christians who believe in a
literal interpretation of the Bible.

Natural Health World and the Naturopath
1920 Kilpatrick St.
Portland, OR 97217
(503) 695-0213
Monthly magazine, covering natural, organic, and related
health aspects.

Northwest Labor Press
PO Box 13150
Portland, OR 97213
(503) 288-3311
Semi-monthly labor tabloid.

Oregon Episcopal Churchman
11800 S.W. Military Lane

Portland, OR 97219
Episcopal tabloid published nine times a year.

Oregon Motorist, The
600 S.W. Market
Portland, OR 97201
(503) 222-6729
Bimonthly newsletter, covering motoring, travel, and highways legislation.

Regal Courier, The
15300 S.W. 16th Ave., No. 11
Portland, OR 97224
(503) 639-5414
Monthly local interest magazine.

RFD Publications
6960 S.W. Sandburg St.
Tigard, OR 97223
(503) 620-4140
Publishes *This Week* magazine and *The Downtowner*.

Ruralite
PO Box 558
Forest Grove, OR 97116
(503) 357-2105
Monthly magazine serving specific consumer-owned utilities in Alaska, Washington, Oregon, California, Idaho, and Nevada.

Salmon Trout Steelheader
PO Box 02112
Portland, OR 97202
(503) 653-8108
Bimonthly magazine, featuring sport fishing for salmon, trout, and steelhead.

Skies American Airline Network
9600 S.W. Oak, No. 310
Portland, OR 97223
(503) 244-2299
Publishes monthly inflight magazines for the following airlines: Midway, Horizon, San Juan, Braniff, and United Express.

Union Register, The
721 S.W. Oak St.
Portland, OR 97205
(503) 228-0780
Monthly labor tabloid.

US West Direct
1800 S.W. First Ave.
Portland, OR 97201

(503) 790-2204
Publisher of telephone directories.

Metal Products

For networking in the **metal products** industry, contact the following trade organizations, some of which are listed in Chapter 5:

PROFESSIONAL ORGANIZATIONS:

Pacific Northwest Steel Fabricators Association, Portland
United Metal Trades Association, Portland
Washington Metal Trades, Seattle

For additional information, you can write to:

American Cast Metals Association
455 State St.
Des Plaines, IL 60016

American Powder Metallurgy Institute
105 College Road E.
Princeton, NJ 08540

Association of Iron and Steel Engineers
Three Gateway Center, Suite 2350
Pittsburgh, PA 15222

National Association of Metal Finishers
111 E. Wacker Drive
Chicago, IL 60601

PROFESSIONAL PUBLICATIONS:

Assembly Engineering
Design News
Iron Age
Manufacturing Systems
Metal Working Digest

DIRECTORY:

Dun's Industrial Guide: The Metalworking Directory (Dun's
Marketing Services, Mountain Lakes, NJ)

EMPLOYERS Seattle/Puget Sound Area:

Alaskan Copper Cos.
3223 Sixth Ave. S.
Seattle, WA 98134
(206) 623-5800
Metal and fabricated pipe products, including heat exchangers and process equipment.

Atlas Foundry & Machine Co.
3021 S. Wilkeson
Tacoma, WA 98411
(206) 475-4600
Steel and stainless steel castings, as well as fabrication and machining.

Builders Hardware & Supply Co.
1516 15th Ave. W.
Seattle, WA 98119
(206) 281-3700
Wholesale finish hardware, hollow metal and specialties.

Capital Industries
5801 Third S.
Seattle, WA 98108
(206) 762-8585
Metal fabrication.

Davis Walker Corp.
19411 80th Ave. S.
Kent, WA 98032
(206) 872-8910
Fabricated wire products.

Graham Steel Corp.
13210 N.E. 124th
Bellevue, WA 98005
(206) 823-5656

Isaacson Steel Service Center (ISSC Steel)
3660 E. Marginal Way S.
Seattle, WA 98134
(206) 343-0700

Jorgensen Steel/Forge Division
8531 E. Marginal Way S.
Seattle, WA 98108
(206) 762-1100
Steel and other metal products.

Seattle Steel
2414 S.W. Andover

Building D, Suite 100
Seattle, WA 98106
(206) 938-6800
Processes steel and other metal products, including bolts,
fasteners, and track spikes.

EMPLOYERS Portland Area:

Anodizing, Inc.
7933 N.E. 21st Ave.
Portland, OR 97211
(503) 285-0404
Aluminum extrusion, anodizing, fabrication.

Cascade Steel Rolling Mills
3200 N. Highway 99W
McMinnville, OR 97128
(503) 472-4181
Rebar, flats, smooth rounds, steel products.

Columbia Machine
107 Grand Blvd.
Vancouver, WA 98661
(206) 694-1501
Steel products, industrial machinery, materials handling
products.

Columbia Steel Casting Co.
10425 N. Bloss Ave.
Portland, OR 97203
(503) 286-0685
Steel castings.

Consolidated Metco
13940 N. Rivergate Blvd.
Portland, OR 97203
(503) 286-5741
Aluminum castings, die castings, heavy-duty truck parts.

ESCO Corp.
2141 N.W. 25th Ave.
Portland, OR 97210
(503) 228-2141
Cast steel alloy parts for mining, construction, dredging,
logging.

Oregon Steel Mills
14400 N. Rivergate Blvd.
Portland, OR 97203
(503) 286-9651
Steel plate, heat treated plate.

Precision Castparts Corp.
4600 S.E. Harney Drive
Portland, OR 97206
(503) 777-3881
Investment casting, especially giant castings for the
aeronautics industry.

Reynolds Metals Co.
N.E. Sun Dial Road
Troutdale, OR 97060
(503) 665-9171
Aluminum ingots.

Schnitzer Steel Products Co.
3200 N.W. Yeon Ave.
Portland, OR 97210
(503) 224-9900

Ted Nelson Co.
10750 S.W. Tualatin
Portland, OR 97201
(503) 639-4151
One of top four companies nationwide engaged in
manufacturing steel forms for use in casting concrete.

Vanalco, Inc.
5701 N.W. Lower River Road
Vancouver, WA 98660
(206) 696-8661
Primary aluminum and extrusion billet.

Vanexco/Division of Alcoa
5509 N.W. Lower River Road
Vancouver, WA 98666
(503) 696-8724
Extruded aluminum shapes.

Western Wire Works
4025 N.W. Express Ave.
Portland, OR 97210
Personnel: (503) 222-4598
Wire and other metal products.

Zidell Explorations
3121 S.W. Moody Ave.
Portland, OR 97201
(503) 228-8691
Carbon steel butt weld fittings, pipe valves and fittings,
athletic equipment, machining and fabrication.

Office Supplies

For additional information about the **office supplies** industry, you may wish to write to:

PROFESSIONAL ORGANIZATIONS:

National Office Machine Dealers Association (NOMDA)
12411 Wornall Road
Kansas City, MO 64145

National Office Products Association (NOPA)
301 N. Fairfax St.
Alexandria, VA 22314

Office Products Manufacturers Association
PO Box 248
Glen Oaks, NY 11004

Wholesale Stationers' Association
1701 E. Woodfield Road, Suite 403
Schaumburg, IL 60173

Western Office Machine Dealers Association (WOMDA)
2659 Commercial St. S.E., Suite 260
Salem, OR 97302

PROFESSIONAL PUBLICATIONS:

Modern Office Technology
The Office
Office Administration & Automation
Office Products Dealer
Today's Office

DIRECTORIES:

Geyer's "Who Makes It" Directory (Geyer-McAllister Publications, New York, NY)
Modern Office Technology: Buyer's Reference, January issue (Penton Publishing, Cleveland, OH)
Product Buying Guide & Industry Directory, Office Products Dealer, December issue (Hitchcock Publishing, Wheaton, IL)

EMPLOYERS Seattle/Puget Sound Area:

Action Office Interiors
212 Third Ave. S.
Seattle, WA 98104
(206) 382-9818

Arvey Paper & Supplies
2930 First Ave. S.
Seattle, WA 98134
(206) 622-9232
Contact: Verlin Brown, Manager
Branch location:
1910 132nd Ave. N.E.
Bellevue, WA 98005
(206) 643-4333
Contact: Dan O'Day, Manager

Barclay Dean Interiors
155 108th Ave. N.E., Suite 110
Bellevue, WA 98004
(206) 454-8301

Boise Cascade Office Products
20202 84th Ave. S.
Kent, WA 98032
(206) 872-7878
Has no personnel manager; unsolicited resumes will be returned.

Britain's Office Supply
22001 Highway 99
Edmonds, WA 98070
(206) 774-9535
Contact: Cathy White, Office Manager

Budget Office Furniture
2244 First Ave. S.
Seattle, WA 98134
(206) 447-0393

Business Environments
1145 Broadway Plaza, Suite 150
Tacoma, WA 98402
(206) 627-1767
Other locations in South Seattle and Bellevue.

Clark Office Products
12750 Lake City Way N.E.
Seattle, WA 98125
(206) 362-1250

Crawford's Office Furniture
435 Westlake Ave. N.
Seattle, WA 98109
(206) 623-4210
Contact: Edward E. Webb, Owner/Manager

Firstline Office Supply
18825 33rd Ave. W.
Lynnwood, WA 98036
(206) 775-3551
Contact: John Tabb Sr., President

John L. Bird Co.
1725 Westlake Ave. N.
Seattle, WA 98101
(206) 285-9555
Contact: Don Olson, Personnel Manager

Keeney's Office Products
10541 N.E. Fourth
Bellevue, WA 98004
(206) 454-7555
Contact: Lisa Keeney, President

Kopy King Corp.
351 S. 25th
Tacoma, WA 98402
(206) 572-8187

Office Furniture To Go
133 Westlake Ave. N.
Seattle, WA 98109
(206) 682-3000
Branches in Bellevue and Tukwila.

Olympic Office Supply
1950 130th Ave. N.E.
Bellevue, WA 98005
(206) 883-0303
Contact: Rick Rosen, Office Manager

Record Stationery & Office Supply
801 Houser Way S.
Renton, WA 98057
(206) 255-3444
Contact: Lowene Dickinson, Office Manager

Seattle Office Furniture
3035 First
Seattle, WA 98121
(206) 728-5710

The Stationer's
711 St. Helens Ave.
Tacoma, WA 98401
(206) 838-1434
Contact: Doug Bergrund
Second outlet in Kent.

Trick & Murray
300 Westlake Ave. N.
Seattle, WA 98109
(206) 622-1440
Contact: Missy Ross, Director of Human Resources
Several retail stores in Seattle, Tacoma, and Auburn.

Vanguard Office Systems
10715 Silverdale Way
Silverdale, WA 98383
(206) 698-1666
Seven stores statewide, including Tacoma.

Westlake Office Furniture
222 Westlake Ave. N.
Seattle, WA 98109
(206) 623-9222

Xerox Corp.
6400 Southcenter Blvd
Tukwila, WA 98188
(206) 241-1428

EMPLOYERS Portland Area:

Automated Office Systems
12100 S.W. Garden Place
Portland, OR 97223
(503) 620-2800
Office supplies and equipment dealer, printing services.

B & I Interiors
115 N.W. Fifth Ave.
Portland, OR 97209
(503) 227-3107
Office furniture dealer, space planning services.

Boise Cascade Office Products
4660 N. Channel Ave.
Portland, OR 97217
(503) 283-2211
Office supplies and equipment dealer.

Business Commercial Furniture
2800 N.W. 29th Ave.

Portland, OR 97210
(503) 227-3401
Office furniture dealer, space planning services.

City Liquidators
823 S.E. Third Ave.
Portland, OR 97214
(503) 238-4477
Office furniture dealer, space planning. Five locations in the metropolitan area.

Commercial Office Machines
6650 N. Basin Ave.
Portland, OR 97217
(503) 289-9009
Office supplies and equipment dealer. Three locations in the metropolitan area.

Environetics, Inc.
17380 S.W. Boones Ferry Road
Lake Oswego, OR 97035
(503) 635-8141
Office furniture dealer, space planning services.

Far West Office Systems
5105 S.E. 25th Ave.
Portland, OR 97202
(503) 239-4404
Office supplies and equipment dealer, printing services.

Gill, J.K.
6800 S.W. Beaverton-Hillsdale Highway
Portland, OR 97225
(503) 297-1759
Office supplies and equipment dealer with 12 metropolitan area locations.

Graham's Book & Stationery
460 Second St.
Lake Oswego, OR 97034
(503) 636-3562
Office supplies and equipment dealer, printing services. Four locations in the metropolitan area.

Kilham Stationery & Printing Co.
509 N.W. 10th Ave.
Portland, OR 97209
(503) 228-8433
Office supplies, equipment, and furniture dealer; services include printing, space planning.

431

Mart, The
2202 E. Burnside St.
Portland, OR 97214
(503) 233-7665
Office furniture dealer, space planning services.

Office Interiors
210 N.W. Broadway
Portland, OR 97209
(503) 226-3399
Office furniture dealer, space planning services.

Pacific Office Furnishings
421 S.W. Second Ave.
Portland, OR 97204
(503) 242-3550
Office furniture dealer, space planning services.

Pacific Stationery & Printing Co.
8303 N.E. Killingsworth St.
Portland, OR 97220
(503) 255-8900
Office supplies and equipment dealer with three metropolitan area locations.

Peter's Office Supply Co.
338 N.W. Ninth Ave.
Portland, OR 97209
(503) 228-6357
Office supplies, equipment, and furniture dealer; services include printing, space planning.

Smith Brothers Office Environments
135 N.W. Park Ave.
Portland, OR 97209
(503) 226-4151
Office supplies and equipment dealer, printing services.

Thayer, The J., Co.
11755 S.W. Third Ave.
Beaverton, OR 97005
(503) 646-9191
Office supplies, equipment, and furniture dealer; services include printing, space planning. Three metropolitan area locations.

Total Office Products and Printers
3461 N.W. Yeon Ave.
Portland, OR 97210
(503) 228-2395
Office supplies, equipment, and furniture dealer; services

include printing, space planning. Four metropolitan area locations.

Western Office Products
8380 S.W. Nyberg Road
Tualatin, OR 97062
(503) 692-4422
Office supplies, equipment, and furniture dealer; services include printing, space planning.

Paper/Packaging/Forest Products

For networking in **paper** and related industries, check out the following professional organizations:

PROFESSIONAL ORGANIZATIONS:

American Plywood Association, Tacoma, WA
Industrial Forestry Association, Portland
Pacific Coast Association of Pulp and Paper Manufacturers, Portland
Public Timber Purchasers Group, Portland
Timber Operators Council, Inc., Tigard, OR
Washington Contract Loggers Association, Olympia
Washington Wood Energy Association, Bellevue, WA
Western Forest Industries Association, Olympia, WA, and Portland
Western Forestry and Conservation Association, Portland
Western Hardwood Association, Portland
Western Red Cedar Lumber Association, Portland
Western Wood Products Association, Portland
Wood Moulding and Millwork Producers, Portland
Woodmen of the World, Portland

For additional information, you càn write to:

American Paper Institute
260 Madison Ave.
New York, NY 10016

Pacific Coast Paper Box Manufacturers Association
2301 Vernon Ave.
Los Angeles, CA 90060

Paper Industry Management Association
2400 E. Oakton St.
Arlington Hts., IL 60005

Technical Association of the Pulp and Paper Industry
Technology Park, PO Box 105113
Atlanta, GA 30348

PROFESSIONAL PUBLICATIONS:

Good Packaging Magazine
Packaging
Paper Trade Journal
Pulp and Paper
World Wood

DIRECTORIES:

Directory of the Forest Products Industry (Miller Freeman, San
    Francisco, CA)
Good Packaging Magazine Western Packaging Directory (Erich
    Printing & Lithography, San Jose, CA)
Lockwood-Post's Directory of the Pulp, Paper and Allied Trades
    (Miller Freeman, San Francisco, CA)
Paper Yearbook (Harcourt Brace Jovanovich, New York, NY)
Paperboard Packagings International Container Directory (Harcourt
    Brace Jovanovich, Cleveland, OH)

EMPLOYERS Seattle/Puget Sound Area:

Bacon, Henry, Building Materials
2350 104th N.E.
Bellevue, WA 98005
(206) 641-8000

Brazier Forest Industries
Columbia Center, 45th Floor
Seattle, WA 98104
(206) 584-1575
Manufacturer, exporter of high-grade wood products.

Burlington Northern
999 Third Ave.
Seattle, WA 98104
(206) 467-3838
Forest products, natural resources.

Cello Bag Co.
17100 West Valley Highway
Tukwila, WA 98188
(206) 251-8666
Paper bags.

Container Corp. of America
601 Monster Rd. S.W.
Renton, WA 98055
(206) 235-3300
Boxes, folding paperboard.

Harris Group
425 Pontius Ave. N.
Seattle, WA 98109
(206) 382-7410
Consulting and engineering for pulp and paper plants.
Specializes in rebuilding older pulp and paper mills, and
designing plants to process recycled paper.

Ketcham, Henry H., Lumber Co.
2811 E. Madison, Suite 300
Seattle, WA 98112
(206) 329-2700
Wholesaler, broker, and distributor of lumber.

Laird Norton Co.
801 Second Ave., Suite 1300
Seattle, WA 98104
(206) 464-5234
Building materials.

Longview Fibre Co.
PO Box 639
Longview, WA 98632
(206) 425-1550
Operates tree farms, pulp and paper mill producing kraft
paper and containerboard.

Manke Lumber Co.
1717 Marine View Drive
Tacoma, WA 98422
(206) 572-6252
Wholesale lumber and pellet mill, saw mill, wood treatment.

Pacific Lumber & Shipping Co.
1301 Fifth Ave., Suite 3131
Seattle, WA 98101
(206) 682-7262

Paper Fibres/Subsidiary of Rebanco
66 S. Hanford
Seattle, WA 98134
(206) 622-1991
High-grade paper recyling.

Scott Paper Co./Western region
2600 Federal Ave.

Everett, WA 98201
(206) 259-7333
Sanitary paper products.

Weyerhaeuser Co.
Corporate Headquarters
33663 Weyerhaeuser Way S.
Federal Way, WA 98003
(206) 924-2345
World's largest private owner of timber; produces and markets
diversified forest products, including wood products, building
materials, pulp, paper, and packaging products. Chief
subsidiaries include Weyerhaeuser Real Estate Co. and
Weyerhaeuser Financial Services, Inc.
Contact: Personnel by mail only; send resume with cover
letter.

EMPLOYERS Portland Area:

Boise Cascade Corp., White Paper Division
1600 S.W. Fourth Ave.
Portland, OR 97201
(503) 224-7250
Business paper, form paper, other paper products.

Camas Mill/Division, Crown Zellerbach
N.E. Fourth and Adams
Camas, WA 98607
(206) 834-3021
Paper products and related goods.

Chase Packaging Corp.
2550 N.W. Nicolai St.
Portland, OR 97210
(503) 228-4366
Textile bags, multi-wall paper bags, biodegradable erosion
netting.

Estacada Lumber
900 N.W. Mill Road
Estacada, OR 97023
(503) 630-7701
Lumber, wood products.

Fort Vancouver Plywood Co.
Foot of W. 13th St.
Vancouver, WA 98666
(206) 694-3368

Georgia-Pacific Corp., Western Division
900 S.W. Fifth Ave.
Portland, OR 97204

(503) 222-5561
Lumber, wood, plywood, paper products.

Hampton Affiliates
9400 S.W. Barnes Road, Suite 400
Portland, OR 97225
(503) 297-7691
Lumber brokers, lumber and veneer manufacturing.

James River Corp.
1500 S.W. First
Portland, OR 97201
(503) 221-7000
also:
521 S.E. Chkalov Drive
Vancouver, WA 98684
(206) 896-4500
Towel and tissue products, business and printing papers, food
packaging.

Linnton Plywood Association
10504 N.W. St. Helens Road
Portland, OR 97231
(503) 286-3672
Plywood, sawdust.

Louisiana-Pacific Corp.
111 S.W. Fifth Ave.
Portland, OR 97204
(503) 221-0800
Wood products.

Mail-Well Envelope Co.
2515 S.E. Mailwell Drive
Portland, OR 97222
(503) 654-3141

Niedermeyer-Martin Co.
1727 N.E. 11th Ave.
Portland, OR 97208
(503) 287-2411
Forest products, including pressure treated poles, piling,
timbers.

Pope & Talbot
1500 S.W. First Ave.
Portland, OR 97201
(503) 228-9161
Pulp, tissue, diapers, lumber.

Smurfit Newsprint Corp.
472 Main St.

Oregon City, OR 97045
(503) 650-4211
Newsprint, particle board.

Stimson Lumber Co.
PO Box 68
Forest Grove, OR 97116
(503) 357-2131
Lumber, hardboard.

Weyerhaeuser Co.
1601 N.E. 192nd Ave.
Portland, OR 97230
(503) 661-6161
See description under Seattle/Puget Sound Area.

Willamette Industries
3800 First Interstate Bank Tower
Portland, OR 97201
(503) 227-5581
Lumber, plywood, pulp, paper, business forms, boxes, bags.

WTD Industries
10220 S.W. Greenburg Road
Portland, OR 97223
(503) 246-3440
Lumber, plywood, veneer.

Plastics/Rubber

For networking in **plastics, rubber** and related fields, you can contact the following organization:

PROFESSIONAL ORGANIZATIONS:

Society of Plastics Engineers, Pacific Northwest Chapter

For more information, you may want to write to:

Rubber Manufacturers Association
1400 K St., N.W.
Washington, DC 20005

Society of Plastic Engineers
14 Fairfield Drive
Brookfield Centre, CT 06804

Society of the Plastics Industry
1275 K St., N.W.
Washington, DC 20005

PROFESSIONAL PUBLICATIONS:

Modern Plastics
Plastics World
Rubber
Rubber & Plastics News

DIRECTORIES:

Modern Plastics Encyclopedia (McGraw-Hill, New York, NY)
Plastics World Plastics Directory (Cahners Publishing, Newton, MA)
Rubber Red Book (Communication Channels, Atlanta, GA)
Rubbicana: Rubber Directory & Buyers Guide (Crain Communications, Akron, OH)

EMPLOYERS Seattle/Puget Sound Area:

Accurate Plastics
35703 16th S.
Federal Way, WA 98003
(206) 927-4345
Plastic molding.

Burke Rubber Co./Division of Burke Industries
PO Box 1064
Renton, WA 98057
(206) 228-1556
Molding and fabrication.

Cadillac Plastic & Chemical Co.
2427 Sixth Ave. S.
Seattle, WA 98134
(206) 682-7252

Cascade Gasket & Manufacturing Co.
8825 S. 228th St.
Kent, WA 98031
(206) 854-1800

Design Plastics
7495 159th Place N.E.
Redmond, WA 98052
(206) 883-2022
Pressure and vacuum forming.

Dye-Plastics
3000 Lind S.W.
Renton, WA 98055
(206) 251-5405
Rotational molding.

Fabriform Plastics
3300 Airport Way S.
Seattle, WA 98134
(206) 587-5303
Vacuum forming, custom fabricating.

Fiberchem
1120 Andover Park E.
Seattle, WA 98188
(206) 575-0270
Raw plastics, resins distributor.

Fleck Company
3410 A St. S.E.
Auburn, WA 98002
(206) 833-5900
Plastic injection molding.

McCawley Precision Machine Corp.
13405 S.E. 30th St.
Bellevue, WA 98005
(206) 747-4366
Plastic products, injection molding.

Middy Plastic Products
9320 151st Ave. N.E.
Redmond, WA 98052
(206) 883-4600
Pressure and vacuum forming.

Mikron Industries
1034 Sixth Ave. N.
Kent, WA 98032
(206) 226-8020
Custom profile extrusions.

Nerland's Plastic Products
3412 16th Ave. W.
Seattle, WA 98119
(206) 282-5661

Northwest Containers
635 E. 15th St.
Tacoma, WA 98421
(206) 627-2151
Plastic bottles.

Production Plastics
4609 70th Ave. E.
Puyallup, WA 98371
Seattle Tel No.: (206) 624-6506

Rainier Rubber Co.
1083 Andover Park E.
Seattle, WA 98188
(206) 575-1558
Precision custom molding of elastomers.

Scougal Rubber Corp.
6239 Corson Ave. S.
Seattle, WA 98108
(206) 763-2650
Custom molded industrial rubber parts.

Stanley Plastic Manufacturing
28818 112th E.
Buckley, WA 98321
Auburn Tel No.: (206) 939-8442
Custom fiberglass production.

Tacoma Plastics
2416 South C
Tacoma, WA 98402
(206) 383-4836
Injection molding, mold building.

Universal Plastics Co.
650 S. Industrial Way
Seattle, WA 98108
(206) 623-4900
Sheets, rods, tubes, film for industrial uses.

EMPLOYERS Portland Area:

ABC Plastics
116 S.E. Yamhill St.
Portland, OR 97214
(503) 235-6778
Plastic molding.

Bonar Plastics
19705 S.W. Teton Ave.
Tualatin, OR 97062
(503) 692-0560
Plastic molding.

Cascade Rubber Products
1520 N.W. 20th
Portland, OR 97209

(503) 248-1992
Custom rubber molding.

Challenge Manufacturing
9800 S.W. Tigard St.
Tigard, OR 97223
(503) 684-2507
Plastic molding of medical products.

Columbia Rubber Mills
12405 S.E. 82nd Ave.
Portland, OR 97266
(503) 654-5458
Custom rubber products for industry.

Denton Plastics
4427 N.E. 158th Ave.
Portland, OR 97236
(206) 257-9945
Buys and sells scrap plastic.

Fiberchem, Inc.
15757 S.W. Jay
Beaverton, OR 97006
(503) 641-2324

Gage Industries
6710 S.W. McEwan Road
Lake Oswego, OR 97035
(503) 639-2177
Custom sheet extrusion.

Grant & Roth Plastics
1600 N.E. 25th Ave.
Portland, OR 97232
(503) 648-2136
Plastic manufacturing, including computer printer outer shells.

Griffith Polymers
1930 S.E. Minter Bridge Road
Hillsboro, OR 97123
(503) 648-1105
Custom polyurethane products for industry.

Griffith Rubber Mills
2625 N.W. Industrial St.
Portland, OR 97210
(503) 226-6971

Kaso Plastics
11013-A N.E. 39th St.
Vancouver, WA 98686

Portland Tel No.: (503) 227-3064
Injection molding, production, engineering.

Molded Container Corp.
8823 S.E. 13th Ave.
Portland, OR 97202
(503) 233-8601
Plastic molding and decorating for food and industrial
packaging industries.

Multi-Craft Plastics
240 Broadway St. N.
Portland, OR 97227
(503) 281-5157
Plastics for home, commercial, industrial use.

Northwest Rubber Extruders
16748 S.W. 72nd Ave.
Portland, OR 97224
(503) 620-5522
Custom rubber, plastic, and silicone products.

Olshen's Bottle Supply Co.
1204 S.E. Water
Portland, OR 97214
(503) 233-5049

Poly-Cast, Inc.
9898 S.W. Tigard St.
Tigard, OR 97223
(503) 620-9850
Plastic molding.

Printers/Graphic Design

For networking in **printing, graphic design,** and related
fields, check out the following organizations, some of which
are listed in Chapter 5:

PROFESSIONAL ORGANIZATIONS:

**Pacific Printing Industries, Portland and Seattle
    Chapters**
Seattle Design Association
Women in Graphic Arts, Seattle

How To Get a Job

For more information, you can write to:

National Association of Printers and Lithographers
780 Palisade Ave.
Teaneck, NJ 07666

Printing Industries of America
1730 N. Lynn St.
Arlington, VA 22209

Technical Association of the Graphic Arts
Box 9887
Rochester, NY 14614

PROFESSIONAL PUBLICATIONS:

American Printer
Graphic Arts Monthly
Print
Printing News

DIRECTORIES:

Graphic Arts Monthly Buyer's Guide/Directory Issue (Cahners
    Publishing, New York, NY)
Printing Trades Blue Book (A.F. Lewis & Co., New York, NY)
Who's Who In Typesetting (National Composition Association,
    Arlington, VA)

EMPLOYERS Seattle/Puget Sound Area:

Color Control
3820 150th Ave. N.E.
Redmond, WA 98052
(206) 881-5454
Commercial printing.

Cone-Heiden Corp.
3441 Thorndyke Ave. W.
Seattle, WA 98117
(206) 282-3888
Commercial printing.

Craftsman Press
1155 Valley St.
Seattle, WA 98109
(206) 682-8800
Commercial printing.

Emerald City Graphics
22223 68th Ave. S.
Kent, WA 98032
(206) 872-6874
Commercial printing.

Evans/Spangler Design
190 Queen Anne Ave. N., Fourth Floor
Seattle, WA 98109
(206) 285-5522
Graphic design, other marketing services.

Frayn Printing Co.
2518 Western Ave.
Seattle, WA 98121
(206) 441-4222
Commercial printing.

Heath Printers
1617 Boylston
Seattle, WA 98122
(206) 323-3577
Commercial printing.

Hunter Tavernor & LaComa
1101 Alaska Way, Pier 55, Suite 301
Seattle, WA 98101
(206) 625-1774
Graphic design, other marketing services.

Impression Northwest
2001 22nd Ave. S.
Seattle, WA 98144
(206) 328-2770
Commercial printing.

Labels West
17629 130th Ave. N.E.
Woodinville, WA 98072
(206) 486-8484
Specialty printing.

LaserPrint Communications
19026 72nd Ave. S.
Kent, WA 98032
(206) 251-6688
Commercial printing.

Leonhardt Group, The
411 First Ave. S., Suite 315
Seattle, WA 98104

(206) 624-0551
Graphic design, other marketing services.

Martin Lithographics
1741 First Ave. S.
Seattle, WA 98134
(206) 622-1386
Commercial printing.

Print Northwest
PO Box 1418
Tacoma, WA 98401
(206) 545-3741
Commercial printing.

Rockey Company Design Group, The
2121 Fifth Ave.
Seattle, WA 98121
(206) 728-1100
Graphic design, other marketing services.

Rotary Offset Sales Co.
18221 Andover Park W.
Tukwila, WA 98188
(206) 575-0144
Commercial printing.

Sudden Printing
571 S. Michigan St.
Seattle, WA 98108
(206) 767-7611
Commercial printing.

Technigraphic Systems
111 James St.
Edmonds, WA 98020
(206) 672-2963
Graphic design, other marketing services.

Tim Girvin Design
911 Western Ave., Suite 408
Seattle, WA 98104
(206) 623-7808
Graphic design, other marketing services.

United Graphics
1401 Broadway
Seattle, WA 98122
(206) 325-4400
Commercial printing.

Visual Communications Systems
5305 Shilshole Ave. N.W.
Seattle, WA 98107
(206) 784-9000
Commercial printing.

Walter Dorwin Teague Associates
14727 N.E. 87th St.
Redmond, WA 98052
(206) 868-7677
Graphic design, other marketing services.

EMPLOYERS Portland Area:

Daily Journal of Commerce
2014 N.W. 24th Ave.
Portland, OR 97210
(503) 226-1311
Contact: Jorja Orr, Office Manager
Commercial printing.

Deluxe Check Printers
10550 S.W. Fifth Ave.
Beaverton, OR 97005
(503) 646-6171
Contact: Gary Mahone, Staff Specialist
Specialty printing.

Fine Arts Graphics
10955 S.W. Avery St.
Tualatin, OR 97062
(503) 692-3550
Contact: Debi Alioth, Personnel Coordinator
Commercial printing.

Graphic Arts Center
2000 N.W. Wilson St.
Portland, OR 97209
(503) 224-7777
Contact: Personnel Manager Nelva Kibble
One of the largest commercial printers in the West.

Graphic Information Systems, d/b/a PrintRight
27375 S.W. Parkway
Wilsonville, OR 97070
(503) 682-1322
Contact: Patricia Reddemann, Director of Personnel
Commercial printing.

In/Serv Information Services Group
5822 N.E. Skyport Way
Portland, OR 97218

(503) 287-0343
Contact: Su Linch, Director of Human Resources
Specialty printing.

Irwin-Hodson Co.
2838 S.E. Ninth Ave.
Portland, OR 97202
(503) 231-9990
Contact: Virginia Swan, Office Manager
Commercial printing.

John H. Harland Co.
18600 S.W. Teton Ave.
Tualatin, OR 97062
(503) 692-4084
All hiring conducted through Atlanta, GA office.
Specialty printing.

Norwest Publishing Co.
17401 N.E. Halsey St.
Portland, OR 97230
(503) 255-2455
Specialty printing.

Pry Publishing Co.
600 N.W. 14th Ave.
Portland, OR 97209
(503) 235-8335
Commercial printing. Also publishes seven neighborhood
newspapers.

RFD Publications
6960 S.W. Sandburg Road
Tigard, OR 97223
(503) 620-4140
Commercial printing.

Rocky Mountain Bank Note Co.
15201 N.W. Greenbrier Parkway
Beaverton, OR 97005
(503) 645-0954
Contact: Jim Coley, Plant Manager, PO Box 5088, Portland, OR
97208
Specialty printing.

Rono Graphic Communications Co.
535 N.W. 16th Ave.
Portland, OR 97209
(503) 222-4411
Contact: Bindery, Press, Office or Production Manager
Commercial printing.

Times Litho
PO Box 7
Forest Grove, OR 97116
(503) 359-0300
Commercial printing.

Treasure Chest Advertising
6031 N.E. 92nd Drive
Portland, OR 97220
(503) 257-0383
Commercial printing.

Willamette Industries Business Forms Division
5700 S.W. Western Ave.
Beaverton, OR 97075
(503) 641-8700
Contact: Bob Coats, Personnel
Specialty printing.

Wright Business Forms
18440 N.E. San Rafael St.
Portland, OR 97230
(503) 661-2525
Contact: Bob Hebert, Personnel Director
Specialty printing.

Real Estate Developers and Brokers

For networking in **real estate** and related fields, check out the following organizations, some of which are listed in Chapter 5:

PROFESSIONAL ORGANIZATIONS:

Commercial Real Estate Women, Seattle
National Association of Real Estate Executives
Portland Board of Realtors
Washington Association of Realtors

For additional information, you can write to:

International Real Estate Institute
8383 E. Evans Road
Scottsdale, AZ 85260

National Association of Realtors
430 N. Michigan Ave.
Chicago, IL 60611

PROFESSIONAL PUBLICATIONS:

National Real Estate Investor
Real Estate News
Realty and Building
Western Real Estate News (WREN)

DIRECTORIES:

National Real Estate Investor Directory Issue, mid-June
    (Communication Channels, Atlanta, GA)
National Roster of Realtors (Stanats Communications, Cedar
    Rapids, IA)
Western Real Estate News Directory Features (WREN, 3057 17th
    St., San Francisco, CA)
Who's Who in Creative Real Estate (Who's Who in Creative Real
    Estate, Inc., Ventura, CA

EMPLOYERS Seattle/Puget Sound Area:

Advance Properties
17018 15th Ave. N.E.
Seattle, WA 98155
(206) 362-8822
Residential real estate firm with eight Puget Sound offices.

All American Homes
622 S. 320th
Federal Way, WA 98003
(206) 246-1234
Three Puget Sound residential real estate offices.

Bain, William A. Associates
1200 Westlake N.
Seattle, WA 98109
(206) 283-5200
Four Puget Sound area residential real estate offices.

Benton's, Inc. Realtors/Ron Turner, Inc.
4454 California S.W.
Seattle, WA 98116
(206) 932-2500
Residential real estate firm with five Puget Sound offices.

Bruch & Vedrich/Better Homes & Gardens
2955 80th S.E., Suite 103
Mercer Island, WA 98040
(206) 232-4437
Residential real estate firm with nine Puget Sound locations.

Century 21/North Homes Realty
13322 Highway 99
Everett, WA 98204
(206) 355-3298
Residential real estate; four Puget Sound area offices.

Coldwell Banker Commercial Real Estate Services
1200 Sixth Ave., Suite 1600
Seattle, WA 98101
(206) 292-1600
also:
110 110th Ave. N.E., Suite 303
Bellevue, WA 98004
(206) 455-8500
Commercial real estate brokerage.

Coldwell Banker Residential Real Estate
305 108th N.E.
Bellevue, WA 98004
(206) 451-0572
Some 24 offices in King, Snohomish, Pierce, and Kitsap
counties.

Colliers Macaulay Nicolls International
800 Fifth Ave., Suite 3900
Seattle, WA 98104
(206) 223-0866
also:
500 108th Ave. N.E., Suite 700
Bellevue, WA 98004
(206) 453-4545
Commercial real estate brokerage.

Crescent Realty
16119 Pacific Ave.
Spanaway, WA 98387
(206) 531-9400
Residential real estate offices in Spanaway, Lakewood,
Puyallup.

Cushman & Wakefield of Washington
999 Third Ave., Suite 2600
Seattle, WA 98104
(206) 682-0666
Commercial real estate brokerage.

Duryee, D.A., & Co., Real Estate
2721 Wetmore
Everett, WA 98206
(206) 258-3411
Residential real estate; four Puget Sound offices.

ERA Real Estate Northwest
9757 N.E. Juanita Drive, Suite 103
Kirkland, WA 98034
(206) 820-0656
Residential real estate firm with some 28 Puget Sound offices.

Ewing and Clark
2110 Western Ave.
Seattle, WA 98121
(206) 441-7900
Commercial real estate brokerage.

First Western Properties
4232 198th S.W.
Lynnwood, WA 98036
(206) 775-4611
Commercial real estate brokerage with three area locations.

Grubb & Ellis Co.
600 University, Suite 1800
Seattle, WA 98101
(206) 623-8901
also:
11400 S.E. Eighth, Suite 300
Bellevue, WA 98004
(206) 454-3630
Commercial real estate brokerage.

Harper Bond
1500 112th N.E.
Bellevue, WA 98004
(206) 455-9440
Commercial real estate brokerage.

Heller Co.
222 112th N.E.
Bellevue, WA 98004
(206) 454-7299
Residential real estate; three Eastside offices.

Home Realty
12055 15th Ave. N.E.
Seattle, WA 98125
(206) 365-4700
Three Seattle residential real estate offices.

Imperial Real Estate Corp.
1730 Minor Ave.
Seattle, WA 98101
(206) 382-9181
Commercial real estate brokerage.

Kamas Realty
4020 Lake Washington Blvd. N.E., Suite 300
Kirkland, WA 98033
(206) 827-0404
Residential real estate firm with six King County offices.

Kidder Mathews & Segner
12886 Interurban Ave. S.
Seattle, WA 98168
(206) 248-7300
Commercial real estate brokerage with three Puget Sound
locations.

MacPhersons, Realtors
12733 Lake City Way N.E.
Seattle, WA 98125
(206) 364-9650
Residential real estate firm with more than 20 locations in
Pierce, Snohomish, and King counties.

Olympic Properties
22727 Highway 99
Edmonds, WA 98020
(206) 774-3500
Residential real estate; five north King/south Snohomish
County offices.

Page Co., The
1233 Olympic View Dr.
Edmonds, WA 98020
(206) 776-2151
Residential real estate; three Puget Sound locations.

Regency Group
11711 S.E. Eighth St., Suite 310
Bellevue, WA 98005
(206) 454-4000
Commercial real estate brokerage.

Richard James Realtors
10613 N.E. 38th Place
Kirkland, WA 98033
(206) 822-5757
Residential real estate firm with 11 Puget Sound locations.

Scott, John L., Real Estate
10909 N.E. Fourth
Bellevue, WA 98009
(206) 462-5000
Residential real estate firm with some 20 offices in King,
Kitsap, and south Snohomish counties.

How To Get a Job

Sherwood Group, The
910 Fifth Ave.
Seattle, WA 98104
(206) 447-1633
Commercial real estate brokerage.

Wallace and Wheeler, Real Estate
924 Bellevue Way N.E.
Bellevue, WA 98004
(206) 454-5064
Residential real estate. Fifteen offices mainly in King County, including commercial, insurance, and property management offices.

Windermere Real Estate
8401 35th N.E.
Seattle, WA 98115
(206) 522-9600
Residential real estate firm with more than 30 offices in King, Kitsap, Skagit, and Snohomish counties.

Yates Wood & MacDonald
221 First Ave. W.
Seattle, WA 98119
(206) 285-2205
Commercial real estate brokerage with three Puget Sound offices.

EMPLOYERS Portland Area:

Barbara Sue Seal Properties
4103 Mercantile Drive
Lake Oswego, OR 97035
(503) 241-7325
Contact: Lisa Hagerty, Personnel
Residential real estate.

Bullier & Bullier Realtors
707 S.W. Washington St., Suite 1500
Portland, OR 97205
(503) 223-3123
Contact: Carolyn Berg, Office Manager
Commercial real estate brokerage.

Century 21 Columbia Realty
2208 S.E. 182nd Ave.
Portland, OR 97233
(503) 665-0111
Residential real estate.

Coldwell Banker Commercial Group
1300 S.W. Fifth Ave., Suite 2600

Portland, OR 97201
(503) 221-1900
Contact for broker positions: Bob Niehaus, Sales Manager
Commercial real estate brokerage.

Coldwell Banker Residential Real Estate Services
366 Third St.
Lake Oswego, OR 97034
(503) 635-3500
Contact: John Donnelly, Vice President
Residential real estate.

Cronin & Caplan, Realtors
636 N.W. 21st Ave.
Portland, OR 97209
(503) 222-9701
Contact: John Scott, Designated Broker
Residential real estate.

Cushman & Wakefield of Oregon
111 S.W. Fifth Ave., Suite 2400
Portland, OR 97204
(503) 279-1700
Contact for broker positions: Tom Usher, Branch Manager
Commercial real estate brokerage.

Equity Group, Realtors, The
1905 S.W. 169th Place N.W.
Beaverton, OR 97006
(503) 645-0638
Contact for agent positions: Jim Homolka, Sales Manager
Residential real estate.

ERA Borge/LeDoux Real Estate
5501 N.E. 109th Court
Vancouver, WA 98662
Residential: (206) 256-4300
Commercial: (206) 892-6022

Executive Properties
12725 S.W. 66th Ave., Suite 102
Portland, OR 97223
(503) 639-9000
Contact: Linda Christensen, Sales Associate
Commercial real estate brokerage.

Gibson Bowles, Realtors
546 S.E. 106th Ave.
Portland, OR 97216
(503) 256-9723
Residential real estate.

Grubb & Ellis Co.
1001 S.W. Fifth Ave., Suite 700
Portland, OR 97204
(503) 241-1155
Contact for broker positions: Mark Fraser, Senior Vice
President and District Manager
Commercial real estate brokerage.

Lutz Snyder Co., The
14050 S.W. Pacific Highway
Portland, OR 97224
(503) 684-1020
Contact for clerical positions: Dian Lane, Administrative
Manager
Residential real estate; 20 metropolitan offices.

Macadam Forbes
1800 S.W. First Ave.
Portland, OR 97201
(503) 227-2500
Contact: David Egelhoff, President
Commercial real estate brokerage.

Norris & Stevens
610 S.W. Broadway
Portland, OR 97205
(503) 223-3171
Contact for broker positions: Clint Benson, Sales Manager
Commercial real estate brokerage.

Norris, Beggs & Simpson
121 S.W. Morrison St., Second Floor
Portland, OR 97204
(503) 223-7181
Contact: Jan Robertton, Regional Office Manager
Commercial real estate brokerage.

Oregon Realty Co.
8124 S.W. Beaverton-Hillsdale Highway
Portland, OR 97225
(503) 297-2523
Contact: E. John Clark, President
Residential real estate.

Professionals 100
Lincoln Tower 200
10260 S.W. Greenburg Road
Portland, OR 97223
(503) 245-1100
Residential real estate.

Real Estate Association
1901 N.E. Broadway
Portland, OR 97232
(503) 282-5000
Residential real estate.

Realty Group
2386 N.W. Hoyt St.
Portland, OR 97210
(503) 220-1144
Contact: James Raze, CEO
Residential real estate.

Stan Wiley Realtors, Commercial Division
10250 S.W. Greenburg Road, Suite 213A
Portland, OR 97223
(503) 245-5400
Contact: Howard Mudder, Office Manager
Commercial real estate brokerage.

Stan Wiley
9725 S.W. Beaverton-Hillsdale Highway, Suite 200
Beaverton, OR 97005
(503) 646-7826
Contact: Branch Manager
Residential real estate; 15 metropolitan offices.

United Properties
7410 Delaware Lane
Vancouver, WA 98664
(206) 693-1468
Residential real estate.

Recreation/Sports/Fitness

For networking in **recreation** and related fields, check out
the following organizations:

Northwest Athletic Clubs Association, Portland
Pacific Northwest PGA, Portland
Pacific Northwest Ski Areas Association, Seattle
Washington Recreation and Park Association,
    Edmonds
Western Winter Sports Representatives Association,
    Seattle

How To Get a Job

For additional information, you can write to:

PROFESSIONAL ORGANIZATIONS:

National Recreation & Parks Association
3101 Park Center Drive
Alexandria, VA 22302

National Sporting Goods Association
1699 Wall St.
Mt. Prospect, IL 60096

World Leisure and Recreation Association
345 E. 46th St.
New York, NY 10017

PROFESSIONAL PUBLICATIONS:

Amusement Business
Athletic Business
Parks and Recreation
Sporting Goods Trade

DIRECTORIES:

Athletic Business—Buyers Guide issue (Athletic Business, Madison, WI)
AUD Arena Stadium International Guide & Directory (Amusement Business, Nashville, TN)
New American Guide to Athletics, Sports, and Recreation (New American Library, New York, NY)
Parks & Recreation Buyers Guide, March issue (National Recreation and Parks Association, Alexandria, VA)

EMPLOYERS Seattle/Puget Sound Area:

Bellevue Athletic Club
11200 S.E. Sixth St.
Bellevue, WA 98004
(206) 455-1616
Health and fitness club.

Corporate Row
714 N. Northlake Way
Seattle, WA 98103
(206) 947-2825

Downstream River Runner
12112 N.E. 195th

Bothell, WA 98011
(206) 483-0335

First Service Tennis
302 Malden E., #1
Seattle, WA 98112
(206) 325-6148

King County Natural Resources and Parks Division
2040 84th S.E.
Mercer Island, WA 98040
(206) 296-4232

Livingwell Lady
14508 N.E. 20th, Suite D
Bellevue, WA 98007
(206) 641-3751
Health and fitness club.

Longacres Race Course
1621 S.W. 16th St.
Renton, WA 98055
(206) 226-3131

Metropolitan Park District Of Tacoma
10 Idaho St.
Tacoma, WA 98409
(206) 591-3690

NACO-WEST
12301 N.E. 10th Place
Bellevue, WA 98009
(206) 455-3155
Provides camping memberships, related services.

Nautilus Northwest
2306 Sixth Ave.
Seattle, WA 98121
(206) 443-9944
Health and fitness club.

Northwest Outdoor Center
2100 Westlake Ave. N.
Seattle, WA 98109
(206) 281-9694

Northwest Womens Health Clubs
14723 Aurora Ave. N.
Seattle, WA 98133
(206) 363-5962
Health and fitness club.

Olympic Athletic Club
5301 Leary Ave.
Seattle, WA 98107
(206) 789-5010
Health and fitness club.

P.R.O. Sports Club
4455 148th Ave. N.E.
Bellevue, WA 98007
(206) 885-5566
Health and fitness club.

Pacific West Athletic Clubs
32818 First Ave. S.
Federal Way, WA 98003
(206) 622-6202
Health and fitness club.

Pierce County Parks and Recreation
9112 Lakewood Drive S.W.
Tacoma, WA 98499
(206) 593-4176
Pierce County Personnel: (206) 591-7480

Seattle Athletic Club/Northgate
333 N.E. 97th
Seattle, WA 98115
(206) 522-9400
Health and fitness club.

Seattle Club, The
2020 Western Ave.
Seattle, WA 98121
(206) 443-1111
Health and fitness club.

Seattle Mariners Baseball Club
411 First Ave. S., # 480
Seattle, WA 98104
(206) 628-3555

Seattle Mini Golf
1535 15th W.
Seattle, WA 98119
(206) 285-7842, 284-9737

Seattle Parks and Recreation Department
Personnel: (206) 684-7063

Seattle Seahawks
11220 N.E. 53rd St.

Kirkland, WA 98033
(206) 8267-9777

Seattle South K.O.A.
5801 S. 212th
Seattle, WA 98198
(206) 872-8652

Seattle Supersonics
190 Queen Anne Ave. N.
Seattle, WA 98109
(206) 281-5800

Sound Mind & Body
711 Northlake Way
Seattle, WA 98103
(206) 547-2086
Health and fitness club.

Thurston County Parks and Recreation Department
529 W. Fourth Ave.
Olympia, WA 98501
(206) 786-5595

Twin Cedars R.V. Park
17826 Hwy. 99
Lynnwood, WA 98037
(206) 742-5540

Washington Athletic Club
1325 Sixth Ave.
Seattle, WA 98101
(206) 622-7900
Health and fitness club.

Washington State Parks and Recreation Commission
Region 5 Headquarters
1602 29th St. S.E.
Auburn, WA 98002
(206) 931-3907

EMPLOYERS Portland Area:

Adventures Northwest
225 E. Jersey
Gladstone, OR 97027
(503) 655-9576
Fishing and tour service.

Body Moves of Portland
918 S.W. Yamhill
Portland, OR 97205

(503) 227-3578
Fitness center.

Colwood National Golf Club
7313 N.E. Columbia
Portland, OR 97218
(503) 254-5515

Dancercize, Inc.
4419 N.E. Sandy Blvd.
Portland, OR 97213
(503) 249-0534
Aerobic dance classes, corporate fitness programs.

Fox Expeditions
41087 S.E. Fall Creek Road
Estacada, OR 97023
(503) 630-6225
Fishing excursions.

Go-For-It Whitewater Adventures
PO Box 2625
Portland, OR 97208
(503) 645-4337 or 645-7768

Mount Hood Recreation Association
PO Box 342
Welches, OR 97067
(503) 224-7158, Ext. 1600

Multnomah Athletic Club
1849 S.W. Salmon St.
Portland, OR 97207
(503) 223-6251
Social and athletic club.

Multnomah Kennel Club
N.E. 223rd Ave., between Halsey and Glisan
Fairview, OR 97024
(503) 667-7700
Parimutuel greyhound racing, four-floor complex.

Northwest River Outfitters
PO Box 3648
Portland, OR 97208
(503) 293-4990
Fishing excursions.

Oregon Fishing Adventures
726 S.W. 20th Circle
Troutdale, OR 97060
(503) 667-2652

Portland Beavers Baseball Club
1844 S.W. Morrison
Portland, OR 97207
(503) 2-BEAVER
AAA farm team for Minnesota Twins.

Portland Meadows Horse Racing
1001 N. Schmeer Road
Portland, OR 97217
(503) 285-9144

Portland Trailblazers Basketball (NBA)
700 N.E. Multnomah
Portland, OR 97232
(503) 234-9291

Portland Winter Hawks Hockey (WHL)
PO Box 3009
Portland, OR 97208
(503) 238-6366

Ski Bowl
PO Box 280
Government Camp, OR 97028
(503) 272-3206
Portland's closest ski area and America's largest night ski area.

Washington County Fairgrounds
872 N.E. 28th
Hillsboro, OR 97124
(503) 648-1416

Restaurants

For networking in the **restaurant** industry and related fields, check out the following professional organizations, some of which are listed in Chapter 5:

PROFESSIONAL ORGANIZATIONS:

Associated Tavern Owners of Washington, Seattle
Hotel Employees and Restaurant Employees Local 8, Seattle
Northwest Culinary Alliance, Seattle
Oregon Restaurant Association, Portland
Restaurant Association of The State of Washington, Seattle
Washington State Chef's Association, Seattle

How To Get a Job

For further information, you can write to:

Chefs De Cuisine Association of America
Paramount Hotel, Suite 3256
235 W. 46th St.
New York, NY 10036

Council on Hotel, Restaurant, and Institutional Education
Human Development Building
University Park, PA 96802

National Restaurant Association
311 First St. N.W.
Washington, DC 20001

PROFESSIONAL PUBLICATIONS:

Restaurant Business
Restaurant Hospitality
Restaurants & Institutions

DIRECTORIES:

Directory of Chain Restaurant Operators (Business Guides, Inc., New York, NY)
Directory of Food Service Distributors (Business Guides, New York, NY)
Restaurant Hospitality: 500 Issue (Penton Publishing, Cleveland, OH)
Restaurants & Institutions: 400 Issue, July issue (Cahners Publishing, Des Plaines, IL)
Restaurant & Institutions Buyers Guide, March issue (Cahners Publishing, Des Plaines, IL)

EMPLOYERS Seattle/Puget Sound Area:

There are thousands of restaurants and restaurant chains in the Seattle/Puget Sound and Portland metropolitan areas. Here you will find restaurants rated three and four stars by major restaurant critics, as well as restaurant and fast-food chains.

Adriatica
1107 Dexter Ave. N.
Seattle, WA 98109
(206) 285-5000

Azteca Restaurant Enterprises
15735 Ambaum Blvd. S.W.
Seattle, WA 98166

(206) 243-7021
Restaurant chain.

Botticelli Cafe
101 Stewart St.
Seattle, WA 98101
(206) 441-9235

Cafe Alexis (Alexis Hotel)
1007 First Ave.
Seattle, WA 98104
(206) 624-3646

Cafe Sport
2020 Western Ave.
Seattle, WA 98121
(206) 443-6000

Chez Shea
Pike Place Market
Corner Market Building, Suite 34
Seattle, WA 98101
(206) 467-9990

Dick's Drive-In Restaurants
4426 Second Ave. N.E.
Seattle, WA 98105
(206) 634-0300
Chain/franchise restaurants.

Dominique's Place
1927 43rd Ave. E.
Seattle, WA 98112
(206) 329-6620

Fullers
1400 Sixth Ave.
Seattle, WA 98101
(206) 447-5544

Gerard's Relais de Lyon
17121 Bothell Way N.E.
Bothell, WA 98011
(206) 485-7600

Host International
Sea-Tac International Airport
Seattle, WA 98158
Restaurant personnel: (206) 433-5644

Hunt Club, The (Sorrento Hotel)
900 Madison St.

Seattle, WA 98104
(206) 622-6400

Il Bistro
Pike Place Market
93A Pike St.
Seattle, WA 98101
(206) 682-3049

Il Fiasco
1309 Commercial St.
Bellingham, WA 98225
(206) 676-9136

Ivar's Restaurants
Pier 54
Seattle, WA 98104
(206) 587-6500
Seafood restaurant chain.

Labuznik
1924 First Ave.
Seattle, WA 98101
(206) 441-8899

Le Gourmand
425 N.W. Market St.
Seattle, WA 98107
(206) 784-3463

Le Tastevin
19 W. Harrison St.
Seattle, WA 98119
(206) 283-0991

Nikko
1306 S. King St.
Seattle, WA 98144
(206) 322-4905

Pizza Hut District Office
901 Powell Ave. S.W.
Renton, WA 98055
(206) 228-9740

Queen City Grill
2201 First Ave.
Seattle, WA 98121
(206) 443-0975

Restaurants Unlimited
1818 N. Northlake Way

Seattle, WA 98103
(206) 634-0550
Restaurant and bakery owner and franchisor.

Rover's
2808 E. Madison St.
Seattle, WA 98112
(206) 325-7442

Saleh al Lago
6804 E. Green Lake Way N.
Seattle, WA 98115
(206) 522-7943

Sea Galley Stores
6920 220th St. S.W.
Mountlake Terrace, WA 98043
(206) 775-0411
Seafood restaurant chain.

Settebello
1525 E. Olive Way
Seattle, WA 98122
(206) 323-7772

Skipper's, Inc.
14450 N.E. 29th Place, Suite 200
Bellevue, WA 98007
(206) 885-2116
Largest quick-service seafood chain in western U.S.

Union Bay Cafe
3505 N.E. 45th St.
Seattle, WA 98105
(206) 527-8364

Wendco Northwest Limited
1107 S.W. Grady Way
Renton, WA 98055
(206) 235-8570
Wendy's hamburger restaurant subsidiary, operates restaurants
throughout Puget Sound and Portland.

EMPLOYERS Portland Area:

Bread and Ink Cafe
3610 S.E. Hawthorne Blvd.
Portland, OR 97214
(503) 234-4756

Cafe des Amis
1987 N.W. Kearny St.

Portland, OR 97209
(503) 295-6487

Collins Foods International
15800 S.E. Piazza Ave., Suite 204
Clackamas, OR 97015
(503) 650-0476
Kentucky Fried Chicken franchise.

Dairy Queen of the Pacific Northwest
12655 S.W. Center St., Suite 325
Beaverton, OR 97005
(503) 646-3111

Eddie Lee's
409 S.W. Second St.
Portland, OR 97204
(503) 228-1874

Genoa
2832 S.E. Belmont St.
Portland, OR 97214
(503) 238-1464

Grant House
1101 Officers' Row
Vancouver, WA 98661
(206) 696-9699

Heathman Restaurant and Bar, The
1009 S.W. Broadway
Portland, OR 97205
(503) 241-4100

Holland, The
109 W. 17th St.
Vancouver, WA 98660
(206) 694-1521
Burgerville USA, Holland restaurants.

Indigine
3725 S.E. Division St.
Portland, OR 97202
(503) 238-1470

L'Auberge
2601 N.W. Vaughn St.
Portland, OR 97210
(503) 223-3302

McCormick & Schmick Management Services
720 S.W. Washington St.

Portland, OR 97205
(503) 226-3440
Food processing, restaurants.

McDonald's Corp.
10220 S.W. Greenburg Road, Suite 250
Portland, OR 97223
(503) 293-0000

Restaurant Management Northwest
1410 S.W. Jefferson St.
Portland, OR 97201
(503) 241-4900
Burger King franchise.

Ron Paul Catering and Charcuterie
2310 N.W. Everett St.
Portland, OR 97210
(503) 223-2121

Retailers/Wholesalers

For networking among **retailers and wholesalers,** you can contact the following organizations, some of which are listed in Chapter 5:

PROFESSIONAL ORGANIZATIONS:

Oregon Independent Retail Grocers Association, Portland
Oregon Jewelers Association, Portland
Pacific Northwest Jewelers Association, Bellevue, WA
Pike Place Market Merchants Association, Seattle
Washington Retail Association, Olympia, WA
Washington State Food Dealers Association, Seattle

For more information, you can write to:

General Merchandise Distributors Council
1275 Lake Plaza Drive
Colorado Springs, CO 80906

Manufacturers' Agents National Association
23016 Hill Creek Road
Laguna Hills, CA 92654

National Association of Wholesale Distributors
1725 K St. N.W.
Washington, DC 20006

How To Get a Job

National Retail Merchants Association
100 W. 31st St.
New York, NY 10036

PROFESSIONAL PUBLICATIONS:

Chain Store Age
College Store Executive
Stores
Women's Wear Daily

DIRECTORIES:

Fairchild's Financial Manual of Retail Stores (Fairchild Books, New York, NY)
Salesman's Guide Nationwide Directory: Major Mass Market Merchandisers (Salesman's Guide, Inc., New York, NY)
Shelton's Retail Directory (PS & M, Inc., Fairview, NJ)

EMPLOYERS Seattle/Puget Sound Area:

Alberton's, Inc.
11000 N.E. 33rd Place, Suite 102
Seattle, WA 98004
(206) 827-8070
Full-service supermarket. More than 41 stores in Puget Sound area.

Associated Grocers
3301 S. Norfolk
Seattle, WA 98124
(206) 762-2100
Wholesale grocer.

Bartell Drug Co.
4930 Third Ave. S.
Seattle, WA 98134
(206) 763-2626
Chain traditional drug stores. More than 31 locations in King and Snohomish counties.

Bergman Luggage
1930 Third Ave.
Seattle, WA 98101
(206) 448-3000
Seven Puget Sound locations.

Best Products Co.
17500 Southcenter Parkway
Tukwila, WA 98188

(206) 575-9503
General merchandise retailer. More than eight locations.

Bon Marche
Third and Pine
Seattle, WA 98181
(206) 344-2121
Retail department chain with 12 Puget Sound locations; three Bon Home stores.

Consumers Choice
1752 Iowa St.
Bellingham, WA 98226
(206) 671-9623
Employee-owned retail grocer with four stores in northwest Washington.

Costco Wholesale Corp.
10809 120th Ave. N.E.
Kirkland, WA 98083
(206) 828-8100
Membership discount retailer of food and general merchandise. Nine cash-and-carry warehouses in Puget Sound area.

D.P. Enterprises
1300 Dexter N.
Seattle, WA 98109
(206) 283-1300
Lease and sales of mini and micro computers.

E.J. Bartells Co.
700 Powell Ave. S.W.
Renton, WA 98057
(206) 228-4111
Wholesale distributor for refractory and industrial insulation products.

Egghead Discount Software
22011 S.E. 51st St.
Issaquah, WA 98027
(206) 391-0800
Largest personal computer software retailer in North America.

Ernst Home & Nursery
1511 Sixth Avenue
Seattle, WA 98101
(206) 621-6700
Retailer of household goods, hardware, and nursery items. More than 39 area outlets.

Fred Meyer, Inc.
14300 First Ave. S.
Seattle, WA 98168
(206) 433-6404
One-stop shopping centers retail general merchandise, food, apparel, home and garden products, small appliances. More than 15 Puget Sound outlets.

Frederick & Nelson
Fifth and Pine
Seattle, WA 98111
(206) 682-5500
Full-service department store. Seven area stores plus five Red Tag stores.

Haagen's, Inc.
PO Box 489
Bellingham, WA 98227
(206) 733-8700
Progressive up-scale supermarket chain. Six outlets.

Johnny's Food Centers
11120 Kent-Kangley Rd.
Kent, WA 98031
(206) 854-7500
Retail grocer. Six locations in south King County.

K-Mart Discount Stores
13200 Aurora Ave. N.
Seattle, WA 98133
(206) 367-1788
Full-service discount chain with more than 16 Puget Sound area stores.

Keith Uddenberg, Inc.
7520 Soundview Dr.
Gig Harbor, WA 98335
(206) 851-6688
Retail grocery stores operating under several names. More than 27 locations in the Puget Sound area.

Lamonts Apparel
3150 Richards Road
Bellevue, WA 98005
(206) 644-5700
Brand-name family apparel retailer. More than 16 locations.

Magnolia Hi-Fi, dba Magnolia Hi-Fi & Video
3701 Seventh Ave. S.
Seattle, WA 98134
(206) 623-7872
Consumer electronics.

Mervyn's
4126 124th S.E.
Bellevue, WA 98006
(206) 643-6554
Value-oriented family department store, specializing in
clothing and soft goods. More than five locations.

Micro Innovations
11812 North Creek Parkway N.
Bothell, WA 98011
(206) 485-6767
Operates ComputerLand retail chain.

Nordstrom, Inc.
1501 Fifth Avenue
Seattle, WA 98188
(206) 628-2111
Retailer, specializing in fashion apparel and accessories for
men, women, and children. Seven stores in Puget Sound area,
plus three Nordstrom Racks and three Nordstrom Place Twos.

Olson's Food Stores
PO Box L
Lynnwood, WA 98046
(206) 745-1266
Retail supermarket. Ten locations in north King and south
Snohomish counties.

Pay 'n Pak Stores
PO Box 8806
Kent, WA 98081
(206) 854-5450
Hardware retailer with more than 17 area locations.

Pay 'n Save
4045 Delridge Way S.W.
Seattle, WA 98106
(206) 936-6500
Retail drugstore. More than 67 Puget Sound locations.

Pay Less Drug Stores Northwest
14880 N.E. 24th
Redmond, WA 98052
(206) 833-3110
Drug and sundries retailer. More than 19 area locations.

Penney, J.C., Co.
1720 Southcenter Parkway
Seattle, WA 98188
(206) 575-4865
Retail merchandise department store. More than 12 Puget
Sound outlets.

Puget Sound Marketing
2708 E. Main
Puyallup, WA 98372
(206) 845-1782
Grocery and hardware retailer, property leasing agent.
Operates area Piggly Wiggly and Bag & Save stores, two Coast to
Coast stores and shopping centers.

Quality Food Centers (QFC)
10116 N.E. Eighth St.
Bellevue, WA 98009
(206) 455-3761
Largest independent supermarket chain in Seattle and King
County, with 22 locations.

Recreational Equipment (REI)
6750 S. 228th
Kent, WA 98032
(206) 395-3780
Nation's largest consumer co-op retails outdoor recreational
equipment and clothing. Three locations: Seattle, Bellevue,
and Federal Way.

Safeway Stores
1647 140th N.E.
Bellevue, WA 98005
(206) 455-6336
Retail grocer and distributor. More than 88 Puget Sound area
outlets.

Schuck's Auto Supply
15395 S.E. 30th Place, No. 300
Bellevue, WA 98008
(206) 644-2002
Automotive parts and accessories retailer. More than 44 Puget
Sound locations.

Sears, Roebuck and Co.
2212 148th Ave. N.E.
Redmond, WA 98052
(206) 643-3201
Department store chain.

Video Depot
1435 Railroad Ave.
Bellingham, WA 98225
(206) 676-0319
Wholesaling, retailing, and telemarketing of consumer
electronic products.

Weisfield's, Inc.
800 S. Michigan St.

Seattle, WA 98108
(206) 767-5011
Nine-state retail jewelry chain.

Western Drug Distributors
12515 116th Ave. N.E.
Kirkland, WA 98034
(206) 820-1060
Discount drug stores; Drug Emporium, Inc., franchise.

EMPLOYERS Portland Area:

Albertsons Food Centers
10230 S.W. Hall Blvd.
Portland, OR 97223
(503) 661-3900
Retail grocery chain.

Alpha Computers
15110 S.W. Bangy Road
Lake Oswego, OR 97035
(503) 620-7000
Three metropolitan stores.

Beaverton Florists
4705 S.W. Watson Ave.
Beaverton, OR 97005
(503) 644-0129

Businessland, Inc.
1600 S.W. Fourth Ave.
Portland, OR 97201
(503) 227-2367
Computer retailer.

Computer One/Better Computers
9725 S.W. Beaverton-Hillsdale Highway
Beaverton, OR 97005
(503) 297-7953
Computer retailer with four metropolitan stores.

ComputerLand
206 S.W. Morrison St.
Portland, OR 97204
(503) 295-1928
Computer retailer.

Costco Wholesale Corp.
4849 N.E. 138th Ave.
Portland, OR 97230
(503) 252-2243
Wholesale membership club and general merchandise.

How To Get a Job

CTR Business Systems
825 S.W. 14th Ave.
Portland, OR 97205
(503) 227-2414
Computer retailer.

Fabricland, Inc.
2035 N.E. 181st Ave.
Portland, OR 97230
(503) 666-4511
Fabric, notions, patterns.

Fleming Foods
S.E. Milwaukie Expressway at Pheasant Court (Milwaukie)
PO Box 3800
Portland, OR 97208
(503) 654-9551
Wholesale grocery.

Flowers by Tommy Luke
625 S.W. Morrison St.
Portland, OR 97205
(503) 228-3131

Fred Meyer, Inc.
3800 S.E. 22nd Ave.
Portland, OR 97202
(503) 232-8844
Regional retailer, carrying food, hardlines, soft goods.

G.I. Joe's
9805 Boeckman Road
Wilsonville, OR 97070
(503) 682-2242
General merchandise chain, specializing in automotive
supplies and sporting goods.

Gifford-Doving Florists
704 S.W. Jefferson St.
Portland, OR 97201
(503) 222-9193
Four metropolitan locations.

Jacobsen's
111 S.W. Columbia St.
Portland, OR 97201
(503) 224-1234
Florist.

K-Mart Discount Stores
12350 N.E. Sandy Blvd.
Portland, OR 97230

(503) 255-8903
Retail discount department stores.

Kienow's Food Stores
9840 S.E. 17th Ave.
Milwaukie, OR 97222
(503) 659-5220
Grocery chain.

Lamonts
9009 S.W. Hall Blvd., Suite 300
Tigard, OR 97223
(503) 624-0702
Retail family clothing and accessories.

Mains Florist
127 N.E. Third Ave.
Hillsboro, OR 97123
(503) 648-6601
Includes Flowers by Donna in Tigard and Hill Florist & Gifts in
Hillsboro.

Meier & Frank Co.
621 S.W. Fifth Ave.
Portland, OR 97204
(503) 223-0512
Department store.

Mervyn's
Washington Square Plaza
Portland, OR 97223
(503) 620-8800
Retail department store.

Montgomery Ward & Co.
4401 S.W. 110th Ave.
Beaverton, OR 97005
(503) 646-7212
Retail department store chain.

Nordstrom
701 S.W. Broadway
Portland, OR 97205
(503) 224-6666
Retail specialty store.

OmniTek Computers
1509 S.E. 122nd Ave.
Portland, OR 97233
(503) 253-1330
Computer retailer.

Payless Drug Stores Northwest
9275 S.W. Peyton Lane
Wilsonville, OR 97070
(503) 682-4100
Drug/variety store chain.

Penney, J.C., Co.
8900 A N.E. Vancouver Mall Drive
Vancouver, WA 98662
(206) 254-1833
Department store.

Plaid Pantry
10025 S.W. Allen Blvd.
Beaverton, OR 97005
Personnel: (503) 244-8710
Convenience store chain.

Rancho Flowers
8605 S.W. Beaverton-Hillsdale Highway
Beaverton, OR 97225
(503) 292-0154
Six metropolitan locations.

Safeway Stores
16300 S.E. Evelyn St.
Clackamas, OR 97015
(503) 656-1461
Grocery chain with some 100 stores in Oregon and southwest
Washington.

Sears, Roebuck & Co.
11800 S.E. 82nd Ave.
Portland, OR 97266
(503) 238-2311
Department store.

Southland Corp. d/b/a Seven-Eleven Food Stores
10220 S.W. Greenburg Road
Portland, OR 97223
(503) 245-9761
Convenience store chain.

Sprouse!
1411 S.W. Morrison St.
Portland, OR 97205
(503) 224-8220
General merchandise chain.

Target Stores
4900 S.W. Meadows Road
Lake Oswego, OR 97035

(503) 635-3344
Discount retail chain.

United Grocers
6433 S.E. Lake Rd.
Portland, OR 97222
(503) 653-6330
Wholesale grocery cooperative, operates Select Markets chain.

Transportation/Shipping

You may also want to check out the section on **Travel.**

For networking in **transportation,** you can contact the
following organizations, some of which are listed in Chapter 5:

**Northwest Marine Trade Association, Portland and
    Seattle Chapters**
Oregon Railroad Association, Portland
Oregon Trucking Associations, Inc., Portland
**Pacific Maritime Association, Portland and Seattle
    Chapters**
Pacific Merchant Shipping Association
Washington Trucking Associations, Seattle
**Washington-Oregon Shippers Co-op Association,
    Seattle**
Westward Shippers Association, Renton, WA

For more information, you can write to:

American Trucking Association
2200 Mill Road
Alexandria, VA 22314

Association of American Railroads
50 F St. N.W.
Washington, DC 20001

Institute of Transportation Engineers
525 School St., S.W.
Washington, DC 20024

PROFESSIONAL PUBLICATIONS:

AOPA Pilot
Heavy Duty Trucking
Traffic Management
Transportation & Distribution

DIRECTORIES:

Marine Directory, Greater Puget Sound and Washington Coast
   (Jeremy Mattox & Associates, Inc., Seattle, WA)
Moody's Transportation Manual (Moody's Investor's Service,
   New York, NY)
Port Directory (Washington Public Ports Assoc., Olympia, WA)

EMPLOYERS Seattle/Puget Sound Area:

Airborne Freight Corp.
3101 Western Ave.
Seattle, WA 98111
(206) 285-4600
Express delivery; international and domestic freight forwarder.

Bekins Northwest
Aurora Ave. N. & N. 95th
Seattle, WA 98103
(206) 527-7600

Burlington Northern
999 Third Ave.
Seattle, WA 98104
(206) 467-3838
Railroad; passenger and freight.
also:
Burlington Air Express
Transplex Air Cargo Building G
Sea-Tac International Airport
Seattle, WA 98158
(206) 433-5591
Air freight operations.

Chipman Moving & Storage
18821 90th Ave. S.
Kent, WA 98031
(206) 622-1959
Agent of: Mayflower Transit, Inc.

Consolidated Freightways
PO Box 3585
Seattle, WA 98124
(206) 763-1517
Freight forwarding.

Crowley Maritime Corp.
2401 Fourth Ave.
Seattle, WA 98121
(206) 443-8100
Tugboat, towing operations.

Expeditors International of Washington
19119 16th Ave. S.
Seattle, WA 98168
(206) 246-3711
Air and ocean freight forwarder; customhouse broker.

Federal Express
6633 S. 216th St.
Kent, WA 98032
(206) 282-9766

Foss Maritime Co.
660 W. Ewing St.
Seattle, WA 98119
(206) 281-3800
Towing, tugboat operations.

Fritz Air Freight
1200 S. 192nd St.
Seattle, WA 98148
(206) 242-8232
International transportation; warehouse in Kent.

Interstate Distributor Co.
11707 21st Ave. S.
Tacoma, WA 98444
(206) 537-9455
Common and contract motor carrier. Accepts mailed inquiries
only.

Lynden, Inc.
18000 Pacific Highway S.
Seattle, WA 98188
(206) 241-8778
Trucking, barge lines, air freight forwarding, construction.

Matson Navigation Co.
720 Third Ave.
Seattle, WA 98104
(206) 461-9100
Container shipping line.

Municipality of Metropolitan Seattle (Metro)
821 Second Ave.
Seattle, WA 98104
(206) 684-2100
Regional mass transportation provider.

Port of Olympia
915 Washington N.E.
Olympia, WA 98501

(206) 586-6150
Ocean shipping terminal, Olympia, Airport.

Puget Sound Freight Lines
3720 S. Airport Way
Seattle, WA 98134
(206) 623-1600
Tug and barge operation; provider of marine transportation
and warehousing.

Todd Shipyards
1102 S.W. Massachusetts
Seattle, WA 98134
(206) 223-1560
Shipbuilding, ship repair and conversion; tool manufacturing.

Totem Resources Corp.
Metropolitan Park Building, Suite 1100
Seattle, WA 98101
(206) 628-4343
Deep sea domestic transportation of freight.

United Parcel Service
4455 Seventh Ave. S.
Seattle, WA 98108
(206) 767-9700

EMPLOYERS Portland Area:

Alexander's Moving and Storage
3400 N.E. Columbia Blvd.
Portland, OR 97211
(503)
Agent of: Atlas Van Lines

Bekins Moving and Storage Corp.
407 N. Broadway
Portland, OR 97227
(503) 288-5411

Blue Bird Transfer
2410 E. 15th St.
Vancouver, WA 98661
(206) 693-4779 or (503) 233-5271
Agent of: Allied Van Lines

Consolidated Freightways
1621 N.W. 21st Ave.
Portland, OR 97208
(503) 226-4692
Trucking.

EastSide & WestSide Moving and Storage Co.
4836 S.E. Powell Blvd.
Portland, OR 97206
(503) 288-6564
Agent of: Mayflower Moving and Storage

Federal Express
6756 N.E. Alderwood Road
Portland, OR 97218
(503) 224-4175

Fulton Moving and Storage Co.
14305 S.W. Millikan Way
Beaverton, OR 97005
(503) 644-1600
Agent of: United Van Lines

Irvington Transfer and Storage Co.
2321 N.E. Argyle St.
Portland, OR 97211
(503) 287-2700
Agent of: Global Van Lines

Lile International Cos.
15605 S.W. 72nd Ave.
Tigard, OR 97224
(503) 620-8480
Agent of: North American Van Lines

O'Neill Transfer Co.
2233 N.W. 22nd Ave.
Portland, OR 97210
(503) 226-3055
Agent of: Allied Van Lines

Quality Moving and Storage Co.
14101 S.W. 72nd Ave.
Portland, OR 97224
(503) 620-9202
Agent of: Allied Van Lines

Rose City Van and Storage Co.
600 N.W. 14th Ave.
Portland, OR 97209
(503) 227-5791
Agent of: American Red Ball

Southern Pacific Transportation Co.
800 N.W. Sixth Ave.
Portland, OR 97209
(503) 220-4410

How To Get a Job

National common carrier trucking and railroad firm; most hiring handled through San Francisco headquarters.

Swartz Moving and Storage Corp.
2881 N.E. Argyle St.
Portland, OR 97211
(503) 288-6564
Agent of: United Van Lines

Tri-Met
4012 S.E. 17th Ave.
Portland, OR 97202
(503) 233-3511
Local and suburban public mass transit.

Union Pacific Railroad Co.
2745 N. Interstate Ave.
Portland, OR 97227
(503) 249-2711
Freight transportation, railroad.

United Parcel Service
6707 N. Basin Ave.
Portland, OR 97217
(503) 283-7750
Cargo distribution.

WDI
3501 N.W. Yeon Ave.
Portland, OR 97210
(503) 224-0121
Agent of: National Van Lines

Western Transportation Co.
3710 N.W. Front Ave.
Portland, OR 97208
(503) 294-8200
Warehousing and water transportation, intermodal distribution, interchange.

Travel

You may also want to check out the section on **Transportation**.

For networking in the **travel** industry, you can contact the following professional organizations:

PROFESSIONAL ORGANIZATIONS:

Airline Pilots Association
1625 Massachusetts Ave. N.W.
Washington, DC 20036

American Society of Travel Agents
1101 King St.
Alexandria, VA 22314

National Air Transportation Association
4226 King St.
Alexandria, VA 22302

Travel Industry Association of America
1133 21st St. N.W.
Washington, DC 20036

United States Tour Operators Association
211 E. 51st St.
New York, NY 10022

PROFESSIONAL PUBLICATIONS:

AOPA Pilot
ASTA Travel News
Fleet Owner
Frequent Flyer
Travel Agent

DIRECTORIES:

Aviation Directory (E.A. Brennan Co., Garden Grove, CA)
Travel Industry Personnel Directory (Travel Agent Magazine, New York, NY)
Western Travel Sales Guide (Cabell Travel Publications, North Hollywood, CA)

EMPLOYERS Seattle/Puget Sound Area:

AAA Travel Agency
333 Sixth Ave.
Seattle, WA 98109
(206) 448-5353
Ten Puget Sound branches.

Alaska Airlines
19300 Pacific Highway S.
PO Box 68900

Seattle, WA 98168
(206) 433-3200

All-Around Travel
4701 42nd Ave. S.W.
Seattle, WA 98116
(206) 938-3030

American Express Travel Service
600 Stewart St.
Seattle, WA 98101
(206) 441-8622
Branch office:
Business Travel Service
10640 Christensen Road, Suite 105
Seattle, WA 98188
(206) 248-3888

Amtrak
423 Second Ave.
Seattle, WA 98104
(206) 382-4136
Intercity rail passenger service

Carlson Travel Network
425 Pike St., Suite 401
Seattle, WA 98101
(206) 623-6688
Five Puget Sound offices.

Cascade Trailways
2209 Pacific Ave.
Tacoma, WA 98402
1-800-824-8897
Bus charters and tours.

Exploration Cruise Lines
1100 Olive Way, Suite 1500
Seattle, WA 98101
(206) 625-9600

Global Express Travel
129 S.W. 153rd
Seattle, WA 98166
(206) 244-7500
Eleven Puget Sound locations.

Gray Line of Seattle
720 S. Forest St.
Seattle, WA 98134
1-800-544-0739
Bus charters and tours.

Greyhound Charter Service
811 Stewart
Seattle, WA 98101
(206) 628-5526

Holland America Line—Westours, Inc.
300 Elliott Ave. W.
Seattle, WA 98119
(206) 281-3535
Tour and cruise line.

Horizon Air
19521 Pacific Highway jS.
PO Box 48309
Seattle, WA 98148
(206) 241-6757 or (800) 523-1223

Mercer Island Travel
7525 S.E. 24th
Mercer Island, WA 98040
(206) 232-1431
Seven Puget Sound offices, five remote service locations.

Mutual Travel
1000 Second Ave., Suite 1900
Seattle, WA 98104
(206) 461-4600
Twenty-three Puget Sound offices, some located in Washington
Mutual financial centers.

Princess Tours
2815 Second, Suite 400
Seattle, WA 98121
(206) 728-4202
Air, land, and ship tours.

Satellite Travel Systems
1750 112th N.E., B112
Bellevue, WA 98004
(206) 453-1180

Travel Center/Carlson Travel Network Associate
1201 Pacific Ave.
Tacoma, WA 98402
(206) 383-8000
Five Puget Sound branches.

Travel Exchange, The
999 Third Ave., Suite 1000
Seattle, WA 98104
(206) 622-0135

How To Get a Job

United Express
Tri Cities Airport, Building 142
C Ave. and Fourth
Pasco, WA 99301
Contact: Personnel. No phone number available.

US Travel Systems Co. dba Doug Fox Travel/University Travel
520 Pike St., Suite 2800
Seattle, WA 98101
(206) 747-9090 or (206) 682-5200
Thirty-three Puget Sound locations.

Washington State Ferries
Colman Dock, Pier 52
801 Alaskan Way
Seattle, WA 98104
(206) 464-7800
For office, administrative, and other off-ferry jobs, call the Office & Professional Employees International Union (OPEIU) at (206) 441-8880.

EMPLOYERS Portland Area:

AAA Travel Agency dba/Automobile Club of Oregon
600 S.W. Market St.
Portland, OR 97201
(503) 222-6767
Five area locations.

Amtrak
800 N.W. Sixth
Portland, OR 97209
(503) 273-4873
Intercity rail passenger service.

Ask Mr. Foster Travel
818 S.W. Broadway
Portland, OR 97205
(503) 222-3779
Six local offices.

Azumano Travel Service
320 S.W. Stark St.
Portland, OR 97204
(503) 223-6245
Six local offices.

Beaverton Travel
13525 S.W. Canyon Road
Beaverton, OR 97005
(503) 643-9984

Emmett Travel
4949 S.W. Macadam Ave.
Portland, OR 97201
(503) 223-5190

Evergreen Stage Line
400 S.W. Broadway
Portland, OR 97205
(503) 227-3340

Fairview Travel Service
1605 N.E. Fairview Ave.
Fairview, OR 97230
(503) 666-3893

Greyhound-Trailways Bus Lines
550 N.W. Sixth Ave.
Portland, OR 97209
(503) 243-2320

IVI Travel
2701 N.W. Vaughn St.
Portland, OR 97210
(503) 243-3470
Six area locations.

Port of Portland
700 N.E. Multnomah St.
Portland, OR 97232
(503) 231-5000
Port/marine and airport operations, industrial land.

Travel Company, The
121 S.W. Morrison St.
Portland, OR 97204
(503) 224-3533

USTS-Travelwise
7000 S.W. Varnes St.
Tigard, OR 97223
(503) 639-8869
Ten local offices.

Vista Travel Service
200 S.W. Market St.
Portland, OR 97201
(503) 224-5000

Utilities

For networking in **utilities** and related fields, you can contact the following organizations, some of which are listed in Chapter 5:

PROFESSIONAL ORGANIZATIONS:

Electric League of the Pacific Northwest, Bellevue, WA
Northwest Electric Light & Power Association, Portland
Northwest Irrigation Utilities, Portland
Oil Heat Institute of Oregon, Portland
Oil Heat Institute of Washington, Seattle
Public Power Council, Inc., Portland
Utility Contractors Association of Washington, Bellevue, WA
Washington Public Utility Districts' Association, Seattle
Washington State Association of Water Districts, Seattle

For additional information, you can write to:

American Public Power Association
2301 M St., N.W.
Washington, DC 20037

North American Telecommunications Association
2000 M St., N.W.
Washington, DC 20036

United States Telephone Association
900 19th St. N.W.
Washington, DC 20006

PROFESSIONAL PUBLICATIONS:

Electric Light and Power
Electrical World
Public Utilities Fortnightly
Telephony
Western Water

DIRECTORIES:

Brown's Directories of North American Gas Companies (Harcourt
 Brace Jovanovich, Cleveland, OH)
Electrical World Directory of Electrical Utilities (McGraw Hill, New
 York, NY)
Moody's Public Utility Manual (Moody's Investor Services, New
 York, NY)
Sourcebook (North American Telephone Association,
 Washington, DC)

EMPLOYERS Seattle/Puget Sound Area:

Cascade Natural Gas Corp.
222 Fairview Ave. N.
Seattle, WA 98124
(206) 624-3900
Gas distribution.

Contel of the Northwest
1805 Continental Place
Mount Vernon, WA 98273
(206) 428-7778
Telephone company, serving eight Washington counties.

Continental Telephone of the Northwest
1805 Continental Place
Mount Vernon, WA 98273
(206) 428-3100
Provides service in six Washington counties.

FlowMole Corp.
21409 72nd Ave. S.
Kent, WA 98032
(206) 395-0200
Provider of utility services.

GTE Northwest
1800 41st St.
Everett, WA 98201
(206) 261-5321
Telephone company, serving 12 Washington counties,
including King County.

Municipality of Metropolitan Seattle (Metro)
821 Second Ave.
Seattle, WA 98104
(206) 684-2100
Regional utilities.

Puget Sound Power & Light Co.
10608 N.E. Fourth
Bellevue, WA 98004
(206) 454-6363
Investor-owned public electric utility serving eight Puget
Sound counties.

Seattle City Light Department
1015 Third Ave.
Seattle, WA 98104
Personnel: (206) 684-3273
Municipal electric utility.

Telephone Utilities of Washington/Western Division
8102 Skansie Ave.
Gig Harbor, WA 98335
(206) 851-8118
Western and Eastern Divisions combined serve 14 Washington
counties.

U.S. Intelco Networks
99 South Sound Center
Lacey, WA 98503
(206) 456-8844
Consortium of nearly 300 independent telephone companies
nationwide; provides information services to more than 600
telephone companies.

US West Communications
1600 Seventh Ave.
Seattle, WA 98101
(206) 346-8500
Telephone company, serving 19 Washington counties,
including King, Pierce, and Thurston counties.

V & J, Inc.
4616 S. 200th
Kent, WA 98032
(206) 872-8622
Underground utilities (water and sewer).

Washington Energy Co.
815 Mercer St.
Seattle, WA 98109
(206) 622-6767
Holding company with natural gas and other energy-related
operations.

Whidbey Telephone Co.
2747 E. State Highway 525
Langley, WA 98260

(206) 321-1122
Serves two Washington counties.

EMPLOYERS Portland Area:

American Network (Owned by ITT Communications Services)
529 S.W. Third Ave., Suite 300
Portland, OR 97204
(503) 241-4671
Long-distance telephone service, dedicated lines, call accounting systems, voice mail.

Bonneville Power Administration
BPA Building
905 N.E. 11th Ave.
Portland, OR 97232
(503) 230-3000
Federal electric power marketing and distributing agency.

GTE Northwest
17855 N.W. Cornell Road
Beaverton, OR 97075
(503) 645-5581
Telephone utility.

Northwest Natural Gas Co.
220 N.W. Second Ave.
Portland, OR 97209
(503) 226-4211 or (503) 220-2434
Gas utility.

Pacific Power & Light Co.
920 S.W. Sixth
Portland, OR 97204
Employment: (503) 464-6800

Pacific Telecom
805 Broadway
Vancouver, WA 98668
(206) 696-6918
Telephone utility.

PacifiCorp
851 S.W. Sixth Ave.
Mailing address:
920 S.W. Sixth Ave.
Portland, OR 97204
(503) 464-6000
Diversified electric utility. Electricity, mining, telecommunications, leasing (includes Pacific Power & Light

Co., Pacific Telecom, NERCO, PacifiCorp Financial Services, Flight Dynamics, ONSITE Energy, and PacifiCorp Trans, Inc.).

Portland General Electric Co.
121 S.W. Salmon St.
Portland, OR 97204
(503) 226-8333
Electric utility.

Public Utility District of Clark County
PO Box C-005
Vancouver, WA 98668
(206) 699-3000 or (503) 285-9141
Electrical power, water.

United Telephone Co. of the Northwest
902 Wasco St.
Hood River, OR 97031
(503) 386-2211
Serves seven counties in Washington and Oregon.

U.S. West Communications
Employment Office
421 S.W. Oak
Portland, OR 97204
(503) 242-8593

Employers Index

A

A Contemporary Theatre, 279
A/DEC Inc., 403
AAA Travel Agency, 485
AAA Travel Agency
  dba/Automobile Club of
  Oregon, 488
AAA Washington Motorist, 413
ABAM Engineers, a member of
  The Berger Group, 313
ABC Plastics, 441
Absher Construction Co., 271
Accountants Microsystems, 262
Accurate Plastics, 439
Ace Novelty Co., 400
Acme Poultry Co., 323
ACT, Inc., 305
Action Office Interiors, 428
Admac, Inc., 400
ADP Dealer Services, 265
ADP-Automatic Data Processing,
  258, 260
Adriatica, 464
Advance Properties, 450
Advanced Technology
  Laboratories, 302, 372
Adventure Northwest
  Magazine/Leisure Publications,
  413
Adventures Northwest, 461
Aetna Casualty and Surety Co.,
  378
Aetna Life Insurance Co., 380
Agena Corp., 262
Airborne Freight Corp., 480
Aircastle Media Productions, 318
AKA Business Services, 260
Al Bauer Advertising Co., Inc.,
  227
Al Smith Co., 374
Alaska Airlines, 485
Alaska Airlines Magazine, 414
Alaskan Copper Cos., 424
Alberton's, Inc., 470
Albertsons Food Centers, 475
Aldus Corp., 262
Alexander's Moving and Storage,
  482
All American Homes, 450
All Fab Corp., 230
All-Around Travel, 486
All-World Scientific & Chemical,
  254
Allenmore Hospital, 342
Allstate Insurance Co., 378
Alpac Corp., 323
Alpha Computers, 475
Alston-Kline, 396
American Cable &
  Communications, 408

American Cancer Society, Local
  and State Office, 362
American Cancer Society, Oregon
  Division, 368
American Diabetes Association,
  362
American Express Travel Service,
  486
American Heart Association, 362
American Indian Basketry
  Magazine, 420
American Marine Bank, 246
American Motion Pictures, 318
American Network (Owned by
  ITT Communications Services),
  493
American Red Cross, 368
American Red Cross, Seattle/King
  County Chapter, 362
American Savings Bank, 246
American States Insurance
  Co./American Economy
  Insurance Co., 378, 380
Amtrak, 486, 488
Andersen Bjornstad Kane Jacobs,
  313
Andersen Construction Co., 276
Ankrom Moisan Associated
  Architects, 240
Anodizing, Inc., 425
Apex Wholesale, 287
Apple Computer, 265
Applied Microsystems Corp., 262
Architectural Alliance, 238
Archway Cookies, 323
Arco Petroleum Products/Atlantic
  Richfield, 309
Arctic Alaska Fisheries Corp., 323
Arctic Ice Cream Novelties of
  Seattle, 323
Argent Chemical Laboratories,
  254
Argus Weekend, 414
Arrowac Fisheries, 324
Arst Public Relations, 225
Arthur Andersen & Co., 221, 222
Arthur Young and Co., 396, 397
Artistic Drywall, 271
Arvey Paper & Supplies, 428
Ask Mr. Foster Travel, 488
Associated Grocers, 470
Association for Retarded Citizens,
  368
Association for Retarded
  Citizens/National Employment
  Training Program, 362
AT&T, 306
AT&T Business Markets Group,
  302
Atlantic Richfield Co., 310
Atlas Chemical, 256
Atlas Foundry & Machine Co.,
  424
Attachmate Corp., 262

495

Attitudes For Selling, 397
Attitudinal Healing, Northwest Center, 362
Auburn General Hospital, 343
Auburn School District No., 408, 294
Aurion Video Productions, 320
Autism Society of America, 362
Auto-Chlor System of Washington, 254
Automated Office Systems, 430
Avia Group International, 236
Azteca Restaurant Enterprises, 464
Azumano Travel Service, 488

B

B & I Interiors, 430
Back Door Travel, 414
Bacon, Henry, Building Materials, 434
Bain, William A. Associates, 450
Ball-Incon Glass Packaging Corp., 400
Ballard Community Hospital, 343
Ballard Construction, 271
Ballard Convalescent Center, 343
Bank of California, The, 250
Bank of Tacoma, 246
Bank of Tokyo, 250
Barbara Sue Seal Properties, 454
Barclay Dean Interiors, 428
Bardahl Manufacturing Corp., 254
Bartell Drug Co., 470
Bartells, E.J. Co., 271
Bassetti/Norton/Metler/Rekevics Architects, 238
Bateman Eichler Hill Richards, 385
Bathhouse Theatre, 279
Baugh Enterprises, 271
Baugh Industrial Contractors, Inc./Baugh Construction Co., 276
Bayley, Robert E., Construction, 272
Bayliner Marine Corp., 272, 400
Beaverton Florists, 475
Beaverton School District No., 48J, 299
Beaverton Travel, 488
Beck, R.W., and Associates, 313
Bekins Moving and Storage Corp., 482
Bekins Northwest, 480
Bell Industries Illuminated Displays Division, 231
Bell Industries/Farwest Manufacturing Division, 302
Bellevue Art Museum, 280
Bellevue Athletic Club, 458

Bellevue Community College, 291
Bellevue Hilton, 356
Bellevue Philharmonic Orchestra, 280
Bellevue Public Schools District No., 405, 294
Bellowing Ark/Bellowing Ark Society, 414
Belmont School, 299
Bemis Co., 403
Benjamin Franklin Federal Savings & Loan Association, 250
Benson & McLaughlin, P.S., 221
Benton's, Inc. Realtors/Ron Turner, Inc., 450
Bergman Luggage, 470
Berkley Engineering and Construction, 272
Bess Kaiser Medical Center, 349
Best Products Co., 470
Best Western Greenwood Inn, 356
Bethany of the Northwest, 343
Bethel School District No., 403, 294
Betts, Patterson & Mines, 390
Bicycle Paper, 414
Big Brothers of King County, 362
BioPharmaceuticals Corp., 289
BJSS Group, The, 238
Black & Co., 387
Blacksmith's Gazette, 414
Blitz-Weinhard Brewing Co., a Division of G. Heileman Brewing, 329
Blount Oregon Cutting Systems, 403
Blue Bird Transfer, 482
Blue Cross and Blue Shield of Oregon, 380
Blue Cross of Washington and Alaska, 378
Blue Cross of Washington and Alaska Prudent Buyer Plan, 343
Blue Cross/Blue Shield of Oregon Preferred Option Plan, 349
Boatracing Magazine/Muncey Productions, 414
Body Moves of Portland, 461
Boeing Co., The, 231
Boeing Computer Services Co., 258
Boeing Portland/Commercial Airplane Division, 232
Bogle & Gates, 391
Boise Cascade Corp., White Paper Division, 436
Boise Cascade Office Products, 428, 430
Bon Marche, 471
Bonar Plastics, 441
Bonneville Power Administration, 493
Book Buyer, 420

Borden Chemical Division of Borden, 254
Borders Perrin & Norrander, 225
Borders, Perrin & Norrander, 228
Botticelli Cafe, 465
Boy Scouts of America, Chief Seattle Council, 363
Boys and Girls Clubs of King County, 363
Boys Clubs of Portland, 368
Branom Instrument Co., 374
Brazier Forest Industries, 434
BRB Manufacturing, 234
Bread and Ink Cafe, 467
Brems Eastman Glade, 225
Bristol Productions, Ltd., 318
Britain's Office Supply, 428
Brod & McClung-Pace Co., 403
Broome Oringdulph O'Toole, 240
Brost Data Input, 258
Brower Co., The, 272
Brown and Caldwell, 313
Bruch & Vedrich/Better Homes & Gardens, 450
Buchan, John F. Construction, 272
Budget Office Furniture, 428
Builders Hardware & Supply Co., 424
Bullier & Bullier Realtors, 454
Bullivant, Houser, Bailey, Pendergrass & Hoffman, 393
Bumgardner Architects, The, 238
Burke Memorial Washington State Museum, 280
Burke Rubber Co./Division of Burke Industries, 439
Burlington Air Express, 480
Burlington Northern, 434, 480
Burlington Resources, 310
Burns Brothers, 244, 403
Burnside Community Council, 369
Burnside Projects, 369
Burnstead Construction Co., 272
Burr Lawrence Rising + Bates, 238
Bush School, 294
Business Commercial Furniture, 430
Business Environments, 428
Business Space Design, 238
Business Telephone Systems, 302
Businessland, Inc., 475

C

Cable Northwest, 410
Cache Cosmetic Co., 289
Cadillac Plastic & Chemical Co., 439
Cafe Alexis (Alexis Hotel), 465
Cafe des Amis, 467
Cafe Sport, 465

Call A.P.P.L.E./Apple Pugetsound Program Library Exchange, 415
Callison Partnership Ltd., 238
Calma Co., 258
Calvert Manufacturing Co., 234
Camas Mill/Division, Crown Zellerbach, 436
Cameron Productions, 319
Camp Fire, 369
Camp Fire, Seattle/King County Council, 363
Canoe/Canoe America Association, 415
Capital Industries, 424
Care Computer Systems, 262
CareNet, 349
Carlson Travel Network, 486
Carnation Co., 324
Carney Stephenson, 391
Carver Corp., 400
Cascade Business Forms, Division of Vanier Graphics, 400
Cascade Center for Training and Development, 397
Cascade Chemicals, 256
Cascade Corp., 403
Cascade Gasket & Manufacturing Co., 439
Cascade Information Resources, 260
Cascade Natural Gas Co., 310
Cascade Natural Gas Corp., 491
Cascade Rubber Products, 441
Cascade Savings & Loan Association, 247
Cascade Steel Rolling Mills, 425
Cascade Trailways, 486
Catholic Community Services, Seattle/King County, 363
Catholic Services for Children, 369
CB&S Advertising, 228
Cello Bag Co., 434
Centennial School District No., 28J, 299
Center for Human Services, 363
Centex Homes, 272
Central Point Software, 265
Centralia Public Schools District No., 401, 294
Century, 21 Columbia Realty, 454
Century, 21/North Homes Realty, 451
CH2M Hill Northwest, 313, 315
Chaffey Corp., 272
Challenge Manufacturing, 442
Chase Packaging Corp., 436
Chateau Ste. Michelle, 324
Chez Shea, 465
Childhaven, 363
Children's Home Society of Washington, 364
Children's Hospital and Medical Center, 343
Children's Museum, 283

Chipman Moving & Storage, 480
Christian Women Against Crime, 369
Church and Synagogue Libraries, 420
CIGNA HealthPlan of Washington, 343
City Liquidators, 431
City University, 291, 296
Citybank, 247
Clackamas Community College, 297
Clackamas County Bank, 250
Clackamas County Historical Society, 283
Clark College, 292, 297
Clark Office Products, 428
Clark, Nuber & Co., P.S., 221
Clark, W.G., Construction Co., 273
Classi Color Studios, 289
Close, D.W., Co., 273
Clover Park School District No., 400, 294
Coast Oyster Co./Hilton Seafoods Co., 324
Cochran Electric Co., 273
CODA, Inc., 349
Coe Manufacturing Co., 404
Coffman Engineers, 313
Coldwell Banker Commercial Group, 454
Coldwell Banker Commercial Real Estate Services, 451
Coldwell Banker Residential Real Estate, 451
Coldwell Banker Residential Real Estate Services, 455
Cole & Weber, 225, 228
Colliers Macaulay Nicolls International, 451
Collins Foods International, 468
Color Control, 444
Columbia Christian College, 297
Columbia Cosmetics Manufacturers, 289
Columbia Health Service, 380
Columbia Machine, 404, 425
Columbia Rubber Mills, 442
Columbia Steel Casting Co., 425
Columbia Winery, 324
Colwood National Golf Club, 462
Commercial Design Architects, 238
Commercial Office Machines, 431
Communication Services & Engineering, 306
Computer One/Better Computers, 475
ComputerLand, 475
Comtel, Inc., 303
Concept Technologies, 266
Concordia College/Portland, 297
Condominium News, 415

Cone-Heiden Corp., 444
Conner Development Co., 273
Consolidated Freightways, 480, 482
Consolidated Metco, 425
Consumers Choice, 471
Container Corp. of America, 435
Contel of the Northwest, 491
Continental Baking Co., 324
Continental Mills, 324
Continental Telephone of the Northwest, 491
Contractors, Inc., 276
Control Data, 258, 260
Cook Newhouse and Associates, 396
Cooper Vision, IOL, 372
Coopers & Lybrand, 221, 222
Cornish College of the Arts, 292
Corporate Row, 458
Costco Wholesale Corp., 471, 475
CPC Cedar Hills Hospital & Mental Health Clinic, 350
Craftsman Press, 444
Crawford's Office Furniture, 429
Crescent Foods, 324
Crescent Realty, 451
Crisis Clinic, 364
CRISTA Senior Community, 343
Criton Technologies, 231, 303
Cronin & Caplan, Realtors, 455
CrossLand Savings, FSB Utah, 251
Crowley Maritime Corp., 480
CRS Sirrine, 315
CTR Business Systems, 476
Culp, Guterson & Grader, 391
Cushman & Wakefield of Oregon, 455
Cushman & Wakefield of Washington, 451
Custom Software Services, 262

D

D.P. Enterprises, 471
Daily Journal of Commerce, 447
Dain Bosworth, 385
Dairy Queen of the Pacific Northwest, 468
Dammasch State Hospital, 350
Dancercize, Inc., 462
Danmor Co., The, 273
Darigold, Inc., 324
Data Force, 259
Data General Corp., 266
Data I/O Corp., 263
David Douglas School District No., 40, 299
Davis Walker Corp., 424
Davis Wright Tremaine, 391, 394
Davis, Johnson, Mogul & Colombatto Advertising (DJMC), 228
Day-Floren Associates, 398

Dean Witter Reynolds, 385, 387
Deloitte & Touche, 221, 222
Delta Marine Industries, 243
Delta Video Productions, 320
Deluxe Check Printers, 447
Dennis Uniform Manufacturing
 Co., 236
Denton Plastics, 442
DePaul Treatment Centers, 350
Dermacare Pharmaceutical, 289
Design Plastics, 439
Diabetes Supply Club, 289
Dick's Drive-In Restaurants, 465
Discovery Chemical Corp., 254
Dominique's Place, 465
Doubletree Inn at Southcenter,
 356
Doubletree Suites Hotel, 356
Downstream River Runner, 458
DP Enterprises, 263
Drake Beam Morin, 396, 398
Drake, Donald M. Co., 276
Drug and Sundry Supply Co., 287
Dunn, Carney, Allen, Higgins &
 Tongue, 394
Duryee, D.A., & Co., Real Estate,
 451
Duwamish Shipyard, 243
Dye-Plastics, 440
Dykeman Architects, The, 239

E

E.J. Bartells Co., 471
Easter Seal Society for Crippled
 Children and Adults, 364
Eastmoreland Hospital, 350
EastSide & WestSide Moving and
 Storage Co., 483
Eastside Mental Health, 364
Ebasco Services, 314
Ecumenical Ministries of Oregon,
 369
Eddie Bauer, 234
Eddie Lee's, 468
Edgewater Inn, 358
Edmonds Community College,
 292
Edmonds School District No. 15,
 294
Edwards, A.G. & Sons, 385
Edwards, A.G., & Son, 388
Egghead Discount Software, 471
Ehrig & Associates, 225
Eicher-Richards Co., 374
El Centro de la Raza, 364
Eldec Corp., 231, 303, 372
Electro Scientific Industries, 306,
 374
Elgin Syferd, 225
Emanuel Hospital & Health
 Center/Healthlink, 350
Embassy Suites Hotel, 360
Emerald City Chemical, 254

Emerald City Graphics, 445
Emerald Technology, 263
Emerald Terrace, 350
Emerick Construction Co., 277
Emmett Travel, 489
Empty Space Theatre, The, 280
Encore Arts in Performance
 Magazine, 420
Engineering & Design Associates,
 Inc., 316
Enterprises International, 400
Entranco Engineers, 314
Enumclaw Public Schools, 294
Environetics, Inc., 431
Epson Portland, 266
Equicor Preferred, 343
Equity Group, Realtors, The, 455
ERA Borge/LeDoux Real Estate,
 455
ERA Real Estate Northwest, 452
Ernst & Young, 221, 222
Ernst Home & Nursery, 471
ESCA Corp., 263
ESCO Corp., 425
Estacada Lumber, 436
Esterline Corp., 303, 400
Evans/Kraft, 225
Evans/Spangler Design, 445
Everett Community College, 292
Everett Pacific Hotel, 358
Evergreen Bank, 247
Evergreen Pharmaceutical
 Service, 288
Evergreen Stage Line, 489
Evergreen State College, 292
Everylife Nutritionals, 288
Ewing and Clark, 452
Execulodge/Portland Airport, 360
Executive Forum, 398
Executive Properties, 455
Executone Information Systems,
 303, 306
Exotic Metals Forming Co., 231
Expeditors International of
 Washington, 481
Exploration Cruise Lines, 486

F

F O R M A, 239
Fabric Wholesalers, 236
Fabricland, Inc., 476
Fabriform Plastics, 440
Fairview Travel Service, 489
Family Health Plan, 344, 350
Family Services, 364
Famous Pacific Dessert Co., The,
 325
Far West Federal Bank, 251
Far West Office Systems, 431
Farmers Insurance Group, 380
Farmers New World Life
 Insurance Co., 378
Farwest Garments, 234

Fearey Group, 226
Federal Express, 481, 483
Federal Way Public Schools, 295
Ferguson & Burdell, 391
Ferguson Construction, 273
Fiberchem, 440
Fiberchem, Inc., 254, 442
Fifth Avenue Theatre, 280
Fine Arts Graphics, 447
First Choice Health Network, 344

First Independent Bank, 251
First Interstate Bank of Oregon, 251
First Interstate Bank of Washington, 247, 251
First Mutual Savings Bank, 247
First National Bank of Enumclaw, 247
First Service Tennis, 459
First Western Properties, 452
Firstline Office Supply, 429
Fisher Bag Co., 234
Fishing and Hunting News, 415
Flavorland Foods, 329
Fleck Company, 440
Fleming Foods, 476
Flight Dynamics, 232
Floathe & Associates, 226
Flow International Corp., 401
Flowers by Tommy Luke, 476
FlowMole Corp., 491
Fluke, John Manufacturing Co., 303, 373
Flyfishing, 420
Food Services of America, 325
Forest Grove Community Hospital, 350
Fort Vancouver Plywood Co., 436
Foss Home, 344
Foss Maritime Co., 481
Foster, Pepper & Shefelman, 391
Foundation for the Handicapped, 364
Four Seasons Olympic Hotel, 358
FOURGEN Software, 263
Foushee & Associates, 273
Fox Expeditions, 462
FPS Computing, 266
Franklin Pierce School District No., 402, 295
Frayn Printing Co., 445
Fred Hutchinson Cancer Research Center, 344
Fred Meyer, Inc., 472, 476
Fred S. James and Co. of Oregon, 381
Frederick & Nelson, 472
Freedom Socialist/Freedom Socialist Party, 415
Freightliner Corp., 244, 404
Friendly House, 369
Frito Lay, 329
Fritz Air Freight, 481
Frontier Bank, 247

Frontier Museum, 280
Frye Art Museum, 280
Fujitsu America, 266
Fujitsu Microelectronics, 404
Fullers, 465
Fulton Moving and Storage Co., 483

G

G.I. Joe's, 476
Gaco Western, 254
Gage Industries, 442
Gai's Seattle French Baking Co., 325
Gall Landau Young Construction Co., 273
Garvey, Schubert & Barer, 391
GBD Architects/GBD Interiors, 241
General Construction Co., 273
General Hospital Medical Center, 344
Generic Software, 263
Generra Sportswear Co., 234
Genie Industries, 401
Genoa, 468
Geological Newsletter, 421
Georgia-Pacific Corp., Western Division, 436
Gerard's Relais de Lyon, 465
Gerber Advertising Agency, 228
Gerber Legendary Blades, 404
Gerry Sportswear Corp., 234
Gibralter Savings Bank, 247
Gibson Bowles, Realtors, 455
Gifford-Doving Florists, 476
Gill, J.K., 431
Girl Scouts, Totem Council, 364
Glacier Fish Co., 325
Gladstone School District No. 115, 300
Gleaner, 421
Global Express Travel, 486
Go-For-It Whitewater Adventures, 462
Golden Age Fisheries, 325
Golder Associates, 314
Good Health Plan of Washington, 344
Good Samaritan Hospital, 344
Good Samaritan Hospital and Medical Center/Legacy Health Systems, 350
Goodwill Industries, 364
Goodwill Industries of the Columbia Willamette, 369
Gordon, Thomas, Honeywell, Malanca, Peterson & Daheim, 392
Government, City, 332-334, 337-338
Government, County, 334, 338-339

Government, State, 335
Government, U.S., 335-337, 339-341
Graham & Dunn, 392
Graham Steel Corp., 424
Graham's Book & Stationery, 431
Grange News, 415
Grant & Roth Plastics, 442
Grant House, 468
Grant Thornton, 222
Graphic Arts Center, 447
Graphic Information Systems, d/b/a PrintRight, 447
Gray and Co./Portland Foods, 329
Gray Line of Seattle, 486
Gray, R.A., & Co., 277
Great Northwest Federal Savings & Loan Association, 247
Great Western Chemical Co., 256
Great Western Chemical Co./McCall Lubricants, 255
Great Western Savings Bank, 248
Green River Community College, 292
Greenwood Inn, The, 360
Gresham Grade School District No., 4, 300
Gresham Historical Museum, 283
Gresham Union High School District No. U2-20 JT, 300
Greyhound Charter Service, 487
Greyhound-Trailways Bus Lines, 489
Griffith Polymers, 442
Griffith Rubber Mills, 442
Grigsby Construction Co., 277
Group Health Cooperative Central Hospital, 344
Group Health Cooperative Eastside Hospital, 344
Group Health Cooperative of Puget Sound, 344
Grubb & Ellis Co., 452, 456
GTE Northwest, 303, 491, 493
GTE West, 306
Gunderson, Inc., 404
Gunderson, Inc., a Greenbrier Co., 244

H

Haagen's, Inc., 472
Haba Supply Co., 290
Halvorson Osborne Construction Co., 274
Hampton Affiliates, 437
Hanna Carwash International, 244
Hanna, Murphy, Jensen & Holloway, 394
Harborview Medical Center, 345
Harder Mechanical Contractors, 277
Harper Bond, 452

Harper McLean & Co., 385
Harris Group, 314, 435
Harris Group, Inc., 316
Harrison Memorial, 345
Harry J. Prior/Martech Associates, 396
Harry's Mother Runaway Youth Agency, 369
Hart Crowser, 314
HDR Engineering, 314
Health Maintenance of Oregon, 350
HealthGuard Services, 351
HealthPlus, 345
Heath Printers, 445
Heath Tecna Aerospace Co., 231
Heathman Hotel, The, 360
Heathman Restaurant and Bar, The, 468
Heikes Produce Co., 329
Heller Co., 452
Helly-Hanson USA, 234
Helsell, Fetterman, Martin, Todd & Hokanson, 392
Henderson Homes, 274
Henry Art Gallery, 280
Heritage Federal Savings & Loan Association, 248
Heritage Music Review, 415
Herring/Newman Direct Response Advertising, 226
Hewlett Packard Co., Lake Stevens Division, 401
Hewlett-Packard Co., 266, 306
Hewlett-Packard Co., Sales Office, 375
Hewlett-Packard Electronic Instruments, 373
Hewlett-Packard, Lake Stevens Instrument Division, 373
High Sierra Video Productions, 319
High-Purity Chemical, 256
Highline Community College, 292
Highline Community Hospital, 345
Highline Public Schools District, 401, 295
Hill and Knowlton, 226
Hillhaven Corp., 345
Hilton Downtown, 358
Historic Preservation League Of Oregon, 283
HMO Washington, 345
Hoffman Construction Co., 277
Holiday Inn Crowne Plaza, 358
Holiday Inn of Bellevue, 358
Holiday Inn Portland South, 360
Holiday Inn/Portland Airport Hotel and Trade Center, 360
Holiday Inn/Sea-Tac, 358
Holladay Park Medical Center/Legacy Health System, 351

Holland America Line—Westours, Inc., 487
Holland, The, 468
Home Realty, 452
Honeywell, Marine Systems Division, 401
Hooper Memorial Center, 351
Horizon Air, 487
Host International, 465
Howard Needles Tammen and Bergendoff, 314
Hunt Club, The (Sorrento Hotel), 465
Hunter Tavernor & LaComa, 445
Hygrade Food Products Corp., 325
Hyland & Sons, 277
Hyster Co., Headquarters Unit, 404

I

IBM Corp., 263, 266
Icicle Seafoods, 325
IDEA, Inc., 373
Il Bistro, 466
Il Fiasco, 466
Immunex Corp., 288
Imperial Real Estate Corp., 452
Impression Northwest, 445
In/Serv Information Services Group, 447
Indigine, 468
Infotech Corp., 259
Ingrim/Mills, 241
Injury and Illness Incidence, 421
Inland Chemical Co., 255
Input Factory, The, 259
Insight Productions, 320
Instromedix, Inc., 375
Instrumed, Inc., 373
Instrument Sales and Service, 373, 375
Instrumentation Northwest, 373
Instruments for Cardiac Research, 375
Intel Corp., 266
Interlinq Software Corp., 263
Intermec Corp., 401
International Biomedics, 373
Interpoint Corp., 303, 401
Interstate Distributor Co., 481
InterWest Savings Bank, 248
Intiman Theatre, 280
Ioline Corp., 263
Irvington Transfer and Storage Co., 483
Irwin-Hodson Co., 448
Isaacson Steel Service Center (ISSC Steel), 424
Isler & Co., 223
Issaquah School District No., 411, 295

ISSPRO/Instrument Sales and Service, 375
Issue Watch/Municipal League of Seattle, 416
Ivar's Restaurants, 466
IVI Travel, 489

J

J. Marcel Enterprises, 235
J.C. Thomas and Associates, 398
Jacobsen's, 476
James River Corp., 437
JanSport, Inc., 401
Jantzen, Inc., 236
Japanese Community Service, 365
Jay Jacobs, 235
Jeddeloh, Hays, 316
Jensen Krause Schoenleber Associates, 241
Jewish Federation of Greater Seattle, 365
Jewish Transcript, The/Jewish Federation, 416
JIM Enterprises, 398
John Bastyr College of Naturopathic Medicine, 292
John Graham Associates/DLR Group, 239
John H. Harland Co., 448
John L. Bird Co., 429
John, James E. Construction Co., 277
Johnny's Food Centers, 325, 472
Johnson Controls, 375
Jones Chemicals, 255
Jorgensen Steel/Forge Division, 424
Journal of the Association for Persons With Severe Handicaps, 416

K

K-Mart Discount Stores, 472, 476
K2 Corp., 401
Kaiser Permanente, 351
Kaiser Sunnyside Medical Center, 351
Kamas Realty, 453
Karakas, VanSickle, Ouellette, 228
Karol Niemi Associates, 241
Karr Tuttle Campbell, 392
Kaso Plastics, 442
KATU-TV/ABC, 410
KBRD FM, 408
KBSG AM & FM, 408
KCPQ-TV/Kelly Television Co., 408
KCTS-TV, 408

Keeners Inc. dba K & N Meats, 325
Keeney's Office Products, 429
Keith Uddenberg, Inc., 472
Kemp Pacific Fisheries, 326
Kent School District No., 415, 295
Kentrox Industries, 306
Kenworth Truck Co., 243
Ketcham, Henry H., Lumber Co., 435
KEX, 410
Key Bank of Oregon, 251
Key Bank of Puget Sound, 248
KEZX FM, 408
KGON FM, 410
KGW AM/King Broadcasting, 410
KGW-TV/NBC, 410
Kidder Mathews & Segner, 453
Kidder Peabody & Co., Inc., 385
Kienow's Food Stores, 477
Kilham Stationery & Printing Co., 431
KING, 408
King Broadcasting Co., 408, 410
King County Medical Preferred Plan, 345
King County Natural Resources and Parks Division, 459
KINK FM, 411
Kirkland Multi-Service Center, 365
KIRO AM and KIRO-TV, 408
Kistler-Morse Corp., 373
KISW FM, 408
Kitsap Bank, 248
KIXI AM/KMGI FM, 408
KKCW FM, 411
KKEY, 411
KKRZ FM, 411
KLDY AM, 409
KLSY AM & FM, 409
KLTX FM, 409
KMAS AM, 409
KMJK AM & FM, 411
KMPS AM & FM, 409
Knight Vale & Gregory, 221
KNUA FM, 409
Knudsen Erath Winery, 329
KOAP FM, 411
KOAP-TV, 411
Kobasic, Harris & Savage Advertising and Public Relations, 228
Kober/Sclater Architects, 239
KOIN-TV/CBS, 411
KOMO AM, 409
KOMO-TV/Fisher Broadcasting, 409
Kopy King Corp., 429
Korry Electronics Co., 304
KPDX-TV, 411
KPFF Consulting Engineers, 316
KPLZ FM/KVI AM, 409
KPMG Peat Marwick, 222, 396

KQEU, 409
Kramer Video, 319
Kramer, Chin & Mayo, 315
KRPM AM & FM, 409
KSEA FM, 409
KSGO AM, 411
KSTW-TV, 409
KTOL AM, 409
KTZZ-TV, 409
KUBE FM, 409
KUIK, 411
KUPL AM & FM, 411
KVOS-TV, 409
KWJJ AM & FM, 411
KXL AM & FM, 411
KXRX FM, 409
Kyocera Northwest, 404
KZOK FM, 410

L

L'Auberge, 468
Labels & Lists, 259
Labels West, 445
Labuznik, 466
Laird Norton Co., 435
Lake Oswego School District No. 7, 300
Lake Union Dry Dock Co., 243
Lake Washington School District No., 414, 295
Lake Washington Vocational Technical Institute, 292
Lake-Vue Gardens Convalescent Center, 345
Lakeside Industries, 274
Lakeside School, 295
Lamonts, 477
Lamonts Apparel, 472
Lane, Powell, Moss & Miller, 392
Langendorf Baking Co. of Seattle, 326
Lanier Voice Products Division, 306
Lanz International Laboratories, 288
Lariat, The, 421
LaserPrint Communications, 259, 445
Last Day Messenger, 421
Lattice Semiconductor Corp., 267, 316
Laurelwood Care Center, 345
Laventhol & Horwath, 222, 223
Le Gourmand, 466
Le Tastevin, 466
Lease Crutcher Lewis, 274
Lee Grocery Co., 326
Legacy Health Systems, 351
Leonhardt Group, The , 445
Leukemia Society of America, 365
Leupold & Stevens, 405
Leupold and Stevens, 375

Lewis and Clark College, 297
Lewis Packing Co., 330
Liberty Northwest Insurance
Corp., 381
Lile International Cos., 483
Lilly, Eli, and Co., 288
Lindal Cedar Homes, 401
Lindsay, Hart, Neil & Weigler,
394
Linfield College, 297
Linnton Plywood Association,
437
Little Chemical Co., 256
Livingston & Co., 226
Livingston Securities, 388
Livingwell Lady, 459
Lockheed Shipbuilding Co., 274
Logiplex Corp., 267
Longacres Race Course, 459
Longview Fibre Co., 435
Lonigan, William L. Contractors,
277
Lorentz Bruun Co., 277
Loschky Marquardt & Nesholm,
239
Louis Owen, 239
Louisiana-Pacific Corp., 437
Lozier Homes Corp., 274
Lutheran Social Services of
Washington, 365
Lutz Snyder Co., The, 456
Lynden, Inc., 481

M

Macadam Forbes, 456
MacDonald and Wolff, 397
Mackenzie/Saito & Associates,
241
MacPhersons, Realtors, 453
Madigan Army Medical Center,
346
Magni Systems, 375
Magnolia Hi-Fi, dba Magnolia Hi-
Fi & Video, 472
Mahlum & Nordfors, 239
Mail-Well Envelope Co., 437
Mainline Modeler/Hundman
Publishing Co., 416
Mains Florist, 477
Mainstream Youth Program, 351
Mamco Manufacturing Co., 231
Managed Health Care Northwest
d/b/a Caremark, 351
Management Advisory Services,
397
Management/Marketing
Associates, 398
Manke Lumber Co., 435
Mannesmann Tally Corp., 264
Manufacturers Life Insurance Co.
of Canada, 378, 381
Manus Direct Response
Marketing, 226

March of Dimes, 370
March of Dimes Birth Defects,
Puget Sound Chapter, 365
Marco Seattle, 402
Markron Cosmetics, 290
Marontate-Jones, 235
Marriott Corp., 358
Marsh & McLennan, 378
Mart, The, 432
Martech Associates, 398
Martha and Mary Nursing Home,
346
Martin Lithographics, 446
Marvin Stein & Associates, 239
Marx/Knoll, Denight & Dodge,
228
Marylhurst College, 297
Maryville Nursing Home, 352
Matrix Telecommunications, 304
Matson Navigation Co., 481
Mayflower Park Hotel, 358
McCall Oil & Chemical Corp., 256
McCall Oil Co./Division, McCall
Oil and Chemical Corp., 311
McCann-Erickson Seattle, 226
McCaw Cellular Communications,
304
McCawley Precision Machine
Corp., 440
McCormack, W.L., & Co., 278
McCormick & Schmick
Management Services, 468
McCutcheon Associates
Northwest, 398
McDonald's Corp., 469
McDonald, Babb & Clarkson, 229
McDonnell Douglas, 259
McDonnell Douglas/Health
Systems Co., 260
McKinley Architects, PSC, The,
239
McLoughlin House, 283
Meany Hall for the Performing
Arts, 281
Media West, 320
Medina Children's Service, 365
Meier & Frank Co., 477
Memorex Telex 304
Mentor Graphics Corp., 267, 316
Mercer Industries, 405
Mercer Island School District No.,
400, 295
Mercer Island Travel, 487
Merck Sharp & Dohme, 288
Meridian Park Hospital/Legacy
Health System, 352
Merrell-Dow Pharmaceuticals,
288
Merrill Lynch, Pierce, Fenner &
Smith, 388
Merrill Lynch, Pierce, Fenner &
Smith, Inc., 385
Mervyn's, 473, 477
Metheus Corp., 267

Metropolitan Area Communications Commission, 411

Metropolitan Federal Savings & Loan Association of Seattle, 248

Metropolitan Life Insurance Co., Evergreen Branch, 379

Metropolitan Life Insurance Co., Portland Branch, 381

Metropolitan Park District Of Tacoma, 459

Micro Innovations, 473

Microrim, Inc., 264

Microsoft Corp., 264

Middy Plastic Products, 440

Mikron Industries, 440

Milgard Manufacturing, 402

Miller, Nash, Wiener, Hager & Carlsen, 394

Milliman & Robertson, 379

Milwaukie Museum, 283

Mira Film and Video, 320

Mitchell, Lang & Smith, 394

Mithun Partners, 240

Mobil Oil Corp., 310

Modern Manufacturing, 231

Moffatt, Nichol & Bonney, 316

Mogelgaard & Associates, 226

Molded Container Corp., 443

Molin/Cutler Telemarketing Services, 227

Monarch Motor Hotel and Convention Center, 360

Montgomery Ward & Co., 477

MONY Financial Services, 381

MONY Financial Services, Seattle Office, 379

Moss Adams, 222, 223

Mount Hood Community College, 297

Mount Hood Medical Center/Legacy Health System, 352

Mount Hood Recreation Association, 462

Mount St. Joseph's Residence and Extended Care Center, 352

Mount St. Vincent Nursing Center, 346

Multi-Craft Plastics, 443

Multi-Service Centers of North and East King County, 365

MultiCare Medical Center, 346

Multnomah Athletic Club, 462

Multnomah Cable Access-Community Television, 411

Multnomah Education Service District, 300

Multnomah Kennel Club, 462

Multnomah School of the Bible, 297

Municipality of Metropolitan Seattle (Metro), 481, 491

Murphey Favre, 386, 388

Murphy, Donald B. Contractors, 274

Murray Franklyn Group, 274

Muscular Dystrophy Association, 365

Museum Of Flight, 281

Museum Of History & Industry, 281

Mutual Life Insurance Co. of New York, 381

Mutual of Enumclaw Insurance Co., 379

Mutual Travel, 487

Muzak, 402

Myriad Systems and Services, 397

N

Nabisco Brands, 330

NACO-WEST, 459

Nalley's Fine Foods, 326

National Boycott News/Institute for Consumer Responsibility, 416

National Business Systems, 259

National Frozen Foods Corp., 326

National Health Laboratories, 346

National Pacific Asian Resource Center on Aging, 366

National Securities Corp., 386

Nationwide Insurance, 381

Native American Rehabilitation Association of the Northwest, 352

Natural Health World and the Naturopath, 421

Nautilus Northwest, 459

NBBJ Group, The, 240

NCR Corp., 264

NEC America, 306

Neighborhood House, 366

Nendels Corp., 360

NERCO, Inc., 311

Nerland's Plastic Products, 440

Network Management, 346

New Times, 416

New York Life Insurance Co., 379, 382

Newhall Jones, 274

Niedermeyer-Martin Co., 437

Niemi, Holland & Scott, 223

Nike, Inc., 236

Nikko, 466

Nintendo of America, 402

Nintendo, Inc., of America, 264

Nordstrom, 477

Nordstrom, Inc., 473

Norpac Foods (Dayton Plant No. 3), 330

Norris & Stevens, 456

Norris, Beggs & Simpson, 456

North American Post, 416

North Clackamas School District No. 12, 300

North Pacific Bank, 248
North Pacific Insurance Co., 382
North Pacific Processors, 326
North Seattle Community
    College, 292
North Thurston District No. 3,
    295
North Willamette Telecom, 411
Northern Telecom Meridian
    Systems, 304
Northshore School District No.,
    417, 296
Northwest Biotech International,
    288
Northwest Cable Advertising, 410
Northwest Cable TV, 410
Northwest Career and
    Organizational Consulting, 398
Northwest Chamber Orchestra,
    281
Northwest Containers, 440
Northwest Hospital, 346
Northwest Information Services
    (NIS), 307
Northwest Labor Press, 421
Northwest Marine Iron Works,
    245
Northwest National Bank, 251
Northwest Natural Gas Co., 311,
    493
Northwest Outdoor Center, 459
Northwest Packing Co., 330
Northwest River Outfitters, 462
Northwest Rubber Extruders, 443
Northwest Skier, 417
Northwest
    Technocrat/Technocracy, 417
Northwest Test and
    Measurement, 375
Northwest Transforms, 319
Northwest Womens Health
    Clubs, 459
Northwestern Drug Co., 288
Northwestern Mutual Life
    Insurance Co., 382
Norwest Publishing Co., 448
Nurnberg Scientific, 256

O

O'Neill Transfer Co., 483
Oak Knoll Winery, 330
Occidental Chemical Corp., 255
Ocean Beauty Seafoods, 326
Odom Corp., 326
Odyssey Productions, 321
OECO Corp., 307
Office Furniture To Go, 429
Office Interiors, 432
Official Productions, 321
Ogilvy & Mather/West, 227
Oles, Morrison & Rinker, 392
Olin Defense Systems, Aerospace
    Division, 231

Olshen's Bottle Supply Co., 443
Olson's Food Stores, 326, 473
Olympia School District No. 111,
    296
Olympic Athletic Club, 460
Olympic College, 292
Olympic Homecare Products Co.,
    255, 402
Olympic Office Supply, 429
Olympic Properties, 453
Olympic Savings Bank, 248
Omark Industries, 405
OmniTek Computers, 477
On the Boards, 281
OP/Lost Music Network, 417
Opcon, Inc., 304
Oppenheimer & Co., 386
Option Care, 290
Oregon Art Institute/Portland Art
    Museum, 283
Oregon City School District No.
    62, 300
Oregon Dental Service, 382
Oregon Episcopal Churchman,
    421
Oregon Fishing Adventures, 462
Oregon Graduate Institute, 298
Oregon Health Sciences
    University, 298
Oregon Health Sciences
    University Hospital, 352
Oregon Historical Society, 283
Oregon Institute of Technology,
    Metro Campus, 298
Oregon Maritime Center &
    Museum, 284
Oregon Motorist, The, 422
Oregon Museum of Science and
    Industry, 284
Oregon Public Broadcasting, 411
Oregon Realty Co., 456
Oregon Steel Mills, 425
Oregon Symphony Orchestra,
    284
Oroweat Foods Co., 327
Otak, Inc., 316
Overall Laundry Services, 235
Overlake Hospital Medical
    Center, 346
Owens-Corning Fiberglas Corp.,
    257
Owens-Illinois Glass Container,
    405

P

P & C Construction Co., 278
P.R.O. Sports Club, 460
Pabst Brewing Co., 327
PACC Health Plan, 352
PACCAR, Inc., 243, 402
Pacific Affairs Group/Fisher Brady
    & La Brue Advertising and
    Public Relations, 227

Pacific Coast Concepts, 397
Pacific Communications (PACCOM), 319
Pacific Electro Dynamics, 304
Pacific Engineering Corp., 316
Pacific First Bank, 251
Pacific First Federal Savings Bank, 248, 252
Pacific First Securities Limited, 386
Pacific Gateway Hospital, 352
Pacific Health, 346
Pacific Heritage Assurance Co., 382
Pacific Lumber & Shipping Co., 435
Pacific Lutheran University, 293
Pacific Mutual Life Insurance Co., 382
Pacific Northern Oil Corp., 310
Pacific Northwest Ballet, 281
Pacific Office Furnishings, 432
Pacific Power & Light Co., 493
Pacific Science Center, 281
Pacific Stationery & Printing Co., 432
Pacific Telecom, 307, 493
Pacific Trail Sportswear, 235
Pacific University, 298
Pacific West Athletic Clubs, 460
PacifiCare of Oregon, 352
Pacificorp, 311, 493
Page Co., The, 453
Paine Webber, 386, 388
Panlabs, Inc., 289
Pantages Centre, 281
Paper Fibres/Subsidiary of Rebanco, 435
Park Rose Care Center, 347
Parkrose School District No. 3, 300
Parkwood Homes, 275
Parsley Sage & Time/Pike Market Senior Center, 417
Partners National Health Plans, 353
Passages/Horizons Publishing, 417
Pasta and Co., 327
Paul Seibert and Associates, 240
Paulson Investment Co., 388
Pay 'n Pak Stores, 473
Pay 'n Save, 473
Pay Less Drug Stores Northwest, 473
Payless Drug Stores Northwest, 478
Peat Marwick Main & Co., 223
Peco, Inc., 232
Pendleton Woolen Mills, 236
Penney, J.C., Co., 473, 478
Pennwalt Corp., Agchem Division, 255
Pennwalt Corp., Indchem Division, 257
Penwest, Ltd., 327

Pepsi-Cola Bottling Co., 330
Perkins Coie, 392, 394
Permaculture Activist, The/Permaculture Institute of North America, 417
Pesca Y Marina, 417
Peter Pan Seafoods, 327
Peter's Office Supply Co., 432
Peterson Sullivan & Co., 222
Physicians MedLab, 353
Physio-Control Corp., 374
Pierce College, 293
Pierce County Medical Preferred Plan, 347
Pierce County Parks and Recreation, 460
Pihas, Schmidt, Westerdahl Co., 229
Pioneer Federal Savings Bank, 249
Piper Jaffray & Hopwood, 389
Piper, Jaffray & Hopwood, 386
Pizza Hut District Office, 466
Plaid Pantry, 478
Poly-Cast, Inc., 443
Poorman-Douglas Corp., 260
Pope & Talbot, 437
Port Chatham Packing Co., 327
Port of Olympia, 481
Port of Portland, 489
Portland Adventist Convalescent Center, 353
Portland Adventist Medical Center, 353
Portland Ballet/Portland Opera Association, 284
Portland Beavers Baseball Club, 463
Portland Black Repertory Theatre, 284
Portland Bottling Co., 330
Portland Cable Access, 411
Portland Carousel Museum, 284
Portland Center for the Performing Arts, 284
Portland Civic Theatre, 284
Portland Community College, 298
Portland General Electric Co., 494
Portland Hilton Hotel, 361
Portland Impact, 370
Portland Inn, 361
Portland Marriott Hotel, 361
Portland Meadows Horse Racing, 463
Portland Paging, 307
Portland School District No. 1J, 300
Portland State University, 298
Portland Trailblazers Basketball (NBA), 463
Portland Veterans Administration Medical Center, 353
Portland Veterans Administration Nursing Home Care Unit, 353

Portland Winter Hawks Hockey (WHL), 463
Portland Youth Philharmonic, 284
Potentials Development, 397
Precision Castparts Corp., 232, 405, 426
Precision Machine Works, 232
Precor U.S.A., 402
Prescription Instrument Corp./EPIC, 376
Preservative Paint Co., 255, 402
Preston, Thorgrimson, Shidler, Gates & Ellis, 393
Price Waterhouse, 222, 223
Princess Tours, 487
Print Northwest, 446
Production Plastics, 441
Professional Business Services, 259
Professionals 100, 456
Programming Resource Organization, 259
Progress, The, 418
Providence Hospital, 348
Providence Medical Center, 348, 353
Providence Milwaukie Hospital, 353
Prudential Bache Securities, 389
Prudential Insurance Co. of America, Oregon Agency, 382
Prudential-Bache Securities, 386
Pry Publishing Co., 448
Public Utility District of Clark County, 494
Puget Sound Bancorp, 249
Puget Sound Council of Governments (PSCOG) Newsletter, 418
Puget Sound Freight Lines, 482
Puget Sound Hospital, 347
Puget Sound Marketing, 474
Puget Sound Power & Light Co., 492
Puget Sound Savings Bank, 249
Purdy Corp., 405

Q

Qual-Med Health Plan, 347
Quality Food Centers (QFC), 474
Quality Moving and Storage Co., 483
Queen City Grill, 466
Queen Fisheries, 327
Quinton Instruments Co., 374

R

R & H Construction Co., 278
Raden, G., & Sons, 327
Radisson Hotel, 358
Radix Microsystems, 267
Rafn, J.M., Co., 275
Ragen MacKenzie, 386
Ragen, Tremaine, Krieger, Schmeer & Neill, 394
Rainier Brewing Co., 328
Rainier Rubber Co., 441
Rancho Flowers, 478
Rappleyea, Beck, Heiterline, Spencer & Roskie, 394
Ratelco, Inc., 304
Real Estate Association, 457
Realty Group, 457
Record Stationery & Office Supply, 429
Recreational Equipment (REI), 474
Rector Construction, 275
Red Hook Brewery, 328
Red Lion Hotel/Columbia River, 361
Red Lion Hotel/Downtown, 361
Red Lion Hotel/Jantzen Beach, 361
Red Lion Hotels and Inns, 361
Red Lion Inn/Bellevue, 359
Red Lion Inn/Lloyd Center, 361
Red Lion Inn/Sea-Tac, 359
Red Lion/Inn at the Quay, 361
Reed College, 298
Reed, McClure, Moceri, Thonn & Moriarty, 393
Regal Courier, The, 422
Regency Group, 453
Renton Inn, 359
Renton School District No., 403, 296
Reser's Fine Foods, 330
Rest Harbor Extended Care Center, 353
Restaurant Management Northwest, 469
Restaurants Unlimited, 466
Restorative Care Center, 347
Revelation Technologies, 264
Reynolds Metals Co., 426
Reynolds School District No. 7, 300
RFD Publications, 422, 448
Richard James Realtors, 453
Richardson Strang Engel, 229
Riddell, Williams, Bullitt & Walkinshaw, 393
Riedel Resources, 278
Rippling River Resort and Conference Center, 362
Riverdale School District No., 51J, 301
Riverview Savings Bank, 252
Robbins Co., The, 403
Robinson Construction Co., 278
Rockey Co., 227
Rockey Company Design Group, The, 446

Rocky Mountain Bank Note Co., 448
Rodgers Instrument Corp., 376
Rogers Cable TV, 412
Roman Meal Co., 328
Ron Paul Catering and Charcuterie, 469
Rono Graphic Communications Co., 448
Rose City Van and Storage Co., 483
Rose Vista Nursing Center, 354
Rotary Offset Sales Co., 446
Rover's, 467
Royal Video Productions, 319
Rundel Products, 405
Ruralite, 422
Rust International, 317
Ruth Dykeman Children's Center, 366
Ryan Communications, 229
Ryther Child Center, 366

S

Safeco Insurance Co., 383
SAFECO Insurance Co. of America, 379
Safeco Securities, 386
Safeway Stores, 474, 478
Sage Polytron, 267
Saint Cabrini Hospital of Seattle, 347
Saleh al Lago, 467
Salmon Trout Steelheader, 422
Salvation Army, 366
Salvation Army, Cascade Division, 370
Sander Perkins & Co., 223
Satellite Travel Systems, 487
Sauvie Island School District No. 19, 301
Scenic Fruit Co., 331
Schemmer Associates, Inc., The, 240
Schneider Homes, 275
Schnitzer Steel Products Co., 426
Schuck's Auto Supply, 244, 474
Schwabe, Williamson & Wyatt, 394
Scott Paper Co./Western region, 435
Scott, John L., Real Estate, 453
Scougal Rubber Corp., 441
SDL Corp., 275
Sea Galley Stores, 467
Sea-Tac Marriott Hotel, 359
Seafirst Bank, 252
Seafirst Corp., 249
Sears, Roebuck & Co., 478
Sears, Roebuck and Co., 474
Seatoma Convalescent Center, 347
Seattle Art Museum, 281

Seattle Athletic Club/Northgate, 460
Seattle Central Community College, 293
Seattle Children's Home, 366
Seattle Children's Museum, 281
Seattle Children's Theatre, 282
Seattle City Light Department, 492
Seattle Club, The, 460
Seattle Downtown Hilton, 359
Seattle First National Bank, 249
Seattle Fur Exchange, 235
Seattle Group Theatre, 282
Seattle Indian Center, 366
Seattle Mariners Baseball Club, 460
Seattle Mini Golf, 460
Seattle Northwest Securities Corp., 387
Seattle Office Furniture, 429
Seattle Opera Association, 282
Seattle Pacific Industries, 235
Seattle Pacific University, 293
Seattle Parks and Recreation Department, 460
Seattle Repertory Theatre Company, 282
Seattle School District No. 1, 296
Seattle Seahawks, 460
Seattle Sheraton, 359
Seattle South K.O.A., 461
Seattle Steel, 424
Seattle Storytellers Guild, 418
Seattle Supersonics, 461
Seattle Symphony Orchestra, 282
Seattle University, 293
Seattle Urban League, 366
Seattle's Child, 418
Security Pacific Bancorporation Northwest, 249
Security Pacific Bank Washington, 252
Security Pacific Oregon Bancorp, 252
Security Pacific Savings Bank, 249
SEH America, 405
Selectron, Inc., 307
Sellen Construction Co., 275
Senior Scene/Council on Aging, Lutheran Social Services of Washington, 418
Senior Services of Seattle/King County, 367
Sequent Computer Systems, 267
Settebello, 467
Sew It Seams, 418
Shannon & Wilson, 315
Sharp Hartwig, 227
Shearson Lehman Hutton, 387, 389
Sheraton Portland Airport Hotel, 362
Sheraton Tacoma Hotel, 359
Sherwood Group, The, 454

Sherwood Terrace, 347

Shoreline Community College, 293

Short, Cressman & Burgess, 393

Shriners Hospital for Crippled Children, 354

Sidereal Corp., 268

Sierra Geophysics, 264

Signpost/Washington Trails Association, 418

Simon Golub & Sons, 235

Sisters of Providence Good Health Plan of Oregon, 354

Sisters of Providence of Washington, 347

SJO Consulting Engineers, 317

Skagit Valley College, 293

Ski Bowl, 463

Skies American Airline Network, 422

Skilling Ward Magnusson Barkshire, 315

Skipper's, Inc., 467

Smith Barney Harris Upham & Co., 389

Smith Barney, Harris Upham & Co., 387

Smith Brothers Office Environments, 432

SmithKline Bio-Science Laboratories, 348

Smurfit Newsprint Corp., 437

Snoqualmie Winery, 328

Soderstrom Architects, 241

Software Research Northwest, 264

Sokol Blosser Winery, 331

Sound Mind & Body, 461

South King County Multi-Service Center, 367

South Puget Sound Community College, 293

South Seattle Community College, 293

Southern Pacific Transportation Co., 483

Southland Corp. d/b/a Seven-Eleven Food Stores, 478

Southland Corp., North Pacific Division, 328

Southwest Washington Hospitals, 354

Spacelabs, Inc., 374

Spectra-Lux Corp., 232

Speedometer Service and Instrument Co., 376

Spencer Aircraft Industries, 232

Spiritual Women's Times/Silver Owl Publications, 418

Sports Northwest Magazine, 419

Sprouse!, 478

SRG Partnership, 241

St. Joseph Community Hospital, 354

St. Joseph Hospital and Health Care Center, 348

St. Vincent Hospital and Medical Center, 354

Stafford Homes, Inc., 275

Stan Wiley, 457

Stan Wiley Realtors, Commercial Division, 457

Standard Insurance Co., 383

Stanley Plastic Manufacturing, 441

State Capitol Museum, 282

State Farm Insurance Co., 383

Stationer's, The, 430

Steilacoom Historical School District No. 1, 296

Stevens Memorial Hospital, 348

Stewart Greacen, 275

Stimpson-Clarke Advertising, 227

Stimson Lumber Co., 438

Stoel Rives Boley Jones & Grey, 395

Stoel, Rives, Boley, Jones & Grey, 393

Stouffer Madison Hotel, 359

Stusser Electric Co., 305

Sudden Printing, 446

Sulzer Bingham Pumps, Division of Guy F. Atkinson Co., 406

Sun Sportswear, 235

SunAmerica Securities, 387

Sundstrand Data Control, 232

Sverdrup Corp., 315

Swartz Moving and Storage Corp., 484

Swedish Hospital Medical Center, 348

Synergy Video Productions, 319

Sysco/Continental-Portland, 331

T

Tacoma Actors Guild, 282

Tacoma Art Museum, 282

Tacoma Boatbuilding Co., 244

Tacoma Community College, 293

Tacoma Lutheran Home, 348

Tacoma Plastics, 441

Tacoma School District No. 10, 296

Target Stores, 478

TASH, The Association for People With Severe Handicaps, 367

TCI Cablevision, 410

TCI Cablevision of Oregon, Inc., 412

Technigraphic Systems, 446

Ted Nelson Co., 426

Teknifilm Video, 321

Tektronix, Inc., 307, 376

Tel Plus, 305

Telemation Productions, 319

Telepage Northwest, 307

Telephone Utilities of Washington/Western Division, 492
Tempress Measurement and Control Corp., 376
Tex Chemical, 257
Texaco Refining and Marketing, 310
TFB/BBDO, 227
Thayer, The J., Co., 432
Then and Now, 419
Third Avenue Productions, 319
Thompson Valvoda & Associates, 241
Thurston County Parks and Recreation Department, 461
Thurston-Mason Senior News, 419
TIE Systems, 305
TIE Systems, Northwest, 307
Tigard School District No., 23J, 301
Tim Girvin Design, 446
Time Oil Co., 310
Timeline, Inc., 265
Times Litho, 449
Todd Pacific Shipyards Corp., 244
Todd Shipyards, 482
TOM Software, 265
Tonkon, Torp, Galen, Marmaduke & Booth, 395
Topline Inports, 236
Total Office Products and Printers, 432
Totem Resources Corp., 482
TRA Architecture, Engineering, Planning, Interiors, 240
Trailblazer, 419
Training Consultants Co., 397
Transamerica Insurance Group, 383
Transamerica Insurance Group, Main Office, 379
Transamerica Occidental Life Insurance Co., 383
Travel Center/Carlson Travel Network Associate, 487
Travel Company, The, 489
Travel Exchange, The, 487
Travelers Aid Society, 367
Travelers Preferred, 354
Traveling Software, 265
Treasure Chest Advertising, 229, 449
Trend College, 298
Tri-Met, 484
Trick & Murray, 430
Trident Seafood Corp., 328
Tsang Partnership, The, 240
Tualatin Vineyards Winery, 331
Tuality Community Hospital, 354
Tucci & Sons, 275
Turn Around At Vancouver, 354
Turner Construction Co., 276
Turtledove Clemens, 229

Twin Cedars R.V. Park, 461
Twin City Foods, 328
Tyee Productions, 321

U

U.S. Bank of Oregon, 252
U.S. Bank of Washington, 250
U.S. Intelco Networks, 492
U.S. Natural Resources, 311
U.S. Oil & Refining, 310
U.S. Savings Bank of Washington, 250
U.S. Securities Clearing Corp., 389
U.S. West Communications, 494
Union Bay Cafe, 467
Union Pacific Railroad Co., 484
Union Register, The, 422
Unisea, Inc., 328
United Beer Distributors Co., 331
United Cerebral Palsy Association of King-Snohomish Counties, 367
United Communications Systems, 305
United Express, 488
United Graphics, 446
United Grocers, 479
United Indians of All Tribes Foundation, 367
United Instrument, 376
United Marine Shipbuilding, 244
United Pacific Insurance Co., 380
United Parcel Service, 482, 484
United Properties, 457
United States Bakery, 331
United Telephone Co. of the Northwest, 494
United Way of King County, 367
United Way of the Columbia Willamette, 370
Univar Corp./Van Waters & Rogers, 255
Universal Plastics Co., 441
University of Oregon, Portland Center, 299
University of Portland, 299
University of Washington, 294
University of Washington Medical Center, 348
University Place School District No. 83, 296
University Savings Bank, 249
URS Consultants, 315
US Travel Systems Co. dba Doug Fox Travel/University Travel, 488
US West, 308
US West Communications, 492
US West Communications Systems, 308
US West Direct, 422

US West Information Systems, 305
US West NewVector Group, 305
USTS-Travelwise, 489

V

V & J, Inc., 492
Valley Medical Center, 348
Vanalco, Inc., 426
Vancouver Federal Savings Bank, 252
Vancouver Memorial Hospital, 355
Vanexco/Division of Alcoa, 426
Vanguard Office Systems, 430
Vantage, 355
Vernell's Fine Candies, 328
Viacom Cablevision, 410
Video Depot, 474
Video Librarian, 419
Video Presentations, 320
Video Professionals Production Co., 321
View-Master Ideal Group, 406
Viking Industries, 406
Village Theatre, 282
Virginia Manor Convalescent Center, 348
Virginia Mason Health Plan, 349
Virginia Mason Hospital, 349
Vision Productions, 320
Visiting Nurse Association/Legacy Health System, 355
Visiting Nurse Services of Seattle/King County, 368
Vista Travel Service, 489
Visual Communications Systems, 447
Volunteers of America, 368

W

Wacker Siltronic Corp., 406
Wagner Mining Equipment Co., 406
Walker, Richer & Quinn, 265
Wallace and Wheeler, Real Estate, 454
Walter Dorwin Teague Associates, 447
Wang Laboratories, 268
Ward's Cove Packing Co., 329
Warn Industries, 406
Warner Pacific College, 299
Warwick Hotel, 359
Washington Athletic Club, 461
Washington County Fairgrounds, 463
Washington Employers, 397
Washington Energy Co., 310, 492
Washington Federal Savings & Loan Association, 250

Washington Federal Savings Bank, 252
Washington Mutual Savings Bank, 250
Washington Physicians Service, 380
Washington State Ferries, 488
Washington State Historical Society Museum, 282
Washington State Parks and Recreation Commission, 461
Waves/Northwest Passage, 419
WDI, 484
WEA Action, 419
Weisfield's, Inc., 474
Wendco Northwest Limited, 467
Wesley Homes, 349
West Linn School District No. 3 JT, 301
West One Bank, 252
West State, 245
Westcon, Inc., 376
Western Alaska Fisheries, 329
Western Business College, 299
Western Community Bank, 250
Western Drug Distributors, 475
Western Flyer, 420
Western Health Clinics, 355
Western Marine Electronics, 305
Western Office Products, 433
Western States Chiropractic College, 299
Western Telephone, 308
Western Transportation Co., 484
Western Video Services, 320
Western Viking, 420
Western Washington University, 294
Western Wire Works, 426
Westin Benson, The, 362
Westin Hotel, 359
Westlake Office Furniture, 430
Westmark International, 403
Westwood Corp. Developers and Contractors, 278
Weyerhaeuser Co., 436, 438
Weyerhaeuser Information Systems, 259, 265
Whatcom Medical Bureau Alternative Choice Plan, 349
Whatcom Museum of History and Art, 283
Whidbey Telephone Co., 492
Whitehall Laboratories/Division of American Home Products Corp., 289
Whitman Advertising & Public Relations, 229
Wick Construction Co., 276
Wieden & Kennedy, 229
Willamette Falls Hospital, 355
Willamette Industries, 438
Willamette Industries Business Forms Division, 449

Willamette Savings & Loan
Association, 253
Willamette View Convalescent
Center, 355
Williams, Kastner & Gibbs, 393
Wilsey & Ham Pacific, 317
Windermere Real Estate, 454
Wing Luke Asian Museum, 283
Woodland Park Hospital, 355
Woodworth & Co., 276
Wright Business Forms, 449
Wright Schuchart, 276
WTD Industries, 438
Wyatt Software Services, 268
Wyatt Stapper Architects, 240
Wyeth-Ayerst
Laboratories/Division of
American Home Products
Corp., 289

X,Y,Z

Xerox Corp., 430
Yates Wood & MacDonald, 454
Yelm Community Schools, 296
Yergen & Meyer, 223
YMCA of Greater Seattle, 368
YMCA of the Columbia
Willamette, 370
Yost Grube Hall, 241
Young & Roehr, 229
YWCA Downtown Center, 370
YWCA of Seattle/King County,
368
ZGF Interiors, 242
Zidell Explorations, 426
Zimmer Gunsul Frasca
Partnership, 242

General Index

A

Accounting/Auditing: selected firms; professional groups, professional magazines, and directories, 220-223

Advertising/Public Relations: selected agencies; professional groups, professional magazines, and directories, 223-230

Aircraft and Aerospace: selected firms; professional groups, publications, and directories, 230-232

Apparel and Textiles: selected firms; professional groups, publications, and directories, 233-236

Architecture/Interior Design: selected firms; professional groups, professional magazines, and directories, 237-242

Art Galleries: *see Cultural Institutions*

Associations, Local, 123-147

Auditing: *see Accounting*

Auto/Truck/Marine/Transportation Equipment: selected firms; professional groups, publications, and directories, 242-245

B

Banks/Savings and Loans: selected firms; professional groups, publications, and directories, 245-253

Beverage Industry: *see Food/Beverage*

Books: *see Resource Books*

Broadcasting: *see Media, Broadcasting*

C

Cable TV: *see Media, Broadcasting and Cable TV*

Career Analysis: *see Vocational Testing*

Career Consultants, 22-29, 156-157

Career Counseling, 22-40, 156-157

Career Objectives, how to establish, 17-19

Career Transition Issues, 206-207

Chambers of Commerce, 14-16

Chemicals: selected firms; professional groups, publications, and directories, 253-257

Colleges, list of local: *see Educational Institutions*

Computer Industry: selected equipment manufacturers and programming and software companies; trade groups, trade magazines, and directories: Data Processing, 257-260; Hardware and Software, 260-268

Consultants, Career: *see Career Consultants*

Consultants, Vocational: how to choose, 23-24 local listing, 25-29

Consumer Protection Agencies, 29-30, 76

Contractors and Construction: selected firms; professional groups, professional magazines, directories, 270-278

Cooperatives, 91-92

Cosmetics: *see Drugs/Cosmetics*

Counseling, Career, 22-40, 156-157

Counseling, Psychological: as support during job search, 199-200 local resources, 201-206

Cover Letter: *see also Resume* preparation of, 60 sample formats, 67-69

Crisis Centers, 203-206

Cultural Institutions: selected museums, galleries, theaters, symphonies, etc.; professional groups, publications, and directories, 278-284

D

Data Processing: *see Computer Industry*

514

Department Stores: *see Retailers*

Directories, 76-91 *(see also under employment categories)*

Disabled Workers: *see Handicapped Workers*

Drugs/Cosmetics/Biological Products: selected firms; professional groups, publications, and directories, 286-290

E

Economic Outlook of Seattle/Portland area, 4-9

Educational Institutions: selected schools, universities, colleges; professional groups, professional magazines, and directories, 290-301

Electronics/Telecommunications: selected firms; trade groups, trade magazines, and directories, 301-308

Emotional Problems, 199-206

Employers Index, 495

Employment Agencies: listing of local agencies, 152-156 pros and cons of using, 149-152

Employment Services, *see Chapter 6 and the following:* government, 169-172 social service agencies, 163-168 veterans, 171

Energy and Oil: selected firms; professional groups, publications, and directories, 308-311

Engineering: selected firms; professional groups, professional magazines, and directories, 312-317

Executive Search Firms: listing of local firms, 158-163 pros and cons of using, 158

F

Film, Video, and Related Fields: selected studios; professional groups, publications, and directories, 317-321

Financial Institutions: *see Banks/Savings and Loans and Investment Bankers/Stock Brokers*

Financial Management: *see Chapter 8* during job search, 113, 187-189

Fired: *see Chapter 9* coping with being fired, 198-199, 206

Fitness: *see Recreation*

Food/Beverage Industry: selected food and beverage producers and distributors; trade groups, trade magazines, and directories, 321-331

G

Government, Loacal, State, and Federal: professional groups, publications, and directories, 331-341

Government Employment Resources, 169-172

Graphic Design: *see Printers/Graphic Design*

Guidance, Vocational, 22-29; *see also Chapter 2*

H

Handicapped Workers: resource books, 21

Health Care: selected health care facilities; professional groups, professional magazines, and directories, 341-355

Hotels/Motels: selected hotels, motels; professional groups, professional magazines, and directories, 355-361

Hotlines, Telephone, 98, 108-109

Human Services: selected providers; professional groups, professional magazines, and directories, 361-370

I

Information Resources (*see also Resource Books*): career resource facilities, 25-29, *see also Chapter 4* Chambers of Commerce, 14-16 directories, 76-91

job-hunting strategy books, 20-21, 122
job listings, 106-109, 173
libraries, 72-75
magazines, feature, 101-102
magazines, general, 98-100
magazines, trade and special interest, 102-106
network groups (listing of local), 123-147
newspapers, 92-97
small business, 40-46, 147-148
telephone hotlines, 98, 108-109
visitor and relocation information, 3, 9-13
women, 21, 46-49, 137, 147
Instruments: selected firms; professional groups and directories, 372-376
Insurance: selected underwriters and brokers; professional groups, professional magazines, and directories, 376-383
Interviewing:
books on, 186
exploratory, or informal, 116, 182
follow-up correspondence, 185
formal, 182-184
how to succeed in, *see Chapter 7*
personal history in, 175-177
techniques and strategies, 179-181, *also see Chapter 7*
work history in, 178
Investment Bankers/Stock Brokers: selected investment bankers and stock brokers; professional groups, professional magazines, and directories, 384-389

J

Job Listings, 106-109, 173 (*see also Telephone Hotlines*)
Job Market:
local trends, 4-9
researching the job market, *see Chapter 4*
Job Offer:
evaluation of, 213-215
Job Satisfaction, 212
Job Search :
computerized, 3

conducting while employed versus unemployed, 187
handling finances during, 113, 187-189
hotlines, 98, 108-109
how to cope, 111-113, 198-200, 206-209
length of, 111, 197

L

Law Firms: selected law firms; professional groups, professional magazines, and directories, 389-395
Libraries, 72-75

M

Magazines: *see under Information Resources*
Management Consultants: selected firms; professional groups, publications, directories, 395-398
Manufacturers: selected firms; professional groups, publications, directories, 399-406
Media, Broadcasting and Cable TV: selected companies and stations; professional groups, publications, directories, 406-412
Media, Print: local newspaper and magazine publishers; professional groups, professional magazines, and directories, 412-422
Mental Health Centers, 203-206
Metal Products: selected firms; professional groups, publications, directories, 423-426
Mid-Life Career Change: *see Resource Books*
Museums: *see Cultural Institutions*

N,O

Networking (*see Chapter 5*):
as key to job search success, 114

contacts (how to locate), 115-
118, 120-122
executive, 138
exploratory interviews, 116,
182
function of, 114
hiring authority (how to
contact), 120-122
local networks, 123-147
organization and
recordkeeping, 112, 118-119
sample letter, 114-115
telephone networking, 120
Newcomers, Advice for, 9-13
Newspapers:
listing of local newspapers, 93-
97
want-ads and how to answer,
92, 121
Office Supplies: selected firms;
professional groups,
publications, and directories,
427-433
Oil: *see Energy and Oil*
Organizations, Professional, 123-
147 (*see also under employment
categories*)

P

Paper/Packaging/Forest Products:
selected firms; professional
groups, publications,
directories, 433-438
Part-Time Employment, 188-195
Personnel Department, 121
Plastics/Rubber: selected firms;
professional groups,
publications, directories, 438-
443
Printers/Graphic Design:
selected firms; trade groups
trade magazines, and
directories, 443-449
Psychological Counseling, 200-
206
Public Relations: *see Advertising*
Publishers: *see Media, Print*

R

Radio Stations: *see Media,
Broadcasting*
Real Estate: selected firms;
professional groups,

professional magazines, and
directories, 449-457
Recreation/Sports/Fitness:
selected providers;
professional groups,
professional magazines, and
directories, 457-463
References, Use of, 186
Rejection, how to deal with, 111-
113, 198-200
Relocation information, 3
Resource Books:
on career planning, 20
for college students, 20-21
for handicapped workers, 21
on interviewing, 186
on job-hunting strategy, 20-21,
122
for mid-life career change, 21
on part-time employment, 190
for resume preparation, 53
for retirement years, 21
on salary negotiation, 213
for vocational analysis, 20-21
for women, 21, 49
Restaurant Industry: selected
firms; professional groups,
publications, directories, 463-
469
Resume: *see Chapter 3; see also
Cover Letter*
distribution of, 59
function of, 50-51
preparation of, 51-53, 61
professional resume preparers,
53-58
resource books on, 53
formats, 61
sample resumes, 62-66
screening done by employer,
121
Retailers/Wholesalers: selected
companies; professional
groups, professional
magazines, and directories,
469-479

S

Salary Negotiation, 213
resource books on, 213
Service Corps of Retired
Executives (SCORE), 40-41, 44
Shipping: *see
Transportation/Shipping*
Small Business Administration
assistance, 40-41, 44

Small Business Assistance, 40-46, 147-148
Social Service Agencies, 37-40, 163-168
Sports: *see Recreation*
Stock Brokers: *see Investment Bankers/Stock Brokers*

T

Tax Deductible Expenses, 113
Telecommunications: *see Electronics/Telecommunications*
Telemarketing, 193-195
Telephone Hotlines, 98, 108-109
Telephone Networking, 120
Television: *see Media, Broadcasting*
Temporary Employment: *see Part-Time Employment*
Testing, Vocational, 22-40
Theater: *see Cultural Institutions*
Trade Magazines, 102-106
Trade Organizations, 123-147, *see also under employment categories*
Transportation Equipment: *see Auto/Truck/Marine Equipment*
Transportation in Seattle/Portland area, 10-13
Transportation/Shipping: selected firms; trade groups, trade magazines, and directories, 480-484
Travel: selected firms; professional groups, publications, directories, 484-489

U,V

Unemployment Benefits, 195-196
Universities: *see Educational Institutions*
Utilities: trade groups, trade magazines, and directories, 490-494
Video: *see Film, Video, and Related Fields*
Vocational Consultants: *see Consultants, Vocational*
Vocational Objective: how to develop, *see Chapter 2*
self-appraisal exercise, 18-19

Vocational Testing: types of assessment tests, 22-23
where offered, 25-40

W

Want-ads, 92, 121
Wholesalers: *see Retailers/Wholesalers*
Women: career resources, 21, 46-49, 137, 147
resource books for, 21, 49